POPERY AND POLITICS
IN ENGLAND
1660–1688

POPERY AND POLITICS
IN ENGLAND
1660–1688

JOHN MILLER
Fellow of Gonville and Caius College, Cambridge

CAMBRIDGE
AT THE UNIVERSITY PRESS
1973

Published by the Syndics of the Cambridge University Press
Bentley House, 200 Euston Road, London NW1 2DB
American Branch: 32 East 57th Street, New York, N.Y.10022

© Cambridge University Press 1973

Library of Congress Catalogue Card Number: 73–79306

ISBN: 0 521 20236 1

Printed in Great Britain by
Western Printing Services Ltd, Bristol

FOR CAROL

CONTENTS

PREFACE

This book is based on a doctoral thesis on 'the Catholic factor' in English politics under Charles II and James II. A study of anti-Catholicism in the later seventeenth century has led me to consider the way in which the anti-Catholicism, explicit or implicit, of 'Whig' historians has coloured popular attitudes to the seventeenth century in general and to James II in particular. As a non-Catholic I am less familiar than I might be with the spiritual side of Catholic life and I should be grateful if Catholic readers would look with indulgence on any errors or gaucheries that they might find.

I have received a great deal of help from many people during my research for the thesis and the book, but my thanks are due first of all to Professor J. H. Plumb who suggested the topic to me in the first place and who, as my research supervisor, guided my work and watched over the development of the thesis. I am also very grateful for the valuable advice that I have received from Professor J. P. Kenyon, Professor J. R. Jones, Mr J. A. Williams, Mr P. R. Glazebrook, Dr B. Neveu and Professor T. A. Birrell. My thanks are due also to the duke of Marlborough, the marquis of Bath, the marquis of Salisbury and Mr R. J. R. Arundell for allowing me to use manuscripts in their possession and to Professor C. D. Chandaman for allowing me to quote figures for the revenue from recusants from his unpublished thesis. Having worked in a wide variety of archives and libraries, I have benefited from the expert knowledge, kindness and helpfulness of many people, but I should like in particular to express my thanks to Miss Elisabeth Poyser of the Archives of the Archbishop of Westminster, to Fr Charles Burns of the Vatican Archives and to the staffs of the Cambridge University Library (especially the Anderson Room), the British Museum Manuscripts Room, the Rolls Room in the Public Record Office, duke Humfrey's library in the Bodleian, the library of St John's College, Cambridge and Dr Williams's Library. Neither the thesis nor the book would have been completed as quickly as they have been if the Master and Fellows of Gonville and Caius College had not elected me into a research fellowship; for this and for much else I should like to express my thanks. Finally, my greatest debt is to my wife for all her support, moral and financial, during the last five years.

JOHN MILLER

Gonville and Caius College
Cambridge
November 1972

ABBREVIATIONS

AAW   Archives of the Archbishop of Westminster
AOFM   Archives of the English Province of the Order of Friars
    Minor, The Friary, Forest Gate
Arundell MSS   MSS of Arundells of Wardour and Lanherne in
    the possession of Mr R. J. R. Arundell
ASJ   Archives of the English Province of the Society of Jesus
Baschet   Baschet transcripts of French ambassadors' dispatches
    in the PRO, ref PRO/31/3
BM   British Museum
Bodl.   Bodleian Library
brs.   broadside
Cal. Clar. S.P.   *Calendar of Clarendon State Papers*, 5 vols.,
    Oxford, 1872–1970
Cibo MSS   Archivio di Stato, Massa, Archivio del cardinale
    Alderano Cibo
CJ   *Commons Journals*
CPA   Ministère des Affaires Etrangères, Paris, Archives Diplo-
    matiques, Correspondence Politique, Angleterre
CRS   Catholic Record Society volumes
CSPD   *Calendar of State Papers, Domestic*
CSPVen   *Calendar of State Papers, Venetian*
CTB   *Calendar of Treasury Books*
CUL   Cambridge University Library
DNB   *Dictionary of National Biography*
EHR   *English Historical Review*
Grey   A. Grey, *Debates in the House of Commons 1667–94*,
    10 vols., London, 1763
HJ   *Historical Journal*
HMC   Historical Manuscripts Commission reports
JEH   *Journal of Ecclesiastical History*
LJ   *Lords Journals*
Morrice MSS   Dr Williams's Library, London, Roger Morrice's
    Entering Book, vols. 1 and 2 (MSS 31P and 31Q)
Nunz. Div.   Vatican Archives, Nunziature Diverse
Nunz. Fian.   Vatican Archives, Nunziatura di Fiandra

PC/2/ Privy Council Registers in the PRO

P & P   Past and Present

PDB   Papists (Disarming and Removal) Bill, House of Lords
R. O., Main Papers, no. 321 (3 December 1680)

POAS   Poems on Affairs of State 1660–88, 4 vols., New Haven,
1963–8; ed. (i) G. de F. Lord, (ii) L. F. Mengel, jnr, (iii)
H. H. Schless, (iv) C. M. Crump

Portland MSS   Nottingham University Library, MSS of the
first duke of Portland, ref. PwA

PRO   Public Record Office

Prop. Ang. Archives of the Congregation 'de Propaganda
Fide', Rome, 'Scriture referite nei congressi dal 1627 al
1707, Anglia I'

RH   Recusant History

Rom. Tr.   Roman transcripts in the PRO, ref PRO/31/9. The
folio numbers used are those at the bottom of each sheet
in blue pencil

*Somers Tracts   A Collection of scarce and valuable Tracts…
selected from … libraries, particularly that of … Lord
Somers*, ed. Sir W. Scott, 13 vols., London, 1809–15

SP/   State papers in the PRO

SS Ing.   Vatican Archives, Segretaria di Stato, Inghilterra

State Trials   W. Cobbett and T. B. Howell (eds.), *State Trials*,
33 vols., London, 1809–26

VCH   Victoria County History

Wing   D. Wing, *Short-Title Catalogue of Books, 1641–1700*,
3 vols., New York, 1945

NOTE ON SPELLINGS AND DATES

Spelling in English and in French has been modernised throughout. Dates in the text are old style but the year is taken as starting on 1 January. Where the dates of dispatches in the footnotes are new style, I have marked them NS.

INTRODUCTION

In the reign of Charles II only a small minority of the population of England was Roman Catholic. This minority had owed its survival after the Reformation to the firmness in the faith of the Catholic nobility and gentry, who provided most of the financial support for the priesthood and many of its members. The Catholic community under Charles II was much as it had been at the end of Elizabeth's reign and much as it was to remain until the massive Irish immigrations at the time of the Industrial Revolution. It was primarily aristocratic and rural and it depended on priests trained in seminaries abroad. There were fearsome laws in force against all aspects of Catholic life, but they were enforced comparatively little except in times of crisis. Most Protestant magistrates showed a considerable practical tolerance in their dealings with their Catholic neighbours.

In view of this it may seem surprising that the politics of the period 1660–88 should have been dominated by a violent and often hysterical anti-Catholicism. One must seek the explanation of this apparent anomaly in the religious policies of Charles II and even more in the conversion to Catholicism of James, duke of York, the king's brother and heir-apparent, who eventually succeeded to the throne as James II. In the early part of Charles's reign English anti-Catholicism was latent but far from dead. The attitude to Catholicism of English Protestants had been formed by their interpretation of a century and more of religious conflict since the Reformation. If many Protestants were tolerant of the few Papists among their neighbours, they retained a vigorous fear and hatred of 'Popery', especially of 'Popery' at the royal court or among those in positions of power. Memories of the reign of Queen Mary and the present experience of that of Louis XIV combined to give a frightening picture of the behaviour of Papists in power towards their Protestant subjects. Thus in 1673, when the duke of York's conversion became known, the dreadful prospect of a Catholic king became the central issue of politics. It led directly to the attempts to exclude James from the throne and resulted incidentally in a fierce persecution of Catholics. Traditional Protestant images of Catholics and Catholicism also coloured the attitudes of James's subjects when he became king, and strongly influenced their interpretation of his actions and of his intentions. Deep-rooted suspicions of James's motives, which sprang mainly from the fact that he was a Catholic, played a major part in preparing the way for his expulsion.

The first three chapters of this book are concerned with the nature and position of the Catholic community and with the enforcement of the penal laws. The fourth discusses the nature and development of English anti-Catholicism, and the remainder of the book is concerned with the impact of the 'Catholic question' on English politics between 1660 and 1688 and, to a lesser extent, with the impact of political developments on the English Catholics. The last three chapters are concerned with specific aspects of James II's reign: his unhappy relations with Rome, his efforts to turn the rather somnolent Catholic mission into an instrument of evangelism and the type of opposition which his policies aroused. I hope to show that although many of his subjects' assumptions and suspicions were ill-founded, the fact that they were so widely and deeply held meant that James's policies were extremely foolhardy and that they were doomed to eventual failure.

I

THE CATHOLIC LAITY

The form which English Catholicism was to take in the seventeenth and eighteenth centuries was largely determined by what happened in Elizabeth's reign. The English church had been ill-prepared, materially and psychologically, to face the challenge of the Reformation. The disposal of many of its richest benefices to clerics employed in the royal and ecclesiastical administrations tended to leave the church weakened and impoverished at the parochial level. Contemporary complaints of the pomp and venality of the higher clergy and the ignorance and incompetence of their inferiors had a firm basis in fact, but were both exaggerated and to some extent misdirected. However scandalous it might seem to humanist or Protestant intellectuals that many parish priests knew hardly a word of Latin, it mattered less to their illiterate parishioners who knew none at all. The old church may have been concerned mainly with outward observances, it may have taken over and endorsed pre-Christian practices and superstitions and it may have instilled no deep spiritual understanding into the people at large. It did however provide a series of 'ingrained observances which defined and gave meaning to the cycle of the week and the seasons of the year, to birth, marriage and death'. It also provided and enforced a rudimentary moral code.[1]

The old church maintained a vigorous if crude spiritual life, but it was one whose beliefs, at a popular level, could not be described as informed or clearly articulated. The old ways had seldom been openly challenged and the church was unused to defending itself; neither clergy nor laity had ever known anything different. Then, suddenly, the habits of centuries were disrupted

---

[1] J. Bossy, 'The Character of Elizabethan Catholicism', in T. Aston (ed.) *Crisis in Europe 1560–1660* (London, 1965), p. 223; H. Aveling, *Northern Catholics: The Catholic Recusants of the North Riding of Yorkshire 1558–1790* (London, 1966), p. 49.

3

by the break with Rome, the swing to Protestantism under Edward VI, the reversion to Catholicism under Mary and the re-establishment of Protestantism, finally as it turned out, under Elizabeth. The average parishioner was faced with a bewildering series of changes, back and forth: services in English, the removal of images and crucifixes, the suppression of monasteries, the prohibition of pilgrimages and many traditional processions. A minority reacted violently: the Lincolnshire rebels of 1536 feared, among other things, that their church plate would be taken away; the Cornish rebels of 1549 complained that they could not understand the new English service (at which Cranmer snidely asked if they had understood the old Latin one).[2] Most conformed outwardly as they had always done, with a bewilderment tinged with resentment at the disruption of age-old routines. Some pre-Reformation practices, like beating the bounds at Rogation Tide, were taken over by the Church of England. The traditional Corpus Christi plays were performed at York until the later 1570s.[3] Those Catholic practices which the Church of England refused to adopt were gradually stamped out. For some time, however, it was far from obvious that the 1559 settlement was to be permanent; Elizabeth nearly died in 1562 and there were many prophecies that the old religion would be restored. Catholic vestments were stored away in the 1560s in the belief that they would soon be needed again.[4] There were as yet few people who could be described definitely as either Catholic or Protestant. The bulk of the population was bewildered and uncertain. Most of the old parish clergy conformed to the new order; they were not pressed to conform in every detail at first, as there were too few Protestant ministers to take their places. Some of these 'conservative conformists' among the clergy were later squeezed out as the authorities came to demand a greater measure of con-

---

[2] M. E. James, 'Obedience and Dissent in Henrician England: The Lincolnshire Rebellion, 1536', *P & P*, 48 (1970) 15–16; A. Fletcher, *Tudor Rebellions* (London, 1968), pp. 58–9.

[3] Aveling, *Catholic Recusancy in the City of York 1558–1791* (CRS monograph no. 2, 1970), pp. 31–4, 54.

[4] Aveling, *Northern Catholics*, pp. 20–3, 75, 79; Aveling, *The Catholic Recusants of the West Riding of Yorkshire 1558–1790* (Proceedings of the Leeds Philosophical and Literary Society, vol. x, 1963), p. 205; K. V. Thomas, *Religion and the Decline of Magic* (London, 1971), pp. 405–8.

4

formity; many more died and were replaced.[5] The universities began to produce enthusiastic Protestant ministers, whose mission was to convert England to Protestantism. The process of evangelisation had proceeded some way in the South and East even before Elizabeth's accession but in the North and West, not to mention Wales, it had hardly started. It was to be a long process, never more than partially successful.

In the 1560s religion in England was in a state of flux. The old church, its rituals and its sacraments had been taken away but the new church had not yet developed a character of its own. Both Catholics and Protestants had to try to learn 'to do what the past had not prepared them for – to maintain a faith as the result of an individual choice, very largely unsustained by institutions and a solid framework of social habits'.[6] The 1559 Act of Uniformity required everyone to attend his parish church. Deprived of direction, most conservatives did so,[7] but many refused the sacrament and paid little attention to the service, and so were called 'mislikers' of the new religion. There were as yet few conscious Catholics who clearly recognised the difference between the new form of worship and the old; indeed, however Protestant its doctrine might be, the form of worship imposed by the Church of England was not so unlike the traditional form as to make it intolerable to the vast mass of theologically unsophisticated conservatives of all classes.[8] Elizabeth's government was content to imprison and silence the leading conscious Catholics, notably Mary's bishops, in the hope that the rest would eventually conform if deprived of leadership. This did not happen, thanks largely to the efforts of small groups of Catholic intellectuals, many from the universities, who fled to the continent early in the reign and settled first at Louvain. Outstanding among them were William Allen, who eventually became a cardinal, and Robert Parsons, the Jesuit. The exiles' writings, which included a Catholic English Bible, clarified a Catholic position in danger of

[5] Aveling, *Northern Catholics*, pp. 25–33; Aveling, *West Riding*, pp. 196–200; K. R. Wark, *Elizabethan Recusancy in Cheshire* (Chetham Soc., 1971), p. 2; most of the old priests in the West Riding were dead by 1577: Aveling, *West Riding*, p. 203.

[6] Aveling, *Northern Catholics*, p. 49.

[7] Aveling, *Northern Catholics*, p. 35; Bossy, p. 226.

[8] This point was made by J. Berington, *Memoirs of Gregorio Panzani* (Birmingham, 1793), p. 17.

being lost through lack of definition and direction. Equally important, the exiles founded a series of schools, starting with the English college at Douai in 1568. These performed a double function: they provided, for the sons of English Catholics, the Catholic education which they were increasingly denied at home, and they trained the new generation of 'seminary priests' who were sent on missions to arrest and reverse the decay of Catholicism in England.[9]

The coming of the 'seminary priests' finally ensured the survival of English Catholicism. But even before they arrived, in the later 1570s and early 1580s, there were signs that in some cases undifferentiated conservatism and 'misliking' were hardening into a more conscious Catholicism. More Catholics became 'recusants' – they stayed away from the Protestant services in their parish churches. There were several reasons for this hardening. The minority of Marian priests who had refused to conform were partly responsible.[10] Works written by the exiles were imported in large numbers and must have made an impression on literate Catholic laymen.[11] There were also little cells of Catholic teaching. At first Catholics were not forbidden to attend the universities. At Gonville and Caius College, Cambridge, John Caius and his successor Dr Legge were accused by the fellows of being 'fosterers of Papists by drawing them into fellowships, encouraging others with maintenance, countenance and example ... which for many years have made the college as a seminary to poison the commonwealth with corrupted gentlemen'. However, by the end of the 1580s the college had lost its Catholic associations as most others had done some time before.[12] Prisons were rather surprisingly another source of Catholic teaching.

[9] P. Guilday, *The English Catholic Refugees on the Continent 1558–1795* (London, 1914); A. C. F. Beales, *Education under Penalty* (London, 1963), chaps. 3–4.

[10] Some Marian priests had got faculties abroad to reconcile to the church those who had attended Protestant services: Aveling, *West Riding*, p. 208; Aveling, *Northern Catholics*, p. 87.

[11] Aveling, *City of York*, pp. 41–2, 45–6; Aveling, *Northern Catholics*, p. 106; L. Rostenberg, *The Minority Press and the English Crown 1558–1625* (Nieuwkoop, 1971), chaps. 2–3.

[12] J. Venn, *Caius College* (Cambridge, 1901), pp. 55–8, 65–6, 77–80, 85; M. H. Curtis, *Oxford and Cambridge in Transition 1558–1642* (Oxford, 1959), pp. 168–9.

Catholic priests and laymen were imprisoned for varying periods and carried on a mission there. The prisons, though noisome, were run for profit by private individuals and a wealthy prisoner could enjoy a substantial amount of freedom. Mass was often said in gaols and people went from outside to hear it. In 1582 four priests climbed into York castle prison to say Mass, one being captured on the way out. In 1611 it was found that some prisoners were running a dame school for Catholic girls in another of the York prisons. In 1612 the keeper of Newgate was said to have made it 'rather a chapel for superstitious service than a prison or gaol for strait keeping'.[13]

Another reason why conservatism developed into recusancy was because the government's attitude hardened after the rebellion of the Northern earls in 1569 and the pope's excommunication of the queen in 1570. Catholics now seemed a potential fifth column, ready to rise against the queen on behalf of a Catholic invader. The Privy Council spent much time and energy on the surveillance and harassment of leading Catholics. This drove some into temporary or permanent conformity with the established church, but it also forced others to think more clearly about their religious position. The turning point of the reign came in 1578–82. Until then the government had tried to pick off and silence the natural leaders of English Catholicism, hoping that without leadership their following would gradually be eroded. But the increasing self-consciousness of the surviving Catholic minority was now being strengthened by the mission of the seminary priests, who helped to give backbone to the love of traditional observances by inculcating a sense of identity based on membership of the one true church. The government came to realise that the old religion was not going to wither away just as the danger to the Protestant state from Catholicism was reaching its height. The claims to the throne, first of Mary Queen of Scots and then of Philip of Spain, were eagerly supported by a number of the exiles, including Allen and Parsons. Faced with this danger, the government cracked down hard on the English Catholics. The penalty for absence from church was raised from one shilling a week to £20 a month. It was made a capital crime for a priest to come into England, or for him to convert anyone,

13 Aveling, *City of York*, pp. 59–65, 82; P. Caraman, *The Years of Siege: Catholic Life from James I to Cromwell* (London, 1966), pp. 66–7.

or for anybody to harbour him. The martyrdoms which followed this new legislation strengthened the Catholics' steadfastness and sense of identity.

The energy and determination of the first generation of Elizabethan Catholics ensured the survival of the faith in England. It could never again be the religion of the majority, after the twenty years of uncertainty and erosion at the start of the reign. The efforts of the government and of the Protestant clergy ensured that Catholic numbers did not increase, and probably fell, in the seventeenth century. But Catholicism had sufficient strength among the nobility and gentry to be proof against sporadic attempts to exterminate it. The Catholics soon realised that they were doomed to remain a minority in a Protestant nation: 'The state seems now to be settled against the religion of our forefathers and not unlike so to continue,' wrote a priest in 1608.[14] Most therefore relapsed into passivity, resigned to exclusion from public life, asking only to be left alone. The political activism of a minority of the exiles against the Protestant state had never found much of an echo among the Catholic squirearchy and now virtually disappeared.[15] The Gunpowder Plotters were an atypical minority. After a period of severe persecution after the Gunpowder Plot, the government's attitude relaxed. Charles I was more concerned to raise money from the Catholics than to crush Catholicism. Only two priests were executed between 1625 and 1640.

The Parliamentarians' fierce hatred of Papists and the king's identification with them ensured that many Catholics fought for the king in the Civil Wars, although the majority remained neutral.[16] Catholics suffered more severely than other Royalists from mob violence on the eve of the war and from the depredations of the Parliamentary forces; the butchering of the predominantly Catholic garrison of Basing House in 1645 was one of the few real atrocities of the Civil War.[17] After the war,

---

[14] Caraman, p. 21.

[15] Guilday, p. xviii; Bossy, pp. 243–6.

[16] K. J. Lindley, 'The Part Played by Catholics in the English Civil War' (unpublished Ph.D thesis, Manchester, 1968), passim.

[17] R. Clifton, 'The Popular Fear of Catholics during the English Revolution', *P & P*, 52 (1971), 31–2; S. R. Gardiner, *History of the Great Civil War* (4 vols., London, 1893), ii, 363–4.

Catholic 'delinquents' (those who had fought for the king) were supposed to lose four-fifths of their lands and mere Papists two-thirds. But by compounding or fictitious sales many avoided having their lands confiscated or quickly recovered them; most emerged at the Restoration with a heavy load of debt but with most of their lands intact. Apart from the confiscations, Catholics were not vigorously persecuted under the Protectorate, although a greater measure of repression was envisaged through the new penal legislation of 1657.[18] With the Restoration, the English Catholics recovered most of their lands and hoped for some relaxation of the penal laws as a tangible recognition of their loyalty to Charles I.

THE NUMBER OF CATHOLICS

Any estimate of the number of Catholics in England under Charles II must be largely conjectural. Petitions for a bishop in 1660 and 1664 gave figures of 100,000 and 200,000 respectively, but in 1679 the earl of Castlemaine put the figure as low as 50,000.[19] According to the census taken in 1676 on the orders of Henry Compton, bishop of London, there were 11,867 Catholics over the age of sixteen in the province of Canterbury.[20] Opinions vary on the accuracy of this census; its purpose was to show how few non-Anglicans there were and it included only those Catholics and Protestant Dissenters who stayed away from church – not 'church-papists' or occasional conformists. Within those limitations, the figures it gave were probably not a great underestimate.[21] The census did not include figures for the province of

---

18 M. Greenslade, *A List of Staffordshire Recusants, 1657* (Staffs. Record Soc., 1958), pp. 72–4.
19 AAW A32, pp. 187, 469; R. Palmer, earl of Castlemaine, *The Compendium* (1679), p. 85. (Castlemaine was, of course, trying to minimise the threat from Catholics to the Protestant nation.) At least one non-Catholic, Sir Peter Pett, accepted Castlemaine's figure: *The Happy Future State of England* (1688), p. 149. In 1637 the papal agent Panzani had estimated the English Catholic population as being 150,000: B. Magee, *The English Recusants* (London, 1938), p. 104.
20 A. Browning (ed.), *English Historical Documents 1660–1714* (London, 1953), pp. 413–14.
21 J. A. Williams, *Catholic Recusancy in Wiltshire, 1660–1791* (CRS monograph no. 1, 1968), pp. 253–7; S. A. Peyton, 'The Religious

9

York and its compilers very rashly assumed that, as its population was one-sixth that of the province of Canterbury, it would include one-sixth the number of Papists (1978). This was clearly nonsense. In 1687 the Catholic bishop John Leyburn toured the North and Midlands and confirmed nearly 20,000 people, including 17,290 in the province of York.[22] It is difficult to guess what relation this figure might bear to the Catholic population of the North. Leyburn was the first Catholic bishop to visit the area for well over fifty years, so the great majority of the Catholic population could not have received the sacrament of confirmation before and would probably have taken the opportunity to do so. But it is possible that the surviving lists are incomplete (there are none for Cheshire, for instance) and that not all Catholics were able to meet Leyburn, especially those living in remote areas. Nevertheless I think it is not unreasonable to see the number of those confirmed as only a modest under-estimate of those over the age of seven in the North. The number of confirmations in Yorkshire (3369) squares quite well with the rev. Aveling's estimate of 4170 Catholics, adults and children, in the county in the 1680s.[23]

Census of 1676', *EHR*, xlviii (1933), 100–1; S. C. Ratcliff and H. C. Johnson (eds.), *Warwick County Records*, vii (Warwick, 1946), pp. lxxviii–c: the census showed 675 Papists in Warwickshire over the age of sixteen, and 509 Popish recusants were presented at quarter sessions; in 1687 bishop Leyburn confirmed 1024 Catholics over the age of about seven in the county: T. B. Trappes-Lomax, 'Bishop Leyburn's Visitation in 1687', *Newsletter for Students of Recusant History*, iv (1962), 20. The detailed census returns that are in Lambeth Palace Library (MS 639, fols. 163–9, 252–9) do not fill one with confidence about the precise accuracy of the figures.

[22] Trappes-Lomax, pp. 16–21; I have deducted the figures for those confirmed in Northants., Lincs., Staffs. and Warwicks., which counties are in the Province of Canterbury, and I have added the 529 for Garswood, Lancs., to which Trappes-Lomax refers. Even if other lists have been lost which would push the total up to the 20,859 given in the original, the total for the Northern province could not exceed 18,665. The arithmetic of the original lists (AAW A35, pp. 13–400) is erratic, that of Brig. Trappes-Lomax contains only a few minor errors.

[23] Seven was the minimum age which the church recommended, although a few of those confirmed may have been younger: *Catholic Encyclopedia* (New York, 1908), iv, 216; Trappes-Lomax, p. 21. For Aveling's figures, see his essay 'Some Aspects of Yorkshire Catholic Recusant History', in G. J. Cuming (ed.), *Studies in Church History*, iv (Leiden,

Thus one may assume that there were, very approximately, 15,000 adult Catholics in the province of Canterbury, allowing for 'church-papists'. If so, and if half the population was under sixteen,[24] the total number of Catholics in the province would be about 30,000. It seems unlikely that the Catholic population of the province of York could have exceeded the same figure.[25] This would give a total of 60,000 Catholics, or between 1.1 and 1.2 per cent of a population of five to five and a half millions.[26] This figure may well be too high. Professor Dickens and the rev. Aveling have each put the Catholic population of the comparatively strongly Catholic county of Yorkshire, in 1604 and in the later seventeenth century, at 1.5 per cent or a little less; according to Mr Williams, Catholics comprised only about 0.4 per cent of the population of Wiltshire. The bishop of Peterborough knew of only sixty-six Popish recusants in his diocese in 1683.[27]

Some historians have suggested that the figure should be much higher. Professor Kenyon suggests 260,000, apparently using the figure in the Compton census with a multiplier of twenty.[28] It is quite clear, however, that the census includes all persons over sixteen, not just heads of households, and that it is useless for the province of York. Bryan Magee put the figure even higher, but his method of calculation was extremely unreliable. He took a list of convicted recusants drawn up in 1671, which he wrongly

1967), 108–10; the Compton census gave only 574 Catholics in the diocese of York (which did not include the whole of Yorkshire): Lambeth Palace Library, MS 639, fol. 297.

24 This is not necessarily correct – forty per cent might be a more accurate estimate: Williams, *Wiltshire*, p. 256, n. 11.

25 If the figure of 18,000 Catholics over seven were at all accurate, the total would only be 24,000 if one allowed a very generous estimate of twenty-five per cent for the proportion of the population under seven.

26 Browning, *English Historical Documents*, pp. 516–17; D. V. Glass, 'Gregory King's Estimate of the Population of England and Wales', in D. V. Glass and D. E. C. Eversley (eds.), *Population in History* (London, 1965), pp. 203–4.

27 A. G. Dickens, 'The Extent and Character of Recusancy in Yorkshire in 1604', *Yorks. Archaeological Journal*, xxxvii (1948–51), 33; Aveling, *Studies in Church History*, iv, 111; Williams, *Wiltshire*, p. 256 and n. 11 (I have divided 250 into 66,373); Bodl., Rawl. MS D 1163, fols. 14–15.

28 J. P. Kenyon, *The Popish Plot* (London, 1972), pp. 24–5 and note.

ascribed to 1677, and compared it with a full list of Catholic peers and gentry made in 1680. Finding that only one-tenth of these peers and gentry were on the first list, he assumed that only one-tenth of all Catholics were convicted of recusancy. He then multiplied the 54,000 convicted recusants (allowing for children) by ten to give the huge figure of 540,000 or about ten per cent of the population.[29] This procedure is littered with pitfalls. First, many names occur on the 1671 list more than once, as convicted several times. Secondly, it is wrong to assume that all convicted recusants were Catholics when many, probably the majority, were Quakers and other Protestant Dissenters.[30] Thirdly, one can draw no conclusions about the extent to which Catholics were convicted later in Charles II's reign from the convictions in the years before 1671 when the laws were enforced sporadically and unevenly.[31] In short, these statistics are quite valueless. More useful are those which purport to show that the Catholic peers and gentry (as described in the 1680 list) comprised about ten per cent of the peers and gentry of England, although again I feel that Magee's figures here are rather too high, and that his original estimate of seven per cent might be more accurate.[32] This serves to illustrate the social top-heaviness that was so characteristic of English Catholicism in the seventeenth century.

RURAL CATHOLICISM

Since Elizabeth's reign, rural Catholicism had survived mainly in pockets centred on the households of the Catholic peers and gentlemen who alone could afford to maintain the priests who

[29] *The English Recusants*, pp. 115–17; the editor of the 1671 list, printed in *Miscellanea* (CRS vol. vi, 1909), gives the date as 1677, but it contains no record of any convictions after 1671 and the original (BM Add. MS 20739) is clearly marked as being drawn up in 1671. The 1680 list is the PDB, partly printed in *HMC House of Lords 1678–88*, pp. 225–37.

[30] See Appendix 2; Williams, *Wilts.*, p. 272; W. M. Wigfield, 'Religious Statistics concerning Recusants of the Stuart Period', *Theology*, xli (1940), 94–102.

[31] Williams, *Wilts.*, p. 272; Appendices 1 and 2.

[32] Magee, pp. 169–71. It is true that some Catholic peers and gentry do not appear on the list, but some of those who do are flattered by being accorded gentry status, particularly in the towns and in Monmouthshire and Herefordshire.

kept the old religion alive. A document of 1660 stated that the Catholic aristocracy kept 'vulgi innumerabilis multitudo' stead-fast in the faith. When John Gavan SJ, who was later executed during the Popish Plot, made his profession under the Royal Oak at Boscobel, surrounded by the neighbouring Catholic gentry, the occasion in many ways epitomised the spirit of English Catholicism – it was aristocratic, rural and Royalist.[33] The zeal of Catholic peers and gentlemen varied considerably. Some made converts among their servants and tenants, others merely kept them firm in the faith and there must have been others like lord Thomas Howard who said that 'he never trusted them [Catholics] with any secret and used Protestants only in all business of im-portance'.[34] William Blundell, on the other hand, boasted that there was not a Protestant, a beggar or an alehouse in his hamlet of Little Crosby.[35]

Catholicism was strongest in the more backward areas of the country where old, personal landlord–tenant relationships sur-vived longest: in the North, especially in Lancashire, and in the west Midlands, particularly in Herefordshire and Monmouth-shire.[36] Its strength in the last-named area owed much to the hereditary local dominance of the Somerset family, earls and later marquises of Worcester. There were several vigorous complaints to parliament about the continuing protection of Popery by the first Protestant head of family, who was created duke of Beau-fort in 1682. (There were also other local issues behind the com-plaints.)[37] In Lancashire there was no single dominant family; a list of the incomes of the leading Catholics in 1682 showed

33 AAW A32, pp. 187–9; Bodl., Rawl, MS A 136, pp. 126–8, 171.
34 Aveling, 'The Catholic Recusancy of the Yorkshire Fairfaxes, part II', *RH*, iv (1957), 87; J. Bossy, 'Four Catholic Congregations in Rural Northumberland', *RH*, ix (1967), 107–9 and Passim; Bossy, 'More Northumbrian Congregations', *RH*, x (1969), 11–29; A. G. Dickens, *Yorks. Archeological Journal*, xxxvii, 37–42; Evelyn, 25 Aug. 1678, *Diary*, iv, 142; see also Pepys, *Diary*, 17 Jan. 1668.
35 M. Blundell, *Cavalier: Letters of William Blundell of Crosby to his Friends* (London, 1933), p. 251.
36 The figures in Appendix 3 can be taken as a rough guide to Catholic strength in various counties; see also Browning, *Historical Documents*, p. 415.
37 *LJ*, xii, 450–1; *CJ*, ix, 466–9; M. M. C. O'Keeffe, 'The Popish Plot in South Wales and the Marches' (unpublished M.A. thesis, University College, Galway, 1969), chap. 6.

13

none higher than £3500, whereas the Somerset estates had been worth £23,000 a year in 1642.[38] The survival of the faith in Lancashire depended on lesser men like William Blundell and even on Catholic yeomen like the Tickles of Altcar. It was helped by the geographical isolation of some of the most strongly Catholic areas, especially in the West Derby hundred; Formby, like Little Crosby, remained predominantly Catholic into the eighteenth century.[39] In these remote areas, the survival of Catholicism was made easier by the weakness of the established church. Its parishes were very poor, and so attracted mediocre clergy; they were also very large and sparsely populated and often contained decayed or disused chapelries. At Llanfair-Cilgoed in Monmouthshire, the tithes were actually used to support a Catholic chapel. The bishop of Sodor and Man complained in 1688 that the Manxmen, though supposedly Protestant, continued a number of superstitious, pre-Reformation practices.[40] Clearly, a century and more of Protestant evangelism had left these remote areas comparatively untouched.

Very few Catholics took an active part in politics during this period; some who did, like the earl of Bristol, probably did the Catholics more harm than good. Catholic peers continued to sit in the House of Lords until 1678, but apart from the duke of York and the erratic Bristol they had no real spokesmen or leaders. Indeed during this period the Catholic nobility lost its most distinguished members. From 1662 to 1677 the dukedom of Norfolk was held by a lunatic and from 1683 to 1701 by a Protestant. The marquisates of Worcester and Winchester and the earldom of Shrewsbury fell to Protestants. Between 1660 and 1678 the number of Catholic peers varied between twenty-nine and thirty-two; it fell to twenty-four in 1681–4 and rose to twenty-eight in 1687 and thirty-two in 1688 with the help of conversions and new

---

[38] Lancs. R.O., DDKe/7/21: lord Molyneux's income was £3500 p.a., that of Richard Sherburne was £3000; H. R. Trevor-Roper, *The Gentry 1540–1640* (Economic History Review Supplement no. 1, 1953), p. 54.

[39] *HMC Kenyon*, p. 138; *VCH Lancs.*, iii, 51–2.

[40] F. O. Blundell, *Old Catholic Lancashire* (3 vols., London, 1925–41), i, 134–5; R. Howell, *Newcastle upon Tyne and the Puritan Revolution* (Oxford, 1967), pp. 63–71; *Miscellanea* (CRS, vol. ii, 1906), p. 303; Bodl., Tanner MS 28, fol. 176.

creations. These figures exclude the duke of York but include six to seven peers with Scots or Irish titles only, as well as minors, dotards, a lunatic, and several lukewarm and dubious Catholics like the second lord Widdrington and earl Rivers. Only twenty titles were in Catholic hands throughout the period; of these, six did not carry membership of the House of Lords and one, the barony of Abergavenny, was held by minors from 1666 to 1686. The only leaders the Catholic peerage had were the duke of York and elderly peers of the second rank like Arundell of Wardour, Bellasis and Powis. Few of James II's advisers came from the old Catholic nobility; most were Protestants (like Sunderland and Jeffreys), converts (Perth, Melfort, Peterborough and Sir Nicholas Butler) or members of his personal following as duke of York (Dover, Tyrconnel and Fr Petre).

It is probable that the Catholic community suffered a slow erosion during the seventeenth century, and that apostasies among Catholic peers and gentry outnumbered conversions to Catholicism.[41] It seems clear that the financial burdens on recusants were not crippling, although they might be irritating. When that most persistent of Elizabethan recusants, Sir Thomas Tresham, ran into debt, his large recusancy fines were only one cause among several.[42] More surprisingly, few Catholics were totally ruined by sequestration and decimation during the interregnum.[43] In fact many Catholics prospered; the penal laws were just one more hazard for a landed family in economically parlous times and there is no evidence that Catholics proved any less capable of managing their estates than their Protestant neighbours. There are numerous references to Catholic gentlemen who

---

[41] Aveling thinks that the North Riding's Catholic population grew slightly in the seventeenth century, though it grew slower than the population as a whole; on the other hand, he thinks that that of the West Riding declined: Aveling, *Northern Catholics*, p. 352; *West Riding*, p. 245.

[42] Aveling, *Northern Catholics*, pp. 125–35; *West Riding*, p. 246; M. E. Finch, *The Wealth of Five Northamptonshire Families 1540–1640* (Northants. Record Soc., 1956), pp. 76–8; on the other hand, the Babthorpe family *did* blame their impoverishment on their recusancy fines, Aveling, *Post-Reformation Catholicism in East Yorkshire 1558–1790* (E. Yorks. Local History Soc., 1960), p. 45.

[43] Aveling, *West Riding*, pp. 233–4; *Northern Catholics*, pp. 310–17; R. Meredith, 'The Eyres of Hassop and their Forfeited Estates', *RH*, viii (1965), 28ff.

went in for enclosure, mining and even foreign trade.[44] Whether or not a landowner prospered depended less on his religion than on accidents of personality and mortality.[45]

In many ways there was little to distinguish Catholic peers and gentlemen from their Protestant neighbours. They enjoyed the same primary source of income, land, the same leisured lifestyle, the same interests and pleasures: estate management, the stable, the race-meeting, the chase. Catholics and Protestants were often related: in 1603 over a third of the armigerous families of the North Riding of Yorkshire had Catholic connections. (Nevertheless, the question of mixed marriages could often prove delicate.)[46] There is ample evidence of friendship and neighbourliness between Catholic and Protestant. While the pious earl of Anglesey was planning a book against the Jesuits, he dined with lord Baltimore and received and visited his Catholic neighbours, Mr Fermor of Tusmore, Mr Dormer of Leigh and lord Carrington.[47] Kentish gentlemen and Lancashire apprentices found it quite possible to discuss their differences of religion in a friendly manner.[48] Some Protestant magistrates went out of their way to protect their Catholic friends from the operation of the penal laws, and there is also evidence of Catholic gentlemen living on good terms with Protestant Dissenters and trying to protect them.[49] In a crisis gentlemen and even priests might stress that

---

[44] Finch, pp. 74, 146–8, 154–63; *HMC Downshire*, i, 13–14; ASJ, Stony-hurst MSS, Anglia VI, p. 475; Meredith, *RH*, viii, 14–17; *DNB*, Sir John Winter; *CSPD 1664–5*, p. 485; Blundell, *Cavalier*, pp. 119, 131; Lord Lumley owned the greatest coal-mines in the North: R. North, *Lives of the Norths*, ed. A. Jessopp (3 vols., London, 1890), i, 173.

[45] Aveling, *Northern Catholics*, pp. 70–1.

[46] *ibid.* p. 169; Aveling, *RH*, iv, 85–7; *HMC Rutland*, ii, 7–10.

[47] BM Add. MS 18730, fols, 1, 3, 15, 16, 27, 28; there are no references to such contacts after 1678. See also J. Morris, *The Troubles of our Catholic Forefathers* (3 vols., London, 1872–7), i, 402–5; *Constable Papers* (CRS, xxvii, 1927), pp. 261–73; J. A. Hawkes, *Sir Roger Bradshaigh of Haigh* (Chetham Soc. Miscellanies, 1945), p. 41; A. à Wood, *Life and Times*, ed. A. Clark (5 vols., Oxford Historical Soc., 1891–1900), ii, 281; *HMC 6th Report, Appendix* p. 370; Aveling, *West Riding*, p. 255.

[48] Lambeth Palace Library, MS 1391; W. L. Sachse (ed.), *The Diary of Roger Lowe* (London, 1938), pp. 64, 66.

[49] PC/2/60, pp. 331, 336; Bodl., Rawl. MSS A 135, pp. 174–5, A 136,

although they were Papists, they were also gentlemen; during the Popish Plot Sir Thomas Gascoigne was found not guilty on a charge of treason by a jury of his Yorkshire neighbours.[50]

In other ways, too, a Catholic squire had much in common with his Protestant neighbours. Sir John Arundell of Lanherne in Cornwall served as an officer of the militia in 1667; he presented to two Anglican benefices; he was consulted about the pricing of tin by no less a person than the lord treasurer and he had a dominant interest in parliamentary elections for the small Cornish borough of Mitchell until the *quo warranto* against its charter in 1684.[51] Yet despite this men like Sir John could not assume fully that responsibility for running the shire to which their rank entitled them, for they were excluded by law from public office and from serving as members of parliament. This could be damaging in financial terms; exclusion from lucrative offices removed one means of offsetting losses incurred elsewhere. It also had a more serious and insidious effect which was described, with surprising sympathy, by the Protestant marquis of Halifax:

To have no share in business, no opportunity of showing his own value to the world; to live at the best an useless and by others to be thought a dangerous member of the nation where he is born, is a burden to a generous mind that cannot be taken off by all the pleasure of a lazy unmanly life, or by the nauseous enjoyment of a

pp. 278–9, D 1283, fols, 15–16; *HMC Buccleuch (Montagu House)*, i, 329–30; Blundell, *Cavalier*, pp. 210–11; C. E. Whiting, *Studies in English Puritanism 1660–88* (London, 1968), pp. 36, 416; *An Account of the Convincement . . . of Richard Davies* (Newtown, 1928), pp. 122, 147–8; PRO, PRO/30/53/7, fol. 167; Aveling, *Northern Catholics*, pp. 343–4; *HMC Leeds*, p. 18.

50 BM Add. MSS 29563, fol. 228, 34730, fol. 32; *State Trials*, vii, 959ff.; A. Browning (ed.), *Memoirs of Sir John Reresby* (Glasgow, 1936), pp. 197–8.

51 Arundell MSS, 'Letters to and from Sir J. Arundell', lord Bath to Sir J. A., 29 July 1667 and 3 Dec. 1684; presentations dated 10 June 1671 (Ideford) and 24 Jan. 1686/7 (Phillock); Sir R. Edgecumbe to Sir J. A., 11 Feb. 1687; 'Bellings Letters', Sir J. A. to Sir R. Bellings, 9, 20 and 30 March 1685, 10 June and 26 July 1686. Another Catholic family with a sizeable parliamentary interest was the Howards (earls of Norwich and dukes of Norfolk) at Castle Rising: A. Bryant, *Samuel Pepys: The Years of Peril* (London, 1948), pp. 105–7.

dull plenty that produceth no food for the mind, which will ever be considered in the first place by a man that hath a soul.[52]

Despite the penal laws, despite sequestration during the Interregnum, despite exclusion from office, Catholic numbers dwindled only slowly and most Catholic landed families remained steadfast in the faith. Not all were saints of course. Few were as spectacularly sinful as the second earl of Castlehaven who was executed for rape and sodomy in 1631. But many must have felt like the bluff old soldier lord Bellasis who remarked that he had done much in his life that he was ashamed of; even the clergy were not free from accusations of drunkenness and wenching.[53] Many Protestants claimed that Catholics clung to their religion out of inertia and purblind conservatism, that they refused to abandon 'the old religion' simply because it was the one professed by their forefathers; there was much truth in this.[54] But their steadfastness was far from unthinking. Their conservatism was reinforced by confidence that the Catholic church, by virtue of the apostolic succession, was the sole legitimate source of spiritual authority.[55] Catholic controversialists laid great stress on the church's authority and on the need for unthinking submission to its dictates; they argued that the divisions among Protestants showed clearly that to rely on the Bible alone as a source of authority bred confusion, not certainty.[56] This authority and certainty were clearly the feature of Catholicism which appealed most to Charles II, James II and other converts.[57]

It would be wrong to see the Catholics' attachment to their

[52] Halifax, *Complete Works*, ed. J. P. Kenyon (Harmondsworth, 1969), p. 84. Some claimed that their freedom from county business gave Catholics more time to see to their estates: Reresby, *Memoirs*, pp. xxxviii, 70.

[53] *State Trials*, iii, 402ff.; Bodl., Rawl. MSS A 136, p. 119, D. 1283, fols. 12–13, 21–2.

[54] Halifax, *Works*, pp. 82–3; Caraman, pp. 21–3, 135–8.

[55] Lambeth Palace Library, MS 1391, fols, 2, 5–6.

[56] L. I. Bredvold, *The Intellectual Milieu of John Dryden* (Ann Arbor, 1956), pp. 76–98; I. Brown, *An Unerrable Church or None* (Douai, 1678); S. Cressy, *I. Why are You A Catholic?* (2nd edn, 1673); J. Gother, *A Papist Misrepresented and Represented* (1685), pp. 36–42.

[57] *State Tracts* (2 vols., 1689–92), ii, 273–4; G. Burnet, *History of My Own Time* (6 vols., Oxford, 1823), iii, 186–7; *The Autobiography of Symon Patrick* (Oxford, 1839), pp. 112, 114; Caraman, pp. 47–50; BM Add. MS 40160, fol. 45.

religion as resting on blinkered conservatism, unreasoning submission and ignorance. The Papist peers and gentry were far from uneducated. A few attended Oxford and Cambridge, although there was no Catholic teaching there and they could not take degrees. Rather more attended the Inns of Court.[58] Many went to the English schools and colleges abroad, where they received a good education; an unwilling non-Catholic student at the Jesuit school at St Omers admitted that he had learnt more there in a short time than he had done in seven years in Wales.[59] Although some Catholic gentlemen doubtless conformed to Macaulay's caricature of bucolic simplicity, one could not say that of Anthony à Wood's friend and fellow antiquary 'the great Sheldon' or even of the impoverished squire of Little Crosby, who grumbled at his twelve year old grandson's poor Latin and ignorance of Greek.[60] Despite the foreign education of gentry and priesthood, there remained something distinctively English about English Catholicism. It escaped the baroque extravagances of continental spirituality, especially those that grew around the cult of the Virgin Mary. Despite the emphasis on unquestioning faith and reliance on the church, the tone of Catholic spiritual writing was temperate and reasoned and had much in common with that of contemporary Protestant devotional works. It is significant that several leading Catholic controversialists – John Sergeant, Serenus Cressy, John Gother – were converts from Protestantism.[61] There were several reasons for this moderate tone. English Catholics tried hard to show that, whatever their religion, they were still good Englishmen. More important, continental spirituality was built on magnificent churches and the massive institutional apparatus refurbished by the Counter-Reformation. Such a basis was lacking in England, with hidden and

58 E. A. B. Barnard, *A Seventeenth Century Country Gentleman* (2nd edn, Cambridge, 1948), pp. 11–35, 41–4; *Grays Inn Admission Register*, pp. 289 (G. Knipe), 292 (T. Ireland), 295 (R. Allibone and C. Ingleby), 307 (lord Arundell of Wardour), 309 (H. and J. Hall), 312 (R. Sherburne), 313 (R. Hansby), 317 (Sir F. Radcliffe), 318 (lord Carrington), 321 (C. Byerley and R. Dormer), 326 (J. Towneley), 333 (Sir R. Throckmorton), 334 (Sir T. Clifton and R. Bartlett).
59 Longleat, Coventry MS xi, fols. 204–5.
60 T. B. Macaulay, *History of England* (2nd edn, 5 vols., London, 1849–61), ii, 332–4; *DNB*, Ralph Sheldon; Blundell, *Cavalier*, pp. 177–80.
61 Sister Marion Norman, 'John Gother and the English Way of Spirituality', *RH*, xi (1972), 306–17.

makeshift chapels and an underground priesthood. However strong the pull of family tradition and inherited principles, membership of the English Catholic community could not be entirely unthinking. Although the laws were normally laxly enforced, there was always the possibility that they *might* be enforced to the full. English Catholics consciously chose a life that was completely satisfying spiritually at the cost of sacrificing certain social and political advantages and with the constant fear of real persecution in time of crisis. Although the laws were not fully enforced and although many Catholics compromised and equivocated under pressure, this should not blind one to the fact that most of the aristocratic leaders of the Catholic minority ultimately put principle before expediency and by so doing ensured the survival of Catholicism in England between the reign of Elizabeth and the Industrial Revolution.

URBAN CATHOLICISM

Compared with the countryside, Catholicism was weak in provincial towns in the seventeenth century. In most towns, the population was small and closely packed, so that everyone knew everyone else's business. Most municipal authorities actively supported Protestant evangelism by appointing Puritan ministers to town churches and by providing Puritan lectureships. They also tried hard to suppress Popery. At York and Richmond, Yorkshire, for instance, the council on its own initiative doubled the statutory one shilling a week fine for absence from church.[62] In most towns residual Catholicism, the conservatism of the first years of Elizabeth's reign was gradually crushed, at least among the wealthier citizens.[63] There remained a few Papists among the poor, but the main strength of Catholicism in the larger towns came to be among the servants, dependants and suppliers of Catholic gentry who lived in the town for part or all of the year.[64] At York forty out of eighty-five persons presented as recusants in 1623 and forty-five out of seventy-two in 1633

[62] Aveling, *City of York*, pp. 53–4; *Northern Catholics*, pp. 17–18. At Lincoln the penalty was raised to 1s 8d: Sir J. W. F. Hill, *Tudor and Stuart Lincoln* (Cambridge, 1956), p. 99.
[63] Aveling, *City of York*, chaps. 1–2.
[64] Williams, *Wilts.*, pp. 214–17, 233–4, 255; Williams, *Bath and Rome, the Living Link* (Bath, 1963), chaps. 1–2; *VCH Staffs.*, viii, 271; Blundell, *Old Catholic Lancashire*, i, 49–50, ii, 25, 34, 48.

were associated with the Palmes and Thwing families who lived on the edge of the city. There were also a few professional men, notably doctors, who could get a training in a university abroad; at York there were three generations of doctors by the name of Alexius Vodka.[65] In most towns, even in strongly Catholic areas, the number of resident Catholics remained small until it was swollen by migrants from the countryside and from Ireland in the second half of the eighteenth century.[66]

The one exception was London. There Catholics had the advantage of being able to attend Mass more or less openly at the royal chapels and at those of the French, Spanish, Portuguese, Venetian and (later) Florentine representatives. Their were two royal chapels from 1662 to 1669 and one thereafter. The queen mother, Henrietta Maria, had a chapel at Somerset House served by a lord almoner, the abbé Montagu, six to ten French Capuchins and two Oratorians. She left most of these behind when she returned to France in 1665 and the chapel remained open until her death in 1669, when the king ordered that it be closed and the chaplains returned to France.[67] Queen Catharine arrived in 1662 with six Portuguese chaplains; none was a Jesuit as the Jesuits were so hated in England. Her chapel at St James's Palace opened that September and soon provided sermons in English. Attached to it were communities of six English Benedictines and twelve Portuguese Franciscans. The lord almoner, Louis Stuart, sieur d'Aubigny presided over a variegated establishment which included Philip Howard, a Dominican and a future cardinal, and Patrick MacGinn, an Irishman and an active intriguer at court.[68] After the queen mother's death, the queen

---

[65] Aveling, *City of York*, p. 85

[66] There were few Catholic recusants at Newcastle, but rather more at Durham: J. Rogan, 'Episcopal Visitations in the Diocese of Durham 1662–71', *Archaeologia Aeliana* (1956), p. 96; Howell, *Newcastle upon Tyne and the Puritan Revolution*, pp. 73, 75–6. For eighteenth century migrations, see Bossy, *RH*, x, 21–2.

[67] A. S. Barnes, 'Catholic Chapels Royal Under the Stuart Kings', *Downside Review* (1901), pp. 160–5; *CSPVen 1669–70*, p. 133.

[68] *Cal. Clar. C.P.*, v, 201; Barnes, *Downside Review* (1901), pp. 232–49; B. Weldon, *Chronological Notes ... of the English Congregation of the Order of St Benedict* (London, 1881), p. 196; BM Add. MS 10117, fol. 132; Prop. Ang., fol. 17; H. Foley, *Records of the English Province of the Society of Jesus* (7 vols. in 8, London, 1877–83), i, 174; *CSPD 1684–5*, p. 269.

moved from St James's to the more accessible chapel at Somerset House, where in 1670 she had an establishment of twenty-eight priests, maintained at the king's expense. Charles allowed the duke of York only a private chapel. In 1675 all the English and Irish priests were banished from the court, except for John Huddlestone, the Benedictine who had helped save the king's life after the battle of Worcester and who was to reconcile him to the church on his deathbed.[69] In 1680 Charles ordered the queen to move her chapel back to St James's, out of the public eye; by that time, of seventeen priests in her household only Huddlestone was English.[70]

In the early part of Charles II's reign there were many references to the freedom with which Catholics worshipped in London.[71] In 1671 the Venetian resident reported that the four ambassadorial chapels could not hold all those wishing to use them and even in 1680 two to three hundred people, mostly women, attended the queen's chapel.[72] The diarist John Evelyn attended a Catholic wedding at the queen's chapel in 1664 and a Catholic baptism there in 1671, at which the king was one of the godfathers.[73] At Easter 1672 the French ambassador publicly displayed a life-size tableau of the Last Supper; in the same year a printed broadsheet enumerated the spiritual benefits that Catholics could obtain by joining the confraternity of Our Blessed Lady of Succour at the queen's chapel. Even in 1678, after William Staley had been executed for treason, his Catholic friends arranged for his body to lie in state and openly said requiem masses for him.[74] From 1673 the Privy Council tried to

---

[69] Barnes, *Downside Review* (1902), pp. 39–53; J. G. Dolan, 'English Benedictine Missions', *Downside Review* (1898), pp. 144–8; Prop. Ang., fols. 635, 637; not all English priests left: the Franciscans' chapter meetings were still held at Somerset House and Christopher Davenport OFM died there in 1680: J. B. Dockery, *Christopher Davenport* (London, 1960), p. 135.

[70] BM Add. MS 25359, fols. 236–7; Barnes, *Downside Review* (1902) p. 53.

[71] Nunz. Fian. 49, fols. 221–2; *Dominicana* (CRS, vol. xxv, 1925), p. 273; Prop. Ang., fols. 635, 637; Foley, i, 267; L. Magalotti, *Travels of Cosimo III, Grand Duke of Tuscany, through England, 1669* (London, 1821), p. 458.

[72] *CSPVen 1671–2*, p. 76; *CSPD 1680–1*, p. 47.

[73] *Diary*, 9 June 1664, 19 Aug. 1671 (iii, 373, 585).

[74] *ibid.* 4 Apr. 1672 (iii, 612); *A Summary Relation of the Holy Congregation of Our Blessed Lady of Succour* (1672); *State Trials*, vi, 1511–12.

prevent Londoners from using the ambassadors' chapels, but its efforts were neither very sustained nor particularly effective. Ever since Elizabeth's reign, the English government had tried sporadically to restrict their use; by law they should have been used only by the ambassadors' domestic servants and not by the population at large, but in practice many English Catholics attended them and Catholic ambassadors, especially those of Spain, extended their protection to many who were not their menial servants. (It was a moot point whether ambassadors could appoint English chaplains.) These practices led to a number of incidents, in some of which diplomatic immunity was violated and the Council had to apologise. The Council always had to tread carefully in such matters for fear of provoking reprisals against English embassies in Catholic countries.[75]

The size of London's Catholic population was probably well below the ten to twelve thousand suggested by Agretti, a papal agent, in 1669. The Compton census revealed 2069 Catholic recusants in the diocese of London. In 1680 a list was drawn up of 1582 suspected Papists from the cities of London and Westminster and four suburban parishes who had not yet taken the oaths of allegiance and supremacy. I have identified 1278 Catholic recusants who were convicted in the county of Middlesex.[76] There were few Papists in the city of London. I have found only fifty-one convicted Catholic recusants and a survey of 1680 showed only seventy-seven Papists or reputed Papists.[77] The great majority of the London Catholics lived in the western suburbs and especially in the city of Westminster. This area contained the most fashionable residential districts, the foreign embassies

75 BM Add. MS 25358, fol. 22; *CSPD 1676–7*, pp. 349, 386; PC/2/68, pp. 208–9, 328–9; Bodl., Rawl. MS A 136, pp. 77–80; W. R. Trimble, *The Catholic Laity in Elizabethan England* (Cambridge, Mass., 1964), pp. 17, 64–5; Caraman, p. 16; W. R. Trimble, 'The Embassy Chapels Question', *Journal of Modern History*, xviii (1946), 97–107; B. Zimmerman, *Carmel in England* (London, 1899), pp. 245–8; Kenyon, *Popish Plot*, pp. 220–1. For ambassadors who distributed Catholic books, see Rostenberg, pp. 141–5; E. M. Thompson (ed.), *Hatton Correspondence* (2 vols., Camden Soc., 1878), i, 138; *CSPD 1676–7*, pp. 262, 269.

76 AAW A32, p. 469; Browning, *Historical Documents*, p. 413; *HMC House of Lords 1678–88*, pp. 225–6; Appendix 1. Not all Papists were convicted of recusancy.

77 *HMC House of Lords 1678–88*, pp. 169–71.

and the court. Here I have found 1169 convicted Catholic recusants.[78] Since the beginning of the century the main concentration of Catholics had moved westwards, from parishes in the
western suburbs like St Andrew, Holborn, and St James, Clerkenwell, to the three Westminster parishes of St Martin's in the Fields,
St Giles in the Fields and St Margaret's, which contained 869
recusants between them, two-thirds of the total for the county.
To some extent this drift westwards must have reflected the
increasingly Catholic tone of the Stuart court.[79]

Using the occupational descriptions of those convicted of
recusancy, one can get an impression of the social composition of
London Catholicism. Of the 1273 recusants of whom some
description was given, 411 were women – spinsters, wives and
widows. Of the men, 192 were of the rank of gentleman or
above.[80] Only thirty-three were labourers and only thirteen can
be identified as domestic servants. Of the rest 358 were described
vaguely as 'yeomen' (craftsmen or shopkeepers of some kind)
and 265 had specific occupations ascribed to them. Of these,
much the largest group consisted of those involved with clothing
and textiles (ninety-four, including fifty-three tailors), followed
by food and drink (forty), medicine (thirty, including doctors,
surgeons, barbers and apothecaries), metal goods (twenty-one),
building (eighteen) and a variety of luxury trades (also eighteen).
There were a variety of others, including two dancing-masters.
There were only nine merchants, although it is possible that some
of those described as 'gentlemen' were really merchants. Thus
although there was a strong representation of gentry among the
Catholic recusants of London and although many London Papists
no doubt depended on the patronage of the Catholic aristocracy,

[78] Those parishes with most Catholics were St Martin's in the Fields
(493), St Giles in the Fields (268), St Margaret's Westminster (110),
St Paul's Covent Garden (97), St Clement Danes (85), St Andrew
Holborn (63) and St Mary Savoy (41). I have counted only definite
Catholics who were convicted of recusancy under Charles II, see
Appendix 1.

[79] A. Dures, 'The Distribution of Catholic Recusants in London and
Middlesex, *c.* 1580–1629', *Essex Recusant*, x (1968), 77–8.

[80] Ten peers, nineteen knights and baronets, fifty-three esquires and 110
'gents'. These figures do not include 141 peers and gentlemen convicted in 1680 for St Giles in the Fields in order to keep them from
coming within ten miles of London: PDB, c3.

the embassies and the court, there did exist in London a vigorous urban Catholicism of artisans and shopkeepers which did not exist in other towns and which seems to have been less noticeable earlier in the century.[81] This vigour doubtless owed much to the accessibility of chapels and to the ease with which priests could move around; not only was it easier for them to remain unnoticed in London than it was in the country, but they could also usually carry on an independent mission there, not tied to one Catholic family.[82]

CATHOLICISM AT COURT

From the time of Charles I's marriage to Henrietta Maria of France, the court of the Stuart kings became increasingly associated with Catholicism. Charles II showed a strong preference for Catholic ladies both as possible wives and as mistresses; his brother James, even before he became a Catholic, showed a market fondness for Catholics and Irishmen as personal companions (men like Henry Jermyn and Dick Talbot), although some of his mistresses were Protestants. Charles's queen, Catharine, was a Catholic and had many Catholic servants; for a while she even had the Portuguese ambassador as her chamberlain.[83] James's first wife was converted to Catholicism shortly before her death; his second wife, Mary Beatrice, had a number of Catholic servants, including the notorious Edward Coleman as her secretary. With the large Catholic clerical establishment at the royal chapels there were always many priests at court, some of them active intriguers, like Patrick MacGinn and Dick Talbot's brother Peter, who in 1669 became titular archbishop of Dublin. Whitehall palace, a great rabbit-warren of apartments and corridors, was ideally suited to intrigue, especially under a king like Charles II, who always preferred informal means of consultation and procedure. Protestants noted with anxiety the

---

[81] Dures, pp. 70–1. He thinks about half of the convicted recusants of 1580–1629 were gentry and about one-eighth were servants.

[82] *ibid.* pp. 73–4; Zimmerman, pp. 207–15, 222–6, 265–6.

[83] *CSPVen 1673–5*, p. 443. The queen's servants were exempt from conviction for recusancy, and this protection was extended to some who were not her menial servants, like Daniel Arthur, a merchant, who acted as the financial agent of many Catholics: PC/2/64, p. 419; *CSPVen 1673–5*, p. 375.

French ambassadors' frequent attendance at court and the ease with which they obtained access to the king. In 1673 Charles ordered that all Papists should leave the court, but some soon trickled back. In 1675 most of the English, Scots and Irish priests were driven out; in 1678 most of the lay Catholics left too, except for a few of the queen's servants. When James II came to the throne, Catholics flocked to court once more, but it was James's old courtier friends not the Catholic gentry of the shires, who exercised political influence.

The distinction between 'court' and 'country' Catholics during this period has long been noted by historians.[84] The Catholicism of the court tended to be alien and cosmopolitan; the court was full of foreigners and Irish. The comte de Grammont felt quite at ease there; one doubts whether many English Catholic squires would have done. At times strange dreams of the reconversion of England sprang up in this exotic atmosphere, which would soon have withered had any attempt been made to put them into practice.

The Catholicism of the shires, on the other hand, remained much as it had been under Elizabeth: seigneurial, unambitious, concerned with survival and with being left alone to practise its own form of worship. Many Catholics were conscious of their vulnerability and sought to behave with circumspection. Henry Howard, later duke of Norfolk, whose brother Philip became a cardinal, wrote in 1667:

[We] do not desire at this time any alterations or innovations, or new rules or authorities to be procured, for . . . the poor Catholics of England are not really under such a heavy persecution as may be supposed . . . . if we do but continue sober and humble, we shall not I hope have severe laws put in execution upon us, for the indiscretion of some few impertinent, over-zealous busy coxcombs.[85]

He argued that Rome should not heed the counsels of those whose estates and persons were not in peril. He swore that if he received any letters from Rome that looked incriminating he would take them to a secretary of state and protest his innocence; this he

---

[84] Macaulay, ii, 332–5; D. Mathew, *Catholicism in England 1535–1935* (London, 1948), pp. 93–100.
[85] M. V. Hay, *The Jesuits and the Popish Plot* (London, 1934), p. 106; see also p. 102.

did.[86] Similarly many Catholics had considerable reservations about the wisdom of James II's aggressive Catholicising policies. Catholics under Charles II mostly accepted exclusion from national life as the price of maintaining their own form of belief. Although their hopes of open toleration were occasionally raised, most realised from bitter experience that the most they could expect was toleration by connivance: anything more was likely to excite fresh persecution; like Henry Howard, they distrusted grand schemes and innovations. A few were always liable to behave tactlessly, especially when they were drunk. Thomas Gunter told the vicar of Abergavenny that he had kept a priest under Cromwell and would keep one now. In Nottinghamshire in 1661, Papists were said to be approaching former soldiers, 'telling them that they, meaning the Papists, should have a day for it'. One threatened to kill a parson if he preached on 5 November.[87] Such incidents helped keep alive fear and hatred of Papists and offset much of the good done by the quiet demeanour of most Catholics. Such stories spread most at times of political tension, in which the Catholic question was involved: the tension helped give rise to the stories, which in turn reinforced the tension.[88] The importance of such incidents involving Papists was secondary and supplementary: the primary cause of anti-Catholic excitement was not the behaviour of Catholics in the localities, but the religious policies of the court and the political situation at the national level.

[86] BM Add. MS 15395, fols, 28–9; Hay, p. 104; T. A. Birrell, 'English Catholics without a Bishop, 1655–72', *RH*, iv (1958), 152.

[87] Longleat, Coventry MS xi, fols. 120–7, 132; *CJ*, ix, 467; L. Hutchinson, *Memoirs of the Life of Colonel Hutchinson*, ed. C. H. Firth (London, 1906), pp. 339–40.

[88] For instance, for 1666 see 'London's Flames Revived', *State Tracts*, ii, 27–46; *HMC le Fleming*, p. 41; *CSPD 1666–7*, p. 127 (Mr Dormer of Grove Park).

2

ENGLAND AND ROME:
THE CATHOLIC CLERGY

In this chapter I shall consider two further aspects of the situation of the English Catholics; each is concerned with the relationship of the surviving Catholic minority to the pope and the court of Rome. First, the breach with Rome left Catholics with the problem of reconciling two traditional and ingrained loyalties, to the king and to the pope, which were no longer strictly compatible. Although Catholics tried to reconcile the two by obeying the king in temporal matters and the pope in spiritual matters, their position was made more difficult by the wording of the oath of allegiance which the English state imposed on them in 1606. Secondly, starting in Elizabeth's reign, the English clergy and the papacy had started to build a new ecclesiastical organisation to help meet the spiritual needs of a persecuted minority. The strains and squabbling inevitable in such a situation were made more serious by the attempt of a section of the secular clergy to set up an organisation, based on a bishop and chapter, which would be independent of Rome for most practical purposes. Disputes about the legality of the Chapter complicated and exacerbated the disputes over the oath of allegiance which rent the clergy, and with them the laity, through most of the seventeenth century. Usually the secular priests (those belonging to no order, the equivalent of parish priests in Catholic countries), advocated greater submission to the English state and greater independence of Rome, while the regulars were more sensible of their duty to uphold the rights of the church and of the pope.

The papal primacy over the church before the breach with Rome had been, in Professor Scarisbrick's words, 'a cold, juridical fact, obvious and necessary enough in the institutional life of the Christian Church, not a central, compelling, gratifying truth in the experience of the individual Christian'.[1] When Henry VIII broke with Rome, there had been no question at first of changing the form of worship and so, to those who did not think too hard about it, it could seem quite possible to be both a good Catholic and a good subject. Under Elizabeth, when the state had established a heretical religion, the question of the Catholics' allegiance to the pope and the queen became more immediate and more delicate. The theorists of the Counter-Reformation were reviving and embellishing many of the highest claims of papal authority made when the medieval papacy had been at its apogee. These included the claim that the pope could excommunicate princes, declare them deposed and absolve their subjects from their allegiance. Taken to its logical conclusion, this involved the justification of tyrannicide, for an excommunicated prince was *ipso facto* a tyrant. Rome seldom tried to put into practice the full implications of this theory, but it was used to justify the excommunication of Elizabeth in 1570 and the papal sponsorship of the Spanish armadas and of the invasions of Ireland. The discomfiture created among English Catholics by the excommunication of 1570 was only partly mitigated by an explanatory bull of 1580, which said that the obligation to execute the sentence of excommunication was not binding on Catholics until it could be put into effect.[2] Most English Catholics, however, continued quietly loyal to the crown; few even among the exiles openly approved the papacy's actions against the English state. Most Catholics would not deny that the deposing power was taught by the church, but most agreed that it should not be put into practice, except perhaps as a warning; the annotators of the Catholic English Bible were typical in counselling patient submission to the state.[3]

By the early 1600s few Catholic writers outside Spain and Italy would entertain even the theoretical justification of tyrannicide. Following the Gunpowder Plot, the attempts on the life of Henry IV of France and the outcry against the writings of the

[1] J. J. Scarisbrick, *Henry VIII* (Penguin edn, Harmondsworth, 1971), p. 318.
[2] P. MacGrath, *Papists and Puritans under Elizabeth I* (London, 1967), pp. 69–72, 162.
[3] T. H. Clancy, *Papist Pamphleteers* (Chicago, 1964), pp. 74–6, 88–9, 95–6; Caraman, p. 20; MacGrath, pp. 162–3.

Jesuits Mariana and Suarez, the French Jesuits grew alarmed at their order's growing reputation as the defenders and practitioners of the assassination of princes, especially as they relied heavily on Henry IV's protection. Their pressure forced the Society to forbid its members to engage in controversies on the justifiability of tyrannicide; in practice this meant withdrawing from controversies on all aspects of the power to depose.[4] The church officially retained the theory of the deposing power, while taking no steps to put it into practice. In 1679, when the duke of York was in temporary exile at Brussels, he complained that an Irish friar had vigorously upheld the deposing power at the university of Louvain; the Brussels internuncio said that the friar could not be made to recant, as it was not an inadmissible opinion; it had been very tactless of the friar to uphold it at that time, however, and he was sent away from the university.[5]

Rome and the English Catholics eventually came to accept the permanence of the Protestant regime in England. Conspiracies came to an end. Charles I and Charles II were sympathetic towards the Catholics. At Rome the fiery zeal of the Counter-Reformation cooled; the new institutions ossified and the curia slowly relapsed into a bureaucratic caution which verged at times on total immobility and which often seemed to lose touch with practical realities: a letter bearing cardinal Barberino's seal was sent off, addressed simply to 'Most Reverend Walter Routse [?], Missionary at London, London'.[6] Faced with an English regime favourable to the Catholics, Rome soon became content to acquiesce in whatever it saw fit to do; to follow an independent line would be futile and dangerous. Relief for the English Catholics had to come from the crown, and Rome knew it.[7]

Many English Catholic writers of the seventeenth century denied that the deposing power was an article of faith. A few condemned it out of hand;[8] most regarded it as at best problematical:

[4] Clancy, pp. 96–106, 197.
[5] Tanari to Cibo, 26 Aug. 1679 NS, Rom. Tr. 100 A, fols. 187–8.
[6] AAW A33, pp. 19, 21, 33, 195 etc.; CRS, xxv, 44–5.
[7] P. Hughes, *Rome and the Counter-Reformation in England* (London, 1942), pp. 272–4; Wood, ii, 170.
[8] E. Cary, *The Catechist Catechiz'd* (1681), pp. 89–91, 129; W. H., *English Loyalty Vindicated by the French Divines* (1681), preface; *CSPD 1675–1676*, p. 52.

This pretended article of faith is by such new *de-fide* men grounded either on the actions of certain popes since pope Gregory VII, which both for their own sakes and ours it is to be wished had never been done, or might be blotted out of men's memories; or upon the decrees of some councils not received or acknowledged by Catholic churches.[9]

As early as 1603, thirteen priests signed a declaration of loyalty to the crown which in effect denied the deposing power. The whole problem of Catholics' allegiance was reopened and embittered when the oath of allegiance was imposed in 1606, following Gunpowder Plot. Quickly condemned by Rome, the oath demanded a repudiation of the deposing power in terms designed to divide Catholics and to force conscientious ones to reveal themselves. They were required to swear: 'I do from my heart abhor, detest and abjure as impious and heretical this damnable doctrine and position that princes which be excommunicated and deprived by the pope may be deposed or murdered by their subjects or any other whatsoever.'[10] Many Catholics were unwilling to describe any power claimed and used by popes in the recent past as impious and damnable, let alone heretical, even though they believed that the promise of allegiance could lawfully be made. As one pamphleteer wrote: 'When I detest from my heart all opinions offensive to government, that manner of expressing, which adds nothing of security to my prince, but evidently causes a rent among Christians and cast[s] dirt upon our forefathers ought to be carefully avoided.'[11] Sir John Winter's attitude was that of many Catholic laymen:

Although they hold communion with the church of Rome *in spiritualibus* and acknowledge (as their ancestors did) that the pope is the supreme spiritual pastor ... yet the Roman Catholics do not hold it as part of their faith that the pope is infallibly free from error, or that he can absolve subjects from their obedience to their

9 [S. Cressy], *Reflexions upon the Oathes of Supremacy and Allegiance* (1661), pp. 61–2. Wing (S 2588) attributes it to John Sergeant, but the copies in the Bodleian and Trinity College, Cambridge, are marked as being by Cressy. See also Berington, *Memoirs of Gregorio Panzani* p. 326n.
10 J. P. Kenyon, *The Stuart Constitution* (Cambridge, 1966), pp. 458–9.
11 *A Letter concerning the Iesuites* (1661), p. 6; see also Foley, v, 460–2; Cary, *The Catechist Catechiz'd*, pp. 31–62, 112–16, 126.

natural prince, or from the obligation of faithful upright dealing with their neighbours, though such their prince or neighbour be not of their religion, or were excommunicated . . . And all this (say they) they will cheerfully testify upon their oaths, without equivocation or mental reservation, if an oath in clear terms expressing as aforesaid be tendered unto them.[12]

William Blundell expressed his opinion more simply: 'All Catholic subjects of a lawful Protestant king (such as king Charles the 2nd) are obliged faithfully to adhere to that king in all invasions whatsoever, though made by Catholic princes or even by the pope himself.'[13]

Under Charles II most of the Catholic clergy consistently opposed the taking of the oath.[14] In 1679–82, a period of acute stress for English Catholicism, a small minority (mostly secular priests) defended the oath and sought the opinion of the Sorbonne on the lawfulness of taking it.[15] Some allowed the laity to take it; a few took it themselves and even took the oath of supremacy as well.[16] Rome expressed anxiety about the orthodoxy of some of the clergy and two English pamphlets were condemned by the Inquisition.[17]

It was usually the laity, not the clergy, who weakened and took the oath. Lord Petre quarrelled with his confessor, a Jesuit, when he took it in 1675; he was not alone: at least ten other Catholic peers had taken it the previous year.[18] Only six or seven of those

[12] *Sir John Winter's Observations upon the Oath enacted 1, Eliz.* (1679), pp. 17–18.

[13] Blundell, *Cavalier*, pp. 202–3; see also *ibid.* p. 185; Hay, p. 107; G. Digby, earl of Bristol, *Two Speeches* (1674), p. 11.

[14] AOFM, Acta Capitularum 1625–1746, p. 161; Vecchi to Secretary, 3 July 1660 NS, Rom. Tr. 98, fol. 157; Foley, v, 80–1n.; ASJ, Cardwell Transcripts, i, fols, 83, 94–100, 113; AAW A34, pp. 783–6.

[15] AAW A34, pp. 541–9, 652–5; Tanari to Cibo, 13 March and 24 April 1682 NS, Rom. Tr. 100A, fols. 281–2, 284; J. Kirk, *Biographies of English Catholics in the Eighteenth Century*, ed. J. H. Pollen and E. Burton (London, 1909), pp. 179–80.

[16] Bodl., Rawl. MSS A 135, p. 356, A 136, pp. 17–18, 91–2; *State Trials*, vii, 714, 722; Morrice MS P, p. 369.

[17] C. Dodd (*vere* H. Tootell), *Church History of England* (3 vols., 'Brussels', 1742), iii, 385–6; AAW A 34, p. 735; the works condemned were those by Cary and 'W. H.' mentioned in n. 8 above.

[18] A. W. Thibaudeu (ed.), *Autograph Letters in the Collection of Alfred Morrison: Bulstrode Papers* (1 vol. only, London, 1897), i, 291; *LJ*, xii, 674, 606, 607, 610–11, 620, 639, 641. The ten were lords Berkshire,

who sat in the Lords avoided taking it; an order of the House
of 30 April 1675 removed the necessity.[19] The duke of York said
later that he had taken it without knowing that it was condemned,
and added that he now saw that he had been wrong to do so.[20]
Sir Thomas Strickland thought that all Catholics would take the
oath; a Jesuit in 1681 thought that at least a third of the English
Catholics were against it, which would suggest that the majority
were prepared to take it.[21] During the persecution which followed
the Popish Plot, some laymen were imprisoned for refusing the
oath but many found doctrinal purity hard to maintain – they
had estates to lose. There were several attempts to have the oath
modified. In 1660–3 there were a number of suggestions, including
one which the Chapter discussed with Clarendon; one formula
seems to have had the king's approval, and was tentatively offered
to Rome, but without success.[22] There were other attempts in
1674 and 1677.[23] Throughout, the chances of finding a formula
that would satisfy both Rome and the English parliament were
virtually nil. So, it was still popularly believed that the English
Catholics approved a tenet which few in fact wholly accepted,
simply because many could not stomach the form of words in
which the state required them to renounce it.

THE ORGANISATION OF THE MISSION

Under Charles II one can distinguish two main types of Catholic
mission: the chaplaincy, where the priest lived in the house of a
Catholic peer or gentleman, who provided a chapel, and the
independent 'circuit', where the priest lived in rented rooms or

Cardigan, Stourton, Audley, York, Bristol, Widdrington, Bellasis,
Norwich, Stafford.

19 *LJ*, xii, 671–3. Of the list on p. 671 only Petre took the oath; lord
Teynham was not on the list but does not seem to have taken it.
20 Tanari to Cibo, 30 March and 8 June 1680 NS, Rom. Tr. 100A, fols.
223–4, 237.
21 *HMC le Fleming*, p. 154; Foley, v, 81n.; Kirk, pp. 179–80
22 Vecchi, 13 Nov. and 4 Dec. 1660 NS, Rom. Tr. 98, fols. 259–60,
263–4, 278; Nunz. Fian. 47, fol. 10; *Cal. Clar. S. P.*, v, 43, 358; AAW
A32, pp. 284, 287, 294, 393; St George's Cathedral, Southwark, MS
106e, p. 391.
23 Dodd, iii, 385; Tanari, 9 April 1677 NS, CUL Add. MS 4878, fol.
642; Courtin au Roi, 8 April 1677 NS, Baschet 135.

travelled around with his portable altar and massing-stuff, saying Mass and finding shelter where he could. A few missions fell somewhere between the two main types; the priest served a circuit, but operated from the house of one person – a yeoman, perhaps, or a widow – who provided him with shelter, food and perhaps fodder for his horse, but no salary.[24] Over most of the country the resident chaplain was the norm; 'These secular priests and regulars are almost all in the houses of wealthy laymen, which are the parishes of England,' wrote the papal agent Agretti in 1669. Of thirty-four members of the Chapter in 1684, eight lived in London, three abroad, twenty-one with particular Catholics and only two had no place of abode ascribed to them. In 1692 all the secular priests in Hampshire, Staffordshire, Worcestershire and Gloucestershire lived as chaplains; in 1701 bishop Leyburn knew of 219 Catholic peers and gentlemen who kept priests of some kind. Most Benedictines and most Jesuits outside London lived as chaplains.[25] Chaplaincies were less common among the Franciscans; in 1716, of thirty-two whose mission was described, ten lived as chaplains, ten lived in London, eight had circuits and four operated the intermediate type of mission.[26] The chaplaincy remained the most common type of mission and secular priests and the various orders vied for control of particular great families.[27]

The resident chaplaincy reflected the nature of Catholic congregations in many parts of the country, with a nucleus of the servants, tenants and dependants of a Catholic notable, who could afford to maintain a priest and who exerted his social authority to keep his inferiors steadfast in the faith. His household, with its chapel, provided the focus of spiritual life.[28] The

---

[24] For this intermediate type see AOFM, 'Mr Anthony Parkinson's State of the Province, anno 1716', pp. 10–12.

[25] AAW A33, pp. 324–5, A34, pp. 793–6, A38, no. 2; CRS, ix, 107–8, 112–13; Foley, i, 1–2. Two of the three Franciscans in Hampshire, however, had independent circuits: AOFM, Parkinson's State of the Province, pp. 17–19.

[26] AOFM, Parkinson's State of the Province, *passim*.

[27] Williams, *Wilts.*, p. 110.

[28] *ibid.* pp. 189–92; Aveling, *Northern Catholics*, pp. 170, 181; Aveling, *West Riding*, p. 228; Caraman, pp. 12, 38–41. There were many similarities between devout households, whether they were Anglican, Puritan or Catholic: Aveling, *Studies in Church History*, iv, 105.

priest usually ministered to the poor Catholics of the surrounding area, though some, like Mr Mason of Worcester, refused to do so. Many travelled long distances on broken-down horses to visit Catholics too poor to pay their expenses; they might be lonely, seeing other priests only rarely, and their dependence on their host might prove embarrassing or even humiliating. Some acted as stewards, or as tutors for their hosts' children. A few wealthy Catholic families, like the Throckmortons or the Carylls, kept several priests, one for the household, the rest for the surrounding area, but the one-man mission was the norm.[29]

An independent mission was easiest in London. It was relatively easy to remain unobserved; a large Catholic population was concentrated in a small area, including many wealthy Catholics who could provide a priest with plenty to live on. In case of emergency, some priests could find protection in one of the Catholic embassies. Fr Bede, a Carmelite, described how he lived in lodgings and carried on an active mission among the poor and those in prison as well as among the well-to-do.[30] There were at least nine independent missions in provincial towns in the 1690s, at least one of them dating back before James II's reign; they were maintained either by wealthy individuals or by those whom the mission served; if need be, they were subsidised from common funds.[31] There were also independent rural missions, mostly in poor, remote, sparsely populated areas in Yorkshire, Lancashire, Northumberland and the Welsh marches. The money to maintain these missions (sometimes as little as £7 a year) came either from endowments or from the common funds of the clergy. The secular clergy of several counties had funds of their own to

---

29 CRS, ix, 113; W. Price, 'Three Jesuits at Plowden Hall in Shropshire in the Eighteenth Century', *RH*, x (1969), 165–9; AAW A38, no. 2; J. G. Dolan, 'English Benedictine Missions', *Downside Review* (1900), pp. 169–70; Caraman, p. 38; Williams, *Wilts.*, pp. 114–15.

30 Zimmerman, pp. 204, 207–15, 222–5, 245–8, 265–7; Foley, i, 1–2; *CSPVen 1673–5*, p. 40.

31 AAW A38, no. 2. That at Tamworth went back thirty years; the others were at Edgbaston, Wolverhampton, Newcastle, Durham and York. There were Franciscan missions at Hexham, Edgbaston and Abergavenny, all founded under James II, and there had been another at Hereford in 1684–8: AOFM, Parkinson's State of the Province, pp. 1, 9, 13; Fr Thaddeus, *The Franciscans in England* (London, 1898), p. 154.

maintain independent missions and to support aged and infirm priests.[32]

The financial position of the mission was always a little precarious and much depended on the continued willingness of individual Catholics to maintain priests. A resident chaplain would receive a salary as well as full board; a 'riding missioner' received fees for weddings, burials etc., payments for masses for the dead and perhaps other payments for expenses from those whom he served; these were sometimes supplemented by money bequeathed to the circuit. This was normally adequate for the priests' needs, and most were expected to save some of their income and to give or bequeath money to the common funds.[33] The mission depended on two other types of income. First, the personal wealth of priests. One had £700 out at interest; another described 'a good purse' as the 'conditio sine qua non' of the Yorkshire mission. All at the general Chapter of 1667 gave money, mostly between £2 and £5, for the English college at Lisbon.[34] Secondly, legacies of money or property. These could be considerable; in 1689 lands held in Monmouthshire for various orders totalled over a thousand acres and brought in over £250 a year. Such bequests 'for superstitious uses' had to be kept secret; the Jesuits' Derbyshire district lost almost all its property in the early 1680s. When all else failed, the missions had to fall back, as always, on the gifts of the faithful.[35] The English mission seems to have received no financial help from abroad, although the Spanish government sent ten thousand crowns for payment to aged and suffering priests in 1667 and Propaganda agreed to provide for ten priests in Scotland in 1677. The English college

[32] AAW A38, no. 2; CRS, ix, 107–12; Blundell, *Old Catholic Lancashire*, i, 7, 27; Williams, *Wilts.*, pp. 96, 107; Thaddeus, pp. 179–82. For the distribution of the priests in the North Riding between chaplaincies and circuits, see Aveling, *Northern Catholics*, pp. 344–8.
[33] AOFM, Parkinson's State of the Province, passim.
[34] *CTB*, vii, 17, 295; AAW A33, pp. 147–8; BM Egerton MS 2260, fols. 129–30; for example of priests who depended on their own incomes, see AOFM, Parkinson's State of the Province, pp. 1, 10, 11.
[35] CRS, ii, 299–303 (of 24 properties, the annual value is given for 15, which brought in a total of £246 0s 4d a year); AAW A34, pp. 185, 757, 836–7; *CTB*, viii, 1290; Foley, vii, pp. cxlix–cli; Thaddeus, pp. 87–94; R. Meredith, 'The Eyres of Hassop from the Test Act to Emancipation', *RH*, ix (1967), 10–13.

at Douai received a papal pension and Rome gave twenty thousand florins to the English colleges in Flanders in 1679.[36]

Under Elizabeth almost all the missioners were secular priests from the new seminaries; a few Jesuits also came over[37] and disputes soon arose between some of the seculars and the Jesuits, disputes which were embittered by the psychological strain imposed by persecution. They were partly concerned with apparently trivial issues of precedence and prestige, but also the association with Spain of a small minority of the clergy, including some leading Jesuits, drove other priests to assert their loyalty to the English crown in extravagant terms. The government encouraged these divisions. In 1598 matters came to a head; Rome appointed one Blackwell 'archpriest' and head of the clergy. Many seculars saw him as a tool of the Jesuits; their protests were ignored by Rome and this convinced them (not without reason) that the Jesuits had stopped them from getting a fair hearing.[38]

The makeshift archpriest system continued, unsatisfactorily, for some years. It became obvious that England was not going to revert to Catholicism and that a permanent organisational structure was needed which would take account of the peculiar situation of a Catholic minority in a non-Catholic country. Following a softening in the government's attitude towards Catholics during the negotiations for the Spanish marriage, such a structure was provided for the secular clergy and the regular orders. In 1623, after some hesitation, Rome appointed William Bishop titular bishop of Chalcedon, with jurisdiction over England. From the outset there was some disagreement as to the precise extent of his authority. Rome regarded him as a 'vicar apostolic', with authority derived entirely from a special commission from the Holy See, which was therefore wholly revocable, as distinct from an 'ordinary', a bishop whose authority was derived from the tenure of an established diocese. In April 1624

---

36 *CSPVen 1666–8*, p. 123; Altieri to Paris Nuncio, 2 Aug. 1677 NS, Cibo to Tanari, 3 June 1679 NS, Rom. Tr. 100A, fols. 87, 174; Guilday, pp. 69, 340n.

37 In 1598 there were over 400 secular priests in England, but only fourteen Jesuits, MacGrath, p. 285.

38 *ibid.* pp. 274–89; Clancy, *Papist Pamphleteers*, pp. 82–5; Hughes, pp. 277–306; J. Sergeant, *An Account of the Chapter erected by William, Titular Bishop of Chalcedon*, ed. W. Turnbull (London, 1853), pp. 7–20

Bishop died; his successor was Richard Smith. Bishop had already set up a rudimentary ecclesiastical organisation under the overall supervision of a chapter of canons. Whether Bishop, as a vicar apostolic, had had the authority to create such a chapter was dubious. The Chapter claimed that its foundation was valid, that Bishop and Smith had been ordinaries and that Rome had recognised this at least tacitly.[39] Smith left England in 1631 after a bitter feud with the regulars; he remained abroad until his death in 1655. So from 1631, this body of dubious legality, which claimed to exercise episcopal authority first in the bishop's absence and then *sede vacante*, was the only immediate superior that the secular clergy had.

Faced with attacks on its authority, the Chapter tried spasmodically to obtain a successor to Smith on terms which would not involve the annihilation of its authority. Under Charles II the full Chapter consisted of the Dean, who was vicar-general of the London district, five or six other vicars-general, nineteen archdeacons and ten or eleven other canons, making a total of thirty-six.[40] It seldom met as a whole but 'consults' of leading members were often held in London. The Dean acted as chairman and titular head. He was responsible for maintaining good relations with the court and the Catholic ambassadors and for the discipline of the London clergy. He was assisted by a treasurer and a secretary.[41] The vicars-general each supervised a group of counties. Their function was to examine and to give faculties to missioners and to provide for local needs. Every two years they were supposed to visit the archdeacons in their districts. The archdeacons each supervised two or three counties and were supposed to visit the clergy there annually, and to try to maintain moral and pastoral standards among the clergy.[42] Under Charles II the Chapter does seem to have tried to maintain standards. Frequent exhortations were made to perform visitations regularly.[43] The Chapter tried to prevent priests from publishing

[39] For arguments against the Chapter, see Bodl., Rawl. MS D 840, fols. 258–72; for arguments for the Chapter, see Sergeant, pp. 31–45, 65–80. The latter are not very convincing.

[40] AAW A32, pp. 288–9, A34, pp. 793–6, 813–14; Williams, *Wilts.*, pp. 96, 241–2.

[41] BM Egerton MS 2260, fols. 134–9.

[42] *ibid.* fols. 139–41.

[43] AAW A32, pp. 583–5, A34, pp. 57–8, 405–6, 822–3, 827, 832–5;

opinions contrary to the teachings of the church or the wishes of the state.[44] It is uncertain how effective the exhortations to diligence were; most vicars-general and archdeacons lived in or near their districts and vacancies mostly seem to have been filled quickly.[45] There is evidence of meetings of clergy on a county level to discuss pastoral matters; in 1685–6 the Staffordshire and Hampshire clergy agreed to follow the broad lines of policy laid down by the Chapter. But the Chapter's directives against immorality, gaming and the frequenting of alehouses in the 1680s show that the situation was far from satisfactory.[46]

The organisation of the regular orders followed a similar pattern. England was made a vice-province of the Society of Jesus in 1619 and a province in 1623. By 1676 the country was divided into nine larger districts, or 'colleges', and five smaller ones, or 'residences'. The provincial, who usually lived in London, was directly subordinate to the general of the Society in Rome.[47] A mission from the Benedictine houses on the continent began in the first years of the seventeenth century; after years of negotiations, English monks from the Spanish, English and Italian congregations were united in an English congregation in 1621, the form of which was laid down by a papal bull, *Plantata*, in 1633. At the head of the congregation was a president-general; below him, and independent of each other, were the English Benedictine houses on the continent and the two missionary provinces of Canterbury and York, each with a provincial and various subordinate officers. The congregation's supreme legislative and appeal body was the general chapter, which met every four years.[48] The restoration of the English province of the Franciscans began in 1618 but was not completed until 1629. In 1647 it was divided into eight districts each with a guardian; by 1672 the number had grown to eleven. Not all guardians were resident and the provision that guardians should visit their districts annually proved impossible to enforce. The Franciscans

B. Hemphill (*vere* Whelan), *The Early Vicars Apostolic of England* (London, 1954), pp. 161–4.

[44] AAW A34, p. 406; BM Egerton MS 2260, fols. 130–2.
[45] AAW A34, pp. 793–6, 813–14.
[46] AAW A34, pp. 805–7, 832–5, 951–2, 1075–9.
[47] Foley, i, 1–2 and passim.
[48] Weldon, pp. 45–6, 94–119; H. N. Birt, *Obit. Book of the English Benedictines 1600–1912* (Edinburgh, 1913), pp. xxvi–xxix.

also held regular chapter meetings.[49] A small Carmelite mission began in 1615 and a small Dominican mission in 1617; an English Dominican province was created in 1622.[50]

The size of the English mission under Charles II fluctuated and is hard to assess. Agretti's estimate in 1669 was probably fairly accurate – 230 seculars, 120 Jesuits, eighty Benedictines, fifty-five Franciscans and a few Carmelites and Dominicans.[51] Claims by the Chapter that there were 500 secular priests in 1660 or 800 missioners in 1664 were probably exaggerated.[52] The number of Benedictines on mission remained fairly constant, between forty-eight and sixty-two, while the number in the English order as a whole remained between 108 and 118; there was a small increase under James II, the whole order reaching a peak of 159 in 1693 and the mission one of seventy-nine in 1710.[53] Jesuit numbers fluctuated more. The number on mission fell from 151 in 1660 to between 122 and 139 between 1664 and 1678; it then fell sharply to ninety in 1679–80, recovered to 110 in 1683 and rose to 145 in 1687, when every available priest was sent over. Numbers fell sharply at the Revolution, to just over a hundred in 1689–90. The size of the province as a whole remained between 261 and 297 from 1660 to 1682, rising to 324 in 1687 and 337 in 1689. The Jesuit mission was smaller under Charles II than it had been in the 1630s; the average number on mission in 1635–40 was 176.[54] I have come across no reliable figures for the number of secular priests.

One problem common to all orders was that of discipline. The situation of a mission in a non-Catholic country was alien to the traditional organisation of the Catholic church. Normally priests fitted into a well-defined place in an established ecclesiastical structure, either a parish or a religious order under the close

[49] Thaddeus, pp. 30–7, 46–9, 56–8; AOFM, Acta Capitularum 1625–1746, pp. 130–1.
[50] Guilday, pp. 348, 402.
[51] W. M. Brady, *The Episcopal Succession* (3 vols., Rome, 1877), iii, 109; Foley, v, facing p. 214, gives 122 Jesuits on mission in 1669, while Aveling gives 62 Benedictine missioners in the same year: Aveling, 'The Education of Eighteenth Century English Monks', *Downside Review*, lxxix (1961), 135–6.
[52] AAW A32, pp. 187, 469.
[53] Aveling, *Downside Review* (1961), pp. 135–6.
[54] Foley, vii, pp. lxxxviii–ciii, and facing p. clxviii.

supervision of their superiors. But on the English mission priests found shelter where they could; domestic chaplains especially were dependent on the laity in a way that priests in a Catholic country never were. The problems of discipline thus created were made worse by conditions of persecution; many missioners lived far away from their superiors, who were further hampered by the need to operate in secret. The need for disguise meant that priests had to wear secular dress and the anonymity that this conferred can have done nothing to improve their moral standards. In such circumstances it is not surprising that some priests went spectacularly off the rails; one seduced his host's wife; another seduced his host's niece and murdered the resultant child; another had to be treated for venereal disease; another was killed in a duel.[55] Fr Heton SJ accused Edward Turner SJ of drunkenness while Turner accused Heton of seducing servant-maids in the confessional.[56] By far the worst offenders were the foreign regulars – Irish, French, Spanish, Portuguese and Italian – who abounded in London; Agretti gave the names of seventeen Irish priests in London in 1669, some of whom, the followers of Peter Walsh, were under the protection of the English government.[57] Many of these foreign regulars were unused to and unfitted for life outside the cloister; they had no superiors in England and so did as they pleased, saying masses as and when they liked and ignoring their superiors' orders to return home.[58] Some apostasised and caused scandals; one left France with a nun and set up as an innkeeper. Even the king complained of foreign nuns 'gadding about' instead of remaining in their cloisters.[59]

55 *HMC Rutland*, ii, 115; *A Strange and Wonderful Relation of a Barbarous Murder Committed by James Robinson* (1679), pp. 6–8; M. Prance, *The Whore of Babylon's Pockey Priest* (1681); BM Add. MS 10117, fol. 73.
56 Bodl., Rawl. MSS D 1283, fols. 12–13, 21–2, A 135, p. 487; see also AOFM, Acta Capitularum 1625–1746, p. 90, for a Franciscan suspected of keeping a mistress.
57 Brady, iii, 114–16.
58 Prop. Ang., fols. 510, 609, 638; Nunz. Fian. 46, fols. 91–2; Cibo to Tanari, 24 Aug. 1680 NS, Rom. Tr. 100A, fol. 241; BM Add. MSS 15395, fols. 401–5, 25374, fols. 65–6, 41804, fols. 34, 36, 53.
59 *HMC le Fleming*, p. 77; *HMC Portland*, iii, 335; Prop. Ang., fols. 635–41; CRS, xxv, 47–9. The queen mother's servants claimed that the French Capuchins were less bad than their enemies made them out to be, Prop. Ang., fol. 17.

However despite the aberrations of foreign regulars and of a few English priests, it would be misleading to suggest that immorality was rampant on the English mission. Most priests were decent, conscientious men and the most common problems were laxness, mediocrity and preferring comfortable positions in London or in great houses to the rigours of an itinerant mission. These problems were greatest among the secular clergy, at once the most numerous body and the only one lacking the firm, uncontested superior authority which alone could solve such problems.[60] The task of providing such a superior authority was far from simple. Earlier divisions and doubts about the Chapter's validity were increased and complicated by Rome's failure to appoint a successor to bishop Smith, who died in 1655, and by the growth of Blackloism among the secular clergy.

BLACKLOISM AND THE SEARCH FOR A BISHOP

Rome had regarded Smith as somewhat suspect because of his associations with Gallicanism, and suspected him, wrongly, of being a Jansenist. Thomas White, alias Blacklo, a leading secular priest, went further and his theological writings were condemned by Rome.[61] With Sir Kenelm Digby and two priests, Henry Holden and Peter Fitton, Blacklo was one of a small group of Catholics who tried to secure a promise of toleration from the leaders of the army in 1647 in return for a comprehensive promise of allegiance to the regime in power. At the time this seemed far from indefensible. The king himself was involved in negotiations with the army and Catholics clearly had more to hope for from the relatively tolerant army leaders than from the rigidly intolerant majority in parliament. Those involved in this approach included a number of leading Catholic laymen and representa-

---

[60] However, where an uncontested authority did exist, it might be slow to act. Alphonsus Smithson OFM was reported at the Franciscan Chapter of 1665 to be living with a woman and heavily in debt, but it was not until 1668 that he was expelled from the mission and his faculties were withdrawn; AOFM, Acta Capitularum 1625–1746, pp. 90, 101.

[61] R. Clark, *Strangers and Sojourners at Port Royal* (Cambridge, 1932), pp. 10–13 and chap. 11; R. I. Bradley, 'Blacklo and the Counter-Reformation', in C. H. Carter (ed.), *From the Renaissance to the Counter-Reformation: Essays in Honor of Garrett H. Mattingly* (New York, 1965), pp. 348–70.

tives of the secular clergy and all the religious orders, including the Jesuits; the move also had the guarded approval of Rome.[62] There was considerable disagreement among those involved over the extent to which they were prepared to renounce the papal deposing power, but the negotiations were brought to an end by the king's escape from the army and the start of the Second Civil War. Unlike other Catholics, the Blackloites continued their approaches to the army and the Rump even after Charles I's execution. In 1649 Digby came to discuss with Cromwell the possibility of toleration but the Council of State ordered him to leave the country. He returned in 1654–5, when he clearly enjoyed Cromwell's favour and friendship.[63] The Blackloites also differed from other Catholics in combining their denial of the deposing power (in order to secure a toleration) with claims of the complete validity of the Chapter, which they claimed had the right to elect a new bishop in place of the ailing Smith, whether Rome gave its consent or not. Moreover, they were prepared to seek the opinion of French Gallican divines on these matters if Rome proved refractory. Fitton wrote to Digby in 1647: 'Relying on the justice of our cause, we shall seek to redress ourselves the best way we can, and I hope we shall not be blamed if we chance to set certain questions on foot which the divines on this side of the Alps [*n.b.*] do hold may be disputed without breach of unity of the Church.'[64]

Blackloism represented one extreme reaction to the conflict implicit in the position of all who were Englishmen and Catholics, the conflict between loyalty to the church and loyalty to the state. For most English Catholics, it remained implicit; they made no demands on Rome, Rome made no impossible demands on them; nor did the state if they kept quiet and out of politics. But the Blackloites had some extreme demands to make; they hoped to secure at a stroke toleration for Catholics, a bishop for the clergy (who would legitimise the authority of the Chapter) and the expulsion of the Jesuits from England.[65] Like the Gallicans

62 R. Pugh, *Blacklo's Cabal* (1680, reprinted Farnborough, 1970), pp. 26, 30, 59–60; St George's Cathedral, Southwark, MS 106e, p. 21; ASJ, Foley MS i, fols. 166–75.
63 R. T. Petersson, *Sir Kenelm Digby* (London, 1956), pp. 234–6.
64 Pugh, *Blacklo's Cabal*, p. 28 and passim.
65 *ibid.* p. 28.

in France, they ignored the centralisation of the church in the Counter-Reformation and claimed to represent a pre-Reformation tradition of national churches' independence of Rome, except in purely spiritual matters. 'This hath been the practice heretofore in Catholic times in England, is now in France and in all other Catholic states and kingdoms,' wrote Henry Holden.[66] This attitude expressed in an extreme form the latent dislike of subordination to Rome, the desperate desire for an ecclesiastical government on an *English* basis, unexceptionable to the state, which underlay the Chapter's pressure for a bishop. At the heart of this attitude lay a resentment of the imputation that one could not be both a good Catholic and a good Englishman. This feeling gave an added edge to the Chaptermen's desire to hold onto the direction of the affairs of the secular clergy. In fact the Blackloites' extremism did the Chapter more harm than good. It divided the secular clergy and started a bitter feud between George Leyburn, president of the college at Douai, and the leading junta of Chaptermen.[67] It discredited the Chapter among Catholics and Royalists as disloyal to the monarchy.[68] It made Rome deeply suspicious of the Chapter's orthodoxy and made it easy for its opponents to use the slurs of Blackloism, Gallicanism and Jansenism against it.[69]

It is probable that only a small minority of the secular clergy were really Blackloites. A consult of the Chapter in 1661 and a general Chapter in 1667 declared their abhorrence of Blacklo's doctrines; in 1667 and 1676 the Chapter ordered that no priest should publish anything that had not been approved by the London consult.[70] But the Chapter continued its tradition of independence of Rome; in 1667 it refused to subscribe a form of full submission to Rome preparatory to obtaining a bishop.[71] It

---

[66] *ibid.* p. 33.
[67] Prop. Ang., fols. 706–10; *An Encyclical Epistle sent to their Brethren by the Venerable Dean and Chapter* (1660).
[68] Birrell, *RH*, iv, 142–3; E. Hyde, earl of Clarendon, *The Life of* (3 vols., Oxford, 1827), ii, 112.
[69] Prop. Ang., fol. 342; Nunz. Div. 232, fol. 159; Kirk, p. 98.
[70] Vigilio to Vecchi, 23 Oct. 1660 NS, Rom. Tr. 98, fols. 238–9; *A Manifest Publisht to their Brethren by the General Chapter of the Catholick English Clergy* (1661), pp. 2–3; AAW A34, pp. 406, 429–32; Prop. Ang., fol. 648; BM Egerton MS 2260, fols. 130, 132.
[71] Pugh, *Blacklo's Cabal*, pp. 110–25.

continued to insist that Smith's successor should be an ordinary, not a vicar apostolic, so that the Chapter's validity would be confirmed. If Rome refused, then the Chapter would continue to stand on its own alleged authority, without papal confirmation. Rome refused to confirm the authority of a body of whose orthodoxy it harboured deep suspicions.[72] The situation was changed by the Restoration: 'Our business now is at a full stop till the inclinations of the state be known.'[73]

The Chaptermen hoped to persuade the king to insist that the clergy needed an ordinary, not a vicar apostolic, and then to use his insistence as a major bargaining asset in future negotiations with Rome. Gage, the clergy's agent in Rome, thought an ordinary

> infinitely more consonant with his [Majesty's] prerogative than those of the court of Rome . . . If as we hope the king grow absolute and continue not disaffected towards our religion, we may under his protection prescribe unto this court what laws we please, in order both to the power and person of our superior.[74]

This policy failed because Charles was not very interested in the problem. He was friendly enough to the Chapter but was probably influenced more by priests at court, like Howard, d'Aubigny, MacGinn and Peter Talbot, than by the Chaptermen. In 1661 a consult of the Chapter denied the pope's deposing power, claiming that the king wanted it to do so, but the general Chapter of 1667 said that this denial should not be regarded as an act of the Chapter. In 1665, 1667 and 1670 Chaptermen stated that the king would not admit a vicar apostolic.[75] It is doubtful, however, whether Charles really cared what sort of superior the clergy had, although in 1661 it seems that he did express a preference for an ordinary.[76] But his main concern was that his kinsman d'Aubigny should be made a cardinal; he had no objection to his being made a vicar apostolic as well. In 1663

72 Birrell, *RH*, iv, 144–5; Nunz. Fian. 45, fol. 323; AAW A33, p. 218; Brady, iii, 110–12.

73 AAW A32, p. 61.

74 *ibid.* pp. 75–6.

75 *ibid.* pp. 294, 624–5; AAW A33, p. 511; Sergeant, pp. 91, 94; BM Egerton MS 2260, fol. 126.

76 Sergeant, pp. 88–9; d'Aubigny to d'Estrades, 24 Aug. 1661 NS, CUL Add. MS 4878, fols. 559–65; Dockery, p. 156.

Richard Bellings was sent to Rome to press for d'Aubigny's elevation, but despite the efforts of his supporters (who included the Jesuits) Alexander VII refused.[77] When Vecchi, the internuncio at Brussels, came to England in 1664, Charles urged that d'Aubigny be promoted without delay; he was persuaded to agree to his being made vicar apostolic as well. This time Rome did agree to d'Aubigny's promotion but he died in 1665, before the news could reach him.[78] After his death Charles seems to have lost interest. In 1670 another internuncio, Airoldi, told Charles that the clergy needed a superior to keep them in order. The king replied that he had had several turbulent priests transported, at the request of Philip Howard; for the rest he made only general expressions of his goodwill towards the Catholics.[79]

For some years the Chapter demanded an ordinary while Rome received its advances with suspicion. From about 1668 the situation began to change. An obvious episcopal candidate, Philip Howard, now stood out; he claimed that under the queen's marriage treaty he, as her almoner, should be given the title of bishop.[80] Rome, which regarded the king's approval as essential, now believed that he favoured the idea of the clergy having a new superior.[81] After Agretti's visit to England in 1669, a congregation for English affairs approved in principle Howard's appointment as vicar apostolic and sent Airoldi to investigate the situation.[82] Airoldi thought that a superior was certainly needed and that circumstances were favourable for appointing one. Howard was the obvious choice. (Though many Chaptermen did not want Howard, they realised that they might have to accept him.)[83] Airoldi found Ellis, the Dean, and other leading Chaptermen more moderate than he had expected; they stressed the need for a bishop to remedy abuses and

---

[77] Clark, pp. 90–1; ASJ, Ang. Epist. Gen. 1642–98, fols. 246–55.
[78] Nunz. Fian. 48, fols. 74–5, 78–9, 83; CRS, xxv, 267–8; Clark, p. 96. There is no mention in Vecchi's dispatches of the threats of schism described by the French ambassador in his reports which are of dubious reliability: Cominges to Lionne 29 Sept. 1664 NS, Baschet 113.
[79] Prop. Ang., fols. 628–9; Dockery, p. 158.
[80] Prop. Ang., fols. 338, 342–3; CRS, xxv, 266.
[81] Instructions to Internuncio, Apr. 1668, Rom. Tr. 99, fol. 355; Birrell, *RH*, iv, 158.
[82] Prop. Ang., fols. 425–30, 535–6; Birrell, p. 162.
[83] AAW A33, pp. 139, 145, 147, 181, 511.

claimed that the Chapter had maintained discipline among
the clergy since Smith's departure. They suggested that the pope
should choose a bishop from a list of candidates drawn up by
the Chapter.[84] Airoldi thought that this could be allowed, if it
was understood that it could not stand as a precedent. It would
leave the Chapter no excuse for opposing the person appointed
and would ensure that he would be acceptable to the English
court. He added that it might be possible to reconstitute the
Chapter later, changing its members.[85] Following Airoldi's report,
in April 1672 the congregation for English affairs appointed
Howard a vicar apostolic with the title of bishop. It was too late;
the project was shelved during the Dutch War and the strength
of anti-Catholicism in England from 1673 made it far too
dangerous to try to set up a new Catholic ecclesiastical authority.[86]
In 1675 Howard was forced to leave England and was made a
cardinal. Rumours in 1675–6 that a bishop would be appointed
were quite unfounded, although Rome still thought it desir-
able.[87]

To conclude it is clear that the need for a superior was
generally recognised. The priests available were being used badly,
being concentrated in private houses and in London to the neglect
of the poorer Catholics and of the provinces. A bishop could help
to remedy this and to prevent quarrels and the abuse of faculties,
especially by foreign regulars.[88] It is also clear that Rome would
not grant an ordinary or recognise the Chapter, fearing that it
was tainted with Blackloism and might try to elect its own bishop
in the future. Rome therefore decided to appoint a vicar
apostolic, whom it could control and whose very existence, far
from confirming the Chapter's authority, would tend to nullify
it.[89] The Chapter's attempts to coerce Rome proved ineffectual,
primarily because it failed to win over the king. Rome would
grant no superior until it was sure that Charles was favourable,

---

[84] Prop. Ang., fols. 643–6; part of the report is summarised in Brady, iii,
119–27.

[85] Prop. Ang., fols. 646–7, 652.

[86] Birrell, *RH*, iv, 165.

[87] *CSPVen 1673–5*, pp. 362, 429; Sir G. Treby, *A Collection of Letters*
(1681), p. 90; BM Add. MS 17990, fol. 9.

[88] Instructions to Internuncio, Apr. 1668, Rom. Tr. 99, fols. 349–50;
Prop. Ang., fols. 427–9; AAW A34, pp. 57, 103.

[89] AAW A34, pp. 104–6.

or at least not hostile. The Chapter's agent at Rome was told in 1669:

This court desired nothing but to give [the] clergy gusto and satisfaction in all things, but that we must consider that we did not clear the main point, viz., his Majesty's consent and approbation without which, said he, 'twere imprudence to hazard by such a change the bringing another persecution on the heads of the laity.[90]

Rome began to act only when it was convinced that Charles was not unfavourable and appointed a vicar apostolic immediately after Charles had issued the Declaration of Indulgence.[91] The distinction between a vicar apostolic and an ordinary was important to Catholics because of the wider issues involved; several enemies of the Chapter alleged that the name of bishop was odious in England.[92] It is unlikely, however, that Protestants would have been aware of the difference, and the crucial point was the attitude of the king. When James II asked for a vicar apostolic, and then for three more, the matter was quickly arranged, despite the continued opposition of the Chapter.

The majority of Catholics, even the majority of priests, were not involved in these disputes, but were concerned primarily with living a normal Catholic life. The concerns of the priesthood were primarily spiritual and they saw their mission in that light. The political activism of Allen and Parsons had never touched more than a small minority of the Elizabethan priesthood and was dead long before 1660. Apart from one or two meddlers at court the English Catholic clergy were not involved in any politics other than the ecclesiastical controversies just described. Even if they had wanted to meddle in secular politics, they had had little opportunity during their long exclusion from the centres of power. Yet the myth of the political activism of the English priesthood lived on and has been accepted as valid by many Whiggish historians. This myth was part of a larger one, that of the continued militancy of the Catholic church, which in fact had subsided by now into a cautious determination to maintain the *status quo*. One of the most persistent clichés of Protestant his-

[90] AAW A33, p. 221; see also *ibid.* pp. 106, 115, 188.
[91] Instructions to Internuncio, 1668, Rom. Tr. 99. fol. 355; Charles's sister 'Madame' told the Paris nuncio in 1670 that the king wanted the clergy to have a bishop: Prop. Ang., fol. 526.
[92] Prop. Ang., fols. 299, 338, 342.

toriography concerns the incredible political guile, the incorrigible militancy and the total unscrupulousness of the Jesuits.[93] Whatever the order's record on the continent might be, as far as the English Jesuits are concerned there is virtually no evidence to support this belief in this period. No English Jesuit had exercised any appreciable political influence since Robert Parsons. There were no Jesuits at court, except for one or two, well hidden, in the duke of York's household.[94] As for the notorious Edward Petre, there is no hard evidence that he exerted any but the most general influence over James II. Unlike Sunderland and James's other lay advisers, Petre had no political experience and his main concerns seem to have been the maintenance of his own ascendancy among the ecclesiastics at court and the securing of a cardinal's hat for himself.[95] Nowhere is the Jesuits' lack of cunning and of political acumen seen more clearly than in their treatment of Titus Oates; they accepted his professions of conversion and repentance with naive enthusiasm and later refused on principle to give him the small sums of money that would have kept his mouth shut.[96] It is significant that when the general of the society first heard of the plot, he stated that if the English Jesuits *had* been meddling in politics they deserved to be persecuted.[97]

By Charles II's reign, then, the English mission was carried on in a minor key, more concerned with holding Catholics in the faith than with making large numbers of conversions; that was no longer possible: a century of Protestant evangelism, indoctrination and propaganda had done their work. Most Englishmen abhorred 'Popery' even if they were not too sure what it really was. Foley's figures for conversions made by the Jesuits do not suggest that a Catholic revival was taking place; in the three years

---

[93] See for instance Pollock's tortured attempt to blame the murder of Sir Edmund Berry Godfrey onto the Jesuits: Sir J. Pollock, *The Popish Plot* (London, 1903), sect. ii.

[94] Peter Talbot had been a Jesuit for a while but was one no longer.

[95] See below, chap. 12.

[96] I am unconvinced by Professor Kenyon's rather cynical explanation of Oates's acceptance by the Jesuits, viz. that some of them were attracted rather than repelled by Oates's homosexuality: Kenyon, *Popish Plot*, pp. 47–51.

[97] J. Warner, *The History of the English Persecution of Catholics and the Presbyterian Plot*, ed. T. A. Birrell (CRS, xlvii–xlviii, 1953, 1955), p. 203.

1669–71, when the clergy enjoyed freedom from persecution, the Society reconciled a total of less than 2000 persons to the faith.[98] This was enough to offset apostasies and the extinction of old Catholic families, but not much more. Fears of the growth of Popery had their source in the strength of Catholicism at court, near the centre of power, not in the nation as a whole.

[98] Foley, i, 270–2.

3

THE PENAL LAWS
AND THEIR ENFORCEMENT

Between 1559 and 1610 parliament passed a series of acts which together made up a fearsome body of laws against Catholic recusancy and all aspects of Catholic life. If these laws had been fully enforced they would have broken English Catholicism by executions, imprisonment and fines. However, in the sixteenth and seventeenth centuries it was far easier to make a law than to ensure that it was enforced. The ferocious punishments imposed by statute for a wide variety of offences were intended to deter potential offenders and so to compensate to some extent for the gross practical inadequacies of the machinery of law enforcement. There was no effective police force. The central administration was minute by modern standards. Local administration and day-to-day justice were the responsibility of gentlemen amateurs who were unpaid and overworked and retained prejudices and feelings of their own. The inferior officers who were supposed to enforce their orders were all too often inept, underpaid and venal. Communications between the centre and the localities were poor. Therefore it needed constant vigilance and prodding of J.P.s on the part of the Privy Council if the penal laws were to be enforced in the shires. Even in the worst times, between about 1580 and 1620, the laws were never enforced to the full, but they were enforced sufficiently to cause considerable distress and inconvenience to Catholics; a number of priests and laymen were executed and others died in prison. Under Charles II the Privy Council became concerned to enforce the laws only after 1673, and particularly in the years following the outbreak of the Popish Plot in 1678. Even then the task of enforcement was hampered at every stage by unwillingness and incompetence. For much of the reign, the Catholics felt the weight of the laws very seldom. This chapter is concerned with the various laws affecting Catholics; with the procedures used to enforce the most basic of these, the recusancy laws and the ways in which these procedures were in-

adequate; and with the extent to which the laws kept Catholics
out of civil and military office under Charles II.

The penal laws against Catholics created and imposed penalties
for two types of offence – those of omission (recusancy and the
refusal of the oath of allegiance) and those of commission (actions
pertaining to the leading of a full Catholic life, such as receiving
priestly orders, saying and hearing Mass, providing Catholic
education and so on). The offence of recusancy was created by
the 1559 Act of Uniformity (1 Eliz., cap. 2) which imposed a
fine of twelve pence a week for absence from the parish church;
the fine was to be levied by the churchwardens and spent on the
relief of the poor. Offenders could be proceeded against in the
queen's courts, before judges, and in the ecclesiastical courts. The
church courts' chief penalty was excommunication, which could
lead to imprisonment on a writ of *de excommunicato capiendo.*
This seems to have happened occasionally as late as Charles II's
reign. By then excommunication was used primarily against
Protestant Dissenters and does not seem to have been greatly
feared. The sheer number of excommunicates made it impossible
to proceed against them all.[1] The most serious civil disability of
an excommunicate, that of being unable to plead at law in cases
between party and party (except those involving his own real
property), or to act as an executor, was imposed on all convicted
recusants by 3 & 4 Jac. I, cap. 5.[2] This would not concern poor
recusants; nor would exclusion from the Anglican sacraments as
they did not want to go to church anyway. The only problems
poor excommunicates might face were discrimination by land-
lords or employers and denial of burial in consecrated ground.
(Catholics had no objection to being buried in Anglican church-
yards as they regarded them as validly consecrated before the
Reformation; if in doubt, they could always put a piece of
consecrated earth in the coffin.)[3] However feeble a deterrent ex-

[1] Williams, *Wilts.*, pp. 70–2; R. A. Marchant, *The Church Under the Law 1560–1640* (Cambridge, 1969), pp. 222, 227.
[2] W. Cawley, *The Laws of Q.Elizabeth ... concerning ... Recusants* (1680), pp. 193, 216–18; J. Keble, *An Explanation of the Laws against Recusants &c Abridged* (1681) is very similar to Cawley. For William Blundell's legal difficulties, see Blundell, *Cavalier*, pp. 173–5.
[3] P. Caraman, *The Other Face: Catholic Life Under Elizabeth I* (London,

communication had become, Restoration bishops continued to inquire into absence from church and the weakened church courts still went through the motions of summoning Popish and Protestant recusants and excommunicating them when they failed to appear.[4]

The main burdens imposed on recusants were in statutes enforceable in the secular courts. The first statute that greatly increased the penalties for recusancy was 23 Eliz., cap. 1, which imposed a penalty of £20 per month. Of this the inhabitants of the parish and the informer (if there was one) could each sue for one-third.[5] 28 & 29 Eliz., cap. 6 stated that this fine was to run on from the time of conviction until the recusant conformed or died. If he defaulted he was to forfeit all his goods and two-thirds of his land to the crown, not in lieu of the fine, but as a further penalty for defaulting.[6] This act also extended the procedure for convicting recusants; following a recusant's indictment at the queen's suit or on a private information, instead of his being convicted in the usual way, a proclamation could be made at the next sessions of assize or gaol delivery ordering him to surrender himself to the sheriff before the following sessions; if he defaulted it was to stand as a conviction in law. Finally, any conveyances made to evade the penalties of 23 Eliz., cap. 1 were declared void.

The most important seventeenth century penal statutes were passed in 1606, after Gunpowder Plot. 3 & 4 Jac. I, cap. 4 systematised earlier legislation and added various new measures. Recusancy was now extended to include failure to take the sacrament according to the rites of the Church of England at least once a year; for this additional penalties were imposed. The provision was designed to prevent occasional conformity by 'church-papists'. The act clearly laid down the procedure to be followed in recusancy cases. Churchwardens and constables

1960), p. 270; Blundell, *Cavalier*, pp. 243–4; Aveling, *West Riding*, p. 252; Marchant, *The Church under the Law*, pp. 220–1; Zimmerman, p. 266.

4 *The Remains of Denis Granville*, ed. G. Ornsby (2 vols., Surtees Soc., 1861, 1867), ii, 213–48.

5 Cawley, pp. 71–2, 78. Under 28 & 29 Eliz., cap. 6 the chief financial officers of the crown could designate one-third of the fines received for the relief of the poor.

6 Cawley, pp. 105, 171.

were to make annual presentments of absentees from church, which were to be recorded by the clerk of the peace or town clerk. Rewards were to be paid when presentment led to conviction and fines were to be levied on those who failed to present or to record presentments. Judges or J.P.s were to hear and determine cases, issue proclamations etc. (as laid down by 28 & 29 Eliz., cap. 6). Convictions were to be certified into the Exchequer so that the crown's financial officers could take steps to levy the fines due to the king or to have juries empanelled to inquire into the value of the recusants' lands. The £20 a month fine was to be run on until conformity. The king could now choose whether he wished to levy the fine or to seize two-thirds of the recusant's lands. The one shilling a week fine was still to be levied as well as that of £20 a month.[7] By this statute a master's liability for his servant's recusancy, implied in 35 Eliz., cap. 1, was made explicit. A husband was not made liable for his wife's recusancy until 7 & 8 Jac. I, cap. 6, although it had been possible to proceed against them by an action for debt under 35 Eliz., cap. 1.[8]

The statutes just described, which can broadly be called recusancy statutes, would affect all Catholics and also many Protestant Dissenters. Their existence drove 'church Papists' to conform outwardly. Recusancy offences were peculiar in that conformity, duly shown, would free a recusant at once from the penalties of the law, although it would not lead to a recovery of fines paid. 3 & 4 Jac. I, cap. 4 also created another means of convicting Catholics by introducing the oath of allegiance. The 1559 Act of Supremacy (1 Eliz., cap. 1) had introduced the oath of supremacy to be taken by all office-holders, clergymen and university graduates; the only penalty for refusal was ineligibility for office and for university degrees. The new oath, drawn up at a time of strong anti-Catholic feeling, was designed to force conscientious Catholics to identify themselves. It made it possible for the procedures by which Catholics were convicted to be extended. By 3 & 4 Jac. I, cap. 4 any bishop or two J.P.s could examine suspected recusants or suspicious strangers on oath and ask whether they went to church or took the sacrament. They could also tender them the oath of allegiance; if they refused to take it, they could be imprisoned until the next assizes

[7] *ibid.* p. 190.   [8] *ibid.* pp. 122–3.

or general sessions. There, if they refused again, they were to suffer the penalties of the Statute of *Praemunire* – forfeiture of all property and imprisonment at pleasure, or outlawry. Married women were to remain in prison until they took the oath. 7 & 8 Jac. I, cap. 6 extended the procedure so that two J.P.s together could tender the oath to any commoner over the age of eighteen; a single J.P. could, upon notice, require a person to take it if he found and could show good reason for doing so. If the person refused, he was to be imprisoned until the next sessions, as above.

Other statutes dealt with specific areas of Catholic life. 23 Eliz., cap. 1, besides raising the penalties for recusancy, made it high treason to reconcile someone or to be reconciled to Rome and imposed heavy fines for saying and hearing Mass, already forbidden by 1 Eliz., cap. 2. 13 Eliz., caps. 1 and 2 made it treason to deny the queen's supremacy or title or to bring in any papal instrument or bull. 27 Eliz., cap. 2 made it treason for a priest to enter or remain in England and felony, a capital offence, to harbour him. A series of acts tried to prevent the establishment of Catholic schools in England and the sending of English children to Catholic seminaries abroad. 35 Eliz., cap. 2 forbade Catholics to move more than five miles from their homes without licence.

The fullest range of disabilities imposed on Catholics (i.e., on convicted recusants or those unwilling to take the oaths of supremacy and allegiance) was imposed by 3 & 4 Jac. I, cap. 5. Under this act, a Catholic could not come to court, except at the king's express command; he could not come within ten miles of London, unless he had a trade or menial occupation in the city or had no abode elsewhere; he could practise no profession and hold no office of any kind. Catholic marriages, and any transfers of land that they might involve, were not valid in law. A Catholic was not allowed to possess Catholic books or devotional articles or to keep arms and munitions. Subsidy acts under Charles I provided that Catholics should pay double; this happened only once under Charles II, in the act for raising the last of the old type of subsidies in 1663 (15 Car. II, cap. 9).

All these statutes remained in force between 1660 and 1688. Two new acts were passed. Since 7 & 8 Jac. I, cap. 6 all office-holders had had to take the oath of allegiance as well as the oath of supremacy. The 1673 Test Act prescribed that all office-holders also had to subscribe a declaration against transubstantiation and take the sacrament according to the rites of the Church of England. The latter provision may also have excluded some Dissenters from office, but in fact many were prepared to take the sacrament and to make the declaration required by the 1661 Corporation Act if need arose.[9] The 1678 Test Act excluded Catholics from both Houses of Parliament, and particularly from the House of Lords, by requiring all members of each House to make a declaration designed to be offensive to Catholics. In terms of new legislation Charles II's reign was much harder on Dissenters than on Catholics.

The aim of all this penal legislation was to dissuade Catholics from retaining their religion and to put pressure on them to conform to the Church of England. Behind this aim lay the theory, which in the sixteenth century was usually confirmed in practice, that divisions of religion within a state were dangerous and usually led to upheaval and bloodshed. By the middle of the seventeenth century these laws had largely achieved their object. The Catholics had been reduced to a small if resilient minority, mostly resigned to exclusion from national life. The strength of the anti-Catholic tradition ensured that this largely harmless minority could not be granted open toleration. At times of political crisis, when fears of Popery were high, the government tried to have the penal laws enforced to the full but its efforts never resulted in an all-out persecution of the Catholic peers and gentry in the shires. There were two main reasons for this. First, the procedures laid down by statute for presentment, conviction and fining were extremely complicated and clumsy and would have taxed the capabilities of an administrative system far more sophisticated that that of seventeenth century England. Secondly, the men who were supposed to enforce the laws in the localities very often proved incompetent, dilatory or simply unwilling to act.

As the procedures laid down by statute were so complex it needed constant vigilance and prodding from the Privy Council to ensure that the laws were enforced. Pressure from the Council was greatest between 1580 and 1610 when the danger from international Catholicism was greatest. J.P.s were bombarded

[9] K. H. D. Haley, *The First Earl of Shaftesbury* (Oxford, 1968), pp. 324–5; *CJ*, ix, 281; *CSPD 1676–7*, p. 232, *1679–80*, pp. 564–5; Burnett, ii, 243.

with demands for information about the number of Catholics and with orders to convict them, fine them and keep them under surveillance. The Council tacitly recognised the inadequacy of the statutory procedures by resorting to various types of administrative action resting on the royal prerogative. The most simple, which was used mainly in periods of acute emergency, was simply an expression of the Council's concern for national security. Leading Catholics were summoned for interrogation and pressed to conform by means of conferences with Anglican divines and short spells of imprisonment.[10] A second procedure involved the creation of special recusancy commissions. Some were ecclesiastical, diocesan commissions on the lines of the Court of High Commission. These had much in common with the normal ecclesiastical courts but could impose much heavier penalties. These were the most active agencies for the repression of Catholicism in Elizabeth's reign. They were gradually superseded by commissions to groups of laymen, issued on a county basis. These, like the Council, were concerned primarily with security and surveillance. Most could not convict recusants but could only imprison them temporarily, pending indictment. The use of commissions was revived in 1627 when commissioners were appointed to seize and lease out recusants' lands or else to arrange for the recusants to compound for them.[11] A third procedure was that laid down by 3 & 4 Jac. I, cap. 4 – tendering the oath of allegiance and subjecting those who refused it to the penalties of *praemunire*. This seems to have been used only occasionally[12] although it was undoubtedly quick and efficient. Presumably this was because the penalties involved were so severe. Charles I (and even James I) did not want to ruin the Catholics although he was quite determined to mulct them. Under Charles II, although some Catholics were imprisoned for refusing the oath, I know of none whose property was confiscated as well.

One must consider the enforcement of the penal laws under Charles II in the context of their past history. The situation after

---

10 Trimble, *Catholic Laity in Elizabethan England*, pp. 76–80, 92–7, 105–14, 134–45, 155–9. The use of conferences with divines died out *c.* 1630, Aveling, *Northern Catholics*, p. 215 and *West Riding*, p. 256.

11 R. B. Manning, 'Elizabethan Recusancy Commissions', *HJ*, xv (1972), 23–34; Aveling, *Northern Catholics*, pp. 146–8, 219–35; M. J. Havran, *The Catholics in Caroline England* (Oxford, 1962), pp. 93–5.

12 Aveling, *Northern Catholics*, pp. 214–15.

1660 was in one respect greatly changed. The abolition in 1641 of the Court of High Commission and the Council of the North had removed the two main agencies for the persecution of Catholics, especially in the North. After the abolition of High Commission, there could be no more diocesan ecclesiastical commissions. Its disappearance and the failure to revive it further weakened the ecclesiastical courts, already considerably decayed after twenty years of disuse during the Interregnum. However, the old procedures were revived, with the old recusancy legislation, at the Restoration. Special commissions were still sometimes issued to inquire into the value of recusants' lands or to tender them the oaths of allegiance and supremacy. The other important change after 1660 was in the attitude of the king and of the Privy Council. They were concerned neither to punish nor to mulct the Catholics and were usually prepared to leave them alone, unless they came under considerable pressure from parliament to enforce the laws against them. Even then, as in 1666–7, the Council's orders to enforce the laws could amount to little more than a gesture. Only in 1673 did it begin to consider seriously the working of the laws and only after the outbreak of the Popish Plot did it act with real vigour.

There was always a certain ambivalence in Protestant attitudes towards Catholicism and Catholics. Men who inveighed against Popery at court and the malevolent designs of international Catholicism might well be on good terms with the few Catholics who lived near them, with whom they had ties of neighbourliness and common social status and interests. Consciously or unconsciously, they distinguished between Popery as a malign political force and Papists as people. Among those who were meant to enforce the penal laws there were always a few whose greed or anti-Catholic zeal pushed them beyond the limits of the law into extortion, but the general impression is one of inertia, of reluctance to put the laws into operation without a sharp external stimulus. Many J.P.s, like Sir Edmund Verney, signed presentments 'very unwillingly, hating to do anything like an informer, though never so legally'.[13] Not all the Anglican clergy were persecutors either. In about 1665, the bishop of Chester was in dilemma. Faced with a large number of presentments of

[13] M. M. Verney, *Memoirs of the Verney Family* (4 vols., London, 1892–9), iv, 178.

Popish recusants, he wrote: 'It is a great scandal and offence to let them alone, though I wish the sectaries were but as quiet and yet inoffensive as they are. To make pecuniary mulcts on them is base, to proceed by church censures is vain, to leave them unobserved is to multiply them.'[14] That was written at a time of comparative calm. From 1673 fear and hatred of Popery came increasingly to dominate politics. Magistrates came under considerable pressure to enforce the laws both from an anxious Privy Council and from the fears in their own minds. They began to convict Catholics of recusancy in large numbers and, to a lesser extent, to levy fines on them and confiscate their lands.

Reluctance to enforce the laws began in the parishes. There is ample evidence of the ineptitude and venality of all kinds of petty officials.[15] There were many complaints that constables and churchwardens were not making presentments; this was especially likely if a lax diocesan administration failed to keep the churchwardens on their toes.[16] (The churchwardens were supposed to present the names of recusants to both the secular and the ecclesiastical authorities.) Mr Williams has found that constables and churchwardens in Wiltshire and elsewhere often presented recusants for three weeks' absence from church, at a shilling a week, rather than for a month's or several months' absence, at £20 a month. This happened less often in 1678–81.[17] This showed an unwillingness to squeeze recusants too hard. Even the one shilling fine was not usually collected. There was little point in fining poor recusants anyway; regular fining would leave them in need of poor relief and there is evidence of poor Papists actually benefiting from recusancy fines in this way.[18] Churchwardens and constables might prove reluctant to present if the

---

[14] Bodl., MS Add. c. 307, fol. 68 (The letter is undated, but the writer, George Hall, was bishop from 1662–8, and a reference to the plague suggests that the letter was written in 1665); cf. M. H. Lee (ed.), *The Diaries and Letters of Philip Henry* (London, 1882), p. 232.

[15] T. G. Barnes, *Somerset 1625–1640* (Oxford, 1961), pp. 76–7, 96, 135–41; Aveling, *Northern Catholics*, pp. 13, 132–4, 213–14; Rostenberg, pp. 36, 78, 100.

[16] Lancs. R. O., QSV/11/2, fols. 22, 51; Bodl., Rawl. MS D 1163, fols. 16–18.

[17] Williams, *Wilts.*, pp. 85–6.

[18] Lancs. R. O., QSV/11/2, fols. 50, 59, 63; Aveling, *Northern Catholics*, pp. 122–3; Williams, p. 74.

parish was dominated by a Catholic squire. In 1662 Sir Philip Constable supplied the local constable with the protest that he was to deliver when he was told to present recusants; the protest quoted the king's remarks about tender consciences in the Declaration of Breda.[19] Some notable Catholics escaped conviction, if not presentment; Sir Francis Jerningham does not appear on the recusant rolls for Norfolk; nor does the duke of Norfolk, although he was presented as a recusant in 1680.[20]

At quarter sessions obstructions often occurred, even during the Plot. In 1663 the North Riding clerk of the peace set aside four hundred presentments on the ground that he dared not proceed to the conviction of persons of quality without a special warrant.[21] In 1674 Yorkshire grand juries were reluctant to accept presentments and the judges levied only the one shilling fine. As the laws had not been enforced for some years many J.P.s were unsure of the procedures involved.[22] The failure of J.P.s to act according to the Council's directives could be due to misunderstanding, inertia or deliberate obstruction. This is seen most clearly during the Exclusion Crisis when many J.P.s jibbed at tendering the oaths of allegiance and supremacy to suspected recusants and 'prosecuting them to a *praemunire*' if they refused. This procedure was both of dubious legality (as far as the use of the oath of supremacy was concerned) and imposed excessively severe penalties. Many J.P.s, particularly in Lancashire, Yorkshire, Herefordshire and Monmouthshire, persistently failed to obey the Council's orders and proved more receptive to the pleas of the recusants' counsel.[23]

There was always the possibility of obstruction by the Papists which, combined with the inertia or sympathy of the J.P.s, could prove very effective. The Papists could employ counsel, exploit legal technicalities and undertake complex conveyances and other legal subterfuges too intricate for sluggish or overburdened J.P.s to probe very deeply. The law worked slowly enough anyway; William Blundell's attorney told him in August 1673 that he could not be convicted before the next summer assizes and in fact

---

[19] Aveling, *Northern Catholics*, pp. 323–4.
[20] *CSPD 1679–80*, p. 624, *1680–1*, p. 61.
[21] Aveling, *Northern Catholics*, p. 324.
[22] *HMC le Fleming*, pp. 109–10.
[23] See below, pp. 166–8.

he was not convicted until late in 1675.[24] Less legal devices included a simple failure to appear, as in Lancashire and Warwickshire in 1680.[25] Catholics could also dodge the law by moving to another county.[26] In Monmouthshire two score Papists clapped on their hats and walked out of the court when the justices asked them why judgment should not be passed on them. The undersheriff refused to fetch them back, and three of the five J.P.s present refused even to fine them for contempt.[27] There were many allegations that the authorities in Monmouthshire showed open favour to Papists. The sheriff was said to have discharged four Papists and to have distrained on five Dissenters for recusancy in 1677. Henry Milborne, J.P. for four counties, was said to have two Popish clerks and to have rescued one by force from a constable. In 1679 the Council ordered that Milborne be prosecuted for keeping a Jesuit (his sisters were Catholics) and for speaking dangerous words on the bench.[28] John Arnold, who made most of these allegations, was the leader of a local faction that was trying to break the marquis of Worcester's political hold on the area. Arnold's allegations were certainly exaggerated; other Monmouthshire J.P.s described them as full of falsehoods and misrepresentation. But there clearly were many Catholics in Monmouthshire; many of them were open in their religion to the point of boldness and that boldness owed much to Worcester's protection. For instance, Worcester himself remarked that the income of the Jesuit residence at Combe, Herefordshire, was only £40 a year, not £300 as Arnold claimed.[29]

Even if Papists were convicted there was no certainty that they would be made to pay fines or that their lands would be seized. Sheriffs might fail or refuse to act. It might prove too difficult and expensive to inquire into the value of a Papist's

---

24 Blundell, *Cavalier*, pp. 150–1, 171; A. W. Thibaudeau (ed.), *Autograph Letters in the Collection of Alfred Morrison:* 2nd Series (3 vols., London, 1887), ii, 247.

25 *HMC le Fleming*, p. 167; PC/2/68, pp. 422–3.

26 *HMC le Fleming*, p. 168; Bodl., Rawl, MS A 135, p. 170; Aveling, *Northern Catholics*, p. 127 and *East Riding*, pp. 38–9.

27 *LJ*, xiii, 621–2.

28 *CJ*, ix, 468; PC/2/68, p. 242.

29 O'Keeffe, chap. 6; Bodl., Carte MS 130, fols. 19–20; *CJ*, ix, 466–9; *LJ*, xii, 450–1; Grey, viii, 130; *HMC Beaufort*, pp. 88, 114.

lands if his ownership of the land was obscured by a tangle of trusts and conveyances. Partly in recognition of this the government connived at the breach of its own rules. The Warwickshire Papists who failed to appear in court did so 'in hopes to compound [their forfeited recognisances] in His Majesty's Court of Exchequer and thereby escape the proceedings against them according to law'.[30] Some Lancashire recusants compounded for their recusancy and there was an unsuccessful attempt to get the rest to do so in order to avoid the rigmarole of inquiring into the value of their lands and then confiscating two-thirds.[31] Viscount Montague was allowed to pay £20 a month rather than lose two-thirds of his lands; for him, no doubt, it was cheaper.[32] At times fines were dispensed with altogether. In 1677 both the Meynells of Kilvington and Simon Scrope secured writs of *supersedeas*, suspending the operation of the penalties of the law; so did indigent old Cavaliers from 1683.[33]

If all else failed there was the possibility of violent self-help. In September 1680 some Papists were rescued from the custody of the sheriff of Lancashire. In 1681 women at Wigan beat bailiffs who tried to carry off a widow's goods and the town authorities did nothing to stop them.[34] At Altcar, Lancashire, in 1682 two bailiffs were almost killed when a score of Papists tried to prevent them from seizing the goods of John Sutton and Margery Tickle. The town officers dared present nobody for recusancy 'for fear of the Tickles'.[35] In 1680 there was a Papists' riot in Abergavenny.[36]

It would be misleading to suggest that violent self-help by Papists or deliberate refusal by J.P.s to enforce the laws were in any way normal. Most of the examples cited took place in the Catholic strongholds of Lancashire and Monmouthshire. They were probably more unusual than cases of extortion. Some sheriffs demanded £20 per month from recusants who had

[30] PC/2/68, pp. 422–3.
[31] *HMC le Fleming*, pp. 181–2; *HMC Kenyon*, p. 130.
[32] PC/2/69, p. 322.
[33] Aveling, *Northern Catholics*, p. 326; CTB, vii, 989, 1019, 1081.
[34] *CSPD 1680–1*, pp. 32, 49, 51–2; PC/2/69, p. 113; *HMC le Fleming*, p. 181; *HMC Kenyon*, pp. 128, 132.
[35] *HMC Kenyon*, pp. 137–8.
[36] PC/2/68, p. 528.

already forfeited two-thirds of their lands.[37] Individuals motivated by bigotry or greed exploited the laws to the utmost. The Council paid rewards to priest-catchers. The undersheriff of Northumberland discovered Papists' lands worth £4859 per annum, and no doubt profited from his discovery.[38] Some cynically exploited Papists' vulnerability, especially during the Plot. Two of the informers, Dugdale and Bolron, had lost their positions as stewards for dishonesty, and now accused their former employers of complicity in the Plot. Lady Portland's steward kept £1000 of her money and claimed that as a convicted recusant she could not sue for its recovery; the Council ordered him to repay it. The tenants of the Giffards of Blackladies refused to pay their rent on the same pretext.[39] In Devon the clerks of the peace, the assizes and the bishop's court ran a 'protection racket'; eighty Popish recusants paid a sum each year to escape presentments and conviction. When they could no longer pay, they were harried for the full £20 a month.[40]

For the most part the behaviour of English Protestants avoided either of these extremes. Between them constables, churchwardens, J.P.s, sheriffs and the Exchequer seem to have failed to convict Papists or, if they were convicted, they seem to have failed to fine them and to confiscate their lands. For most of the period they were under little pressure from the Council. Even when they were convicted, most Papists got off lightly in financial terms except perhaps in the early 1680s when there was the most determined attempt to raise money from recusants.[41] For most Catholics the psychological strain was probably greater than the financial one. When the Catholic question did not dominate politics most Protestants were prepared to leave alone the attenuated minority of Catholics in their neighbourhood. In most counties there were a few Protestant bigots among the J.P.s, but generally the Protestant gentry proved more tolerant in practice than in theory of their Catholic neighbours.[42]

* * *

37 *CTB*, vii, 752; *CSPD July–Sept. 1683*, p. 324.
38 PC/2/68, pp. 28, 32, etc.; *CTB*, vii, 138–9.
39 PC/2/68, pp. 109–10; *HMC House of Lords 1678–88*, p. 128; *CSPD July–Sept. 1683*, p. 324.
40 PC/2/65, p. 514.
41 See below, chap. 9.
42 Aveling, *Northern Catholics*, pp. 324–5, 332–3.

There remains to be considered one further aspect of the enforcement of the laws. Catholics were by law excluded from public office, civil, military and ecclesiastical. Even before the 1673 Test Act all office-holders were required to take the oaths of allegiance and supremacy. One or two Catholics exercised offices through a deputy.[43] Other Catholics were prepared to take these oaths in order to qualify for office and it is probable that others, with the government's connivance, managed to avoid having the oaths tendered to them. There were some individuals whose Catholicism was so circumspect or marginal that it is difficult to decide whether they can be called Catholics at all. The second lord Widdrington seems to have taken both oaths and the test but two of his sons were Jesuits and he and his wife died as Catholics. The third lord Widdrington was so circumspect that in 1680 the House of Lords did not know whether or not he was a Papist; he never came to take the oaths but was not marked as a recusant when the House was called. He was later convicted of recusancy and by 1686 considered it safe to be regarded as a Catholic.[44]

Some Papists were so circumspect that they managed to be elected M.P.s. Sir Solomon Swale became a Catholic in 1660 but sat for Aldborough, Yorkshire, until he was expelled from the Commons in 1678.[45] Sir Thomas Strickland, M.P. for Westmorland, was expelled from the House in 1677. He had not taken the oaths and test (as he should have done) in 1673 and he had been convicted of recusancy in 1676. He had even been appointed a receiver of recusant revenues in the North Riding in 1675.[46] Sir Jordan Crosland was M.P. for Scarborough from 1661 until his death in 1670; he was keeping a priest in 1665. Sir Philip

---

[43] C. H. Hartmann, *Clifford of the Cabal* (London, 1937), p. 314; W. D. Christie (ed.), *Letters Addressed from London to Sir Joseph Williamson 1673–4* (2 vols., Camden Soc., 1874), i, 53–4; *CTB*, i, 2.

[44] The second baron was governor of Berwick 1661–75; colonel of a regiment which went to Ireland 1673–5; his commission was dated 5 June 1673, after most dismissals for refusing the test had taken place. See [F. J. A. Skeet], *History of the Families of Skeet ... Widdrington ... etc.* (London, 1906), pp. 101–2; *LJ*, xiii, 628; *CSPD 1686–7*, nos. 267–8.

[45] Aveling, *Northern Catholics*, p. 319; Grey, vi, 106–7; Browning (ed.), *Historical Documents*, p. 248.

[46] *CJ*, ix, 393; *HMC le Fleming*, pp. 101, 130; *CTB*, iv, 750.

Tyrwhitt was elected M.P. for Grimsby in 1667 but the election was voided on petition, apparently because of the incompetence of his counsel. His Catholicism was so circumspect that his wife was not sure that he was a Catholic when she married him.[47]

Charles II was cautious in his employment of Catholics. He commissioned a few Catholic army officers in 1660–7, in 1672–3 and (in rather exceptional circumstances) in 1678.[48] He employed even fewer Catholics in civilian posts and hardly any of these survived the imposition of the test in 1673. The most eminent was probably lord Bellasis who had served Charles I with distinction in the Civil War. He was lord lieutenant of the East Riding of Yorkshire and governor of Hull from 1661 to 1673, governor of Tangier from 1664 to 1666 and was chosen lord steward of Hull by the mayor and burgesses. Lord Langdale was lord lieutenant of the West Riding until his death in August 1661.[49] A few Catholics were made governors of garrisons, sheriffs and J.P.s. Sir Jordan Crosland was governor of Scarborough from 1660 to 1670. Sir Edward Charlton was made governor of Hartlepool in 1666 and lord Molyneux was governor of Liverpool castle at the time of its demolition in 1667. Colonel John Fitzgerald was appointed governor of Yarmouth in 1672.[50] In 1670 the spasmodically Catholic earl of Bristol and his Protestant son purchased the governorship of Deal castle.[51]

I have identified four sheriffs who were Papists or probable Papists: Sir Francis Salkeld in Cumberland in 1662–3, Sir Solomon Swale in Yorkshire in 1670–1, Henry Hall in Oxfordshire in 1671–2 and Thomas Ireland in Shropshire in 1672–3.[52] At least three Catholic J.P.s survived until 1680: lord Hunsdon (expelled from the Lords as a Papist in 1678), Sir Philip Tyrwhitt

47 *Returns of Members of Parliament* (London, 1878), i, 532; Aveling, *Northern Catholics*, p. 343; *CJ*, ix, 24; C. Robbins (ed.), *Diary of John Milward* (Cambridge, 1938), p. 134; Burnet, ii, 94.

48 J. Miller, 'Catholic Officers in the Later Stuart Army', *EHR*, lxxxviii (1973), 43–5.

49 *CSPD 1660–1*, pp. 429, 526, *1673*, p. 194, *1660–85 Addenda*, p. 119, *1670*, p. 388.

50 *CSPD 1660–1*, p. 327, *1666–7*, pp. 64, 517, *1670*, pp. 402–3, *1671–2*, p. 236.

51 *CSPD 1670*, p. 421.

52 For evidence of Catholicism: Salkeld, PDB c12; Swale, expelled from Commons; Hall, PDB c28; Ireland, Sir G. F. Duckett, *Penal Laws and Test Act 1687–8* (2 vols., London, 1882–3), ii, 183.

and Sir Thomas Strickland in Westmorland. (Strickland had been expelled from the Commons in 1677 and put out of the North Riding commission of the peace in 1678.)[53] Another Catholic J.P. to survive the Test Act was Sir Edward Morgan, put out of the Monmouthshire commission in 1676.[54] A few other Catholics served as J.P.s earlier in the reign but they were never more than a tiny majority. A glance through the commissions of the peace for 1661 reveals a little over twenty, many of them marginal or circumspect.[55] The fact that there were any Papists in office would concern greatly those alarmed at the prevalence of Popish counsels in government. By 1678 parliamentary debates were concerned with the employment of favourers of Popery rather than actual Papists which would imply that few or no Catholics were left in office. Of those Catholics who were employed, in some cases (like that of Sir Solomon Swale) the government may not have known that they were Catholics; in others (like that of lord Bellasis) the king clearly connived at a breach of the law.

The very small number of Catholics who squeezed into public office and the fact that for much of Charles II's reign the penal laws were laxly enforced tend to confirm the picture of the Catholic community given in the first two chapters. The Catholics, then, were a tiny minority of the population; they accepted their exclusion from government and politics; they lived quietly and on good terms with their Protestant neighbours, who for their part recognised that they were mostly harmless, decent people. Yet much of the politics of the period 1660–88 was dominated by a virulent anti-Catholicism. To explain this apparent anomaly one must consider the peculiar nature of the English anti-Catholic tradition and the actual course of political events in this period.

[53] *HMC House of Lords 1678–88*, pp. 180, 183, 191; *HMC Finch*, ii, 45.
[54] *HMC Finch*, ii, 44.
[55] BM Add. MS 36781, fols. 36–75. Those definitely identifiable as Catholics are Sir H. Moore (Berks.); Sir T. Longueville (Bucks.); Sir F. Salkeld (Cumb.); W. Fitzherbert (Derbys.); G. Hussey (Dorset); lord Petre (Essex); Sir W. Thorold, Sir R. Dallison, P. Tyrwhitt, lord Bellasis, H. Hildyard, W. Fitzwilliams (Lincs.); R. Yallop (Norfk.); E. Lloyd (Salop.); Sir C. Shelley (Sussex); T. Braithwayte (Westmor.); lord Langdale, Sir M. Stapleton (Yorks.). Circumspect and marginal Catholics included Sir W. Blakiston (Durham); earl Rivers and lord Morley (Essex), lord Widdrington (Lincs. and Northumb.) and Swale, Strickland and Crosland (Yorks.).

4

THE DEVELOPMENT OF
THE ANTI-CATHOLIC TRADITION

If the Catholics really were so few and so harmless, how is one to explain the ferocious anti-Catholicism of this period? The answer lies partly in the Protestant view of Catholics and Catholicism, as it had developed over more than a century, and partly in the way that this view of Catholicism affected Protestants' interpretation of current political events. The Protestant version of history since the Reformation showed Papists as obedient slaves to the pope, whose greatest ambition was to root out Protestantism with the maximum of bloodshed and cruelty; this gave a distorted picture even of the Catholics of Elizabeth's reign, since which time circumstances had changed so that it bore only a minimal resemblance to reality. However, the myth of the bloodthirsty Papist seemed to acquire new relevance from two important contemporary developments. The first was the emergence of Louis XIV as the most powerful ruler in Europe and the self-styled champion of Catholicism. However weak the Catholics might seem in England, in Europe as a whole they were very much in the ascendant. In the words of Professor Kenyon: 'When the Thirty Years' War ended, Protestantism had been driven out to the periphery of Europe, where it was precariously lodged in North Germany, Holland, Scandinavia, England and Scotland; all, with the exception of Holland, poor, thinly populated, second-class nations.'[1] The emergence in this situation of a new Catholic super-power to offset the decline of Spain made the second new development particularly ominous. From 1673 it was clear that James, duke of York, the king's brother and heir-apparent, had become a Catholic. This raised the spectre of a regime in England like that of Louis XIV in France, complete with the bloody persecution of Protestants. From the time of his conversion to the time he left England in December 1688, English Protestants' attitude to James reflected less what he had actually

---

[1] Kenyon, *Popish Plot*, p. 2.

done than what it was assumed he would try to do. These assumptions were based partly on the current behaviour of Louis XIV and partly on a view of the nature and principles of Catholicism which was the product of Protestant propaganda and of the Protestant interpretation of sixteenth and seventeenth century European history. The validity of these assumptions has been accepted uncritically by many historians, especially those writing in the 'Whig' tradition. Much of this book will be concerned to show that their validity is very much open to question. The purpose of this chapter is to show how the English anti-Catholic tradition developed.

PROTESTANTISM AND POPERY

The Protestant reformers looked at the church of Rome, compared it with the primitive church of the New Testament and found it wanting. It was not surprising that vast changes had taken place. A supranational institution was bound to develop a bureaucracy and laws in a way that scattered underground congregations could not have done. Its head, the pope, extended his pretensions as the power of the institutional church increased. New claims, new religious orders, new ceremonies, new fiscal devices and new administrative practices were developed. By no means all these developments could be ascribed solely to the overweening ambition of popes and priests. Many were the offshoots of a deep and developing, if often crude, medieval spirituality. Protestant controversialists were not disposed to recognise this spirituality, however. 'This church of Rome now present,' wrote John Foxe, 'cannot be fathered on the apostles . . . but is of another author, whom here I will not name'.[2] The differences were ascribed to usurpations and human inventions. It was polemically convenient to relate the changes in the church to the growth of the powers and pretensions of the papacy in order to show that it was not merely justifiable but essential for all true Christians to separate from the church of Rome.

Protestant writers were the more concerned to stress the degeneration of the Roman church from primitive purity because

---

[2] J. Foxe, *Acts and Monuments*, ed. S. R. Cattley (8 vols., London, 1841), i, 7.

of the Catholic emphasis on the continuity of the visible church from the days of the apostles and on its consequent claims to unquestionable authority in spiritual matters. 'Where was your church before Luther?' Catholics asked. Protestant writers therefore sought to show first, that this continuity did not exist but that the church of Rome had been so corrupted by accretions and usurpations that it was no longer the same church as that which had existed in the first centuries after Christ. Secondly, they claimed that the Protestant churches represented the institutional crystallisation of a tradition of pure Christianity stretching back to the apostles. This was an invisible church, remaining pure while the visible church became corrupt, manifesting itself in the medieval heresies (Albigensians, Hussites, Lollards, etc.) which revolted against the pomp and pride of Rome and so were savagely persecuted.

To Foxe and others the growth of the institutional church and the papacy had led to the spiritual essence of Christianity being almost wholly lost in a welter of vain and irrelevant ceremonies.[3] Protestant writers explained the development of these ceremonies in terms of the arrogance and cupidity of popes and priests: 'Look over the whole body and all the parts of Christian religion,' wrote Peter du Moulin the younger, an Anglican divine, 'and see whether any parcel of it was by them left sound that could be screwed to feed the ambition and covetousness of the clergy'.[4] The pamphleteer Henry Care took a similar line:

All the points controverted between us and the Romanists arose either from ambition or avarice and were at first only the private opinions of certain fanatical heads, sprung up in times corrupt and ages of ignorance; which being found to make for the base interests of what they called the church those mercenary hucksters of divinity were concerned and accordingly made it their business to bring them in credit with the people.[5]

Thus transubstantiation and auricular confession were seen as means whereby the priesthood increased and maintained its authority over the laity; purgatory, indulgences, masses for the dead, etc. were seen as designed solely for the clergy's financial

[3] *ibid.* i, 61, 70, 85, etc.
[4] *A Calm Answer to a Violent Discourse* (1677), p. 16.
[5] *The Weekly Pacquet of Advice from Rome, or the History of Popery* (4 vols., 1678–82), ii, 65.

profit.[6] To keep the people from becoming aware of these tricks and innovations the clergy kept them ignorant and denied them the Bible in their own language.[7] Clerical celibacy and monasticism were at best unnatural and at worst hid rampant sexuality and nameless vices behind a facade of chastity.[8] Popery was thus shown as a vast cheat imposed by a priestly caste on a laity deliberately kept in an ignorance from which it could be freed only by the light of the Gospel. The tyranny of priests over laymen, of popes over princes was constantly emphasised.

Most of the corruptions of the Roman church were blamed on to the pope. To William Lloyd, who eventually became bishop of Worcester, what made a Papist was 'an undue adhesion to the bishop of Rome in principles or practices falsely pretended to be Christian'.[9] If Protestants might believe some good of the English Catholics, they could believe none of the pope; he and his emissaries, endowed with satanic cunning, were implacably dedicated to the extirpation of Protestantism and had the recapture of England especially at heart.[10] In order to achieve this end, Catholics were alleged to be allowed, nay encouraged, to equivocate, lie, break any oath made to a Protestant and even die with a lie in their mouths[11] – allegations which had their source in a highly hostile reading of the moral casuistry of some Jesuit writers.

The arguments of the reformers were used repeatedly in seventeenth century theological controversy, at all levels, to little effect. The religious divisions of the theologically conscious part of the nation were now hard and distinct. Hostility to many features of Catholicism was widespread and deep-rooted and

---

6 *ibid.* i, 197, 211–12, ii, 65–70, 78, 89–90, iii, 235, 301, 583; A. Marvell, *An Account of the Growth of Popery and Arbitrary Government* (1677), pp. 6–7; *Popery Manifested or the Papist Incognito Made Known* (1673, Wing P 2376), pp. 26–32, 49.

7 Care, ii, 170, 225, iii, 61; Marvell, p. 6; du Moulin, *A Calm Answer*, pp. 23–5.

8 Pepys, 26 May 1662, *Diary*, iii, 93; Care, i, 41–3, 170–2, ii, 361–6, iii, 37–8; *POAS*, ii, 79–80, iv, 179.

9 *Considerations Touching the True Way to Suppress Popery* (1677), p. 2.

10 du Moulin, *A Replie to a Person of Honour* (1675), p. 43. This belief rested on the feudal vassalage to the pope entered into by king John and Richard II.

11 *State Trials*, vii, 482, 543–70, 679, etc.

lost little strength from being based so often on a crude caricature of Catholic practice. Deeply embedded in the consciousness of all kinds of Protestants by generations of teaching, discussion and propaganda, this hostility provided a reservoir of common ideas and prejudices to which Protestant polemicists could appeal. This mixture of informed dislike and garish misrepresentation of salient features of Catholicism formed only the implicit basis of seventeenth century anti-Catholicism. The explicit basis was in no way a coherent ideology but consisted of a succession of images, mostly lurid, which were the product of successive phases in the historical experience of English Protestantism. Anti-Catholic propaganda was concerned to show, not only the ridiculousness, impiety and superstition of Popery, but also its dreadfulness as a *political* phenomenon as evidenced by English Protestants' past struggles with Catholicism.

The first and least important element in the formation of the anti-Catholic tradition stemmed from the Henrician reformation. Writers claimed, incorrectly, that papal taxation had been a heavy burden[12] and alleged that if Catholicism were ever restored in England, the church would demand back the monastic lands confiscated by Henry VIII.[13] By 1660 this was quite anachronistic. Many Catholics as well as Protestants owned abbey-lands and their recovery after more than a century would have posed insuperable administrative problems. Nevertheless there were some who took the idea seriously. To James II only fears for their property could explain the reluctance of Englishmen to turn Catholic; he subsidised the production of a pamphlet which reassured them on that point.[14] For all their reiteration, the spectres of swingeing taxation and forfeited lands were only part of the

---

12 T. Staveley, *The Romish Horseleech* (1674), parts of which were plagiarised by Care in the *Weekly Pacquet;* Scarisbrick, *Henry VIII*, p. 656.
13 Foxe, vii, 34–5; Care, ii, 31–2; Marvell, pp. 13–14; P. Sarpi, *The Papacy of Paul IV* (1673); W. Lloyd, *A Seasonable Discourse* (5th edn., 1673), pp. 21–5; J. Willes, 'Abby and other Church-lands Not Yet Assured to Such Possessors as are Roman Catholicks', *State Tracts*, ii, 326–30.
14 J. Y. Akerman (ed.), *Moneys Received and Paid for Secret Services of Charles II and James II 1678–88* (Camden Soc., 1851), p. 179; the pamphlet was N. Johnston, *The Assurance of Abby and Other Church Lands* (1687).

pageants of horrors paraded before Protestants' eyes as the inevitable consequences of the re-establishment of Popery; they formed part of a wider tradition which began with the reign of 'Bloody Mary'.

QUEEN MARY: POPERY AND BLOODY PERSECUTION

One work stood out in forming English Protestant attitudes to the Marian persecutions, the *Acts and Monuments* of John Foxe. This was more than a mere martyrology. It contained lengthy accounts of the trials of the martyrs and extracts from their writings. In an unsystematic way it was a theological apology for the Reformation, for it tried to show why as well as how the martyrs died. Foxe placed the martyrs and the English Reformation in an historical perspective. He saw history as continuous with Scripture: both recorded the working out of God's will in the world. Thus the prophecies of the Bible, especially those of the book of Revelation, could be used to explain the past and foretell the future.[15] Foxe produced two rather different chronologies of the history of Christendom, based on the prophecies of Revelation. In each the world was seen as in the final stage of its history – not hard to believe for a generation which had seen the age-old hegemony of the Catholic church cracked again and again. The struggle of Protestantism and Catholicism was depicted as the final cataclysmic conflict of the forces of Christ and the forces of Antichrist which was to end only on the Day of Judgment.[16] The Marian persecutions were shown as part of a continual history of persecutions of true Christians which began with the earliest Christian martyrs.

Foxe also developed a sense that already existed of the central place of England in world and Christian history, as the 'elect nation'. This sense had been expressed by medieval chroniclers and it was now revived and popularised by those of the sixteenth century. Foxe followed medieval writers in giving the English

---

[15] W. Haller, *Foxe's Book of Martyrs and the Elect Nation* (London, 1963), pp. 130–6.

[16] Foxe, i, 4–5, ii, 722–7. The first chronology had Satan bound from the death of Christ to *c*. A.D, 1000, the second from the end of the first persecutions (*c*. A.D. 300) to the accession of Boniface VIII in *c*. 1300.

church an origin independent of Rome, alleging that it had been
founded by Joseph of Arimethea in A.D. 63. Most seventeenth
century writers, Protestant and Catholic, accepted that the
English church had been founded sometime in the first century,
some giving the credit to St. Paul.[17]

To Foxe and the other returning exiles, Elizabeth's accession
must have seemed the dawning of a new age. Foxe portrayed her
as a new Constantine, an archetypal 'godly prince',[18] and encouraged expectations of her that verged on the messianic. Despite her brushes with parliaments and Puritanism, the expectations found their consummation in the defeat of the Catholic challenge, in the shape of the most powerful Catholic kingdom in
Europe, and the securing of the Protestant state. Foxe and a host
of lesser chroniclers, preachers and propagandists created the
expectation and proclaimed the fulfilment of the Elizabethan
achievement. They helped to transmit to later generations a cult
of Protestant patriotism centred on Elizabeth which was at least
partly spontaneous[19] and which acquired a greater leaven of
myth and legend as time went on. In fact, for most of Elizabeth's
reign the position of English Protestantism had seemed extremely
precarious, with so much depending on the queen's own survival;
it was little wonder that the optimism attending her accession was
soon tempered by a deep, even desperate, anxiety.[20] But after her
death the anxiety and the conflicts were forgotten, leaving an
image of her reign as a golden age of harmony and patriotism.
The Elizabethan myth provided a yardstick against which the less
unequivocally Protestant Stuarts could be measured and found
wanting. The practice of celebrating Elizabeth's accession day
(17 November) revived early in James I's reign, despite attempts

17 Haller, pp. 19, 141–53; Foxe, i, 306–14; BM Add. MSS 10118, fol. 82,
25370, fol. 198; S. Cressy, *The Church-History of Brittany* (1668),
pp. 10–34; Evelyn, 26 Aug. 1662, *Diary*, iii, 333; W. Lloyd, *An
Historical Account of Church Government* (1684), p. 48; E. Stillingfleet, *Origines Britannicae* (1685), chap. 1; Sir W. Temple, *Introduction to the History of England* (1695), p. 50.

18 Foxe, viii, 600–2; Haller, pp. 84–9.

19 Haller, pp. 97–103, 225, 228ff.; R. C. Strong, 'The Accession Day of
Queen Elizabeth I', *Journal of the Warburg and Courtauld Institutes*,
xxi (1958), 86–103; J. E. Neale, *Essays in Elizabethan History* (London,
1958), pp. 9–13.

20 C. Z. Wiener, 'The Beleaguered Isle: A Study of Elizabethan and
Early Jacobean Anti-Catholicism', *P & P*, 51 (1971), 27–62.

to have his accession celebrated instead.[21] This practice and that of burning the pope in effigy were revived in the 1670s and reached a peak in the Exclusion Crisis. This was one expression of the fears aroused by the religious and political leanings of the court; the veneration of Elizabeth implied a condemnation of her successors. During the great pope-burning ceremonies of 1679–81 a huge statue of Elizabeth was set on Temple Bar, decked out, as the Tory Roger North sourly remarked, like a heathen idol; a broadside of 1680 expressed the veneration for Elizabeth:

> Behold the genius of our land!
> England's Palladium! May this shrine
> Be honoured still and ever stand
> Than Pallas' statue more divine.[22]

Other versifiers invoked the Virgin Queen as a guardian angel:

> See here she comes, the great ELIZABETH
> Who the great Romish Babylon with her breath
> Threw to the ground: Rome's daubers ne'er were able
> Since her blest reign yet to rebuild their Babel.
>
> So now near four-score years after her death
> Rome's terror still is great Elizabeth.[23]

> Your Popish Plot and Smithfield threat
> We do not fear at all,
> For lo, beneath Queen Bess's feet
> You fall, you fall, you fall.[24]

Even republicans joined in:

> A Tudor! A Tudor! We've had Stuarts enough,
> None ever reign'd like old Bess in her ruff.[25]

Foxe also bequeathed to future generations a graphic account of the Marian persecutions which gave Popish cruelty and perse-

---

[21] Strong, p. 103; Neale, p. 14.

[22] *HMC 7th Report, Appendix*, p. 477; R. North, *Examen* (1740), p. 577; *The Solemn Mock Procession of the Pope, Cardinals, Jesuits, Fryers, etc.* (1680), brs.

[23] *A Poem on the Burning of the Pope* (1679), brs.

[24] *London's Defiance to Rome* (1679), p. 4; see also J. D., *The Coronation of Queen Elizabeth* (1680), a play acted at Bartholomew and Southwark fairs.

[25] *POAS*, i, 281; see also *ibid.* ii, 157–8.

cution a central place in the anti-Catholic tradition. Accounts of the St Bartholomew's Day massacres and Gunpowder Plot were added to later editions.[26] Later writers continued the story with the Irish massacres of the 1640s, the Piedmontese persecutions of the 1650s and the slowly intensifying persecution of the Huguenots which began in the 1660s.[27] A typical mid-century work was the *General Martyrology* of Samuel Clarke.[28] This was avowedly for those with no time to plough through such weighty works as that of Foxe. It cut out the history and documentation and concentrated on gruesome details of the persecutions. Clarke followed Foxe as far as he went, adding horrific accounts of the Irish massacres of 1641, as well as details of the harrying of Puritan preachers by archbishop Laud. The difference between the works of Clarke and Foxe was graphically shown in the contrast between Foxe's carefully executed woodcuts and Clarke's crude line drawings, which showed eighty-seven different ways in which martyrs had been put to death.

The Marian persecutions continued to hold an important place in Protestant memories and were cited as evidence of Popish cruelty during the Exclusion Crisis. One writer referred to the future James II as 'Queen Mary in breeches'.[29] Henry Care asked his readers to imagine:

Yourselves forced to fly destitute of bread and harbour, your wives prostituted to the lust of every savage bog-trotter, your daughters ravished by goatish monks, your smaller children tossed upon pikes, or torn limb from limb, whilst you have your own bowels ripped up ... or else murdered with some other exquisite tortures and holy candles made of your grease (which was done within our memory in Ireland), your dearest friends flaming in Smithfield, foreigners rendering your poor babes that can escape everlasting slaves, never more to see a Bible, nor hear again the joyful sounds of Liberty and Property. This, this gentlemen is Popery.[30]

26 These were in both the 1641 and the 1684 editions; nothing further was added.
27 'An Account of the Bloody Massacre in Ireland', (1678), *Somers Tracts*, viii, 89–96; *A Brief Relation of the Persecution and Sufferings of the Reformed Churches of France* (1668); 'A Remonstrance of the Popish Clergy of France' (1677), *Somers Tracts*, viii, 50–4; *Popery and Tyranny, or the Present State of France* (1679), pp. 5–6.
28 First published 1651; third edition 1677.
29 'Vox Populi, Vox Dei' (1681), *Somers Tracts*, viii, 302.
30 Care, iii, 160 (dated 19 Nov. 1680).

This piece appeared only four days after the House of Lords had rejected the Exclusion Bill in November 1680. It was unusually hysterical but by no means unique.[31] It reflected a deep-seated belief in the cruelty of Papists in power. Even basically gentle monarchs, it was thought, could be turned by their priests into savage persecutors, as Mary had been by her bishops.[32] Propaganda like Care's touched a deep chord in Protestants' minds. Moreover the basis that it had in historical fact was reinforced by contemporary events both in 1641, with the Irish massacres, and in the 1680s, with Louis XIV's persecution of the Huguenots.

QUEEN ELIZABETH: POPERY AND TREASON

After an initial period of uncertainty and ambiguity the relationship between the Elizabethan regime and the papacy became one of embattled hostility. The pope's excommunication of the queen, the invasions of Ireland with the papal blessing, the mission of the new priests, the Spanish armadas – all these were manifestations of that hostility, as was the English government's intensified persecution of the Catholics.

As Foxe had depicted the Marian persecutions as the latest example of the oppression of the godly by the ungodly, so Elizabeth's government represented the queen's conflicts with Rome as being analogous to earlier clashes of popes and princes. The queen's excommunication was compared to that of the emperor Henry IV in 1074.[33] The regime tried to defend its persecution of Catholics on non-theological grounds, hoping thus to make its defence acceptable to Catholic opinion abroad and also to avoid the Catholic position that the repression of religious deviants by a church with a monopoly of truth was not only justifiable but essential. It thus tried to turn the question of Elizabeth's relationship with Rome into one of the political relations between a sovereign state and the pretensions of an unsurped supranational authority, and so represented the religious dissent of Catholic

---

[31] C. Blount (?), 'An Appeal from the Country to the City' (1679), *State Tracts*, i, 401–2; *POAS*, ii, 27, 31–2, 300–1.

[32] Grey, vii, 403–5, viii, 279; *The Narrative of John Smith* (1679), pp. 3–4; E. Settle, 'The Character of a Popish Successor' (1681), *State Tracts*, i, 156–7.

[33] W. Cecil, *Execution of Justice* and W. Allen, *Modest Defence of the English Catholics*, ed. R. M. Kingdon (Ithaca, 1965), pp. 21–9.

priests as the political offence of treason. Lord Burghley asserted in *The Execution of Justice in England* (which was reprinted in 1675 and 1688) that priests and their abettors were executed as 'traitors against their sovereign and queen in adhering to him [the pope], being the notable and only open hostile enemy in all actions of war against her Majesty and kingdoms and people'.[34] He alleged that even if they had committed no overt act of treason they were at the least spies and accessories for traitors, sent by the pope to stir up the people. He utterly denied that they were executed for their religion.[35] But in practice the issue could be seen neither as purely religious nor as purely secular. Men of the sixteenth century saw society as an organic whole, both spiritual and secular, in which religious and political dissidence were equally destructive. Politics and religion were not separate, but were both facets of a divinely decreed order, within which harmony was essential for the stability and wellbeing of society. Catholics and Protestants each tried to concentrate on one aspect, religion or politics, to the exclusion of the other. Most of the Catholic martyrs probably did not meddle in politics. Their offence was given a political colouring only by the tendering of the 'bloody questions' about the pope's deposing power. But a few certainly were involved in political intrigues; the government knew this and so treated all priests as suspect.[36]

The extent of the Elizabethan regime's exploitation of anti-Catholicism was almost always conditioned by political circumstances; it was a dispensable secondary element in government propaganda. Burghley employed Puritan scribblers and regius professors of divinity to write pamphlets, but he wrote one himself in 1588 which contrasted the loyal demeanour of most Catholics during the Armada crisis with that of the minority of incendiaries.[37] The government's approach to the Catholic question

---

34 *ibid.* p. 15. The reprints of 1675 and 1688 were in *A Collection of Several Treatises Concerning ... the Penal Laws;* this collection was also appended to E. Stillingfleet, *The Jesuits Loyalty Manifested* (1677).
35 Cecil, pp. 5–9, 36–9.
36 For a balanced discussion of this question see MacGrath, pp. 177–86.
37 C. Read, 'William Cecil and Elizabethan Public Relations', in S. T. Bindoff, J. Hurtsfield and C. H. Williams (eds.), *Elizabethan Government and Society: Essays Presented to Sir John Neale* (London, 1961), pp. 36–8; C. Read, *Lord Burghley and Queen Elizabeth* (London, 1960), pp. 248, 251, 255, 431–3.

was essentially pragmatic; it probably regarded its persecuting measures as forced on it by the behaviour of the activists among the Catholics. Plots were exploited to create a sense of Protestant solidarity and government spokesmen sometimes made strongly anti-Catholic speeches in parliament.[38] But for the most part the government's concern was simply to survive; it would prefer Catholicism to be destroyed by erosion rather than by evangelism.

Seventeenth century Protestants continued to deny that English Catholics were persecuted for their religion as the Huguenots were in France.[39] Time and again the plots against Elizabeth and Gunpowder Plot were used to show the implacable hostility of popes and Papists to the English Protestant state. The clashes of medieval popes with emperors and kings and the assassinations of Henry III and IV of France, allegedly with papal approval, were cited to show that Popery was incompatible with any monarchy, Protestant or Catholic. Even when Louis XIV showed how compatible Popery and absolutism were and fears proliferated of Popery and arbitrary government, it was said that Papists could not be faithful subjects to any prince as their first obedience was always to the pope.[40] If they refused the oath of allegiance, they did so because it involved a denial of the papal deposing power, which many saw as the central tenet of Popery. 'Treason [is] a sign of true Roman religion,' wrote the Oxford don Henry Foulis.[41] The same tired old historical illustrations were trotted out again and again; significantly, few dated from much after 1605. Still, Protestants argued that if the deposing power was not being used and if the Catholics seemed loyal, this

---

[38] Read, 'Elizabethan Public Relations', pp. 26–7, 33, 35, 39, 52–3; J. E. Neale, *Queen Elizabeth and her Parliaments* (2 vols., London, 1953, 1957), i, 382–4, ii, 28–31, 195–201.

[39] W. D. Cooper (ed.), *Savile Correspondence* (Camden Soc., 1858), pp. 209–10; H. Foulis, *The History of Romish Treasons* (1671), p. 413; P. du Moulin, *A Vindication of the Sincerity of the Protestant Religion* (1664), p. 52; E. Stephens, *A Discourse concerning the Original of the Powder Plot* (1674), p. 128; W. Denton, *The Burnt Child Dreads the Fire* (1675), pp. 10–16, 123–5.

[40] Marvell, *Growth of Popery*, p. 11; T. Barlow, *Popery* (1679), pp. 3–4 and passim; *A Word in Season, or the Great Plot for Restoring Popery* (1663), p. 50.

[41] Foulis, *Romish Treasons*, preface, sig. [d4] and pp. 715–16; Stillingfleet, *The Jesuits Loyalty*, p. 3; du Moulin, *Replie to a Person of Honour*, p. 32.

was only because they were too weak to rebel at present. 'Why should we not fear,' asked an anonymous writer, 'that their malice, though not their power, is as great now as heretofore? And why may we not expect, if opportunity should offer itself to them, to see as many villainies transacted as in times past, for all their pretended loyalty to the king?'[42]

Roman theologians had not abandoned the deposing power as a theoretical concept, but by 1660 the popes had not the slightest intention of using it in practice. It was a common Protestant practice to cite individual Catholic authors or councils and parade their opinions as the officially approved teaching of the church. Protestant writers were not concerned whether such points were taught by the church as articles of faith or were merely allowed as permissible opinions. Nor did they consider, if the views were still held, whether or not the church showed any signs of acting on them. Instead they trotted out clichés about the pope's unfailing malice and the church's claims of infallibility. Catholic arguments that the deposing power was not an article of faith were easily countered by pointing out that popes had claimed and used it in the past.[43] Seventeenth century Englishmen were not inclined to recognise that times and situations were changing. They saw history not as a continuous progression but as a cyclical one; the battles of the past had, in essence, to be fought over again. The Common Law tradition of historical writing and the myth of the Ancient Constitution tended to inhibit the development of any concept of historical change or progress. This tendency was reinforced by political considerations as parliamentarians, in laying claim to 'ancient' rights and liberties, ascribed to them an antiquity which they did not possess but which alone could make them acceptable to men who sought political legitimacy in precedent.[44] Although

---

[42] *Popery Absolutely Destructive to Monarchy* (1673), p. 118; see also Marvell, pp. 9, 13; Lloyd, *Seasonable Discourse*, p. 15; *State Trials*, vii, 1300–1.

[43] *State Trials*, vii, 133, 1517–18; J. Tillotson, *A Sermon Preached November 5 1678 at St Margaret's Westminster* (1678), p. 24.

[44] J. G. A. Pocock, *The Ancient Constitution and the Feudal Law* (Cambridge, 1957) passim, especially chap. 2; Q. R. D. Skinner, 'History and Ideology in the English Revolution', *HJ*, viii (1965), 151–61; V. F. Snow, 'The Concept of Revolution in Seventeenth Century England', *HJ*, v (1962), 167–74. After 1660 one does find some affirmations of the

Protestant writers were aware of changes in the Catholic church over the centuries, this merely reinforced and justified their desire to return to the perfection of the past, to the values and institutions of the primitive church. There is a parallel between the Church of England's adoption of the belief in a first century foundation for the English church and the Common Lawyers' claims of the immemorial antiquity of the Common Law and of parliament. In a mental climate so inimical to any awareness of historical change, it is not surprising that Restoration Protestants saw little reason to regard the political and religious attitudes of the Elizabethan past as irrelevant; instead they regarded the accumulated experience of the past as an invaluable asset in understanding the present. In this they were not entirely wrong. They still had reason to fear Popery, not because of any danger from the papacy or the Catholics but because of the tendencies of the Stuart court towards Catholicism, which became increasingly associated with arbitrariness in government.

CHARLES I: POPERY AND ARBITRARY GOVERNMENT

The Gunpowder Plot was the last and greatest influence in the formation of Protestant belief in Popish disloyalty and treason. The enormity of the Plot, its apparent nearness to success and the involvement of the Jesuits (now the chief bogeymen of English Protestants) made a great impact on Protestant minds.[45] But even in 1605 the Plot was something of an anachronism. James I had shown himself unexpectedly friendly to Catholics and became so again during the negotiations for the Spanish marriage. Changes in the international situation made foreign invasion far less likely. Some priests were already trying to come to terms with the state. The English Catholics were relapsing into a

possibility of progress linked with an awareness that Popery is not really dangerous. Sir Peter Pett, for example, argued that the eventual triumph of Protestantism was assured because of the greater economic progress and population growth of Protestant countries, *The Happy Future State of England* (1688), passim. See also Thomas, *Religion and the Decline of Magic*, pp. 427–32.

45 In this context it is irrelevant whether the Plot was genuine or contrived by Robert Cecil. All Protestants and many Catholics regarded it as genuine.

quietism from which most had never stirred.[46] Meanwhile, the consensus of ruler and ruled which had held together, at times rather precariously, in the face of alien and Catholic threats to the Protestant state, began to break up, even before Elizabeth's death, as those threats declined. The Catholic question was both a cause and a symptom of the gradual alienation of 'court' and 'country'. As late as 1605 it had brought king and nation together; by 1640 it was being used to explain the breach between them.

It was hardly surprising that James I failed to live up to the Elizabethan myth. The very success of Elizabeth in securing the Protestant state made it unnecessary for him to do so. Nevertheless he and his son were measured against the myth and found wanting. In particular, their failure to intervene effectually on the Protestant side in the Thirty Years' War was bitterly criticised. Their deviations from Elizabethan perfection were not only negative. They began to show definite signs of friendliness to Rome and to Papists. Taken in conjunction with Charles I's tendencies towards absolutism during the 'personal rule', with the contemporaneous strengthening of the French monarchy and with the weakening of representative bodies throughout Europe, this gave rise to the celebrated identification of Popery with arbitrary government.

The court first showed signs of favouring Popery in the 1620s, with the Spanish and French marriage negotiations, the temporary suspension of the penal laws and the repayment of fines.[47] The queen pressed Charles to suspend the penal laws entirely. Several major government posts were held by Catholics or crypto-Catholics, like Windebank, Cottington and Weston. Only Laud and Strafford showed a desire to enforce the laws to the full. In fact the laws were still enforced to some extent, with the aim of raising money from the Catholics rather than of harassing or crushing them.[48] Rome soon realised that the court was friendly;

[46] D. H. Willson, *James VI & I* (London, 1956), pp. 217–19; Bossy, *Crisis in Europe*, pp. 243–6.

[47] S. R. Gardiner, *Constitutional Documents of the Puritan Revolution* (3rd edn, Oxford, 1951), p. 208; G. Albion, *Charles I and the Court of Rome* (London, 1935), p. 64.

[48] Albion, pp. 109, 112–13; Havran, p. 59 and chap. 6; Lindley, pp. 225–42; Clarendon, *History of the Rebellion*, ed. W. D. Macray (6 vols., Oxford, 1888), i, 63, 194.

agents were exchanged and the curia hoped for Charles's conversion.[49] The strength of Catholicism at court was obvious; the queen and others flaunted their religion.[50] Meanwhile the growing stress on ritualism and clericalism in the Laudian church seemed to many perilously close to Popery, especially as Puritans were harried more than Papists. The distinction between Laudianism and Popery was often hard to draw and many were not concerned to draw it. Not much separated Anglo-Catholics like Windebank from Catholic reunionists like Franciscus à Santa Clara. Laud was twice offered a cardinalate. One of his bishops, Goodman, became a Catholic; of 149 Laudian clergymen who went into exile during the Interregnum, fourteen became Catholics, although one later recanted.[51] The Catholics' contribution to the Scottish war in 1639 and the presence of Catholic officers in the army must further have increased concern about the court's religious leanings.

When the Long Parliament met a fierce anti-Catholicism was one expression of the wide-ranging hostility to the personal rule. The sheer number of anti-Catholic incidents and their tendency to coincide with periods of high political excitement suggest that the anti-Popery of 1640–2 was not produced merely by agitation and manipulation. On the contrary it expressed the fears engendered in many sorts of people by the king's actions and represented a normal seventeenth century reaction to a crisis in which the Catholic question was involved. Even innocent actions by Papists, like buying in large stores of provisions, could give rise to fears and perhaps to violence against them; such incidents, reported in London, reinforced the tension there. The extremeness of Protestant reactions can be explained by the belief that Catholics would stick at nothing to achieve their ends; stories of plots were readily credited as they fitted in with preconceived ideas. As parliament had virtually no police or military force at its disposal, it tended to act first and investigate the truth of rumours later.[52] The pattern was similar in the Popish Plot crisis.

[49] Albion, pp. 92–5, 248 and passim.
[50] *ibid.* p. 227; Havran, chap. 3; Caraman, pp. 95–6.
[51] Albion, chap. 7; H. R. Trevor-Roper, *Archbishop Laud* (2nd edn, London, 1965), pp. 306–7; R. S. Bosher, *The Making of the Restoration Settlement: the Influence of the Laudians 1649–62* (London, 1951), pp. 284–94.
[52] This paragraph and part of the next are based on some of the argu-

John Pym skilfully exploited the army plots and the Irish rebellion and massacres to back up his allegations of the danger from Papists and so keep anti-Catholic excitement alive. Attempts to place unprecedented checks on the prerogative destroyed the earlier unanimity of parliament. As the radicals came closer to attacking the king directly, so they intensified the anti-Popish element in their propaganda, accusing the court of plotting to bring in Popery and absolutism. They tried to excite deliberately what had been initially a spontaneous response to a highly tense political situation. The propaganda use of anti-Catholicism intensified as the number of popular outbursts of anti-Popery declined. After the summer of 1642 the polemical use of anti-Catholicism was not matched by numerous anti-Catholic incidents.

Even some who later fought for the king believed in 1641 that the personal rule had been part of a great plot to impose absolute monarchy on England and subject it to the pope.[53] The Commons' full-scale apology, the Grand Remonstrance, stated:

The root of all this mischief we find to be a malignant and pernicious design of subverting the fundamental laws and principles of government, upon which the religion and justice of this kingdom are firmly established. The actors and promoters hereof have been:

1. The Jesuited Papists, who hate the laws as the obstacles of that change and subversion of religion which they so much long for.

2. The bishops and the corrupt part of the clergy who cherish formality and superstition as the natural effects and more probable supports of their own ecclesiastical tyranny and usurpation.

3. Such councillors and courtiers as for private ends have engaged themselves to further the interests of some foreign princes or states to the prejudice of his Majesty and the state at home.[54]

The Remonstrance went on to say that the conspirators had tried to divide Protestants while introducing into the church such

ments and material in R. Clifton, 'The Fear of Catholics in England 1637 to 1645', (unpublished Oxford D.Phil. thesis, 1967); see also Clifton's article in *P & P*, 52, pp. 27–33, 39–47, 52 and passim; Clarendon, *History of the Rebellion*, i, 327–8; B. H. G. Wormald, *Clarendon: Politics, Historiography and Religion 1640–60* (Cambridge, 1951), pp. 16–18.

53 S. R. Gardiner, *History of England 1603–42* (10 vols., London, 1883–4), ix, 227–30.

54 Gardiner, *Constitutional Documents*, pp. 206–7.

ceremonies as were consonant with Popery: 'There must be a conjunction between Papists and Protestants in doctrine, discipline and ceremonies; only it must not yet be called Popery.'[55] Few of the 204 articles which followed dealt directly with Catholics;[56] most were concerned with specific grievances, with attacks on the bishops and Catholic peers and with further allegations of plotting. The conspiracy theory reflected a common Protestant belief that there were innumerable secret Papists who would come forward only when the time was right.[57] This belief was shared by James II.

From this it was but a short step to the purely propaganda assertion, virtually a Parliamentarian orthodoxy, that all Cavaliers were Papists or crypto-Papists. This gradually lost credence as the war went on,[58] but for a while pamphleteers like William Prynne, the lawyer, controversialist and M.P., depicted the war as parliament's resistance to a king surrounded by Catholic influences who constantly favoured Papists.[59] (Convention still decreed that the king should not be attacked directly, but only as misled by evil advisers.) Rather illogically, Prynne combined this with a firm belief in the Habernfeld Plot, an alleged Jesuit conspiracy to murder the king and Laud. Others less bigoted and more clear-sighted than Prynne pointed out that this was inconsistent with the more widely held belief in the plot to bring in Popery and absolutism.[60] The identification of Popery with arbitrary government was now so complete that only two of the many plots of the early 1640s – Habernfeld's and another – involved the assassination of the king; the rest involved attacks on parliament and Protestants.[61] A transition had taken place from a situation where Popery was seen as the enemy of crown and nation to one where Popery and the crown were seen as dangers to the Protestant nation. This was one expression of the breakdown of the consensus of court and country since the reign of Elizabeth.

[55] *ibid.* pp. 207, 216.
[56] *ibid.* pp. 219–20 (articles 88–94).
[57] *ibid.* p. 230 (article 194); see also Wiener, *P & P*, 51, pp. 37–8.
[58] Clifton, thesis, chap. 6; Caraman, pp. 141–2.
[59] Prynne, *The Popish Royall Favorite* (1643), pp. 34–5, 56–9, 71–4.
[60] Prynne, *Romes Master-peece* (1643), passim; W. M. Lamont, *Marginal Prynne* (London, 1963), pp. 124–37.
[61] Clifton, *P & P*, 52, p. 54.

REGICIDE AND RESTORATION

Suspicions that Charles I was a Papist in disguise were dispelled by his impeccably Anglican martyrdom. Writers of the Restoration ascribed his troubles to his *seeming* too friendly to Papists or else blamed everything on the queen.[62] It was left to the neurotically anti-Popish Prynne to find a way for Protestants to escape the obloquy of having put to death a Protestant king.[63] By the end of 1648 Prynne was convinced that the army had been infiltrated and taken over by priests and Jesuits.[64] Pride's Purge was, to him, as great a blow to parliament as Gunpowder Plot would have been, had it succeeded. He wrote on 26 December 1648:

All [the army's] present exorbitant actings against the king, parliament [and] government and their new-modelled representative are nothing else but the designs and projects of Jesuits, Popish priests and recusants who bear chief sway in their counsels to destroy and subvert our religion, laws, liberties, government, magistracy, ministry, the present and all future parliaments, the king, his posterity and our three kingdoms, yea, the general, officers and army themselves, and that with speedy and inevitable certainty, to betray them all to their foreign and Popish enemies.[65]

The horrid act of regicide confirmed his suspicions: the army had acted on the Jesuits' maxims of deposing and killing kings.[66] He saw considerable continuity between the actions of Charles I and those of the army; both had shown hostility towards parliaments and the ancient laws. He explained this by saying that the Jesuits had at first influenced the king but that they were working now through the army. He cited as evidence Cromwell's lenient

---

[62] Clarendon, *Life*, ii, 107; Halifax, *Works*, p. 78.

[63] Prynne, 'A Briefe Memento to the Present Unparliamentary Junto' (1649), *Somers Tracts*, v, 180–1; Prynne, *The First and Second Part of a Seasonable Legal and Historical Vindication* (2nd edn, 1655), Introductory epistle, sig. N4.

[64] The idea that secretaries were Papists in disguise probably did not originate with Prynne (Clifton, *P & P*, 52, pp. 33–4), but he certainly did far more than anyone else to popularise it.

[65] *Mr Prynne's Demand of His Liberty to the Generall* (1648), brs.

[66] Prynne, *First and Second Part*, Introductory epistle, sig. C2; Prynne, *The Substance of a Speech* (1649), pp. 80 (misnumbered 48), 107.

treatment of Catholics and his friendship with men like Sir Kenelm Digby.[67] Prynne developed his theory throughout the 1650s and it was taken up by Richard Baxter, Peter du Moulin and others in answer to Catholic jibes at Protestant disloyalty. Thus even the Civil War was blamed on to the Papists; the Habernfeld Plot was hesitantly adduced to back up the story, which was incorporated in the introduction to Titus Oates's narrative in 1679.[68]

A variant of the Prynne theory was used by some Anglican writers, who represented the growth of Puritanism as part of a Catholic plot to destroy Protestantism by dividing it rather than by frontal attack.[69] Prynne himself accused Quakers and other sectaries of being Papists in disguise and the accusation was extended to all Dissenters by Tory pamphleteers and even by Tory gentlemen like Mr Solicitor Finch, Sir John Birkenhead and Sir Peter Leicester.[70] This explanation of the origin of the sects was not universally taken up however; Prynne's fellow-Presbyterian Clement Walker barely mentioned it in his *History of Indepen-*

[67] *First and Second Part*, Introductory epistle, sigs. F, F4–G3; *Substance of a Speech*, p. 103 and passim; Prynne, *A True and Perfect Narrative* (1659), pp. 19–20, 43, 57–63.
[68] Lamont, *Marginal Prynne*, pp. 138–48; R. Baxter, *A Key for Catholicks* (1659), pp. 315–64; *A Word in Season or the Great Plot*, pp. 13–14, 19–22, 25–9; P. du Moulin, *Vindication of the Sincerity*, passim (du Moulin got his account of the Papists' involvement in Charles's death from Prynne: *Replie to a Person of Honour*, p. 9); *Pyrotechnica Loyolana* (1667), pp. 120–2; Denton, *The Burnt Child Dreads the Fire* (reissued in 1679 as *The Ungrateful Behaviour of the Papists*), pp. 4, 6, 31–2, 56, 60–4; C. Stanley, earl of Derby, *The Jesuites Policy to Suppress Monarchy* (1678), pp. 8, 21–2; for Oate's story, see below, pp. 155–6.
[69] W. Lloyd, *The Late Apology in Behalf of the Papists Reprinted and Answered* (1667), p. 46; *The Jesuite and Priest Discovered* (1663), pp. 6–14; A. Egan, *The Romanists Designs Detected* (1674), passim; Clifton, *P & P*, 52, pp. 33–4.
[70] Prynne, *A New Discovery of Some Romish Emissaries* (1656), passim; S. Graveson (ed.), *History of the Life of Thomas Ellwood* (London, 1906), p. 202; *The Jesuites Letter of Thanks to the Covenanters of Scotland* (1679); G. Hicks, *The Spirit of Popery Speaking out of the Mouths of Phanatical Protestants* (1680); J. Nalson, *Foxes and Firebrands* (1680), pp. 1–6, 26–33; Nalson *A Letter from a Jesuit at Paris* (1678), pp. 6–8; Grey, i, 162, v, 252; Kenyon, *Stuart Constitution*, p. 464.

dency.[71] Some Tory writers of anti-Catholic works could remind their readers that the 'fanatics' were even worse than the Papists.[72] This point was repeatedly rammed home by that most prolific and effective of Restoration pamphleteers, Roger L'Estrange, and found wide acceptance.[73] The slogan 'forty-one is here again' was effective during the Exclusion Crisis precisely because it expressed Tory fears that Presbyterians and republicans were once more using anti-Catholicism in an effort to overthrow the monarchy and the church.

There are some grounds for supposing that anti-Catholicism might have waned after 1660. Those not carried away by Prynne's fantasies must have realised that most Catholics had behaved loyally in the Civil War, more loyally than the Dissenters. Statistics, particularly those of the Compton census, were used by some writers to show how small the Catholic minority was and thus to reinforce a slowly growing awareness that a Catholic king would find it quite impossible to impose Popery.[74] After the Restoration, too, there were the beginnings of a more rational and tolerant spirit and of an acceptance of the existence of religious groups outside the national church. The Puritan failure to build a new godly society during the Interregnum and the obstinate failure of the world to come to an end greatly reduced the attractiveness of prophecies about the immediate future based on the books of Daniel and Revelation and, incidentally, also

---

[71] The only references I can find are in *The Compleat History of Independency* (1661), Part II, pp. 15, 28–9, 43–4, 46, 64, 68.

[72] Foulis, *Romish Treasons*, preface, sigs. e–c2.

[73] *POAS*, i, 315; 'Alazonomastix Philalethes', *Free-Parliament Queries Proposed to Tender Consciences* (1660), p. 5; T. Bruce, earl of Ailesbury, *Memoirs*, ed. W. E. Buckley (2 vols., Cambridge, 1890), i, 26–7; Hawkes, *Sir Roger Bradshaigh*, pp. 38–9; E. Bohun, *Diary and Autobiography, 1677–97*, ed. S. W. Rix (Beccles, 1853), pp. 40–1, 45–6.

[74] J. Glanvill, *The Zealous and Impartial Protestant* (1681), pp. 46–50; 'A Seasonable Address to Both Houses' (1681), *Somers Tracts*, viii, 235 (Wing ascribes this to Halifax but this is almost certainly incorrect); J. Nalson, *The Countermine* (2nd. edn, 1677), p. 15; M. R., *Three Great Questions concerning the Succession* (1680), p. 17 (this states that the census took place in 1672); E. Settle, *The Present State of England* (1684), pp. 8–9; Pett, *Happy Future State of England*, pp. 101, 104, 117–19, 139–50; *A Letter to Mr S., a Romish Priest* (dated 1672, but probably published *c.* 1680), brs.; 'England's Concern in the Case of His R.H.' (1680), *Somers Tracts*, viii, 174–5.

reduced the attractiveness of an apocalyptic interpretation of the conflict of Catholicism and Protestantism.

However, the anti-Catholic tradition remained strong. Its roots struck deep into English Protestants' consciousness of religion, politics and history. The Prynne theory offered a way out for those who did not wish to recognise the Catholics' loyalty in the Civil War. The statistics of the Compton census were not published in full and, then as now, statistics could have little influence on those determined to disbelieve what the figures purported to prove. The increase in tolerance was very far from universal and even among the most tolerant there was a reluctance to include the Papists. John Locke argued that the Catholics should not be allowed toleration as they were primarily subjects of the pope rather than of the civil state.[75] In short, the habits of thought of generations could not be changed overnight. Mr Hill has suggested that the identification of the pope with Antichrist declined rapidly after 1660[76] but I can find little evidence for this. It is true that Puritan writers greatly reduced their emphasis on the prophecies of Daniel and Revelation and ceased to proclaim their expectation of an imminent millennium.[77] It is also possibly true that the belief that the pope was Antichrist was less general among members of the Anglican hierarchy after 1660. But a number of Laudians had denied in the 1630s that the pope was Antichrist, and the opinion that he *was* Antichrist was far from inadmissible under Charles II. A book called *The Man of Sin*, which maintained just that, was licensed by the archbishop of Canterbury in 1677. A future archbishop, John Tillotson, said in a sermon of 1678 that he was uncertain whether or not the pope was Antichrist.[78] Restoration Englishmen were steeped in the language and rhetoric of the Bible and references to 'Antichrist' and 'Babylon' abound.[79] One writer tried to identify

[75] J. Locke, *Epistola de Tolerantia/A Letter on Toleration*, ed. R. Klibansky and J. W. Gough (Oxford, 1968), pp. 131–5.

[76] C. Hill, *Antichrist in Seventeenth Century England* (Oxford, 1971), pp. 146–54, 158–60.

[77] P. Toon, 'Conclusion', in Toon (ed.), *Puritans, the Millennium and the Future of Israel* (Cambridge, 1970), p. 128; W. M. Lamont, 'Richard Baxter, the Apocalypse and the Mad Major', *P & P*, 55 (1972), 80–3.

[78] Hill, pp. 34–40, 152–3; W. Hughes, *The Man of Sin* (1677); Tillotson *A Sermon Preached November 5 1678*, p. 28.

[79] Care, ii, 155, iii, 147–8; Grey, iii, 336; *POAS*, iv, 106; P. du Moulin

Oates and Bedloe with the two witnesses whose coming was prophesied in Revelation. In 1688 the Seven Bishops were described as the seven angels of the seven churches. Even archbishop Sheldon, the first man at Oxford to deny formally that the pope was Antichrist, could still refer to the Roman church as the 'whore of Babylon'.[80]

It is of course a common trait of collective psychology to explain disasters or adverse circumstances in terms of conspiracies or machinations by those regarded as hostile to the general well-being of society, be they Jews, Communists, trade unionists or the 'Gnomes of Zurich'. For seventeenth century Englishmen, steeped in the Protestant version of the past, the conspirators had to be the Papists. But what strikes one most about later seventeenth century anti-Catholic works is the anachronism of many of their arguments and illustrations. They rest on what had happened long before, usually before 1605, when the danger to English Protestantism from the papacy and international Catholicism had been much more real and apparent. One reason for this was that the Popery which men now feared was that rampant in the royal family which could not be attacked directly in conditions of censorship. Also most seventeenth century Englishmen had a strong sense of the immediate relevance of past history to present situations which showed little awareness of changing circumstances. Ritual or stereotyped actions, apparently referring to the long-dead past, could arouse strong political emotions if they seemed relevant to present situations, as with the cult of Queen Elizabeth during the Exclusion Crisis. Even where fears of Popery had a rational and realistic basis, they were often expressed in apparently irrelevant and anachronistic terms.

the elder, *The Papal Tyranny as it was Exercised* (1674), pp. 55–7 and the two appended sermons of the younger du Moulin (who was an Anglican divine); *Pyrotechnica Loyolana*, pp. 9, 29–30, 71; *The Solemn Mock Processions, or the Trial and Execution of the Pope* (1680), p. 5; R. S., *Rome's Thunder-bolt, or Antichrist Displaid* (1682); *The Burning of the Whore of Babylon* (1673); *Babylon Blazon'd, or the Jesuit Jerked* (1679); for a variant view, that the whole Roman church was Antichrist, see E. Bagshaw (of Christ Church, Oxon.), *A Discourse of Christ and Antichrist* (1661), pp. 17–29.

[80] E. C., *A Full and Final Proof of the Plot from the Revelations* (1680); A Tindal Hart, *William Lloyd 1627–1717* (Church Historical Soc., 1952), p. 98n.; G. R. Abernathy, jnr, 'Clarendon and the Declaration of Indulgence', *JEH*, xi (1960), 67.

The anti-Catholic tradition of Charles II's reign was a complex phenomenon which can best be understood in terms of successive phases of English historical experience. It was expressed not only in antipathy to the Catholic religion but also in fear and hatred of 'Popery and arbitrary government' which at times of crisis could reach panic proportions. Far from being moribund the tradition continued to develop; the Great Fire added yet another element, a belief in the fire-raising propensities of Jesuits and Papists. Within the broad spectrum of anti-Catholicism there existed differing and sometimes contradictory elements, which interacted and reinforced one another. The tradition retained its vitality and re-emerged to dominate politics when given a stimulus by events. This stimulus was provided, first when Charles II's court began to arouse fears of Popery and arbitrary government and the duke of York became a Papist, and secondly when Louis XIV emerged as the most powerful and aggressive monarch in Europe and as the sporadic champion of militant Catholicism. Bishop Burnet saw the year 1672, when Charles II issued the Declaration of Indulgence and Louis XIV swept through the Low Countries, as the beginning of the fifth and, he hoped, the last great crisis of the Protestant religion. In this crisis a particularly parlous phase opened in 1685, with the accession of a Catholic king in England and the revocation of the Edict of Nantes in France.[81] Much of the anti-Catholicism of the period 1660–88 now seems silly and vicious, exaggerated and misdirected; but beneath it all lay firmly based fears for the future of Protestantism and of representative institutions in England and Europe.

---

[81] Burnet, i, 534–58, iii, 69; for anxiety about the European situation see *The Prophecy of Bishop Usher* (1687), pp. 1–3; Grey, iii, 336, viii, 328; *CJ*, ix, 642; Longleat, Coventry MS xi, fols. 157, 164; H. Care, *History of the Damnable Popish Plot* (2nd edn, 1681), pp. 73–6. Dr Lamont suggests that Richard Baxter was unwilling to cast doubt publicly on the accepted views of the apocalypse 'even as late as 1686' because to do so would 'dishonour the memory of the Protestant martyrs' (*P & P*, 55, pp. 80–90). Baxter's reasons were much simpler and much more compelling; in 1686 the Protestant cause seemed threatened from all sides and it was natural that, as one of the accepted leaders of English Protestantism, Baxter should avoid any action that might prove divisive.

5

THE RESTORATION SETTLEMENT
AND AFTER (1660–9)

The Restoration settlement confirmed the abolition of some of the
institutions abused by Charles I during the personal rule; but it
left the crown's prerogatives little diminished, notably in its right
to summon and dismiss parliaments and in the ill-defined areas
where prerogative action could shade into illegality. In one way
Charles II was potentially stronger than the early Stuarts. They
had governed under the shadow of the Elizabethan myth, but
now there was a new myth, that of the royal martyr. An important section of the political nation never got over the trauma of
the Civil War. They remembered sequestration and decimation,
the overthrow of the monarchy and of the old political order, the
threats to the social order – and they wanted no repetition.
Whenever the spectre of another civil war appeared, such men
would rally to the crown far more uncritically than their fore-
bears under Charles I would have done. There was thus potential
after 1660 for a stronger monarchy, using the 'Cavalier backlash'.

The monarchy was far from absolute, however. Lacking a large
standing army and a politically neutral bureaucracy, the crown
had to have a measure of co-operation from those of its subjects
who ran the local administration and the militia. Charles II's
finances were not constantly bedevilled by inflation as his father's
had been, but because of an initially inadequate provision, exacerbated by royal extravagance, he remained for most of his reign
financially dependent on parliament, at least for his foreign wars.
This meant that to some extent he had to respect the prejudices
of his servants and supporters in parliament and the localities –
the 'church and king' men, the old Cavaliers, the Tories. The
Civil War and Charles I's martyrdom had identified the Church
of England more closely than ever with the monarchy. The Cavalier element, the potential basis of support for strong monarchy,
was solidly Anglican, and expected the king to pursue a 'Cavalier'
policy: to find jobs for 'church and king' men, to follow a
Protestant but cheap foreign policy, to rule according to law

and to repress religious nonconformity, whether Puritan or Popish.

However, neither Charles II nor James II would conform to the religious and political expectations of their natural supporters. It is a testimony to the intrinsic strength of the restored monarchy that Charles II not only survived the Exclusion Crisis but emerged from it stronger than ever, even though the Tories had had little joy from the court in terms of either places or policies during the last twenty years. Charles had tried to tolerate Popery, James became a Catholic. They had seldom followed a 'Cavalier' policy, although when they had tried one (as in 1669–71) it had been far from unsuccessful. Even after James's conversion Danby's attempt at a 'Cavalier' line was a partial success. After the Exclusion Crisis, with the divisions in the political nation re-opened, the Tory reaction raised the royal authority to the highest point it reached in the seventeenth century. The position thus achieved was then demolished at breakneck speed by the Catholicising policies of James II.

Charles II also failed to play an active role in administration and government. Although his administration and his intelligence service were probably much more efficient than those of his father, the traditional picture of Charles putting pleasure before business is far from inaccurate, especially for the early years of the reign. He also failed to appreciate, until too late, that M.P.s, however loyal and willing, were independent creatures and needed organising. His most serious failures, however, were in his general policies, especially those concerned with religion, rather than in his administration. It was the misfortune of Charles II and James II that the temperament of the former and the religious leanings of both made them disinclined to follow that line of policy which would attract the support necessary to maintain and increase the power of the monarchy.

Basically the situation under Charles II was simple. The king wanted to remove some of the penal laws on Catholics. Parliament, which spoke for the Protestant nation, did not. The king's actions and those of his government were conditioned in this context largely by the extent to which the Catholic question dominated politics at any given time. Clarendon, Charles's lord chancellor, thought that the king wanted to remove those of the penal laws that affected life and limb and that he would not enforce the others so long as the Catholics behaved as good subjects.[1] Charles often expressed his goodwill towards the Catholics and his appreciation of their loyalty and help during the civil wars and during his exile. The French ambassador wrote in 1663:

Ce que je puis vous assûrer, c'est que le roi de la Grande Bretagne ne fera rien contre notre religion que forcé par les Chambres, parce que je le trouve persuadé qu'aucune autre n'est si propre pour l'autorité absolue, outre qu'il a en particulier quelque reconnaissance pour l'assistance et les faveurs qu'il a reçues des Catholiques Romains.[2]

Charles was finally received into the Catholic church on his deathbed. During his reign he connived at the non-enforcement of the laws and tried to give Catholics a measure of open toleration in conjunction with some or all Protestant Dissenters. These attempts aroused a vigorous anti-Catholic reaction and Charles drew back. But between 1669 and 1672 changes occurred from which there was no going back. Charles began his long-term alignment with France from which parliament shook him only temporarily, in the late 1670s; at this time Louis XIV came to be regarded as the epitome of absolutism and the greatest enemy of European Protestantism. More serious still, Charles's brother and heir-apparent became a Catholic. From 1673 to 1681 the king was on the defensive; the trust between crown and parliament, never perfect, had broken down, mainly because of the Catholic question. Between 1660 and 1673 anti-Catholicism had been latent and primarily defensive. Most magistrates had been slow to persecute their Catholic neighbours. They were aroused from their inertia by the changes that took place between 1669 and 1672 at court and in government policy. Without James's conversion there would have been little persecution of Catholics in the 1670s, no Popish Plot and no Exclusion Crisis. The anti-Catholicism of the Restoration period expressed not only hatred of Catholics but also fears of 'Popery and arbitrary government' that were far from unfounded.

The efforts of the English Catholics to achieve a measure of toleration in 1660–3 must be seen in the wider context of the

---

[1] Clarendon, *Life*, ii, 100–1, 107–8.

[2] Cominges to Lionne, 12 April 1663 NS, Baschet 111; see also K. H. D. Haley, *Charles II* (Historical Assn, 1966), pp. 9–10.

Restoration religious settlement. Within eight months of the king's return episcopacy had to all intents and purposes been restored. Ecclesiastical patronage was in the hands of Edward Hyde, the lord chancellor, who was made earl of Clarendon in 1661. He was advised by a small group of Anglican clergymen who had been with the king in exile and whom one recent historian has called 'Laudians'; they were high churchmen, determined to return to the *status quo* as it had been before the civil wars. By January 1661 most of the vacant bishoprics and canonries had been filled with their supporters.[3] If the old ecclesiastical structure had been refurbished, the church's articles of faith and form of worship still had to be laid down. The Laudians wanted to restore and enforce the use of the old form of worship and the Book of Common Prayer. They found vigorous support in the strongly Anglican House of Commons elected in the spring of 1661; the majority of its members abhorred religious nonconformity of all kinds. Between 1661 and 1665 this Cavalier House of Commons took the lead in passing through parliament the Act of Uniformity and other acts which enforced strict conformity to the re-established Anglican church and punished those who dissented from it. In such a situation the Catholics' chances of achieving toleration were virtually nil.

There has been some controversy about Clarendon's attitude to Protestant Dissent at this time.[4] It seems most probable that he regarded the full restoration of episcopacy as essential because it was an integral part of the traditional constitutional order.[5] However, he did not hold rigid or dogmatic views about the form of worship or the articles of belief that were to be imposed by the state. He regarded the fundamentals of religion as few and simple and considered that the particular forms adopted should be dictated by convenience and by the needs of the civil state. At the Restoration it was politically expedient to extend the boundaries of the church and to calm partisan differences.[6] Thus to him it could seem quite consistent to try to make the church more accep-

[3] Bosher, chap. 4.
[4] A. Whiteman, 'The Restoration of the Church of England', in G. F. Nuttall and O. Chadwick (eds.), *From Uniformity to Unity 1662–1962* (London, 1962), pp. 55–7.
[5] Wormald, p. 280.
[6] *ibid.* pp. 276–324, especially p. 312.

table to the Presbyterians while bitterly condemning the seditious sermons of some of the Presbyterian clergy.[7]

His attitude to the Catholics is also hard to determine. He had been one of the few Royalists unaffected by the torrent of anti-Catholicism in 1641.[8] He was a close friend of d'Aubigny and supported the move to get him a cardinal's hat.[9] In 1660 he twice expressed approval of the idea that the Catholics should have a bishop, provided he was well-affected to the king.[10] The Jesuits' newsletters described him as not unfriendly towards the Society.[11] On several occasions he acted to help or protect the Catholics. Yet he was later accused of opposing the king's declaration in favour of toleration of December 1662 and of trying to divide the Catholics by discriminating against the Jesuits.[12] The first accusation can be explained by his growing estrangement from the earl of Bristol. For Bristol, himself a Catholic, the main objective was the largest possible measure of toleration for Catholics; he was not concerned whether this involved toleration for other denominations. Clarendon's primary aim was a settlement acceptable to the Presbyterians; this he regarded as essential if serious unrest and perhaps rebellion were to be avoided. He was prepared to consider some measure of relief for Catholics, but this was not to be allowed to jeopardise his main aim. As for the accusation of his dividing the Catholics, it is very possible that his position was similar to that taken by Ormond in Ireland. Ormond did not approve of the enforcement against the clergy of laws affecting life and limb but he firmly supported the use of the 'Remonstrance' (an affirmation of allegiance to the king drawn up by a friar called Peter Walsh) to distinguish between 'loyal' and 'disloyal' Papists and so to divide and weaken the Irish Catholics. Clarendon certainly supported this policy.[13] In 1662 Clarendon

[7] K. G. Feiling, 'A letter of Clarendon during the Elections of 1661', *EHR*, xlii (1927), 407–8.

[8] Wormald, pp. 16, 295.

[9] Clark, *Strangers and Sojourners*, p. 108 and n.4.

[10] Vecchi, 28 Aug. and 16 Oct. 1660 NS, Rom. Tr. 98, fols. 193, 228–9.

[11] Foley, i, 265, iv, 277.

[12] D'Estrades au Roi, 25 July and 29 Aug. 1661 NS, Baschet 109; Burnet, i, 333–8; Warner, pp. 175–6.

[13] T. Carte, *An History of the Life of James, Duke of Ormond* (6 vols., Oxford, 1851), iv, 661–2, v, 151–2; *Essex Papers*, i, ed. O. Airy (Camden Soc., 1890), pp. 150–1; Bodl., Carte MS 46, fols. 158, 308, 323; T. Brown, *Miscellanea Aulica* (1702), pp. 338–9.

discussed with the English Chapter the possibility of modifying the oath of allegiance. The Chaptermen doubtless encouraged any suspicions he may have had concerning the *political* implications of the principles which the Jesuits were alleged to hold; these would, to Clarendon, seem as pernicious as those of the worst Presbyterians. The formula which was agreed on included a firmer denial of the papal deposing power than the Jesuits were prepared to make. The Jesuits, in fact, had not been consulted about the form of the oath, as it was believed they were too addicted to their own ways, but the other regulars took part in the negotiations. This is presumably the origin of the second accusation, that Clarendon tried to divide the Catholics and expel the Jesuits.[14] It is possible that Clarendon was trying to find a way of allowing a modest toleration to those Catholics on whose loyalty the state could absolutely rely, provided that this would not jeopardise the religious settlement as a whole.[15]

In the months before the Restoration groups of Catholics had approached both Charles and a section of the army under general Lambert. Lord Stafford had even offered Charles £100,000 in return for toleration.[16] The Declaration of Breda of April 1660 seemed to augur well for Catholics. In it Charles promised liberty of conscience to those whose religious opinions 'do not disturb the peace of the kingdom' – subject to the approval of parliament.[17] The king presumably intended his promise to include the Catholics but the Presbyterians who were about to call Charles back would take it as applying to themselves.

Most of the pressure for toleration for Catholics in 1660–3 came from a small group associated with the court, most of whom had been with the king in exile. Their leaders were the queen mother and Bristol; they included two priests, d'Aubigny and the abbé Montagu; lord Arundell of Wardour, who became master of the horse to the queen mother in 1663; Sir John Winter, her secretary; Sir Kenelm Digby, her chancellor; Sir John Arundell,

---

[14] St George's Cathedral, Southwark MS 106e, p. 391; Bodl., Clar. MS 92, fols. 198–200; Warner, pp. 175–6: Burnet, i, 335–8; Clarendon, *Life*, ii, 110–11. [15] Abernathy, *JEH*, xi, 72.

[16] P. H. Hardacre, *The Royalists during the Puritan Revolution* (The Hague, 1956), pp. 137–9; *Cal. Clar. S.P.* iv, 511, 524, 534, 565, 632, 667; J. Corker, *Stafford's Memoires* (1681), p. 53; Burnet, ii, 265–6; *HMC Kenyon*, pp. 122–3; Morrice MS P, pp. 286–7.

[17] Kenyon, *Stuart Constitution*, pp. 357–8.

her master of the game; and colonel Samuel Tuke, playwright, courtier and occasional diplomat. When Henrietta Maria returned to England in October 1660 one of her aims was to secure toleration for the English Catholics. There were two meetings of Catholics during her stay. At one Winter failed to persuade those present that the existing oath of allegiance could be taken. (In June secular and regular clergy had agreed that it could not.) Instead Bristol persuaded those present to depute six men to assure the king of their absolute fidelity. At the second meeting nothing much seems to have been achieved.[18] The queen mother remained in England only three months. She had never got on well with Clarendon, Ormond and the old Cavaliers and the main result of her visit was to bring Anglo-French relations to a new nadir.[19]

The government's main concern in 1660 was to reach a settlement with the Presbyterians. Negotiations at Worcester House produced a declaration on 25 October which envisaged considerable changes in the structure of the church. Hyde suggested a clause that would allow 'others' to meet so long as they did not disturb the peace, but the Presbyterians' leader, Richard Baxter, opposed it as allowing liberty to Papists. The declaration contained no concessions to Popery, being specifically for the advancement of the Protestant religion.[20] These negotiations showed clearly that the Presbyterians would resist any settlement which seemed designed to tolerate Papists.[21] Whatever the king's sympathies, he could not appear yet in favour of open toleration for Catholics, but he privately assured the abbé Montagu that the laws against them would not be rigorously enforced.[22] The need for caution was greater because there were widespread suspicions, even among his Anglican courtiers, that he had become a Catholic and hoped to

---

[18] L. von Ranke, *A History of England, Principally in the Seventeenth Century* (6 vols., Oxford, 1875), iii, 340; Vecchi, 3 July and 4 Dec. 1660 NS, Rom. Tr. 98, fols. 157, 278; Bartet to Mazarin, 25 Nov. and 2 Dec. 1660 NS, Baschet 108.

[19] K. G. Feiling, *British Foreign Policy 1660–1672* (London, 1930), pp. 2, 29–33, 55.

[20] Whiteman, pp. 66–72; P. Bayne, *Documents relating to the Settlement of the Church of England* (London, 1862), pp. 63–79.

[21] R. Baxter, *Reliquiae Baxterianae*, ed. M. Sylvester (1696), Part II, pp. 277, 429–30, 433.

[22] Montagu to Mazarin, 9 Dec, 1660 NS, Baschet 108.

bring in Popery. In 1661 an act was passed making it an offence to say that the king was a Papist.[23]

Despite the difficulties, Catholics tried to convince the king and the Protestant nation of their loyalty in the civil wars and of the case for toleration. A small crop of pamphlets to this effect appeared from April 1660.[24] The king received petitions from the Dean and Chapter, the Benedictines and other regulars, Sir John Arundell and Sir Kenelm Digby. The Chapter even described the idea that excommunicated princes could be deposed and murdered as impious, damnable and unchristian.[25] The main bid for toleration came in June 1661. A number of Catholic gentlemen, including Tuke and the son of lord Arundell of Wardour, petitioned the House of Lords to lighten the burden of the penal laws. They stressed the Catholics' loyalty to the king and said that they were willing to take a modified oath of allegiance. The House saw no reason to change the oaths but agreed to hear the Catholics' case. Tuke made a long speech and lord Arundell presented papers to the House.[26] On of these was presumably the one now in the Archives of the Archbishop of Westminster, endorsed as containing the heads proposed by Mr Ellis, Dean of the Chapter, to the Lords' committee. This proposed the repeal of the laws against priests and the removal of the penalties for refusing the existing oath of allegiance. None of this relief was to apply to the Jesuits.[27] Though the committee insisted that the church's position should be secured, a draft bill which included most of the original heads was being prepared by 25 July. The number of priests was to be kept in check by means of a system of registration; they were to take 'an oath of allegiance'. The preamble stressed that the 'peaceable and well-minded Roman Catholic

23 J. Raine (ed.), *York Castle Depositions* (Surtees Soc., 1861), pp. 83, 86, 100, 126, 134; Pepys, 24 Nov. 1662, *Diary*, iii, 266; Carte, iv, 112; Burnet, i, 335–6; Browning, *Historical Documents*, pp. 63–5.

24 R. Caron (?), *A Vindication of the Roman Catholicks* (1660); *The Good Catholick no Bad Subject* (1660); *A Letter from a Person of Quality to a Principal Peer of the Realm* (1661, misdated 1611); *Reasons Why Roman Catholicks Should not be Persecuted* (1662/3); *The Case of Divers Roman-Catholicks* (1662); H. M., *A Letter to a Person of Honour in London* (1663).

25 C. Butler, *Historical Memoirs of English, Irish and Scottish Catholics* (3 vols., London, 1822), iii, 23–34; BM Add. MS 41846, fols. 76–8.

26 *LJ*, xi, 276–7, 281, 286, 291.

27 AAW A32, p. 275; printed, without the endorsement, *LJ*, xi, 310–11.

subjects' were no longer the danger to the state that they had once been. But on 30 July parliament was adjourned. When it met in November the bishops were back in the Lords and the Catholics' chance had gone. An attempt to revive the question failed.[28]

It is doubtful whether there had ever been any real chance of the Lords' accepting the bill, let alone the far less tolerant Commons. Clarendon nevertheless thought that it had had some chance of passing, the majority of peers being favourable or neutral. It had been warmly supported by Bristol and Arundell of Wardour and the king had made it clear that he approved.[29] However, the exclusion of the Jesuits may well have reduced the enthusiasm for the bill of some Catholic peers.[30] Almost all of them voted for the return of the bishops to the House, but they had little option if they hoped for relief from such a strongly Anglican Commons.[31] The idea of excluding the Jesuits presumably came from the violently anti-Jesuit element in the Chapter, for it had been the Chapter which had drawn up the paper for the committee. It was later alleged that it had been a device of Clarendon's, but this was probably a mistake, confusing the Chapter's involvement in the bill of 1661 with Clarendon's discussions with the Chapter about a new oath of allegiance in 1662.[32] There were also allegations that Clarendon had surreptitiously opposed the bill, not because of its contents, but because it had been supported by Bristol.[33] This is one of the first indica-

---

28 AAW A32, pp. 276–7; Nunz. Fian. 45, fol. 603.
29 Clarendon, *Life*, ii, 109; Nunz Fian. 45, fols. 304, 320.
30 J. Lingard, *History of England* (6th edn, 10 vols., London, 1855), ix, 18, states that the Jesuits persuaded the Catholic peers to oppose the toleration bill but his evidence is very unreliable. It consists of W. Kennet, *A Register and Chronicle* (1728), p. 498, which quotes the strongly anti-Jesuit Dodd (*vere* Tootell) in his *The Secret Policy of the Jesuits* (1715), p. 299.
31 AAW A33, p. 324; R. Palmer, earl of Castlemaine, *The Catholique Apology, with a Reply to the Answer* (3rd edn, 1674), p. 33; Warner, p. 175.
32 Warner, pp. 175–6, alleges that Clarendon was the only one to try to excite hatred against the Jesuits. This is clearly nonsense and reduces the credibility of the rest of his allegations. Stafford's claim nineteen years later that Clarendon opposed the bill is even less reliable, Corker, p. 53. Some secular priests had tried to have the Jesuits banished as early as the 1590s, Guilday, pp. 97, 112.
33 D'Estrades au Roi, 25 July and 29 Aug. 1661 NS, Baschet 109.

tions of the feud between Clarendon and Bristol, partly personal, partly on matters of policy, which was to confuse even further the attempts to secure toleration in the next two years. Already Clarendon had reason to be displeased with Bristol; Bristol and the Spanish ambassador had tried to obstruct the negotiations for the king's marriage to a Portuguese princess.[34]

The rift between Clarendon and Bristol became open in March 1662. Parliament was in the process of passing the uniformity bill, which made virtually no concessions to the Presbyterians and gave them the choice of conforming or leaving the church. Clarendon wanted to reduce its rigour by inserting a proviso that would allow the king to dispense with certain requirements laid down by the bill in particular cases. Bristol however suggested that the king should be allowed to dispense altogether with the hearing of Common Prayer; these much more sweeping powers could be used in the interests of Catholics, whereas those suggested by Clarendon could not. Clarendon's proviso was passed by the Lords but rejected by the Commons; Bristol's did not pass the Lords.[35] In May, after the king had given his assent to the uniformity bill, Clarendon reminded the Houses that it was up to the king to execute the laws and that he could distinguish between proud obstinacy and genuine tenderness of conscience. He continued to urge that the king should use his dispensing power to stop the act being enforced against moderate Dissenters; he feared that it might drive them to rebellion, which seemed far from impossible in the six months after the act was passed.[36] He tried to persuade some leading Presbyterians to petition for relief; this they eventually did; most of the Council received them favourably at first, but the petition was rejected, thanks to the fierce hostility of the bishop of London.[37]

---

[34] *HMC 5th Report, Appendix*, p. 159; Feiling, *Foreign Policy*, pp. 39, 48, 52.

[35] Pepys, 21 March 1662, *Diary*, iii, 49 and n.; Feiling, 'Clarendon and the Act of Uniformity', *EHR*, xliv (1929), 289; Abernathy, *JEH*, xi, 59–60.

[36] *LJ*, xi, 476; Abernathy, pp. 62–4; Pepys, 30 June, 19 and 27 Oct., 10 Nov. 1662, *Diary*, iii, 127, 229, 237, 252; BM Add. MS 10117, fols. 45–6; Ranke, iii, 393–5; T. H. Lister, *Life of Clarendon* (3 vols., London, 1838), iii, 198–201.

[37] Feiling, *EHR*, xliv, 290; P. Toon (ed.), *Correspondence of John Owen* (Cambridge, 1970), pp. 129–30; BM Add. MS 10117, fols. 45–6; Bosher, pp. 261–4.

Bristol meanwhile pressed for a full and if possible permanent suspension of the Act of Uniformity. From July 1662 his efforts were seconded by those of the queen mother, who this time remained in England until 1665. They had the powerful support of another of Clarendon's enemies, the new secretary of state, Sir Henry Bennet. Pressure for toleration also came from the Independents.[38] The trend at court was towards toleration; the bishop of Durham was reprimanded for his vigour against the Papists. Clarendon meanwhile discussed with the Chapter possible changes in the oath of allegiance. On 26 December the king issued a declaration in favour of toleration which suspended the operation of the Act of Uniformity. Clarendon had played little part in its formulation, having fallen ill early in the month. The declaration came too late to help the Puritan ministers ejected for failing to conform. As it rested on the royal prerogative it attracted legalist and constitutionalist opposition. Both Anglicans and Presbyterians resented its grateful references to the Catholics' loyalty. It extended only to 'such as shall live peaceably, modestly and without scandal'. There could be no question of open worship for Catholics or of freedom to spread the faith.[39]

When parliament met early in 1663 the king and court beat a hasty retreat. A bill to give the king the powers that he had claimed in his declaration found little support. By the beginning of March the queen mother, Bristol and the court Catholics had decided to abandon any attempt to obtain toleration and to hope instead that the laws would not be enforced.[40] The Commons, now roused, brought in a bill against the growth of Popery; the king countered with a proclamation against priests and Jesuits, blaming them for abusing his kindheartedness. The bill was quietly lost in the Lords.[41] Clarendon argued against further legislation against the Catholics, which would (he said) drive the priests into hiding, not out of the country. He said that the existing laws were adequate, if enforced, and apparently added that only those dangerous to the state should be banished, perhaps a

[38] Abernathy, p. 61; Pepys, 28 July 1662, *Diary*, iii, 148; Burnet, i, 333–334; *Relinquiae Baxterianae*, Part II, pp. 429–30.

[39] G. Ornsby (ed.), *Correspondence of John Cosin*, ii (Surtees Soc., 1872), 97; Abernathy, p. 65; Kenyon, *Stuart Constitution*, pp. 403–6.

[40] Abernathy, pp. 69–70.

[41] *CJ*, viii, 449, 452, 463; PC/2/56, p. 381; Clarendon, *Life*, ii, 214–19; *LJ*, xi, 550, 561, 579–80.

reference to the Jesuits. He also stressed the obligations to some Catholics, notably the Benedictines, that the king had incurred during his exile.[42]

Bristol ascribed the failure of the declaration to opposition stirred up by Clarendon, but although Clarendon expressed considerable reservations about the form and timing of the declaration he does not seem to have opposed it or to have disapproved of the principles on which it was based.[43] In July Bristol tried to impeach Clarendon of high treason, on charges which included that of sending to Rome for a cardinal's hat for d'Aubigny. The impeachment was supported by some Catholic and Puritan peers who regarded Clarendon as the main obstacle to toleration; but the whole business was sadly mismanaged; Bristol fled from the king's fury and conformed for a while to the established church.[44] His favoured position at court and with it his political career had come to an abrupt end. After Bristol's fall there was no further pressure from the English Catholics for toleration; any future moves in that direction were to come from the king and the court.

The uneasy equilibrium that followed Bristol's fall lasted until 1672 when it was upset by growing Catholicising tendencies in government policy. Before 1672, if the court did little to help the Catholics, the laws against them were laxly enforced. In 1665 lord Ashley, the chancellor of the Exchequer, and Bennet suggested that the king should, in effect, sell dispensations from the penal laws. The suggestion was rejected because of the opposition it attracted, as it seemed designed to favour Papists. A similar suggestion in 1668 was equally unsuccessful.[45] The government and

[42] Cominges au Roi, 2 April 1663 NS, Baschet 111; Nunz. Fian. 47, fol. 140; Foley, i, 265; *CSPVen 1661–4*, p. 241.
[43] Lister, iii, 232–3; Abernathy, pp. 66–7, 70–3; see also D. T. Witcombe, *Charles II and the Cavalier House of Commons 1663–74* (Manchester, 1966), p. 211.
[44] Pepys, 10 July 1663, *Diary*, iv, 223–4; *Cal. Clar. S.P.*, v, 323, 327–8; *CSPVen 1661–4*, p. 273; Bodl., Carte MS 130, fol. 20; G. F. Trevallyn Jones, 'The Bristol Affair', *Journal of Religious History*, v (1968), 16–30. This last piece should be used with caution, as the author seems unaware of the work on Clarendon by Abernathy, Wormald and Whiteman.
[45] Clarendon, *Life*, ii, 342–9; R. Thomas, 'Comprehension and Indulgence' in Nuttall and Chadwick (eds.), *From Uniformity to Unity*, p. 203.

parliament were more concerned with Dissent than with Popery; the former kept a watchful eye on conventicles, the latter paid off the scores of the civil war. Parliament's anti-Catholicism received no provocation from a court which showed many signs of dissipation, incompetence and corruption but few of favouring Popery. The Second Dutch War was popular in its early stages and it was followed by that short-lived incarnation of a Protestant foreign policy, the Triple Alliance with Holland and Sweden.

Reaction to the Great Fire of 1666 provided a reminder, if one were needed, of the strength of the anti-Catholic tradition. The rapid and erratic course of the fire convinced many that it had been started deliberately. Rumour blamed the French, Dutch and fanatics but suspicions soon centred on the French and the Papists.[46] There were rumours of thousands of Frenchmen and Papists in arms; citizens rushed to arm themselves. Foreigners, especially Frenchmen, were attacked in the streets; many were arrested and their release by the guards was later regarded as highly suspicious. Some of the guards were said to have behaved suspiciously.[47] The panic spread into the provinces. There were several days of riots round Warwick and Coventry. From elsewhere came reports of Papists behaving oddly and of rumours of plans to bring in Popery.[48] The Commons set up a committee to investigate the fire; it was told that Papists had talked of it or hinted at it before it happened. Anonymous papers scattered in London warned of worse to come.[49] The pattern of spontaneous fear and occasional violence, of exaggerated, misinterpreted or invented incidents and of anonymous letters revealing plots followed that of 1642. There was little or no sign of deliberate manipulation.

The panic slowly subsided and Cavalier magistrates began to

[46] Pepys, 5 and 7 Sept. 1666; W. G. Bell, *The Great Fire of London* (3rd edn, London, 1923), p. 198; Verney, iv, 137–8; *CSPVen 1666–8*, p. 77; *HMC le Fleming*, p. 41.

[47] Pepys, 6 Sept. 1666; Evelyn, 7 Sept. 1666, *Diary*, iii, 462; G. P. Elliott (ed.), *Autobiography and Notes by William Taswell* (Camden Miscellany, ii, 1853), pp. 11–12; *HMC Portland*, iii, 298; 'London's Flames Revived', (1689), *State Tracts*, ii, 31, 35, 36, 44; *Pyrotechnica Loyolana*, pp. 129–30, 133.

[48] *CSPD 1666–7*, pp. 127, 134, 168, 174, 197, 206, 268, 272–3.

[49] *State Tracts*, ii, 40–4; Pepys, 27 Oct. and 5 Nov. 1666; *HMC Portland*, iii, 301–2; *HMC 10th Report, Appendix 4*, pp. 114–16; *Pyrotechnica Loyolana*, pp. 126–8.

accuse the Presbyterians of stirring up the people with fears of Popery. The Commons' committee could find little solid evidence; 'I cannot conceive that the House can make anything of the report from the committee,' wrote one M.P.[50] The Privy Council was sure that the fire had been an accident and so in retrospect were Burnet and others.[51] But many were convinced that it had been started deliberately. A psychological unwillingness or inability to accept such a disaster as an act of God, expressed in terms of the anti-Catholic tradition, received some support from certain peculiar circumstances. The year 1666 had long been expected to be one of dreadful significance, perhaps even of the end of the world. A hundred years before the astrologer Nostradamus had prophesied that there would be fires in 1666; it was said that Roger L'Estrange, the licenser, had cut these prophecies out of the almanacs for the year. Even more mysterious, some 'Cromwellians' arrested in April were reported to have planned to fire the city on 3 September, which date, according to Lilly's almanac, should have been propitious for their designs. This was the day on which the fire began and it was all too easy to claim later that the 'Cromwellians' had really been Papists in disguise.[52] Two versions of the evidence to the Commons' committee were printed; despite government efforts to suppress them they achieved a wide circulation and were later republished in various forms, with accounts of later fires added.[53]

[50] *CSPD 1666–7*, pp. 197, 206, 268, 376, 465–6; *Diary of John Milward*, pp. 68–9.

[51] *CSPD 1666–7*, p. 175; Burnett, i, 403–4; Reresby, p. 62; *Observations both Historical and Moral upon the Burning of London* (1667).

[52] Pepys, 10 Nov. and 13 Dec. 1666, 3 Feb. 1667; *London Gazette*, 23–26 April 1666; *State Trials*, vi, 1447–9; W. Bedloe, *A Narrative and Impartial Discovery* (1679), pp. 14–15.

[53] Bell, *Great Fire*, p. 203; *London's Flames Discovered* (1667) reappeared as *London's Flames* (1679), pp. 1–14. 'A True and Faithful Account of the Several Informations' (1667), *Somers Tracts*, vii, 615–33, was rather more accurate and was reprinted as the first part of 'London's Flames Revived' (1689), *State Tracts*, ii, 27–44. 'A True and Faithful Account' was also the basis for *Trap ad Crucem* (1670), which included various fires from 1670, and for Bedloe's *Narrative and Impartial Discovery* which also included parts of *Trap ad Crucem* and of Oates's *Narrative* and added various fires of 1675–9. There were also references to the evidence in *Pyrotechnica Loyolana*, pp. 126–33, which puts the Papists' alleged complicity in the context of allegations about Jesuits' cunning and malice which draw heavily on Prynne.

The Monument was erected near London Bridge to commemorate the fire; in 1681 an inscription was added which declared that the Papists had started it. James was also accused, unfairly, of having hindered the apprehension of suspects.[54] A belief in Popish pyromania had been added to the anti-Catholic tradition.

Both Charles and James played an active part in fighting the fire. Afterwards, at the request of both Houses, the king ordered that all priests should be banished, that all recusants who refused the oaths of supremacy and allegiance should be disarmed, that all officers and soldiers who refused the oaths were to be dismissed and that those mustered in future were to take the oaths and the Anglican sacrament as well.[55] Three weeks later, however, the searching of Papists for arms was stopped, following the defeat of a small rebellion in Scotland. In April 1667 the Council ordered that new recruits were to take the sacrament within a year of being mustered.[56]

There was a smaller panic in 1667 after the Medway disaster which some blamed on the Papists.[57] However, magistrates complained more about the 'fanatics' whom they accused of hindering the raising of the militia and of turning the people against the government. Fanatics still seemed more dangerous than Papists, although Pepys noted a rumour that the army, under the duke of York (who was still a Protestant), was to be used to set up an absolute monarchy like that in France.[58] In view of this unease, the government tried to forestall possible accusations of negligence when parliament met in October. In September J.P.s were ordered to tender the oaths to all suspected recusants and all office-holders and to investigate cases of conversion to Catholicism. Catholic officers were to be put out of the militia. Parliament,

---

[54] *CJ*, ix, 703; *HMC 10th Report, Appendix 4*, p. 175; Grey, viii, 261.

[55] *CJ*, viii, 641–2, 645; *CSPD 1666–7*, pp. 250–1; PC/2/59, pp. 206–7.

[56] *HMC 3rd Report Appendix*, p. 269; PC/2/59, p. 369; D. Ogg, *England in the Reign of Charles II* (2nd edn, 2 vols., Oxford, 1956), ii, 412.

[57] Pepys, 13–14 June 1667; *CSPD 1667*, pp. 196, 206–7; E. Hockliffe (ed.), *The Diary of the Rev. Ralph Josselin* (Camden Soc., 1908), p. 157.

[58] *CSPD 1667*, pp. 320, 409–10, 428, *1667–8*, p. 89; Pepys, 12 and 27 July 1667.

not fully satisfied, drew up another bill to prevent the growth of Popery, which was lost with the prorogation.[59]

Between 1667 and 1672, when the changes in government policy became obvious, anti-Catholicism played little part in politics. There were unsuccessful attempts to include in the conventicle bills of 1668 and 1670 provisoes that the laws against Papists should be enforced.[60] In February 1671, however, a Commons' committee inquired into the causes of the growth of Popery; it suggested the usual remedies (banishing priests, enforcing the laws and excluding Catholics from office) and asked that the king's subjects be prevented from attending Mass at the royal and ambassadors' chapels and that Popish convents and schools in England be suppressed.[61] This implies that there had been an increase in Catholic activity. An emphasis on Ireland and on the actions of the new Catholic bishops there suggests that the inquiry might have been provoked by the Irish Catholics' petition to the Council for the recovery of their lands. Some suspected that Ormond was behind it as Patrick MacGinn had recently frustrated his efforts to make the Irish Papists take Walsh's Remonstrance.[62] The king responded by issuing a proclamation against priests and ordering his judges and officers to enforce the laws.[63] The Commons had asked the Exchequer to issue out processes against those certified as convicted of recusancy. Since 1660 the Exchequer had received only £147 15s 7d in recusant revenue. Now it drew up a list of convicted recusants and calculated that four or five million pounds were, on paper, due to be paid.[64] But nothing came of this, first attempt to make the laws work and it seems to have been little more than a placatory gesture. The Catholics continued largely unmolested.[65]

In the parliamentary sessions of 1669–71 the court adopted a 'Cavalier' policy which proved very effective, after the previous

[59] PC/2/59, pp. 564, 586, 578–9; *CSPD 1667*, p. 476; *CJ*, ix, 4.
[60] *CJ*, ix, 90; Grey, i, 222.
[61] *CJ*, ix, 203–4, 206.
[62] Colbert au Roi, 2 March 1671 NS, Baschet 126; Nunz. Fian. 60, fol. 213; Prop. Ang., fols. 654–5.
[63] *CSPD 1671*, p. 140.
[64] C. D. Chandaman, 'The English Public Revenue 1660–1688' (unpublished Ph.D. thesis, London, 1954), p. 700; *CTB*, iii, 878; BM Add. MS 20739 (reprinted, not very accurately, in CRS, vi, 1909).
[65] CRS, xxv, 273; Prop. Ang., fols. 638–9.

lack of leadership and organisation. Gestures were made against the Papists, but the real fruits of the policy were money for the king and a renewed persecution of Dissenters. The Conventicle Act of 1664 having expired, a new one was passed in 1670. If the penalties it imposed were somewhat milder, the procedure it laid down for securing convictions was extremely arbitrary and it contained a very high assertion of the royal prerogative. Dissenters were now vigorously persecuted, where earlier the king had tried to shield them from the full weight of the laws.[66] It is possible that the court reversed its policy because the Presbyterians refused to co-operate in any scheme of toleration in which Papists could be included: James II later alleged that the persecution was intended to make them appreciate the benefits of toleration.[67] In April 1669, however, he had told the French ambassador that the Dissenters' support was not worth seeking: 'Au fonds les Episcopaux, ou Protestants, joints avec les Catholiques étaient en bien plus grand nombre et plus puissants et . . . ils étaient tous fort affectionnés à la royauté.'[68] But while the court was building up a strong position in parliament by reverting to a Cavalier policy, that position was being undermined by the king's determination to secure an alliance with Louis XIV and, partly as a consequence of this, by the court's growing association with Catholicism. The Catholic question was brought to the centre of politics as a result of what happened within the court between 1669 and 1672.

[66] Kenyon, *Stuart Constitution*, pp. 383–6; *Statutes of the Realm*, v, 516–20; Haley, *Shaftesbury*, pp. 275–6; Witcombe, pp. 91, 98–104, 125–6; *CSPD 1668–9*, p. 412; *CSPVen 1669–70*, pp. 84–5; *Reliquiae Baxterianae*, Part III, pp. 87–8; *HMC le Fleming*, p. 71.

[67] *Reliquiae Baxterianae, Part III*, pp. 23–4, 28 (misnumbered 36), 35–6; J. S. Clarke, *Life of James II* (2 vols., London, 1816), i, 443–4; M. D. Lee, jnr. *The Cabal* (Urbana, 1965), p. 181; F. A. M. Mignet, *Négociations Relatives à la Succession d'Espagne* (4 vols., Paris, 1835–42), iii, 225.

[68] Colbert au Roi, 25 April 1669 NS, Baschet 121.

6

THE FRENCH ALLIANCE AND 'CATHOLICITY' (1669–72)

Charles II's alliance with Louis XIV and his promise in the Secret Treaty of Dover to declare himself a Catholic have received much attention from 'Whig' historians. Here, they said, was proof positive of Charles's political and religious depravity: a Papist in all but name, he entered into an unholy alliance with the epitome of absolutism and militant Catholicism, with the aim of crushing English parliaments, liberties and religion. The promise to turn Catholic was seen as central to Charles's political strategy, as the corollary of his alleged desire to create an English absolute monarchy. The aim of this chapter is to argue that this view is wrong and that the promise of 'Catholicity' was a temporary and comparatively unimportant tactical move in the negotiations for an Anglo-French alliance, the main purpose of which was a joint war against the Dutch. The alliance and the war were acceptable to all Charles's leading ministers, the notorious 'Cabal', who agreed on little else. The earl of Arlington, the former Sir Henry Bennet, was concerned primarily to maintain the king's favour and to this end he suppressed his own pro-Dutch feelings. Lord Ashley's main concerns at this time were commerce and the securing of toleration for Protestant Dissenters. The duke of Buckingham was also an advocate of toleration for Dissenters, but apart from that he was politically inconsistent, concerned mainly with his own aggrandisement and the destruction of his rivals at court. Lord Clifford, the lord treasurer, was converted to Catholicism during these years and was obsessed with the advancement of his new religion. The fifth member of the 'Cabal', lord Lauderdale, spent most of his time in Scotland. The last important figure at court was the king's brother, James, duke of York, whose conversion to Catholicism affected the course of English history over more than seventy years.

In April 1668, only three months after the signing of the Triple Alliance, Charles began tentative advances to Louis XIV for a personal union or alliance. Louis, initially suspicious, sent over an ambassador to discuss the question in August.[1] Louis XIV's name did not yet terrify English Protestants. Only when he swept through the Low Countries in 1672–3 did they realise the threat that he posed to Europe and perhaps to England. By then he had greatly strengthened his navy, despite Charles's attempts to prevent this. Charles's personal predilections always tended towards France and things French. He clearly wanted another war with the Dutch in order to avenge the humiliations of 1667. Such a war, he hoped, would help English commerce and allow him to strengthen his navy; he might also be able to enlarge the army and even improve his financial position. If he was to make war on the Dutch, an alliance with Louis XIV was essential, for Louis had fought with the Dutch in the war of 1665–7. At this time, also, parliament was critical, parsimonious and obstreperous, though by no means out of control, and this may have strengthened Charles's desire to become the ally of the greatest monarch in Europe rather than the ally of a republic and of a remote Northern kingdom. This desire was far from indefensible in 1668; many of his advisers hated Holland if they did not love France.[2] It would probably not have been unpopular in the nation had it not become entangled with the Catholic issue, partly through the duke of York's conversion to Catholicism and partly through the issuing of the Declaration of Indulgence on the eve of the war.

It is not certain when James's conversion took place, but it was probably late in 1668 or early in 1669. By April 1670 he was impatient to declare himself a Catholic: however he probably did not formally (but secretly) abjure Protestantism until 1672. He continued to attend Church of England services without taking the sacrament until Easter 1676 and did not openly avow his Catholicism until he came to the throne.[3] The other leading convert, Clifford, did not declare himself until 1673 but was showing a strong interest in Catholicism in August 1669.[4] As for the

[1] Mignet, iii, 9–10; Feiling, *Foreign Policy*, p. 289.

[2] Feiling, pp. 290–1.

[3] Clarke, i, 440–1; J. Macpherson, *Original Papers containing the Secret History of Great Britain* (2 vols., London, 1775), i, 49–50; Foley, i, 174; Mignet, iii, 164, iv, 405–6; Nunz. Fian. 59, fols. 292, 305; Ranke, vi, 37.

[4] Hartmann, *Clifford*, p. 189.

king, all things being equal he would have become a Catholic long before his death. He despised the divisions of Protestantism, respected the unity and authority of the Catholic church and no doubt appreciated the obedience it inculcated as being thoroughly compatible with monarchical authority.[5] Claims that he was 'converted' in exile are really meaningless, since he conformed in every respect to the established church. In 1662–3 the agent who was sent to Rome to solicit a cardinal's hat for d'Aubigny was also instructed to put before the pope a project for reuniting the churches of England and Rome; there is no evidence that this had Charles's approval and the proposals put forward envisaged changes in Catholic practice which were far too radical for Rome to accept.[6] Practical political commonsense, then, kept Charles within the established church. The only time he seems to have considered leaving it was in 1669–70.

It is hard to produce a completely satisfying explanation of why he did so. Direct evidence on the 'Catholic decision' is extremely scanty; one has to make deductions about it from the general situation and from subsequent events; in view of Charles's notorious unreliability, this must be done with considerable caution. I find it hard to believe that Charles seriously intended to declare himself a Catholic, as he must have been well aware of what the reaction of his Protestant subjects would have been. If he did not intend to turn Catholic, there were several reasons why he might have said that he intended to do so: in order to get money, or to control the timing of the war, or to force secretary Arlington to accept an alliance of which he disapproved or to give Louis XIV an added inducement to conclude a personal union.[7] Of these four possible reasons only the last is satisfactory. I am inclined to reject the first two for the reasons given below and the third is, I think, over-subtle and has little evidence to back it up. On the other hand it is quite plausible that 'Catholicity' should have been an extra bait for Louis XIV which Charles hastily dropped once the alliance had been secured. Then he and

[5] Feiling, *Foreign Policy*, p. 268; 'Copies of two papers written by the late king Charles II' (1686), *State Tracts*, ii, 273–4; Burnet, i, 158–9, 475; Ranke, iii, 395–8; G. Davies, *Essays on the Later Stuarts* (San Marino, 1958), pp. 11–13.

[6] Ranke, iii, 398–401; Clark, pp. 92–3.

[7] Ogg, *Reign of Charles II*, i, 348–9; Lee, pp. 103–4; Haley, *Charles II*, pp. 16–17 and *Shaftesbury*, p. 270.

Louis concentrated on what was for both of them the main concern, the Dutch war. Charles extricated himself from his commitment to declare himself Catholic with little permanent damage done, apart from leaving Louis with a possible blackmail weapon in the Secret Treaty of Dover, which remained secret.[8] The anti-Catholicism of 1672–3 was aroused by the Declaration of Indulgence, by the conversions of York and Clifford and by a growing fear of France. The Declaration was perhaps a by-product of 'Catholicity', but Charles abandoned it quickly when need arose.

'Catholicity' was raised first in December 1668 when Charles started to use a cipher in his letters to his sister, 'Madame', who was married to Louis's brother.[9] In conversation with James, he apparently expressed a desire to be received into the Catholic church. On 25 January 1669 he asked James, Arundell of Wardour, Clifford and Arlington to suggest the best way to propagate Catholicism in England. It was decided that the best way would be through an alliance with France.[10] Charles apparently did not tell his brother until March of his plan to declare himself a Catholic, as distinct from that for an alliance with France in the Catholic interest.[11] (He never said that he intended to impose Catholicism on England.) He wrote blithely to his sister that it should be easy to calm the fears of the possessors of abbey-lands. He stressed his keenness to declare himself a Catholic, but Louis counselled patience.[12]

Charles said several times that he was making military preparations, either to deal with any opposition which his declaration of Catholicity might arouse, or for the war against the Dutch, but it is hard to find any evidence of this. True, in Scotland Lauderdale tightened his grip on the government and secured an act of parliament that allowed the Scots militia to serve outside Scotland. A militia of 20,000 men was raised and a small experimental

---

8 The first account of the treaty to be published was rather inaccurate and appeared in France in 1683: Dodd, iii, 192–4.

9 C. H. Hartmann, *The King my Brother* (London, 1954), pp. 234–5. It is possible that it had first been raised some months before. See the letter, which could date from 1668 or 1669, in K. G. Feiling, 'Henrietta Stuart, Duchess of Orleans, and the Origins of the Treaty of Dover', *EHR*, xlvii (1932), 642–5.

10 Macpherson, i, 49–50; Clarke, i, 441–2.

11 Hartmann, *The King my Brother*, p. 250.

12 *ibid*. pp. 262–3, 271–6.

measure of toleration allowed.[13] In Ireland Ormond was replaced as lord lieutenant by the Presbyterian lord Robartes in March 1669; he in turn was replaced in May 1670 by lord Berkeley, who sympathised with the Catholics. Ormond's recall was primarily a belated sequel to the fall of Clarendon in 1667 and was engineered by the enemies of both men. His successors were more acceptable to the Irish Catholics; under them the Catholics enjoyed greater liberty and the loyalist Catholic clergy, the Remonstrants, were persecuted by the Catholic bishops. However, there is no evidence of any military changes in Ireland and the Irish army remained firmly closed to Catholics.[14] In England, Charles told Madame, he was fortifying the main ports and was putting reliable men in charge of the garrisons. I can find little evidence that he did so. Some £3500 was spent in 1669 on improving the fortifications at Plymouth and some £1700 at Portsmouth. Those at Gravesend, Tilbury and Sheerness had been improved in 1667–1668. But in March 1669 the castles on the Isle of Wight were found to be in a poor condition and nothing was done about them until September 1670. Nor was anything done about the fortifications of other major ports such as Berwick, Hull, Yarmouth, Chatham and Dover.[15] As for the appointment of reliable garrison commanders, James later referred to four: lord Bellasis at Hull, lord Widdrington at Berwick, the earl of Bath at Plymouth and colonel Fitzgerald at Yarmouth. The first three of these had held their posts since 1660–1, while Fitzgerald was not appointed until March 1672.[16] There was no increase in the size of the English army at this time, nor were any Catholics commissioned in England in 1668–70.[17]

In October 1669 Colbert de Croissy, the French ambassador in London, was brought into the negotiations. In an extraordinary speech, Charles told Colbert that although his plan might seem mad, he hoped to succeed with the help of France. He said that

[13] Ogg, i, 342–3, ii, 413; Burnet, i, 488–96.
[14] Ogg, ii, 396–7; Carte, iv, 344–439; J. C. Beckett, 'The Irish Viceroyalty in the Restoration Period', *Transactions of the Royal Historical Soc.*, 5th series, xx (1970), 62; C. Dalton, *Irish Army Lists 1661–85* (London, 1907), passim.
[15] Hartmann, *The King my Brother*, p. 262; *CSPD 1668–9*, pp. 239, 243, 244, 341, 433, 443, 470 and passim; *CTB*, ii, 177, iii, 663, 793.
[16] Clarke, i, 443; *CSPD 1660–1*, pp. 429, 453, 605, *1671–2*, p. 236.
[17] Miller, *EHR*, lxxxviii, 42–3.

he believed that the Dissenters hated the Anglicans more than the Papists,

que tous les sectaires ne respiraient qu'après la liberté de l'exercice de leur religion; que pourvu qu'ils l'obtiennent, comme c'est son dessein de la leur accorder, ils ne s'opposeront point à son change-ment de religion; que d'ailleurs il a de bonnes troupes qui lui sont bien affectionnées et que, si le feu roi son père en avait eu autant, il aurait étouffé dans leur naissance les troubles qui ont causé sa perte.[18]

He insisted that the only way to save the royal authority was for him to declare himself a Catholic right away and that this declara-tion should precede the war against the Dutch; he even suggested that Louis should declare war without him. He added that he was using every pretext he could to increase his forces and was securing the principal forts. He thought that Ormond could be relied on to hold Ireland. However, he was not increasing his forces and Ormond was no longer lord lieutenant of Ireland. Moreover, less than six months later Charles gave his assent to a new conventicle act which intensified the persecution of Dis-senters; he told Colbert then that he hoped the new act would goad the Dissenters into rebellion and so give him a pretext to enlarge his army.[19] One cannot help feeling, in fact, that Charles was telling Colbert a pack of lies.

In the first draft of the Anglo-French treaty in December 1669 the English asked for a subsidiary of £800,000 and insisted that Catholicity should precede the declaration of war.[20] This might suggest that Catholicity was a means of getting money from Louis or of securing an alliance while leaving the timing of the war to Charles. Neither was in fact the case. The English demands soon fell to £300,000 a year and the figure finally agreed was so in-adequate that Charles had to declare a partial bankruptcy in order to begin the war at all.[21] Once Charles was sure that he had secured his alliance, his ardour for Catholicity cooled rapidly and he ceased to insist that it should precede his declaration of war. After the session of parliament which ended in April 1670, which

---

[18] Mignet, iii, 102.

[19] *ibid.* iii, 102–6; Sir J. Dalrymple, *Memoirs of Great Britain and Ireland* (2 vols., London, 1771–3), ii, Appendix, p. 59.

[20] Mignet, iii, 121–3.

[21] *ibid.* iii, 144–5; Haley, *Charles II*, p. 15 and *Shaftesbury*, pp. 295–6.

had voted him money as well as passing the Conventicle Act, Charles could be more optimistic about the prospects of parliamentary supplies for the Dutch War. The abandonment of his efforts at toleration showed that he no longer took Catholicity seriously. Early in May Colbert reported that Charles wished to delay his declaration of Catholicity and that he now claimed that the Scots and Irish armies were full of Presbyterians and unreliable: 'La concession d'un libre exercice de religion ne peut pas adoucir l'aversion qu'ils ont contre les Catholiques.' He added that the duke of York was still keen to press on.[22] The Secret Treaty of Dover, signed on 22 May, stated that Catholicity should precede the declaration of war. But Madame, who had come over to England for its conclusion, returned to France convinced that Charles had been persuaded, no doubt not unwillingly, to make war first and to postpone Catholicity. Colbert confirmed this. James meanwhile had been kept in London to deal with any disorders that the conventicle act might provoke. When he arrived at Dover he found that Madame had persuaded Charles that the war was the first priority.[23] One is tempted to wonder if he had been kept out of the way deliberately.

By May 1670 Charles was ready to postpone almost indefinitely his declaration of conversion, if he had ever intended to make it at all. Colbert's dispatch of 5 May, before Madame came over, shows that this was not solely the product of her influence. Charles was now expressing doubts which he had not mentioned a year before. In September he was still postponing the declaration, despite James's urging; Charles now said that he wanted to consult Rome. Sensing an excuse for delay, Louis suggested that Charles should use the French agents at Rome to prevent the design leaking out to Spain and to stop the curia from imposing conditions that were too hard; in other words, Louis wanted to control the negotiations.[24] If Charles did not take the negotiations seriously, Clifford did. He and the Benedictine Serenus Cressy drew up detailed instructions for Charles's agent. They stressed the need for assurances on abbey-lands and for other concessions including, if possible, a vernacular service, clerical marriage and

---

[22] Mignet, iii, 153–4, 185.
[23] *ibid.* iii, 185–99; Hartmann, *The King my Brother*, p. 317; Clarke, i, 448–50.
[24] Mignet, iii, 224–5, 230–2.

communion in both kinds for the laity. These Cressy regarded as essential if the English and Roman churches were to be reunited; in fact his demands were never presented.[25] When Airoldi came over in November 1670 he was told nothing of Catholicity, nor of the duke's conversion.

Events in November and December 1670 showed that Catholicity was not being retained as a timing device; at most it was a pretext for an additional French subsidy. Louis had told Colbert in September that he wished to delay making war for a year in order to complete his diplomatic preparations in Germany.[26] In October he told Colbert to tell Charles that he would delay declaring war until the spring of 1672, and to give as a reason Charles's failure to declare himself a Catholic. The new date was to be written into the *traité simulé* that Buckingham was negotiating for the benefit of Charles's Protestant ministers. This provision was to be excepted from a secret clause declaring the *traité simulé* null and void. Charles was thus given a year to declare himself a Catholic, if he still intended to do so before the war.[27]

Charles and James were angry at the delay. They had prepared for the war to start in the spring of 1671 and had called parliament to provide the money for it. Charles complained also at Louis's refusal to pay the £150,000 for Catholicity before he fixed a date for it: it would, Charles promised, be before the war started. He added that he could not make his preparations and fortifications without money. Arlington assured Colbert that the declaration of Catholicity would be made.[28] Louis eventually gave in in order to avoid jeopardising the *traité simulé* which was signed on 21 December. This stated that the war would start in the spring of 1672. At Charles's request this treaty was to stand; he signed a secret clause confirming the Catholicity clause in the Dover treaty. He preferred to abide by the treaty which was known to a wider circle of his advisers. He did not try to evade his commitment to declare war; it was Louis who was unwilling to fix a precise date.[29]

[25] Hartmann, *The King my Brother*, pp 342–8; Hartmann, *Clifford*, pp. 190–200, 318–33.
[26] Mignet, iii, 232–4.
[27] *ibid.* iii, 238–9.
[28] *ibid.* iii, 240–6.
[29] *ibid.* iii, 241, 250–1, 255–6, 260–1, 266–7.

In the spring of 1671 Charles still refused to declare himself a Catholic or to send an agent to Rome. By September he had received his payment for Catholicity. The English war effort was now to be mainly naval; troops were raised for the French service in Scotland and Ireland.[30] Early in 1672 the king made his final preparations for war. The Stop of Exchequer (a suspension of interest payments on the crown's debts) provided some ready money; the payment for Catholicity and the first subsidy had brought him only £225,000, which was not nearly enough to equip the navy for war. In March he sent a priest to tell the queen of Spain of his plans for conversion, presumably hoping that this would dissuade Spain from helping the Dutch.[31] York and Clifford urged him to send an agent to Rome to discuss the terms for reunion: for them the crisis of the 'grand design' had arrived. But Arlington and Colbert advised caution and for both Charles and Louis the war was the main concern. The more York tried to push Charles forward, the more reluctant he became.[32]

The other major preliminary to the war was the Declaration of Indulgence. The government was concerned at the possibility of disorders from the London conventicles during the war. In November 1671, Dissenters were meeting in defiance of the conventicle act and the government was faced with a dilemma: should it allow them toleration, which might be interpreted as weakness, or suppress them, and risk serious disorders? Would it be wiser to give a measure of toleration freely rather than be forced into larger concessions later?[33] In person and through various agents, including the lord mayor and one colonel Blood (who had tried to steal the crown jewels), Charles tried to persuade Nonconformist ministers to meet only in private houses, not in public meeting-houses. Many ministers were open to persuasion, but some were not and others were urged by their congregations to meet publicly, unless prevented by force.[34] For a

---

[30] Hartmann, *The King my Brother*, pp. 348, 352–3; Mignet, iii, 653–4; Colbert au Roi, 28 May and 3 June 1671 NS, Baschet 126.

[31] Haley, *Shaftesbury*, pp. 295–6; Mignet, iii, 701, 703; Hartmann, *The King my Brother*, pp. 347–8.

[32] Mignet, iii, 704; Colbert au Roi, 21 April and 9 May 1672 NS, Baschet 127.

[33] *CSPD 1671*, pp. 554, 563.

[34] *CSPD 1671*, pp. 562–3, 568–9, *1671–2*, pp. 27–9, 44–6, 99.

while the government vacillated uneasily between repression and toleration. The lieutenant of the Tower, Sir John Robinson, urged that the trained bands be used to break up conventicles, but the lord mayor failed to enforce his orders that they should not meet. The government fell back on persuasion and veiled threats. It felt that to use troops against the conventicles would be too provocative and it did not dare disturb five meetings in Southwark composed mainly of sailors and watermen.[35] Secretary Williamson complained that persons close to the king (Buckingham and Ashley?) opposed the suppression of meetings. Whoever they were, they eventually got their way; by 15 March 1672 the Council had agreed to issue the Declaration of Indulgence. As Arlington wrote four days later: 'I add also a late declaration his Majesty has made in favour of the Nonconformists, that we might keep all quiet at home whilst we are busy abroad.'[36]

The Declaration meant different things to different ministers. To Williamson and Arlington it was a security measure; to Ashley and Buckingham it gave the Dissenters a measure of toleration that was long overdue; to York and Clifford it was the first step towards the full toleration and eventual triumph of Catholicism. It also went some way towards earning the money already paid for Catholicity; the French could be told that there might be further moves towards it, depending on the outcome of the war. The war, too, won the approval of those unaware of the Catholic design. Buckingham was one of its foremost advocates, until he realised that he was not going to command the English military contingent, and Ashley later defended it vehemently in his 'delenda est Carthago' speech. Neither the alliance and war nor the Declaration was *necessarily* part of a 'Catholic' policy. Both were compatible with the 'grand design' but both were also acceptable to Protestants at court who knew nothing of Catholicity.

But the war and the Declaration were both unpopular in the nation at large. If the Dutch were not much liked, the French were liked even less,[37] especially when Louis XIV carried all before him in the Low Countries while the Dutch and English

---

[35] *CSPD 1671*, p. 569, *1671–2*, pp. 10, 28, 40, 45, 63.
[36] *CSPD 1671–2*, pp. 45, 608–9; Brown, p. 66.
[37] *CSPD 1671*, pp. 496, 562–3, 569; *Diary of Ralph Josselin*, p. 162; Magalotti, *Travels of Cosimo III*, pp. 396–7.

fleets battered each other inconclusively in the North Sea. Constitutionalists, including lord keeper Bridgeman, were alarmed at the legal and constitutional implications of the Declaration which suspended the penal laws by using powers derived from the king's ecclesiastical supremacy. The Declaration allowed Dissenters to worship publicly under a system of licences and Catholics to worship in their own homes, which they already did largely unmolested. It was this very limited toleration for Catholics which attracted the greatest opposition. Although many Dissenters, especially Independents and members of the more radical sects, rushed to take out licences, Presbyterians and what Baxter called 'episcopal nonconformists' were much more suspicious. Baxter himself thought that the indulgence had been granted only for the Papists' sake. Philip Henry, another Presbyterian, feared that it might divide the Protestants from which only the Papists, 'the common enemy', would benefit; he saw the declaration as a threat to the parochial system. A third Presbyterian, Adam Martindale, would have preferred no indulgence at all to one in which the Papists were included; however, he decided to take advantage of his new-found freedom to preach.[38] The Anglicans too expressed their disapproval strongly. The bishops feared that the number of Dissenters was increasing greatly, but believed that 'the better sort' were remaining firm to the church. The chancellor of the duchy of Lancaster, Sir Robert Carr, wrote that only the fact that it was the king's pleasure could make him 'relish' the declaration.[39] Daniel Fleming, a Lancashire J.P., wrote that at the sessions at Lancaster

the judges were not free to discourse of the tolerating declaration, nor find I any pleased therewith, after such a rate as the Papists run, and I think they'll so overdo their business as in time they'll undo it. It's looked upon as [as] great a prerogative act as hath been done this good while.

Some J.P.s harried Nonconformist preachers, ignoring their

[38] F. Bate, *The Declaration of Indulgence 1672* (London, 1908), passim; Toon (ed.), *Correspondence of John Owen*, pp. 126–7; *Reliquiae Baxterianae*, Part III, pp. 99–101; Lee (ed.), *Diaries and Letters of Philip Henry*, p. 250; R. Parkinson (ed.), *The Life of Adam Martindale, written by himself* (Chetham Soc., 1845), pp. 198–9.
[39] Bodl., Tanner MS 43, fol. 25, MS Add. c. 305, fol. 242; *CSPD 1671–2*, p. 215.

licences, and the Anglican clergy preached vigorously against Popery, despite a rather feeble attempt by the king to stop them.[40] Suspicions of the court's religious leanings were already growing in July 1672,[41] long before York failed to take the Anglican communion at Easter 1673 and he and Clifford showed their Catholicism by laying down their offices rather than take the test. These and other events of the summer of 1673 were to turn general suspicions about the court's religion into a widespread belief that the French alliance was part of a great plot to bring in Popery and arbitrary government.[42]

The negotiations that produced the French alliance and the Secret Treaty of Dover were complicated and are difficult to interpret. *If* Charles can be believed, he was planning to declare himself a Catholic and to use military force to deal with the reaction that this was likely to excite in England. However, there is very little evidence that he made the military preparations necessary to back up such a declaration and some of his statements, as reported by Colbert, were so naive as to be incredible. If it was not backed up by serious military preparations, his talk of Catholicity can have been no more than a diplomatic manoeuvre, pandering to the bigotry and authoritarianism of the French king. Catholicity was, in fact, merely an ephemeral adjunct to the king's main concern of securing an alliance with France and making war on the Dutch. True, he did keep up the pretence. He and Arlington still said that he would fulfil his promise to declare himself a Catholic before the end of the war and they tried to get more money for it from Louis.[43] For James and Clifford Catholicity remained the *raison d'être* of the French alliance. Both urged Charles to press on and Clifford drew up plans for the reunion of the English and Roman churches. Colbert complained in 1672 that York blindly put his religious

---

[40] *HMC le Fleming*, pp. 90 (also the letter of Dr Smith, same page), 92; *CSPD 1671-2*, pp. 396–7, *1672*, p. 26, *1672–3*, pp. 332–3; Burnet, i, 536–7, 589.

[41] W. D. Christie, *The First Earl of Shaftesbury* (2 vols., London, 1871), ii, Appendix, pp. xiv-xv.

[42] See Colbert au Roi, 20 Nov. 1673 NS, Baschet 129 and Mignet, iv, 233–4.

[43] V. Barbour, *Henry Bennet, Earl of Arlington* (Washington, 1914), pp. 188–9; Colbert au Roi, 21 April and 30 June 1672 NS, Baschet 127.

desires before the needs of the state.[44] The fears of Popery and arbitrary government that burst out in 1673 were exaggerated and inaccurate, being based mainly on guesswork and on glimpses of what was going on at court; but they bore some relation to what the king had at one time suggested, albeit insincerely, and to what York and Clifford still hoped to achieve. However large the admixture of fiction, one hard and increasingly inescapable fact was clear to all by the summer of 1673 – the heir-apparent to the throne was a Catholic.

[44] Hartmann, *Clifford*, pp. 153–5; Hartmann, *The King my Brother*, pp. 340–2; Colbert au Roi, 15 Sept 1672 NS, Baschet 127.

7

YORK AND DANBY (1673-8)

The fact of the duke of York's Catholicism underlay all the politics of this period. It broke up the 'Cabal'. Clifford withdrew from the government when his conversion became known and died soon after. Ashley, now earl of Shaftesbury, and Buckingham went into permanent opposition to the court. Arlington, frightened by an attempt to impeach him in 1674, retreated into a cosy apolitical household office. Only Lauderdale remained and he was usually in Scotland. The fact of a Catholic heir-apparent to the throne aroused all the fears and hatreds implicit in the anti-Catholic tradition. But it soon became clear that a direct attack on York or on his right to succeed was something too radical for most parliament-men to contemplate. Instead their fears found an outlet in plans for further legislation against Catholics, in order to minimise the number of supporters the duke would have if he succeeded to the throne, and in attempts to limit the powers of a Popish successor. The court responded with proclamations against priests and orders that the laws against Papists should be enforced. The Venetian resident noted in June 1674:

Since the Catholics are already incapacitated from holding employments or offices of trust about the king, there is not sufficient zeal in any Protestant to persecute them for their faith. They will not suffer for any other reason than that they are made the battleground in the disputes between the king and parliament and the butt for both sides.[1]

From late in 1674 until late in 1677 Charles had to choose between two policies. The first was that advocated by Thomas Osborne, earl of Danby, the new lord treasurer, who rose to prominence following the disintegration of the 'Cabal'. Danby wanted the king to return to the 'Cavalier' line that had been so successful in 1669–71. He demanded loyalty to church and king, equated Dissent with rebellion and expressed hostility to

[1] *CSPVen 1673–5*, p. 268.

Popery and France. He wrote, probably late in 1673, that parliament 'must be gratified by executing the laws both against Popery and Nonconformity and withdrawing apparently from the French interest'.[2] He tried to strengthen the crown's financial position and was prepared to contemplate the use of force if need arose.[3] His efforts to manage the Commons systematically improved temporarily the cohesion of the 'court' party there, but the cohesion was fragile. Most M.P.s were independently minded and Danby's system depended on there being no important issues that would cut across the 'court' party's loyalty to the court. The system collapsed with Danby's fall and the Exclusion Crisis.

York's main concerns were the protection of the Catholics and of the royal prerogative. Thus in 1673–4 he and Danby pressed Charles to stand firm and prorogue parliament. However, late in 1674, when Danby committed himself to a persecuting Anglicanism, James began to heed the advances of the Dissenters, whom he had previously distrusted. He tried to get Catholics and Dissenters to unite to press for a general toleration, the dissolution of the Cavalier Parliament (which had been elected in 1661) and perhaps his own restoration to the admiralty. He even co-operated for a while with Shaftesbury who also wanted a dissolution, believing (correctly) that a new parliament, with fewer old Cavaliers in it would be more anti-Catholic than the existing one and not, as James naively believed, less. By the end of 1677 James was drifting back into agreement with Danby: both wanted war with France. He hoped to regain his lost popularity and perhaps to use the army raised for the war for a *coup d'autorité*.

Charles, for the most part, followed Danby's policy at home but not abroad. He had little sympathy for his brother's viewpoint. He told Courtin, the French ambassador, 'que la nécessité où il était et la défiance qu'on avait en Angleterre de ce qui pouvait arriver à cause de ce que le duc d'York avait fait étaient capables de soulever ses sujets contre lui et de le faire chasser de son royaume'.[4] He thought James's plan to dissolve parliament was very ill-considered. This parliament, he told Courtin, was

<hr>

[2] A. Browning, *Thomas Earl of Danby* (3 vols., Glasgow, 1951), ii, 63–4.
[3] *ibid.* ii, 68–9.
[4] Courtin au Roi, 12 July 1677 NS, Baschet 136.

basically well-affected; any other would be worse as it would contain more Presbyterians 'qui sont tous républicains dans l'âme'.[5] But he did not support Danby wholeheartedly either. He had little sympathy with Danby's intolerant Anglicanism, however politically necessary it might be. He ordered the penal laws against Catholics to be enforced in order to prevent further legislation. Philip Howard reported that Charles had told him that 'He tried by doing this to favour the Catholics, as he foresaw that if he did not do so, parliament would make similar edicts and these would be fundamental and irrevocable laws, whereas if the king does this, he can always use connivance and also revoke them when circumstances permit.'[6] Charles hoped to dispel, with Danby's help, the suspicions aroused by the visible signs of Popery at court, while preventing serious incursions on the prerogative or severe new laws against Catholics. He carefully exploited his power to adjourn and prorogue parliament so as to ensure that bills he disliked were never presented for his consent.

He disagreed with Danby most fundamentally on the question of his relations with France. Charles thought that Louis might be the only friend he had in a crisis and he was afraid that Louis might leak the details of the Secret Treaty of Dover. Danby did succeed in keeping the duke's Catholicism away from the forefront of politics, but only at the cost of bringing much opprobrium onto himself. Without Charles's support, he could never be completely successful; in the words of Sir Keith Feiling, '"church and king", in the sense of exclusive Anglicanism and unfettered monarchy, had ceased to be possible when a Protestant church was governed by a king with a Catholic policy'.[7] While Danby tried to allay the fears of Popery, his authoritarianism and methods of parliamentary management aroused fears of arbitrary government. His anti-Catholic measures were only palliatives and could not touch the Catholicism of the heir-apparent. The Popish Plot and Exclusion Crisis simplified the confused political picture

---

[5] Courtin au Roi, 22 June 1676 NS, Baschet 132.

[6] Nunz. Fian. 59, fol. 410. 'Haveva mirato in ciò a favorirli, poiché prevedéva che il parlaménto in difètto di S. Mtà farebbe egli stésso simil'editto, e che all'hora sarebbe stata una légge fondamentale, e irrevocàbile, dóve che facendolo il Re, può sèmpre S. Mtà usare di connivènza et anche rivocarlo quando le congionture lo permettono.'

[7] K. G. Feiling, *History of the Tory Party 1640–1714* (Oxford, 1924), p. 174; see also Burnet, ii, 90.

of the years 1673–8 by bringing the question of the Popish successor to the centre of politics.

THE COURT IN RETREAT

The year 1673 saw the greatest outburst of anti-Catholic feeling since 1640–2. Between 1660 and 1672 there had been few popular anti-Catholic pamphlets. The two most important ones, du Moulin's *Vindication of the Sincerity of the Protestant Religion* and Lloyd's *The Late Apology in Behalf of the Papists Reprinted and Answered*, were both replies to pamphlets contrasting Catholic loyalty in the Civil War with Protestant disloyalty.[8] For the rest there were some works of controversy, a few minor works excited by the declaration of 1662, some translations of Jansenist attacks on the Jesuits and Foulis's *History of Romish Treasons*, which was a large and scholarly if idiosyncratic work, hardly a popular pamphlet. Anglican writers, like Anglican politicians, were more concerned with Dissent than with Popery. Even overtly anti-Catholic works sometimes stressed that Puritans were as bad as Papists, if not worse.[9]

In 1673–4, however, there appeared a mass of anti-Catholic works of all kinds. Lloyd himself produced four new pamphlets. Very little of this literature was overtly political or related to the present situation. It mostly regurgitated the main features of the anti-Catholic tradition, stressing particularly that Popery was a danger to the state. The duke was not attacked directly, mainly because of the censorship of the press; most libels against him circulated only in manuscript.[10] Few printers would dare to publish an attack on the king's brother. In printed works the clichés of the anti-Catholic tradition were paraded once more in a traditional and stereotyped response to the intrusion of the Catholic question into politics. As the root of the problem could not be mentioned, the pamphlets tried to create and cater for a general fear of Popery and an awareness of how dangerous it was, ex-

---

[8] They were in answer to Sir H. Janson (?), *Philanax Anglicus* (1663) and Castlemaine's *Catholique Apology* respectively.

[9] Foulis, *Romish Treasons*, preface, sigs. e–e2; *The Jesuits Intrigues* (1669), preface (by H. Compton), sigs, a2–a3.

[10] *POAS*, i, 211–12, 214–19, 233 241–2, 248, 250, 269, 281; *CSPD 1673–1675*, pp. 128–32; *Letters to Williamson*, i, 67.

pressed mainly in illustrations from history. They appealed to the nation at large, to parliament and, it was hoped, to the king and court. Only in 1679, after the shock of the Popish Plot and the breakdown of censorship, was the duke attacked directly; only then were the implications of his conversion discussed openly. Similarly, references in parliament to the religion of the heir-apparent were allusive rather than direct until the end of 1678.

When parliament met in February 1673 members stressed how dangerous Popery was to the state, and two blamed Charles I's death on the Papists. Some M.P.s showed that they were already aware of James's conversion. Powle and Vaughan in the Commons and Halifax in the Lords said that they were sure the king's religion was sound but did not know what his successor might be.[11] The Commons attacked both the legal and the religious aspects of the Declaration of Indulgence; even some Dissenting M.P.s argued that it should be withdrawn in order to guard against Popery.[12] The king's advisers were divided. Buckingham, Lauderdale, Shaftesbury and Clifford advised the king to stand by the Declaration; Buckingham and Lauderdale suggested that he should use force if need be. But Arlington advised Charles to abandon the Declaration in order to secure the supply of money, and the advice of Louis XIV to that effect was decisive.[13] After trying to defend it and declaring his willingness to accept any statute that would have the same effect, Charles broke the seal on the Declaration with his own hand. His brother grumbled that he should have stood by it, dissolving parliament if necessary.[14] The Commons now showed that its main fear was Popery; a bill was introduced to allow a modicum of toleration to some of the more moderate Dissenters. In response to an address of 3 March, Charles issued a proclamation for the banishing of priests and for the enforcement of the laws against Papists. On 29 March he gave his assent to the Test Act, which had been attacked violently in the Lords by Clifford, who claimed later to

---

[11] Grey, ii, 16, 32–5, 76; Burnet, ii, 101; Lady Newton, *Lyme Letters 1660–1760* (London, 1925), p. 52.

[12] Burnet, ii, 6–7; Grey, ii, 40.

[13] Dalrymple, ii, Appendix, 89–90, 93–4; Burnet, ii, 8–9; Brown, pp. 98–105.

[14] *CJ*, ix, 246, 256, 266; Bate, pp. 106–23; *CSPVen 1673–5*, p. 27.

have spoken by divine inspiration.[15] Parliament was then adjourned until the autumn.

The session had not been a total failure. Parliament had voted £1,260,000 for the war. The main cause of parliament's anxiety had been religion; the king's foreign policy was scarcely challenged.[16] During the summer he tried to reduce the court's identification with Popery. He declared that he would banish all Papists from the court, except for his brother,[17] and reversed his Irish policy. In Ireland, Catholics were debarred by law from living in corporate towns and from holding public office. Although priests could say Mass under certain circumstances, no man could legally exercise episcopal authority or assert the pope's jurisdiction over Ireland.[18] Until his dismissal in 1669, Ormond had tried to divide the Catholic clergy and keep them under control by making them subscribe to the Remonstrance.[19] Under lord Berkeley the Catholic clergy enjoyed much greater freedom. Their self-appointed leader was Peter Talbot, whom Rome had appointed titular archbishop of Dublin in 1669. It was said that Charles had pressed for his appointment, but Philip Howard was sure that the king's name had been taken in vain. Talbot and Patrick MacGinn were close associates of Arlington, who himself became a Catholic on his deathbed. Howard regarded Talbot as a malicious intriguer and forger of letters while another Catholic, Sir William Throckmorton, thought him 'the lyingest rogue in the world'.[20] In his dealings in Ireland Talbot relied heavily on his influence at the English court and particularly on the favour of York and Buckingham. Buckingham's Catholic associate, Sir Ellis Leighton, came to Ireland as Berkeley's secretary and Berkeley seems to have been either unwilling or unable to prevent Talbot from claiming jurisdiction over all the Irish bishops and excommunicating Remonstrants by virtue of authority delegated to him from Rome. He claimed that he was acting with the king's approval but the earl of Essex, who succeeded Berkeley in February 1672,

---

[15] *CJ*, ix, 252, 259, 261, 281; PC/2/63, pp. 400–1; Colbert au Roi, 3 April 1673 NS, Baschet 128.
[16] K. H. D. Haley, *William of Orange and the English Opposition 1672–4* (Oxford, 1953), pp. 90–7; Brown, p. 98.
[17] *CSPD 1673*, p. 126.
[18] F. C. Turner, *James II* (London, 1948), p. 379; Carte, iv, 582.
[19] *Essex Papers*, i, 150–1; Carte, iv, 436–7, 614.
[20] Nunz. Fian. 54, fols. 15, 17, 163; Treby, i, 68, 81–2, ii, 20.

thought that he based his claim on a letter from MacGinn in Arlington's name. Talbot's tactlessness, his claims to act on authority delegated from Rome and his pretensions to jurisdiction over all Ireland brought him into conflict, not only with Essex, but also with Oliver Plunkett, archbishop of Armagh and Catholic primate of Ireland.[21] Meanwhile Talbot and his brother Richard led the attempt by the Irish Catholics to secure the repeal of the Acts of Settlement and Explanation which had confirmed the Protestant possessors in their lands at the Restoration and perpetuated the dispossession of most Irish Catholic landowners. Their pressure led to a considerable relaxation of the restrictions on Catholics in Ireland. In 1672 they were allowed to live in corporate towns and to trade and hold lands there as freely as Protestants. The king dispensed with their taking the oath of supremacy so that they had to take only the oath of allegiance. By January 1673 Catholics were being admitted to offices, including places on the Dublin common council. The king stressed that while allowing them to hold office he did not intend to abandon the Acts of Settlement and Explanation.[22] This process came to an abrupt halt when it was vehemently attacked by the English parliament. In a sudden *volte-face*, the English Privy Council supported the lord mayor of Dublin's exclusion from the common council of even those Catholics prepared to take the oath of allegiance. In September 1673 Charles ordered that Catholics be disarmed and excluded from offices and corporations; their schools were to be suppressed and all priests (especially Talbot) were to leave the realm.[23] There was to be no further attempt to improve the lot of the Irish Catholics until the reign of James II.

During the summer of 1673 the alienation of parliament from the court greatly increased, despite the king's efforts. York and Clifford made their conversions apparent to all when they laid down their offices rather than take the test. The connection between Popery at court and the French alliance, little considered in the spring, was rammed home by Dutch propaganda. In parti-

[21] *CSPD 1673*, pp. 186, 244–51, *1660–85* (*Addenda*), pp. 322–4; *Essex Papers*, i, 90–1; Carte, iv, 427–39.
[22] Carte, iv, 452–9; *CSPD 1671–2*, p. 166, *1672–3*, pp. 64–5, 432; PC/2/63, p. 172.
[23] Grey, ii, 118–29; B. D. Henning (ed.), *The Parliamentary Diary of Sir Edward Dering 1670–3* (New Haven, 1940), p. 143; *CSPD 1673*, pp. 456–7, 597.

cular Peter du Moulin's *England's Appeal from the Private Cabal at Whitehall to the Great Council of the Nation, . . . Parliament* showed the designs of Louis XIV against European Protestantism, stressed the religious articles in his declaration of war and pointed out the connections with France of some leading English ministers.[24] Meanwhile the pressure on the king to divorce his childless queen, which had started some time before James's conversion, now began again; it came to nothing, but meanwhile James compounded his Papistry by marrying an Italian Catholic princess, a protegée of France.

Rumours that Charles would divorce the queen had started as early as 1667. They revived after the queen's miscarriage in 1669 and continued during the Roos divorce case in 1670, which many thought might serve as a precedent for the king. Buckingham and Bristol were the leading advocates of a divorce; both were enemies of James and of Clarendon, whose heirs would eventually succeed to the throne if Charles had no children.[25] (James's first wife, who died in 1671, was Clarendon's daughter.) Peter Talbot, described as Buckingham's 'grandissimo amico e confidente', was also involved in the intrigue and attracted the hostility of the queen. Airoldi, the Brussels internuncio, told him that he should concern himself with his pastoral duties and not with political intrigues.[26] When James failed to take the Anglican sacrament at Easter in 1673 the divorce question became urgent. Several members of parliament, including Shaftesbury, suggested it.[27] The pressure grew after James's marriage in the autumn. According to MacGinn, the queen considered retiring to a convent, either because she wanted a fuller spiritual life or because she was disgusted by the king's dissoluteness. MacGinn and the Portuguese ambassador tried vigorously to dissuade her. The Brussels internuncio suggested to the papal secretary of state that he should

---

[24] 'A Relation of the Most Material Matters' (1673), *State Tracts*, i, 29; Haley, *William of Orange*, chap. 6; this P. du Moulin was the nephew of Peter du Moulin, the Protestant controversialist, Haley, p. 13. For 'England's Appeal' see *State Tracts*, i, 1–25, especially pp. 10–11, 24.

[25] Haley, *Shaftesbury*, pp. 276–80; Colbert to Lionne, 20 June 1669 NS, Baschet 122; Clarke, i, 438–9; Burnet, i, 452–5.

[26] Prop. Ang., fols. 632–3.

[27] Colbert au Roi, 6 and 17 April 1673 NS, Baschet 128; *CSPVen 1673–5*, p. 35.

send the queen a letter exhorting her not to retire. A month after acknowledging receipt of that letter and of some letters from MacGinn, the secretary replied that he had considered sending a letter to her but doubted whether it would be expedient, since the situation in England was so turbulent. A week later he wrote that he feared that all they could do was trust in divine providence.[28] The project for the divorce foundered on the king's refusal to consider it, although it was revived during the Exclusion Crisis.

After lengthy preliminary inquiries, James chose as his second wife Mary Beatrice of Modena. Rome's behaviour in this affair shows the extent to which its actions were dominated by a rigid legalism. When the marriage negotiations began the young princess was planning to enter a convent. The curia sent a brief exhorting her to marry James in the interests of the faith. This brief was apparently procured by the efforts of d'Estrées, the French ambassador in Rome, and cardinal Barberino, the cardinal protector of England and a relative of the princess. But in September 1673 the curia decided that she would have to have a dispensation to marry the duke, as he was not officially a Catholic (although the secretary of state for one knew that he was a Catholic at least a month earlier). A congregation of cardinals ruled that the dispensation could not be given unless Charles promised the princess the freedom of worship guaranteed in his and his father's marriage treaties.[29]

The curia now withdrew its exhortatory brief. The English court was angry at the delay as it hoped to conclude the marriage before parliament could meet and attack it. D'Angeau, a French agent acting on behalf of James, and the princess's uncle, Rinaldo d'Este, persuaded her mother to consult five priests on the question. These decided that the exhortatory brief and the common knowledge that James was a Catholic were adequate grounds for proceeding with the marriage. The bishop of Modena refused to officiate so it was solemnised by an English priest, the earl of Peterborough standing as James's proxy. The pope and cardinal

[28] Nunz. Fian. 59, fols. 31, 33–4, 305–7.
[29] E. Campana di Cavelli, *Les Derniers Stuarts à Saint-Germain-en-Laye* (2 vols., London, 1871), i, 64–7; Ranke, iii, 563–4; Nunz. Fian. 59, fol. 24; *CSPVen 1673–5*, 125–6. Even in 1677 the secretary of Propaganda was not sure that James was a Catholic, BM, Add. MS 17990, fol. 8.

Altieri were furious; James grumbled about Rome's timidity. Angry that the marriage had taken place, Rome still refused to grant the dispensation without fuller guarantees of the new duchess's freedom of worship than either Charles or Louis could give. It also demanded submission in more and more abject terms for having proceeded with the marriage without the dispensation.[30] Meanwhile the internuncio tried hard to find positive evidence that James had abjured Protestantism. He cited his resignation from his offices and the testimony of MacGinn and of one abbé Balati. The secretary thought that he probably had abjured Protestantism but doubted if Balati's word was sufficient proof and referred the verification to divine providence. He remarked, with presumably unconscious irony, that nobody could regard the marriage as 'una machina di Roma' and added that the curia had shown constancy in adhering to its principles. The French ambassador told Altieri that the curia should have shown greater pragmatism in such an important affair of state.[31] The affair dragged on into 1674. The first contact of Edward Coleman, the new duchess's secretary, with the internuncio was on this matter. He eventually elicited from the secretary vague expressions of goodwill towards James and the English Catholics. As for the marriage, the pope would do what he could, 'having regard always to the proprieties of custom and the respect due to this court'. The marriage eventually received Rome's blessing in March 1675.[32] Throughout the court of Rome had shown little sign of the satanic all-pervading fixity of purpose, the dedication to the extirpation of Protestantism or the Machiavellian unscrupulousness which English Protestants traditionally attributed to it. On the contrary its policy-making was hidebound by a pedantic legalism which, one suspects, many English lawyers would have found quite congenial.

James's marriage raised anti-Catholic excitement in England to an even higher pitch. It seemed to confirm the allegations of

---

[30] *CSPVen 1673–5*, pp. 130–2, 142, 144–50, 157, 164–7, 170–1; R. Halstead (*vere* H. Mordaunt, 2nd earl of Peterborough), *Succinct Genealogies* (1685), pp. 428–9.

[31] Nunz. Fian. 59, fols. 28, 30, 292–3, 305; *CSPVen 1673–5*, pp. 132, 142.

[32] Nunz. Fian. 59, fols. 40–1: 'Salve sèmpre le convenévolezze del costume e dei risguardi della Nòstra Corte'; G. Anstruther, 'Cardinal Howard and the English Court', *Archivum Fratrum Praedicatorum*, xxviii (1958), 330.

Dutch propaganda that the French alliance was part of a plot to introduce Popery and absolutism. During the summer even Buckingham, beceause of his association with the court and the war, found that he was widely suspected of being inclined to Popery. Many of the troops raised for the war were encamped on Hampstead Heath, which increased fears of military despotism.[33] James, meanwhile, became more intransigent and determined. Colbert had reported in April that James still hoped to resuscitate the Catholic design. He had also hoped to command the army when it went to Flanders (where the Test Act would not operate), but the judges had ruled against it. He urged Charles not to recall parliament in October unless peace had been made. If the war had gone well, Charles could then use the army to re-establish his authority and, if necessary, to subdue parliament. Charles rejected his advice.[34] Meanwhile there were rumours that James would be banished or excluded from the throne but he indignantly rejected suggestions that he should withdraw from the court.[35]

On 27 October 1673 parliament met. The Commons petitioned the king not to allow James's marriage to be consummated and resolved to grant no money until the dangers from Popery and Popish counsels had been removed. It also voted the standing army a grievance. James was furious. He always tended to see opposition as motivated by personal animosity or ambition; he and others on the Council saw the Commons' expressions of concern about religion as merely a facade masking factious attacks on himself. But the fears of Popery were real enough. On 5 November there were more bonfires and more popes burnt in effigy than there had been for thirty years. Pope-burnings were so common in London that country people began to regard a 'popemaker' as one of the sights of the capital.[36] Parliament meanwhile

33 *Letters to Williamson*, i, 24, 58, 67, 143, 145–6, ii, 27, 63; 'A Relation of the Most Material Matters', *State Tracts*, i, 33–5; *Diary of Ralph Josselin*, p. 164; *Reliquiae Baxterianae*, Part III, p. 106; Evelyn, 12 June 1673, *Diary*, iv, 13; Bodl., Tanner MS 43, fol. 31.
34 Colbert au Roi, 17 April 1673 NS, Baschet 128; *Letters to Williamson*, i, 60; *CSPVen 1673–5*, pp. 55–6, 76.
35 *CSPVen 1673–5*, pp. 68–9; Nunz. Fian. 59, fol. 241; Colbert au Roi, 10 July 1673 NS, Baschet 128; Haley, *Shaftesbury*, p. 337; Clarke, i, 487–8; Burnet, ii, 37; Dalrymple ii, Appendix, 98.
36 *CJ*, ix, 281, 285, 286; *CSPVen 1673–5*, pp. 174–5; *Letters to Williamson*, ii, 67; BM Add. MS 25122, fol. 165; *CSPD 1673–5*, p. 44.

was so unmanageable that after only eight days Charles prorogued it until 7 January. Apparently on the advice of secretary of state Henry Coventry, the manager of the court interest in the Commons, the king now decided to conciliate his subjects by severe measures against the Catholics. He ignored James's exhortations to take a firm stand, to send 'agitators' to the Tower and to confiscate their estates. On 20 November the king ordered that the penal laws should be enforced and Papists kept away from his person.[37]

The directives of the king and Council and the ominous course of political events now shook the magistrates of the shires out of their inertia. Before 1673 the recusancy laws had been enforced very little in most counties, although there were about five thousand convictions in Lancashire, including many of the Catholic gentry. In Yorkshire most of the Catholic gentry of the North Riding were not presented as recusants until 1674 and many in the West Riding were not presented until 1678. Convictions had been more common in the East Riding.[38] In Wiltshire 220 recusants had been convicted in 1660–72, of whom at least 130 were Dissenters. In 1673 there were 213 convictions, including at least 100 Papists; these were the highest figures for any year of the reign.[39] Only sixty-two recusants had been convicted in Middlesex before 1673 but 739, at least half of them Catholics, were convicted in 1674. Only in Norfolk was the situation different. Before 1673 403 recusants had been convicted, of whom the majority were probably Dissenters; the largest numbers of convictions were in 1664–5, just after the passing of the 1664 Conventicle Act. However, there was no sudden increase in 1674, though this might be due partly to the nature of the evidence,

---

[37] Colbert au Roi, 20 Nov. 1673 NS, Baschet 129; *Letters to Williamson*, ii, 65; *CSPD 1673–5*, pp. 27, 57; *CSPVen 1673–5*, pp. 176–8, 184; BM Add. MS 25122, fols. 171, 173, 176.

[38] *Letters to Williamson*, i, 145–6; CRS, vi, 90–255 (especially Gillow's notes); Aveling, *Northern Catholics*, pp. 324–6 and *West Riding*, pp. 234–5.

[39] Williams, *Wilts.*; the slight disparity between Mr Williams's dates and mine stems from the fact that I have used the date of conviction whereas he has used the recusant roll date, which is often the year before the date of conviction, being perhaps the year in which the offence took place. See below, Appendix 1.

and, while in most counties the numbers of convictions fell sharply in 1675–7, it remained much the same in Norfolk.[40]

In many counties, despite the efforts of the J.P.s, the machinery did not always function smoothly. In Yorkshire there was considerable uncertainty about procedure and juries seemed reluctant to convict.[41] Nevertheless the fact that a real effort was made to enforce the recusancy laws shows the extent of the insecurity created in Protestant minds by the events of 1672–3. As the tendencies of the court towards Popery and absolutism became obvious, fear of Popery struck deep into English life and, for the first time since the Restoration in most counties, really affected the Catholics. Alarmed Protestant gentlemen lashed out in retaliation at those Papists they could touch, in the shires. This might seem illogical, because the Papists were so few, but many Protestants believed that 'hidden' Papists greatly outnumbered those who openly avowed their religion. Signs of Catholic activity, which could be ignored as harmless in normal times, could seem sinister and dangerous now that there seemed to be a plot on foot to impose Popery and arbitrary government. If there was to be a struggle between the Popish court and the Protestant nation, the Catholics would become a dangerous 'fifth column' in the localities and not a harmless and negligible religious minority.

In the next session of parliament, from 7 January to 9 February 1674, anti-Catholicism was still rampant. A manuscript libel of January represented the French alliance and the raising of the army as part of a plot to bring in Popery and absolutism. It accused the duke of being a Papist and asked 'whether it be not high time to consider of settling the succession of the crown so as may secure us from those bloody massacres and inhuman Smithfield butcheries, the certain consequences of a Popish government?' Shaftesbury told the Lords that there were sixteen thousand Papists in London ready to try desperate measures and that nobody's life was safe. A thirteen year old boy told them of a Catholic gunpowder plot. There were reports of scandalous and treasonable speeches by Papists.[42] The king ordered all Papists

---

[40] Appendices 1 and 2.
[41] *HMC le Fleming*, pp. 109–10.
[42] *CSPD 1673–5*, pp. 95–6, 128–32; Ruvigny to Pomponne, 21 Jan. 1674 NS, Baschet 130; *CSPVen 1673–5*, p. 201; *HMC 9th Report, Appendix 2*, p. 37.

to depart from within ten miles of London, except for house-holders and the servants of peers. The Lords ordered all its members to take the oath of allegiance; James refused at first, but later did so. The Commons attacked, individually and in general, counsellors who were 'Popishly affected ... or otherwise obnoxious or dangerous to the government'. 'Fear of the duke makes them every day fetter the crown', remarked one peer in February.[43] Members of both Houses hinted broadly at the dangers from the duke. In the Lords several bills were brought in to restrict his powers if he ever became king, culminating in the earl of Carlisle's bill which envisaged his exclusion from the throne. This was fiercely attacked by the bishops and was allowed to drop. It was clearly too radical for most of the peers.[44] The Commons was not unreservedly hostile to Papists, however. Bernard Howard, the youngest brother of Henry (earl of Norwich and later duke of Norfolk) and Philip (soon to be made a cardinal), petitioned the Commons that he should be exempted from the penalties of the recusancy laws if he could show that he was a good subject. Some M.P.s seemed willing that deserving individuals should be exempted but Howard was eventually told to withdraw his petition. It is uncertain whether this was a personal move or whether it was intended to serve as a precedent for others. The Catholicism of Bernard's brother Henry and nephew Thomas was certainly not aggressive or rigidly sectarian. Even Philip, when Pepys met him, jokingly referred to the pope as 'Antichrist'.[45] The Howards were the most 'English' of Catholics; if any could hope for exemption from the laws, they could; but January 1674 was a bad time to ask for it.

THE ASCENDANCY OF DANBY

After the king had made peace with the Dutch and prorogued parliament, the court set out to recoup its political strength. The

---

[43] *CSPD 1673–5*, p. 102; *LJ*, xii, 604, 607; *CSPVen 1673–5*, pp. 201–2; Ruvigny to Pomponne, 25 Jan. 1674 NS, Baschet 130; *CJ*, ix, 292; *Essex Papers*, i, 174.

[44] *Letters to Williamson*, ii, 156–7; *HMC Kenyon*, pp. 99–100; *CSPVen 1673–5*, pp. 220–1; Haley, *Shaftesbury*, pp. 358–60.

[45] Grey, ii, 358–63; see also, above pp. 13, 26; Pepys, 23 Jan. 1667; Burnet, iii, 78–80; Burnet, *Some Letters Containing an Account* (Rotterdam, 1686), pp. 231–2.

Council ordered the judges to ensure that the penal laws were enforced and chivvied the Middlesex J.P.s to apprehend priests.[46] Despite such measures, however, the basic problem remained. As Ruvigny, the new French ambassador remarked, 'il n'est pas possible d'ôter la cause perpétuelle de leurs défiances touchant M. le duc d'York'.[47] The breakdown of trust between king and parliament had been made worse by Charles's failure to reward the loyalty and to respect the prejudices of his natural supporters. As one M.P., Sir Robert Wiseman, complained, 'the king's conscientious good friends are (as they have always been) little regarded, both in themselves and in the principles they own; . . . undoubtedly if such men and their principles were but at this day regarded, all would speedily do well'. However, some old Cavaliers were now becoming alarmed by the violence of the Commons' proceedings and by the thinly veiled attacks on the duke: 'The old damned Presbyter rides us most vigorously,' wrote Richard Legh, M.P., in March 1673, 'God deliver us from the fate of 1641. These days look too like them.'[48]

It was on men like Wiseman and Legh and a strengthened financial position that Danby based his hopes of regaining the political ground that the court had lost. The peace with the Dutch made possible a reduction of expenditure and an increased customs revenue, but the crown still needed supplies from parliament, so parliament had to be brought under control. To this end Danby set out to recapture the support of the old Cavaliers, the 'church and king' men, which had been obtainable as recently as 1669–71. He was ready to offer them policies that were congenial to them, together with a monopoly of offices and other rewards. He suggested that places should be granted only to those who had fought for Charles I, that the Corporation Act, which theoretically excluded Dissenters from municipal office, should be strictly enforced and that the extra revenue which he hoped to raise from recusants should be used to provide salaries for sheriffs, J.P.s and militia officers 'by which they may be made offices of benefit as well as trust'. He also tried to impose some cohesion on the unorganised supporters of the court in the Commons. By means of

---

[46] Haley, *William of Orange*, chap. 9; PC/2/64, pp. 188, 204, 207, 234.

[47] Ruvigny au Roi, 19 March 1674 NS, Baschet 130.

[48] *Letters to Williamson*, ii, 78; Newton, *Lyme Letters*, p. 55; see also Feiling, *EHR*, xlii, 408; Carte, iv, 269; *CSPD 1667*, p. 428.

a judicious distribution of money and places the idle were induced to attend the House regularly, waverers were kept firm to the court and the venal and indigent were bought.[49]

On the political side, he pushed ahead with the rebuilding of St. Paul's and prepared to erect a statue of Charles I.[50] More fundamentally, he tried hard to induce the king to follow a Protestant, anti-French foreign policy and he began to enforce the laws against recusants and Dissenters. In October 1674 he and Lauderdale began a series of conferences with the bishops, who agreed that the existing laws against Popery were adequate and that they just needed to be enforced. Their recommendations formed the basis of orders in Council of 3 February 1675. These decreed that priests should leave the country and that Papists should not come to court, attend the Catholic chapels in London or send children to the Catholic schools on the continent. The main concern was to ensure that Papists were convicted and that the statutory fines should be levied. Danby ordered the officers of the Exchequer to draw up commissions incorporating the names of those who were returned as having been convicted for recusancy. The commissions were to be sent to commissioners in each county, who were chosen from lists of M.P.s and J.P.s and who were to inquire into the recusants' lands and seize two-thirds of them for the king. One Richard Derham was appointed 'Receiver of the revenue arising from the forfeitures of recusants', to receive the money as it came in. At the same time, the laws against conventicles were also to be enforced and the licences of 1672 were withdrawn.[51]

Danby's religious policy soon produced a reaction. Early in November 1674 some leading Presbyterians had met to consider how to achieve liberty of conscience. Soon after York was said to have welcomed the approaches of some of them 'whereas he has

[49] Browning, *Danby*, ii, 65–6; Browning, 'Parties and Party Organisation in the Reign of Charles II', *Transactions of the Royal Historical Soc.*, 4th series, xxx (1948), 21–36.

[50] Browning, *Danby*, i, 149; Burnet, ii, 53; H. M. Margoliouth (ed.), *Poems and Letters of Andrew Marvell*, rev. by P. Legouis and E. E. Duncan Jones (3rd edn, 2 vols., Oxford, 1971), ii, 341–2.

[51] Browning, *Danby*, i, 147–8; PC/2/64, pp. 364–8; *CTB* iv, 289, 693–4, 739; Bate, pp. 140–1. There had been some uncertainty whether the cancelling of the Declaration had annulled the licences: Bodl.. Tanner MS 42, fols. 7, 110, 112.

previously treated them with contempt and disdained their services, being perhaps doubtful of their loyalty'.[52] James now strove to appear as the protector of Catholic and Protestant nonconformists against Danby's intolerant Anglicanism. In December he obtained pardons for a number of convicted Dissenters. In January he made overtures to some opposition peers which were not rejected. He told Ruvigny that if Louis would lend Charles three or four hundred thousand pounds, Charles would dissolve parliament and not call another. Louis wanted this parliament to be dissolved, but he hoped to achieve his ends far more cheaply.[53]

James does not seem to have realised the full extent of Danby's plans. At the end of January 1675 Ruvigny reported that York accepted that some assurance had to be given that the Protestant religion was secure before parliament could be dissolved. The Venetian resident noted that Danby and Lauderdale were working closely with the bishops, but thought that the king wanted some concessions for Dissenters and Catholics.[54] The order on 3 February to enforce the laws to the full came as a shock to James; he opposed it vigorously and later regarded it as a betrayal. Charles, like Danby, believed that the measures would disarm the parliamentary opposition. James argued that they would set Dissenters as well as Anglicans against the king and that Charles should dismiss Danby and Lauderdale and take a more active part in government.[55] When he failed to persuade Charles not to adopt Danby's religious policy, James began to consider building himself an anti-Danby faction in parliament. The decision to attempt this was made early in February; this can be seen clearly from the change that took place at that time in Coleman's correspondence.

In the summer of 1674 Edward Coleman, secretary first to the duke and then to the duchess of York, sent his first letters to the Brussels internuncio and Louis XIV's confessor. James apparently

52 *CSPVen 1673–5*, pp. 310–11, 316–17.
53 *ibid.* pp. 318–19, 324, 326–7, 330–1; *HMC Portland*, iii, 348; Thomas in Nuttall and Chadwick, pp. 217–18; *Essex Papers*, i, 285; Mignet, iv, 330–1.
54 Ruvigny ou Roi, 4 Feb. 1675 NS, Baschet 132; *CSPVen 1673–5*, pp. 348–50.
55 *CSPVen 1673–5*, pp. 357–9, 366–8; Clarke, i, 499–500; Ruvigny au Roi, 18 Feb. 1675 NS, Baschet 132.

knew of the correspondence, though it is uncertain whether he approved each individual letter.[56] Coleman asked the internuncio if the pope could mediate a peace between France and Spain, to leave one or both of them free to intervene in England and if the pope and emperor would give money to help the duke's designs, which were implied to consist of the reintroduction of Catholicism in England.[57] The internuncio replied that the pope could not provide nearly as much as Coleman wanted and would give nothing without firm guarantees that it would be used for the benefit of the Catholics. He later suggested that Coleman should abandon the whole idea.[58]

Coleman also tried to persuade Louis XIV through his confessors, first Ferrier and then la Chaise, that it would be in his interest to pay Charles to dissolve parliament.[59] On 1 February 1675 he was still writing to his agent at Paris, Sir William Throckmorton, that money was needed to enable Charles to dissolve parliament. But on 12 February and again on 12 March he wrote to the internuncio in different terms. He now said nothing of dissolution but remarked instead that some M.P.s were honest men and for the duke and others could be bought.[60] His aim now was to get money from France to bribe M.P.s to support the duke and to oppose Danby. Unfortunately the situation at Paris was confused; Throckmorton and Peter Talbot each claimed to be James's accredited representative and each put forward different projects to the king's confessor.[61] The situation at Paris was, in fact, frustratingly obscure. One Edmund Everard, who eventually became one of James II's spies in Holland, later alleged that Talbot had been intriguing in Paris to set up Popery in England as early as 1673, when he was banished from Ireland. Everard claimed that he had been imprisoned when he had tried to reveal this. However, when the Council had examined him in 1673 Everard could say nothing of the Talbots except that Peter Talbot had

---

[56] *CJ*, ix, 523; Kenyon, *Popish Plot*, pp. 34–8, 86–8; Ailesbury claimed that James and the duchess did not know of Coleman's correspondence, Ailesbury, i, 27–8.

[57] Treby, i, 4–8, 12–16. The use of trading terms ('merchant' for 'priest', etc.) somewhat obscures the meaning.

[58] Nunz. Fian. 59, fols. 391–2; Treby, i, 23, 25, 26.

[59] Treby, i, 1–2; *State Tracts*, i, 138–40.

[60] Treby, ii, 1–3, 9–11; *State Tracts*, i, 140–2.

[61] Treby, i, 68–70; *HMC Fitzherbert*, pp. 58–9, 66, 69–70.

spent half an hour deep in discussion with the king's confessor in the king's closet.[62] There are indications that the Talbots as well as or instead of Coleman and Throckmorton were intermediaries between James and the French court. It is also possible that the disputes of Talbot and Throckmorton early in 1675 were connected with Talbot's attack later in the year on John Sergeant, a leading Chapterman and a paranoid enemy of the Jesuits. Sergeant had been confessor to Coleman's wife, but he denied any knowledge of Coleman's correspondence.[63]

Whatever was happening at Paris, by 20 February Coleman was writing that James ought to set himself up as a leader in parliament who opposed the debauchery of the court. In this way he could win over the sober Protestants while the Commons destroyed Danby and Lauderdale. James now got the impression that the Dissenters made up the great majority of the population, an impression that recurred when he again wanted the Dissenters' support in 1687–8.[64] Rumours abounded that there would be a rapprochement between James and Shaftesbury and that James would be restored to the Admiralty at the request of the Presbyterians; from that position of power, he would be able more easily to protect Dissenters and Catholics. An unnamed relative of the earl of Berkshire, perhaps Sir Robert Howard or the earl of Carlisle, hoped to insert into a new bill against Popery a proviso that would exempt James from its provisions and restore him to his places.[65] But when parliament met the projects came to nothing. Coleman wrote that James had been persuaded that the risks involved were too great. The chances of success must really have been minimal for parliament was dominated by Anglicans, not by Dissenters. There was also a plan for Catholics to petition

---

[62] Akerman, pp. 150, 163, 169, 195, 207; BM Add. MS 41804, fols. 136–137, 158, 182; Morrice MS Q. p. 148; C. de Witt, *A Letter from Holland Touching Liberty of Conscience* (1688), p. 3; *The Deposition and Examinations of Edmund Everard* (1679); Longleat, Coventry MS xi, fols. 19–49, especially fol. 49.

[63] Hay, pp. 21–7, 154 and passim; Rawl. MS A 135, pp. 153, 156.

[64] Treby, i, 76–7; *CSPVen 1673–5*, p. 367.

[65] Howard had taken a strongly anti-Catholic line in 1673 but was regarded as friendly to James in 1675. He had good reasons of his own for disliking Danby. *CSPVen 1673–5*, pp. 378, 390–2; Treby, i, 102, ii, 20; Haley, *Shaftesbury*, pp. 339–40, 384–5; Browning, *Danby*, i, 138.

parliament for relief, but this also came to nothing and lord Aston, for one, regarded the idea as unnecessary and dangerous.[66]

Danby had delayed meeting parliament until April 1675; the Cavalier policy then had its first trial and was not unsuccessful. The repression of all religious nonconformity must have reassured some anxious Anglicans. 'The Papists and Presbyterians join heartily against the Church of England,' wrote Richard Legh, and again, 'The devil Presbyterian in both houses does all he can to dissolve us and the Lords were never higher but in '42.' The enforcement of the recusancy laws must have taken much of the sting out of anti-Catholic feeling, although there were still the fears of France which were encouraged by the Dutch and other ambassadors. The king was asked to recall English soldiers from the French service.[67] Besides trying to remove the fears of Popery, Danby also appealed directly to the prejudices and self-interest of the old Cavaliers. A new test was proposed in the Lords which included a declaration of the impiety of resistance to duly constituted authority and an oath not to alter the established government in church or state. It would in theory have restricted public office to Anglicans. The attitude of James, as a possible opposition leader, was crucial. The king made it clear to him that he approved of the test and that there could be a connivance at religious nonconformity but no open toleration. James did not desert the court and this, with the attendance of the king, ensured that the measure was approved by the Lords.[68] James did vote for an amendment that would have weakened the bill considerably but on the whole he obeyed his brother and so separated from the other Catholic peers. Four of these (Petre, Audley, Berkshire and Bristol) entered protests against the bill and even earned Shaftesbury's grudging approval.[69]

Shaftesbury's account of the debates about Danby's test, *A Letter from a Person of Quality to His Friend in the Country*, showed how far Danby had changed the political scene. Shaftes-

[66] *State Tracts*, i, 142–3; *CSPVen 1673–5*, pp. 372–3, *CSPD 1675–6*, p. 87.

[67] Lady Newton, *Lyme Letters*, p. 63; idem, *The House of Lyme* (London, 1917), p. 272; *CJ.* ix, 316–19, 333.

[68] *CSPVen 1673–5*, pp. 397–8, 401–2; Browning, *Danby*, i, 153–4; Haley, *Shaftesbury*, pp. 374–80.

[69] 'A Letter from a Person of Quality' (1675), *State Tracts*, i, 45–6, 51, 55.

bury claimed that the Clarendon Code and the Militia Acts had been the start of a Cavalier and Anglican design to wreak revenge for the civil wars, despite the Act of Oblivion. Danby's regime was like that of Laud; his test was designed to prepare the way for the introduction of a military despotism.[70] Shaftesbury's attitude to the Catholics was very confused. He pointed out that they had not been affected by the legislation of the early 1660s and alleged that Clifford had told him that the king could introduce any religion he wanted if he had a large enough army. But although the Declaration of Indulgence had been proposed by Clifford, it gave the Papists nothing that they did not enjoy already by connivance. The bishops and Anglicans had attacked it, ostensibly because it favoured Papists, but really because it gave toleration to Dissenters.[71] Since 1672 the bishops had abandoned their zeal against Popery. They had opposed a bill to prevent princes from marrying Papists. They said that the new test was intended to prevent the establishment of Popery 'if we should have a Popish prince', but they had told the Catholic peers secretly that it was not meant to bear heavily on them. Shaftesbury accused the bishops of being insincere in their pretended opposition to Popery but he tried also not to seem too hostile to the Catholic peers who were for the time being his political allies. He tried to escape from this inconsistency by saying that Catholics should be allowed to enjoy their estates but not to hold office or bear arms.[72] (In a speech to the Lords after his conviction in 1680, lord Stafford said that about this time he had canvassed a number of Protestant peers with some proposals for a measure of relief for Catholics, which Shaftesbury had received quite favourably[73]). Behind Shaftesbury's arguments in this pamphlet lay the fear of a Popish successor, but for the moment it was Danby who was immediately dangerous. Shaftesbury had moved some way since his violent anti-Catholicism of 1673–4 because Danby was now the ruling

---

[70] *ibid.* pp. 41, 44, 49, 55.

[71] *ibid.* pp. 41–3.

[72] *ibid.* pp. 43, 44, 50, 55; cf. Shaftesbury's classification of the political 'worthiness' of the Catholic peers, K. H. D. Haley, 'Shaftesbury's Lists of the Lay Peers and Members of the Commons, 1677–8', *Bulletin of the Institute of Historical Research*, xliii (1970), 92–5.

[73] Corker, p. 53; Burnet, ii, 266; fragment of notes for the speech, AAW B29, packet 12, no. 1; there are no details of the speech in *LJ* or *State Trials*. See also Haley, *Shaftesbury*, pp. 401–2.

figure at court, on whom fears of arbitrary government centred.

In the summer of 1675 Danby was in the ascendant. He continued his attempts to make the recusancy laws financially profitable. But after lists of the names of those convicted for recusancy were returned to the Exchequer, little or nothing was done, 'through whose default is not known'. Coleman thought that the main problem was that Protestant gentlemen were reluctant to participate in the confiscation of the property of their Catholic neighbours. So Danby ordered that the commissions already issued should be renewed and that the names of those recently convicted should be added. He ordered the clerks of the peace to see that the commissions were acted upon. But nearly a year later, in June 1676, he complained that the prosecution of recusants was not proceeding properly, that the commissions were not being acted upon and that no inquiry was made into the lands of poor recusants. As the commissioners were not doing their job, he had decided to revert to the older practice of sending processes to sheriffs.[74] But evidence given to the Commons in April 1678 suggested that this method had not worked either. In four English counties and in all of Wales there had been no convictions at all; in many others no action had been taken after conviction. Only 3s 4d was raised in Middlesex in 1675 although inquiries had been held into the lands of twenty-one convicted recusants. The total raised in the whole kingdom was said to be £78 5s 6d in 1675 and £535 5s 10½d in 1676.[75] On the other hand there were many seizures of Papists' lands in Lancashire, although in most cases they were undervalued. It is also interesting to note that in November 1676 it was alleged that the sheriff of Yorkshire had seized £2300 in recusant revenue in that year and that the previous sheriff had collected £1000.[76] This money clearly did not reach the Exchequer.

The autumn session of parliament, from 13 October to 22 November 1675, followed the pattern of the last. 'There is a strict conjunction between the fanatic and Papist to dissolve this parliament,' announced the speaker on 25 October.[77] Shaftesbury

[74] *Autograph Letters in the Collection of Alfred Morrison*, 2nd Series, ii, 247; *CTB*, iv, 804–5, v, 59.

[75] *CJ*, ix, 470; Middlesex R. O., MR/RRE/1; Prof. Chandaman (p. 704) gives figures of £78 2s 2d for 1675–6 and £245 15s 10½d for 1676–7.

[76] Blundell, *Cavalier*, pp. 172–3; *CTB*, v, 87.

[77] Grey, iii, 345; see also *CSPD 1675–6*, pp. 315–16.

and James both wanted parliament to be dissolved and a vote to address the king to that end narrowly failed to pass the Lords.[78] All that materialised was a prorogation of fifteen months.

In 1676 Danby's position remained strong. Compton's census, whatever its statistical imperfections, showed that the Anglican interest was the surest basis for government, which was what Danby had always said. It convinced the king that he had no need to dissolve parliament. He again ordered that the laws against conventicles should be enforced.[79] James now stopped attending the Anglican service and refused to let Compton prepare his daughter Mary to receive the sacrament at Easter. One account said that Rome received these pieces of news with joy, but cardinal Howard made it clear that Rome's attitude to James was still somewhat reserved and that the memory of his marriage still rankled.[80] In the summer fears of France reached a high level. Fires in various parts of the country gave rise to rumours of a systematic campaign of arson carried on by Frenchmen. One Francis Jenks was gaoled for a speech at Common Hall, London, which blamed the fires on the French and called for a petition for a new parliament. It was printed with another speech 'intended to be given' which stressed the danger of a Popish successor and claimed that the Catholic convents abroad had great hopes of recovering their lands.[81] One Sir Philip Monckton was questioned by the Council after he had said that 'it was the thoughts of many, that the king could be snatched out of our hands so soon as the king of France was at leisure'. He was sent to the Tower. In November Courtin reported that there was a lot of preaching against Popery and about the dangers of a Popish successor.[82] The long interval between sessions of parliament created fears of what might happen if Charles died and brought the question of

---

[78] Haley, *Shaftesbury*, pp. 400–2; *HMC 9th Report, Appendix 2*, p. 79.
[79] Browning, *Danby*, i, 197–9; Browning (ed.), *Historical Documents*, pp. 411–16; Courtin au Roi, 22 June 1676 NS, Baschet 132; *Reliquiae Baxterianae*, Part III, p. 176; *HMC le Fleming*, p. 125.
[80] Nunz. Fian. 59, fols. 459–60; Mignet, iv, 405–6; Treby, i, 81–6, 88.
[81] *HMC le Fleming*, p. 127; *CSPD 1676–7*, pp. 178–82, 184–6, 200–3, 253–6, *1678*, p. 603.
[82] *CSPD 1676–7*, pp. 145–6, 194–5, 207; *Essex Papers*, ii, ed. C. E. Pike (Camden Soc., 1913), p. 63; Courtin au Roi, 3 Dec. 1676 NS, Baschet 134. See also D. Holles, 'A Letter to Monsieur van B— de M—' (1676), *Somers Tracts*, viii, 32–7.

the Popish heir-apparent, never far below the surface, back into the light.

This hatred of France and Popery was not unwelcome to Danby and Lauderdale, who hoped to turn it to the advantage of the court. Courtin thought that they aimed to 'pousser M. le duc d'York' and to persuade Charles to make war on France. Charles said he would do so if parliament gave him the money but at the same time he connived at the raising of recruits to replenish the Scots and Irish regiments in the French service.[83] Courtin was not surprised at the unpopularity of James and of France:

> Il ne faut pas s'étonner si toute l'Angleterre craint que cet attachement [to France] ne lui serve d'appui pour monter sur le trône, quand le cas arrivera, et si elle appréhende qu'un prince qui est capable de s'exposer au péril de perdre une couronne par son zèle pour le religion Catholique ne le soit aussi de se porter à toutes sortes d'extrémités pour la rétablir. Il ne paraît pas qu'il en puisse venir à bout sans le secours de Votre Majesté. C'est la raison pour laquelle tous les Anglais ... croient qu'il leur est important que la puissance de Votre Majesté soit affaiblie si il leur est possible.[84]

These fears were actively encouraged by the Dutch and Spanish ambassadors. Courtin tried to encourage a renewal in the next session of parliament of the alliance of Catholics and Dissenters against Danby. He approached Shaftesbury and the leading Presbyterian peer, lord Holles. Shaftesbury approached James through some of the Catholic peers. James refused to commit himself. He was afraid once again that his succession to the throne would be attacked.[85] In fact he was not attacked, but he and the Catholic peers found Shaftesbury's way of trying to force a dissolution too radical and they voted with the court.[86]

In an effort to reduce the fears aroused by James's religion Danby had two bills introduced in parliament. The first provided that, if a Catholic became king, ecclesiastical affairs should be managed by the bishops and that the royal children should be

[83] Courtin au Roi, 12 Oct., 2, 12 and 16 Nov., 10 Dec. 1676 NS, Baschet 134; Burnet, ii, 114–15.

[84] Courtin au Roi, 31 Dec. 1676 NS, Baschet 134.

[85] Mignet, iv, 434–5; Haley, *Shaftesbury*, pp. 413–14; *CSPD 1676–7*, pp. 541–2.

[86] *CSPD 1677–8*, p. 95; Browning, *Danby*, i, 218–19; Courtin au Roi, 1 March 1677 NS, Baschet 135.

educated as Protestants. James had had to agree to this. It passed the Lords, but in the Commons some M.P.s complained that it did not give sufficient security for the Protestant religion. Some did not trust the bishops and one said bluntly: 'That prince that is Popishly inclined will exercise his prerogative for all this bill.' It was read twice and then was lost in committee.[87] The second bill sent down from the Lords envisaged a system whereby Papists who registered themselves as such and took the oath of allegiance were to pay only a shilling a week for their recusancy and were to be free of all other penalties. They were to be eligible for election to offices, but not able to exercise them and so they would have to pay deputies. Those who failed to register were to have the oaths tendered to them; if they refused to take them, they were to be liable to the full penalties of the law. Priests were to be liable to all the existing laws but were not to be executed for their priesthood without a specific royal warrant. No convert or person who converted someone else was to benefit from the new system. Papists were not to be allowed to possess arms.[88]

Systems of registration had been suggested in 1674 and 1675; they had been attacked as involving a recognition of Popery and because the number of Papists thus revealed would frighten Protestants and encourage conversions to Catholicism.[89] In 1677 the reaction was similar. '[It] puts but twelve pence a Sunday difference betwixt the best Protestant and severest Papist,' complained William Sacheverell. He drew a horrifying picture of the Commons and all public offices filled with Papists or their deputies and deplored the suggestion that priests should not be executed. The House rejected the bill, observing coldly that its sense was very different from its title, which stated that it was a bill for the more effectual conviction of Popish recusants. The Commons brought in their own bill, which aimed to intensify the existing laws and to facilitate the conviction of priests. It still envisaged a procedure based on churchwardens' and constables'

---

[87] Courtin au Roi, 8 March 1677 NS, Baschet 135; Grey, iv, 284–96, 318–26.

[88] A. G. Petti (ed.), *Recusant Documents in the Ellesmere Manuscripts* CRS, lx, 1968), pp. 263–76; Grey, iv, 334–5; Bodl., Carte MS 130, fol. 18.

[89] Grey, ii, 358–63, iii, 15–18.

presentments in which those who were indicted at quarter sessions were to be asked to subscribe a declaration against transubstantiation. The revenue raised from recusants was to be used to augment the income of poor benefices.[90]

There can be little doubt that the bill sent down from the Lords would have increased the revenue from recusants or that this was its aim. Danby had learned from bitter experience that the existing procedures were too cumbersome to work. The bill also represents yet another attempt to use the oath of allegiance to distinguish between loyal and disloyal Papists. Danby encouraged William Lloyd, a leading writer against Popery, to publish a pamphlet which stressed that such a distinction could be made but which was rather vague about how this could be done in practice.[91] The bill tried to forestall most of the obvious objections. It clearly excluded Papists from office while making them liable for the expense of 'chargeable offices', like that of sheriff, to which they were to be liable but which they would be unable to hold. It discouraged conversion to Catholicism, forbade the education of children in foreign seminaries and so on. Yet the Commons rejected it contemptuously and suggested a stiffer but less workable bill on traditional lines. They may have felt that their bill provided a way of distinguishing between Catholic and Protestant recusants by means of the renunciation of transubstantiation, whereas the other bill did not. Apart from that their objections seem to have been based more on principle than on practicality. They were determined to do nothing that could seem like a recognition of or concession to Popery, or that could create a false sense of security with regard to the dangers from the Popish successor and the court. Like so much of the anti-Catholic tradition, the recusancy laws reflected a situation which had long since passed. Their preservation in their entirety seemed necessary primarily because of the political fears excited by James's Catholicism and was justified by the traditional assumption that every Papist constituted a danger to the Protestant state

---

[90] Grey, iv, 335–40; *HMC 9th Report, Appendix 2*, pp. 92–3.
[91] Courtin au Roi, 20 March 1677 NS, Baschet 135; G. P. Elliott (ed.), *Diary of Dr Edward Lake* (Camden Miscellany, i, 1847), pp. 17–18; Lloyd, *Considerations Touching the True Way to Suppress Popery* (1677); Hart, *William Lloyd*, pp. 23–4; Marvell, *Growth of Popery*, p. 67; Burnet, ii, 259.

and nation. Once again past experience fused with present fears and it was the Catholics who suffered. If Danby's bill had passed it is uncertain how many Catholics would have taken the oath of allegiance. Most of the Catholic peers had already taken it. Their suggestion of an alternative form was rejected.[92] Even if the bill had used the existing oath the government should have been able to mulct the recusants steadily and to keep a check on their numbers. This is presumably what Danby intended but the Commons were too afraid of Popery for the bill to be accepted.

<h3 style="text-align:center">THE EVE OF THE POPISH PLOT</h3>

Pressure mounted for a war with France, which Danby encouraged, hoping to be able to turn it to the court's advantage. In a memorandum of April 1677 he pointed out that once the king had an army he could use it against parliament if parliament failed to vote money for the war that it had advocated.[93] Charles was very reluctant to declare war, fearing that it might make his poor financial position worse and perhaps that Louis might make known the details of the Secret Treaty of Dover. He grumbled to Courtin that all the hostility to France had been excited by James's behaviour.[94] In December the court began to prepare for war. James, who hoped to command the army, came out strongly in favour of the war. He abandoned his unproductive flirtation with Dissent and returned to the position he had shared with Danby in 1673–4, that of firmly resisting any attacks on the authority of the monarchy. Late in January 1678 James told Barillon, the new French ambassador who was to remain in England until the Revolution, 'qu'il fallait rétablir l'autorité royale en Angleterre et se mettre dans un état d'agir indépendamment du caprice des gens malintentionnés et ennemis de la royauté'. Charles asked Barillon if Louis would help him to reassert his authority; Barillon replied that he would have to dismiss parliament which Charles said he could not do.[95] In March

---

[92] Courtin au Roi, 8 April 1677 NS, Baschet 135; CUL Add. MS 4878, fol. 642; above, pp. 32–3.

[93] Browning, *Danby*, ii, 68–9.

[94] Courtin au Roi, 12 July 1677 NS, Baschet 136; Mignet, iv, 510.

[95] Barillon au Roi, 10 Jan., 7 and 14 Feb. 1678 NS, Baschet 138; *CSPD 1678*, p. 91.

Barillon reported that James's ardour for war had not made people any more willing to trust him. It was suspected that the court hoped to use the army to establish a more authoritarian regime; those close to James believed that that was precisely his intention.[96]

Andrew Marvell's *An Account of the Growth of Popery and Arbitrary Government* was written late in 1677 and was circulating by February 1678.[97] It took the attack on Danby a stage further than Shaftesbury's pamphlet of 1675 had done. Shaftesbury had accused Danby, not unreasonably, of reviving and exploiting the division of the civil war. Marvell argued that this policy represented a continuation of the tendencies towards Popery and arbitrary government expressed in the breaking of the Triple Alliance and in the Declaration of Indulgence. In fact Danby's 'Cavalier' policy represented a reversal of the 'Catholic' policy of 1669–72 although it also had absolutist implications and, once again, an army was about to be raised. The only evidence that Marvell produced of 'Popish' tendencies in Danby's policies was the bill to remodel the recusancy laws and the fact that the bill to educate all members of the royal family as Protestants had not been passed.[98] He tried to cover up this logical weakness by referring to conspiracies of unnamed persons. The king was not attacked directly: he was merely misled by evil advisers. Nor was James: indeed he was complimented for his honesty and naval leadership. Even the bishops earned a few good words.[99] Marvell quietly ignored the fact that Danby was anti-French and anti-Popish. His authoritarian tendencies and his intolerance of Protestant Dissent were enough to cause concern among those suspicious of executive power and those who saw his Anglicanism as a revived Laudianism, only one step away from Popery. For such people the pamphlet provided a specious rationalisation of dangerous-looking, but in fact unconnected, developments in government policy in the last few years. It signalled the end of the political alliance of Dissenters and Catholics, which had never

[96] Barillon au Roi, 9, 21 and 26 March 1678 NS, Baschet 138.
[97] Margoliouth (ed.), *Poems and Letters of Andrew Marvell*, ii, 357; *CSPD 1677–8*, p. 659. All references are to the 1677 edition (Wing M 860).
[98] *Growth of Popery*, pp. 88, 100.
[99] *ibid.* pp. 15–16, 40, 47, 49, 88, 155.

been more than half-formed. In accusing Danby of Popery it exemplified the growing confusion of the terms 'Popery' and 'arbitrary government' which were soon to be almost interchangeable. This identification had its roots in the anti-Catholic tradition and was greatly strengthened by the example of Louis XIV's regime in France.[100] The allegation of a court conspiracy to impose Popery and absolutism was developed and embellished by the Exclusionist Whigs.

Marvell began with what was perhaps the most succinct and forceful statement of the Protestant case against Popery in the whole period: 'Popery is such a thing as cannot, but for want of a word to express it, be called a religion; nor is it to be mentioned with that civility which is otherwise decent to be used in speaking of the differences of human opinion about divine matters.' It combined all the most 'ridiculous and impious' features of Judaism, 'Turkery' and paganism 'incorporated with more peculiar absurdities of its own in which those were deficient; and all this deliberately carried on by the bold imposture of priests under the name of Christianity'. The priests used all kinds of tricks to maintain their control over the laity, who were compensated for their subjection by being discharged of 'all duty to God or man', all oaths and bonds. The pope's claims to a deposing power made Catholics' temporal obedience unreliable, as was shown by all the Popish treasons against Protestant England, including the Great Fire. There were the usual references to papal taxation and to abbey-lands.[101]

Having reminded his readers of the horrors of Popery, Marvell moved on to his main theme, the conspiracy to bring in Popery and arbitrary government. As Danby had had no real part in the government at the time of the breaking of the Triple Alliance, Marvell refused to name the conspirators, saying that the reader would know who they were. They were not honest open Papists, like those who had laid down their offices rather than take the test – York, Clifford, Bellasis, Sir Thomas Strickland.[102] When these had resigned 'there was never wanting some double-dyed son of our church, some Protestant in grain, to succeed upon the

---

[100] Grey, iii, 17; *Popery and Tyranny or the Present State of France* (1679), passim.

[101] *Growth of Popery*, pp. 5–14.

[102] *ibid.* pp. 14–16.

same conditions. And the difference was no more but that their offices, or however their counsels, were now to be administered by their deputies, such as they would confide in.' The conspirators were 'secure men that are above either honour or conscience, but obliged by all the most sacred ties of malice and ambition to advance the ruin of the king and kingdom . . . under the name of good Protestants'.[103] They were the forerunners, in fact, of the 'Protestant Papists' of the Exclusion Crisis and were the successors of the unprincipled courtiers who had been condemned in the Grand Remonstrance. Marvell tried to show the continuity of their conspiracy. He saw it as starting with the naval failures of the Second Dutch War (which he blamed on France), which were followed by the breaking of the Triple Alliance and by the alliance with Louis XIV, 'the master of absolute dominion, the presumptive monarch of Christendom, the declared champion of Popery and the hereditary, natural, inveterate enemy of our king and nation'.[104] While the Declaration of Indulgence was intended to encourage the spread of Popery, and to serve as a precedent for the suspension of all laws affecting property, England fought alongside France in a war the avowed aim of which was the advancement of Catholicism. The army raised for this war was commanded by Schomberg and Fitzgerald, a Frenchman and a Papist. The war was fought solely for the benefit of Louis XIV who in return was to help the conspirators to achieve their ends. Ten thousand of the king's subjects were trained for this purpose in the French army.[105] However, Louis was kept busy in the Low Countries and so, when parliament proved unco-operative, the conspirators raised the cry that church and king were in danger, 'Forty-one' was here again. 'Those that refused all the money they demanded were to be the only recusants and all that asserted the liberties of the nation were to be reckoned in the classis of Presbyterians.' Cavaliers and sycophants were to have a monopoly of offices. Danby's Test made the conspirators' absolutist intentions clear: the non-resisting oath would have enabled them to impose whatever they wished and they had thousands of troops ready in Scotland and France. The bench of judges was purged to facilitate the design and the independence

103 *ibid.* pp. 45,16.
104 *ibid.* pp. 16–19; see also Grey, iv, 128, 190–1, 202–3, 223.
105 *Growth of Popery*, pp. 33–5, 39–40, 45–6, 55.

of parliament was undermined by means of places and pensions.[106]

This was a convincing and far from inaccurate picture of Danby's actions and intentions. The logical weakness lay in the attempt to represent Danby's policy as the continuation of the equally disturbing but very different policies of 1669–72. It was an indication of the diversity of the anti-Catholic tradition that two lines of policy so dissimilar could both be explained in terms of Popery and arbitrary government. It would be over-cynical to see the depiction of Danby's intolerant Anglicanism as disguised Popery as being solely a polemical device, although it was certainly an effective smear. The anti-Catholic tradition encouraged men to rationalise political and religious phenomena that they disliked in terms of Popery, as with the Prynne theory of the origins of the Civil War and the Anglicans' claim that the Papists had encouraged the rise of Puritanism. Marvell's rationalisation repeated that of 1641, in that it added together signs of Catholicism at court, arbitrary tendencies in government and a persecuting Anglicanism and came up with allegations of a plot to bring in Popery and absolutism. Danby tried to revive the divisions of the civil war and it was natural that this should revive among his opponents some of the fears and arguments of the years preceding the civil war.[107] If the fears of the duke reflected memories of Mary's reign, the fears of Danby reflected memories of the era of Laud and Strafford. The fears of the two men, each expressed in anti-Catholic terms, reflected two separate aspects of the anti-Catholic tradition. Now Danby and York were in agreement on the need for war with France and fears of the two were becoming fused. Marvell claimed that affairs were moving towards a crisis and tried feebly to show Rome's complicity by referring to Howard's being made a cardinal.[108] Whatever the pamphlet's weaknesses it provided a trenchant analysis of some aspects of Danby's policy and no doubt expressed the thoughts and fears of many. When it appeared in February 1678 the crisis that Marvell had predicted seemed to be at hand.

Suspicions grew rapidly that the army raised for the war might be used to establish absolutism. Danby had in fact con-

---

[106] *ibid.* pp. 55–6, 60, 62–3, 66–7, 74–81.
[107] *POAS*, ii, 142–4, 186.
[108] *Growth of Popery*, p. 154.

sidered such a project in the previous year and James clearly saw the army as a possible means of strengthening the crown's position at home:

M. le duc d'York se croit perdu pour sa religion si l'occasion présente ne lui sert à soumettre l'Angleterre . . . [As for the king] son humeur répugne fort au dessein de changer le gouvernement. Il est néantmoins entraîné par M. le duc d'York et par le grand trésorier, mais dans le fonds il aimerait mieux que la paix le mît en état de demeurer en repos et rétablir ses affaires, c'est-à-dire un bon revenu, et je crois qu'il ne soucie pas beaucoup d'être plus absolu qu'il est.[109]

Fears and rumours of a military coup proliferated. A pamphlet called *A Seasonable Argument to Persuade all Grand Juries to Petition for a New Parliament*, which appeared in April, listed the alleged placemen and pensioners in the Commons as men who had sold their votes to help bring in Popery and absolutism. This had been mentioned in *The Growth of Popery*, but the new pamphlet referred to a standing army under 'the bigoted Popish duke', whom Marvell had exonerated from any part in the conspiracy.[110] As fears of the army grew, so did those of Catholicism. John Arnold told the Commons of the strength of Popery in Monmouthshire and of the protection it received from the marquis of Worcester. The House resolved to vote no more money until it was satisfied that more effective measures were being taken against Popery.[111] Danby's parliamentary following, never very co-ordinated, was becoming increasingly hard to control. Danby could not extract enough money to send the troops that had been raised over to Flanders to fight the French, so he had to agree to the king's accepting Louis's peace proposals. As there was now an army but no war to use it in, parliament hastily voted the money needed to disband it, but would grant nothing more.[112] Louis's tergiversations in the peace negotiations led the king to keep up the army. The money given to disband it was used for this so none was available for paying it off. Parliament became even more suspicious; it believed that the

[109] Barillon au Roi, 18 April 1678 NS, Baschet 139.
[110] Barillon au Roi, 28 April and 2 May 1678 NS, Baschet 139; Browning, *Historical Documents*, pp. 237–49.
[111] *CJ*, ix, 463, 466–71; Grey, v, 282; Bodl., Carte MS 130, fols. 19–20.
[112] Browning, *Danby*, i, 274–82; Grey, vi, 95–102.

court intended to keep the new forces permanently on foot and feared that the army contained some Catholics.[113]

The situation on the eve of the Popish Plot was thus extremely tense. There was an army of almost thirty thousand men which York and probably Danby hoped to use for a military coup. Suspicions of arbitrary government were greater than in 1673–1674. They had been increased by Danby's actions and by the raising of an army much larger than that raised for the predominantly naval war of 1672–4. Danby's policies had distracted attention from the existence of a Popish successor but they had themselves revived fears of arbitrary government analogous to those of the years before the Civil War. As in 1640–2 these fears were expressed in terms of the anti-Catholic tradition, of Popery and arbitrary government. In 1677–8 the fears of James revived. His penchant for toughness and authority in government was well-known. Fears of a Popish prince mingled with the fears of arbitrary government that had been excited by Danby as James and Danby came together again after their temporary estrangement in 1675–7. The tensions inherent in the situation were increased when circumstances forced Charles to keep on foot a substantial army, which was found later to contain some Catholics, and which he would probably have been willing to disband. James was still a Papist – the mayor of Chesterfield refused to drink his health, saying that he was a Popish dog[114] – and Charles was not getting any younger. Into this potentially explosive situation came Titus Oates.

[113] Browning, *Danby*, i, 282–3; Haley, *Shaftesbury*, pp. 449–51; Grey, vi, 40–2, 79–86; *CSPD 1678*, p. 260; Evelyn, 28 June 1678, *Diary*, iv, 136; Burnet, ii, 140; Barillon au Roi, 2 and 16 June 1678 NS, Baschet 139.
[114] *CSPD 1677–8*, p. 656.

8

THE POPISH PLOT AND THE EXCLUSION CRISIS (1678–81)

The Popish Plot, breaking on an already tense situation, finally brought into the open the issues raised by James's conversion. After the fall of Danby and the disbanding of the army, James's exclusion from the succession to the throne became the dominant political issue. The Plot tended to die a natural death and was resuscitated with increasing difficulty as time went on. The great wave of popular fear of 1678–9 had long since subsided when the crucial confrontation over the exclusion bill took place in November 1680. There was no violence after the Lords had rejected the bill. The spontaneous and immediate fear of Popery, from which the project had grown, had now cooled. It was terrifying to imagine that the Papists might cut one's throat tonight, but much less so to consider the possibility of this happening at some indeterminate time in the future.

The Whigs' tactics were basically very simple. They played on the fears of Popery and represented James's exclusion from the throne as the only sure safeguard against it. The king's tactics were more complex. First, he enforced the penal laws and investigated the plot in the hope of allaying the popular fears. Secondly, he refused to accept his brother's exclusion and instead offered various limitations on a Catholic successor which both the king and the Whigs believed would prove ineffectual.[1] Thirdly, Charles fought a skilful delaying action in order to prevent a trial of strength over the exclusion bill until he was sure that he would win it. The delay infuriated the Whigs, but it allowed the excitement generated by the Plot to cool and it gave Charles time to arrange for the subsidy from France that would enable him to survive financially without parliament. The Whigs' growing radicalism and demagogy drove the Tories to rally to the king, a trend encouraged by Tory propaganda and by the king's increasingly open favour to the Tories.

This chapter is concerned with four main aspects of the

[1] *CSPD 1680–1*, p. 47.

Catholic question in 1678–81. I shall say little of the Plot itself
or of the Plot trials as these have been well-covered by Professor
Kenyon's *The Popish Plot*. First, in a study of Oates's narrative
and the reaction to it, I shall try to show why it was believed
and why it provoked a nationwide panic in the winter of 1678–9.
Secondly, I shall discuss the court's reaction to the Plot. The
king and Council strove hard to have the penal laws enforced,
either because they believed in the Plot, or because they wanted
to calm popular anxieties or because they wished to avoid any
accusations of dilatoriness. However, these efforts did not always
lead to the laws being fully enforced at the local level. Thirdly,
there was the political exploitation of the Plot. In order to exclude
James from the throne the Whigs had to exploit anti-Catholicism
and the Plot ferociously and unscrupulously, but this helped to
arouse a reaction against the Whigs, which gathered strength as
belief in the Plot slowly declined. Finally, I shall consider popular
pressures and the London crowds in the Exclusion Crisis, with
particular reference to the great pope-burning ceremonies which
took place on 5 and 17 November each year.

OATES'S NARRATIVE AND THE REACTION TO IT

The story that Titus Oates told in 1678, which was printed in
April 1679,[2] was long and ingenious and included a mass of
circumstantial detail. It revamped and embellished earlier stories,
notably the Habernfeld Plot and the Prynne interpretation of
the Civil War, and transposed them into the present.[3] The
printed introduction briefly rehearsed the Prynne theory: the
Papists, especially the Jesuits, had contrived the Civil War and
Charles I's death and had tried to make Cromwell king; Milton

---

[2] There are three versions of the narrative, with slight verbal differences:
(1) *LJ*, xiii, 313–30; (2) *The Discovery of the Popish Plot* (Wing O 34);
(3) *A True Narrative of the Horrid Plot and Conspiracy* (Wing O 59),
reprinted in *State Trials*, vi, 1429–72. An introduction and a conclusion
were added to this version.

[3] See W. C. Abbott, 'The Origin of Titus Oates's Story', *EHR*, xxv
(1910), 126–9; Kenyon, *Popish Plot*, pp. 54–8; Grey, vii, 414. For
Habernfeld's Plot, see *The Grand Design of the Papists* (1678, Wing H
163) and *A True Narrative of the Popish Plot against King Charles I*
(1680, Wing H 164/T 2805).

had frequented a Popish club; Lambert, himself a Papist, had been helped by a priest to draw up the Instrument of Government. The new plot was structurally similar. Again Jesuits, disguised as Presbyterians, were to be sent to stir the Scots to revolt. There was to be a rebellion in Ireland, helped by French troops and Jesuit money. Ormond was to be assassinated. The Jesuits were collecting money for the great cause from their penitents in England, which harked back to the collection among the Catholics for the Scottish war in 1639.[4]

The design for England was twofold. First, the king was to be estranged from his subjects by means of accusations of plans to bring in Popery and absolutism, contemning of his person, betrayal of his counsels, seditious preaching in conventicles, setting up false titles to the succession(!), firing and plundering cities, debasing the coinage, etc. Other points included an account of Jesuits, in the guise of Fifth Monarchy Men, inciting persons to fire the city of London in 1665–6 and references to Coleman and one Smith sending intelligence to Fr la Chaise.[5] Secondly, there was to be a plot against the king's life. After his death twenty thousand Papists were to rise in London and cut the throats of a hundred thousand Protestants. The city was to be fired again.[6] The whole story was embellished with details which would strike a familiar chord in the minds of those well versed in the anti-Catholic tradition. Oates referred to the pope's special claim to England and Ireland, stated that Catholics believed that a heretical prince was *ipso facto* deposed and alleged that one of the conspirators would have had thirty thousand Masses said for him if he had killed the king.[7]

Oates's patron, Israel Tonge, was a religious maniac who eagerly accepted Oates's statement that the Jesuits wanted to kill him for translating an extremely dull Jansenist work called *The Jesuits' Morals*. Oates however was an adventurer with a story to sell. At first Danby and the king seemed the most likely customers. The story was designed for Anglicans and the court. James was exonerated from any complicity and on 30 October 1678 Oates testified positively that he did not believe that James

---

[4] *State Trials*, vi, 1430–1, 1442.
[5] *State Trials*, vi, 1447–9, 1451, 1472; *CSPD 1678*, pp. 426–8.
[6] *State Trials*, vi, 1452–3, 1455, 1457, 1463.
[7] *ibid.* vi, 1441, 1456, 1459, 1470.

was involved.[8] The references to Covenanters, conventicles and speaking against bishops showed a bias against Dissent. The reference to setting up false titles to the succession was hardly compatible with Exclusion. Barillon saw the Plot as a trick of Danby's which was intended to justify his keeping up the army.[9] Oates moved over to the opposition only when he had foolishly ruined his credit with the king by saying that the queen had been in the Plot.[10] Then, once a few irrelevant details had been pared off, he found that it could be used even more profitably against the court. It even mentioned that one of the alternative successors, William of Orange, was an intended victim of the Plot.[11]

Later stories built on the foundations laid by Oates, which became easier as successive narratives were printed. New witnesses added local knowledge and personal grudges, Bedloe from Monmouthshire, Dugdale from Staffordshire, Bolron from Yorkshire. There are signs of collusion between some of the witnesses and a persistent troublemaker and incorrigible liar called Hugh Speke.[12] Their stories contained details that would appeal to Protestant prejudices against barely understood aspects of Catholicism. Thus Oates claimed that the Jesuits requited the queen's promise of £4000 for the English province with '500 masses, 650 pair of beads, 1150 mortifications'; Bolron tried to curdle Protestants' blood with an oath to kill the king which he claimed a priest had given him.[13]

Oates's story was neither very original nor, on its own, very convincing. The king was openly sceptical. Secretary Coventry was impressed by Oates's coherence and assurance but was reluctant to trust the word of one man, who was perhaps not a Protestant even now, in such a weighty affair. By January, however, he was convinced of the truth of the Plot.[14] However, the

[8] *ibid.* vi, 1435, 1438, 1440–5, 1457, 1470–1; *LJ*, xiii, 309.
[9] Barillon au Roi, 10 and 13 Oct, 1678 NS, Baschet 141; Browning, *Danby*, i, 290–1.
[10] *CSPD 1678*, p. 539; Kenyon, *Popish Plot*, pp. 109–15.
[11] *State Trials*, vi, 1454, 1471; PC/2/67, pp. 3–4.
[12] *CSPD 1679–80*, pp. 214, 483; for Speke's activities under James II, see my forthcoming article, 'The Militia and the Army in the Reign of James II', *HJ*, vol. xvi (1973).
[13] *CSPD 1678*, p. 519; R. Bolron, *The Papists Bloody Oath of Secrecy* (1680).
[14] *HMC Ormond, New Series*, iv, 207, 303; Longleat, Coventry MSS lxxxvii, fol. 106, xc, fol. 34.

story, if confirmed, was just the sort to arouse an immediate response in Protestant minds. Its lack of originality was no disadvantage, for it told of the sort of Popish design which the anti-Catholic tradition had made all too familiar to English Protestants. Moreover, it did so at a time when political circumstances made them particularly receptive to such a story. As Sir Robert Southwell, the secretary to the Privy Council, later remarked, 'as for the Plot, . . . it was the preparation of some men's minds and not the witnesses that gave it entertainment'.[15] In the Plot trials, the principles which Catholics were supposed to hold were taken as presumptive evidence of the reality of the Plot, the guilt of the accused and the untrustworthiness of Catholic witnesses. As lord Arundell of Wardour, one of those accused by Oates, plaintively noted: 'Wicked principles are alleged to make good a plot, which being denied the Plot is introduced to make good the principles.'[16]

Oates's story seemed devastatingly and independently confirmed by the murder of Sir Edmund Berry Godfrey, the magistrate who had taken Oates's first deposition, and by Coleman's letters. Coleman's letters were undeniably genuine and were assumed to contain the blueprint for the Popish designs against England. References to the days of the 'pestilent Northern heresy' being numbered made the letters seem more sinister than they really were, but it was bad enough that the duke's secretary should be soliciting French and papal money to bribe the king and the House of Commons. Naturally Coleman's letters did nothing to diminish opposition suspicions of the court and they greatly strengthened Oates's credit.

When the Plot broke both Southwell and Evelyn assumed that the Papists had been encouraged by the indulgence recently allowed to them and Evelyn stressed that they had been very high since James had stopped attending the royal chapel.[17] Much

---

[15] S. W. Singer (ed.), *Clarendon Correspondence* (2 vols., London, 1828), i, 29; Burnet, ii, 191–2; C. E. Whiting (ed.), *Autobiographies and Letters of Thomas Comber* (2 vols., Surtees Soc., 1946–7), ii, 23; BM Add. MS, 38015, fol. 279.

[16] *State Trials*, vii, 133–5, 412–16, 479–85, 1300–1, etc.; Corker, p. 44; Arundell MSS, 'Titus Oates' Plot', lord Arundell's notes for his defence.

[17] Burnet, ii, 150–1; Evelyn, 1 Oct. 1678, *Diary*, iv, 154; *HMC Ormond*, N.S., iv, 462–3.

of the predisposition to believe in the Plot can be explained by a sense of the continuity of the past with the present. Southwell noted the importance of 'the celebration of the fifth of November, applying the present horror of things feared throughout the whole kingdom in one day to the evidence of what had formerly passed'.[18] Certain features of the present situation helped to intensify the excitement. A standing army was on foot, fears of Popery and arbitrary government were widespread and political excitement was at a high level, although it was no doubt somewhat diminished during the summer recess of parliament. Men were unlikely to think too hard whether their fears were of Popery and arbitrary government (excited by the behaviour of Danby and York and apparently confirmed by Coleman's letters), or of Popish treason and massacre (outlined in Oates's story and apparently confirmed by Godfrey's murder), or of the prospect of Popish cruelty and persecution under a possible Popish successor. All three aspects came within the anti-Catholic tradition and all became fused in a general fear of Popery.

In the winter of 1678–9 a great fear of Popery swept the country which was greater than that of 1666 and more like those of 1640–2. The fear was ambivalent, being of a standing army as well as of Popish plots. In November 1678 the Commons tried to persuade the king to allow parliament to raise the militia by a bill; whether the militia was to protect the nation against the Papists or against the army was not made clear.[19] In seventeenth century England communications were poor; there was no effective police force; the only possible peace-keeping forces were the army, deeply distrusted as an instrument of absolutism, and the militia, of which the king refused to surrender control. Although most men realised that open Papists were few, many believed that the vast majority of Papists passed as Protestants and would appear openly only when the time was right. In such a situation, with rumours of Papist risings and invasions in the air, it is not surprising that Protestants all over England should be filled with sudden fear at their vulnerable and unprotected condition. It is also not surprising that such panic should quickly die down when no invasion or massacre ensued and the flimsy forces of law and order were seen to be at work.

[18] *HMC Ormond*, N.S., iv, 471; BM Add. MS 38015, fol. 278.
[19] *HMC Kenyon*, pp. 105, 107–8; Grey, vi, 300–1.

Between October and December 1678 there were many rumours in the provinces of arms found in Papists' houses, of nocturnal gatherings of horsemen and of suspicious behaviour by Papists.[20] Many rumours must have had their source in over-heated imaginations which misinterpreted such innocent actions as the buying of extra supplies. Others were clearly provoked by mysterious anonymous letters.[21] At Yarmouth, when a ship was forced ashore by a storm, there were rumours that thirty or forty Jesuits had landed. On 9 December one Henry Layton wrote from Rawdon, Yorkshire, to secretary Williamson, that when the Plot had first broken 'the crack and noise filled us with great visions and the apparitions of armed men assembled and riding by night'. Strict watches were set and the militia was called out. Papists' houses were searched. Nothing was found, but some gentlemen wrote in the first flush of fear to their friends in London which increased the anxiety there. Layton himself had written to an M.P. that there was no cause for alarm and received the reply that 'the king's refusing to pass their bill for the militia increased their fears very much'. There were rumours that the Spaniards had landed in Ireland and Wales and the French in Scotland and that the great ships had been burned again at Chatham. Layton, who was obviously an embryo Tory, thought that the rumours had been spread by the Presbyterians as a preliminary to rebellion.[22] His letter shows the fears generated by the Plot in a remote area of the West Riding where only a dozen or so Catholic families lived. It illustrates how letters from the provinces could feed the excitement in London and how popular reactions were conditioned by the past. The Medway disaster was quite recent but the fears of Spanish invasion were positively Elizabethan.

By mid-December fears were on the wane. On 30 September lords lieutenant were ordered to have Papists' houses searched for arms and this was being done in the North within ten days. Little was found and, although this convinced some that the arms had been too well hidden or that the search had not been carried out properly, the fact that the houses had been searched must

[20] *CSPD 1678*, pp. 462, 480, 517–18, 521, 558, etc.; PC/2/66, pp. 442–3, 446–9.
[21] Bodl., Rawl. MS A 136, pp. 444, 536–41, 565–9; Longleat, Coventry MS xi, fols. 382–5, 416, 463.
[22] *CSPD 1678*, pp. 557–8, 562–3.

have removed much of the tension.[23] It tended to die anyway for fears could not be kept at a high pitch without repeated stimuli.

By Christmas 1678 the great fear had died down in the provinces. It lasted longer in London and it has, indeed, been argued that the Plot was primarily a metropolitan phenomenon.[24] London had by far the largest concentration of population in the country and it was far more natural to fear a numerous hidden enemy there than in the sparsely populated countryside. It was also the centre of political life and it had a special place assigned to it in the Plot: the city was to be fired and the Protestant inhabitants were to be put to the sword. When the Plot broke families armed to defend themselves and over two thousand men of the trained bands were on watch every night. In January 1679 many daggers were sold bearing Godfrey's name; ladies carried them for protection against the Papists. Chains were kept across the streets at night.[25] In January a great fire at the Temple was blamed on the Papists. James, who came to try to deal with it, left for fear of the crowds who called him a Popish dog.[26] After a lull while parliament was in session there were more fires, which were blamed on the Jesuits, and rumours of Papists waiting all over the city for James to bring an army from France to put all to fire and sword. Terriesi, the Florentine envoy, was amazed that there had not been a general massacre of Papists.[27] After May 1679 the fear of Papists seems to have diminished. Between March and July the nightly guard was gradually reduced from eight companies of the trained bands to two. In September there were complaints that many soldiers of the trained bands were failing to turn out for guard duty.[28] The tension was increased again only by political events connected with exclusion.

---

[22] PC/2/66, p. 409; *CSPD 1678*, p. 451; *HMC le Fleming*, p. 149; Longleat, Coventry MS xi, fols. 282, 289; Bodl., Rawl. MS A 136, pp. 549, 554–7.

[24] Kenyon, *Popish Plot*, p. 239.

[25] *HMC Ormond*, N.S., iv, 473; Barillon au Roi, 26 Jan. 1679 NS, Baschet 142; PC/2/67, p. 21; BM Add. MS 25358, fol. 132; J. T. Rutt (ed.), *Life of Edmund Calamy* (2 vols., London, 1829), i, 83–4.

[26] BM Add. MS 25358, fols. 138–9; for a similar incident in October 1679, see Wood, ii, 466–7.

[27] BM Add MS 25358, fols. 234, 252; *CSPD 1679–80*, pp. 135–6.

[28] D. Allen, 'The Role of the London trained bands in the Exclusion Crisis, 1678–81', *EHR*, lxxxvii (1972), 297; *CSPD 1679–80*, p. 253.

The plot was moribund; later excitement in London was not associated with Popery. In 1680 four drunken gentlemen harangued a crowd in Leicester Square about Popery and arbitrary government and urged the people to attack a nearby house; but one reason they gave was that it was a brothel and brothels were often the object of apprentices' riots. Most demonstrations were closely associated with the pressure for exclusion and often expressed joy rather than anger, as with those celebrating the duke of Monmouth's return to London in November 1679, which gave rise to much exuberance, drinking and rowdyism, with some insults to passing courtiers.[29] There was to be no recurrence of the panic of late 1678 and early 1679.

GOVERNMENT ACTION AGAINST THE CATHOLICS

The Plot placed the king and the court in a very unpleasant position. The fears that it aroused were ambivalent, being concerned with the religious and political leanings of the court as well as with Popish plotters. Charles therefore had to act vigorously in order to try to dispel the impression that the court was implicated in the plot or favourable to Popery, even though he clearly never believed more than a small part of allegations that others accepted in their entirety.[30] The Council investigated the Plot energetically. It was better that the Council should direct the investigations than that a Commons' committee should do so, with the risk that it might reveal something embarrassing to the court. It was also politically essential for some of those accused by Oates and his colleagues to be convicted of treason and executed, even though the king and many of his councillors and judges realised that the witnesses were an unsavoury bunch and some were so inept that the judges had to nurse them carefully through their trials in order that the 'king's evidence' should stand up.[31] Charles had, then, to enforce the laws against Catholics and to act as if the Plot was genuine in order to safeguard James's succession to the throne. He ignored James's warnings that if he disbanded the army his opponents would set up a re-

[29] BM Add. MSS 25359, fols. 308, 319–20, 25360, fol. 13; Haley, *Shaftesbury*, p. 558; *HMC 7th Report, Appendix*, p. 478.

[30] He does seem to have believed one or two of the witnesses, notably Dugdale; Bodl., Rawl. MS A 136, p. 106.

[31] See Kenyon, *Popish Plot*, chaps. 4–6, especially pp. 125–8.

public. He did ask Barillon once for money to keep up the army, but Barillon reminded him that it had been raised for use against France.[32]

Starting in November 1678 Charles issued a long series of proclamations and orders in Council which commanded that the laws against Papists should be enforced, that all Papists (except for householders and tradesmen) should depart from within ten miles of London and that English Papists should be prevented from attending the Catholic ambassadors' chapels. The five mile limit on Papists' movements, imposed by the act of 1593, was now enforced. The laws against priests were to be put into operation and rewards were offered for their capture.[33] These efforts to enforce the existing laws, together with the Whigs' increasing preoccupation with exclusion, helped to reduce the pressure for new legislation against Catholics. Charles did assent to the Second Test Act (1678) which excluded Catholics from either House of parliament. But the court managed to have James exempted from it and it was the only new piece of anti-Catholic legislation to reach the statute book. Other measures were proposed, however. In November 1678 speaker Seymour (who presumably had the approval of the court) suggested that the names of recusants should be registered; those who refused the oaths of allegiance and supremacy and the declaration from the Second Test Act against various aspects of Catholic belief should automatically be convicted of recusancy; the same went for those who attended Mass; those who failed to register were to lose four-fifths of their property. These suggestions were incorporated into a bill in April 1679.[34] Several bills were drafted to banish Papists from the neighbourhood of London; all were similar in content to the king's proclamations to that effect. Another bill was intended to exclude Papists from all trades connected with printing or weapons.[35] More remarkable was the

---

[32] Barillon au Roi, 17 Nov., 12 Dec. 1678, 9 Jan. 1679, 22 Aug. and 3 Oct. 1680 NS, Baschet 141, 142, 146.

[33] R. Steele, *Tudor and Stuart Proclamations* (2 vols., Bibliotheca Lindesiana, Oxford, 1910), i, nos. 3660, 3674, 3686, 3701, 3718–19; *CSPD 1678*, pp. 514–15, 533, 556–7; Blundell, *Cavalier*, pp. 186–9 (the letters quoted are from 1678/9, not 1678).

[34] *HMC Ormond*, N.S., iv, 478–9; *CJ*, ix, 544; *CSPD 1679–80*, pp. 114–115.

[35] *HMC House of Lords 1678–88*, pp. 70–1, 105–8, 130–2, 159–60.

Papists (Disarming and Removal) Bill of December 1680, which may have been based on a similar measure of 1642. Only temporary in operation, this bill listed the leading Papists of each county; those who refused the oaths were to be transported, at their own expense, to a town in another part of the country – from Yorkshire to Exeter, from Lancashire to Norwich and so on. The bill was lost with the prorogation. Like the Commons' resolution *nem. con.* that the best way to suppress Popery was to banish all considerable Papists, the disarming bill can be seen as an expression of frustration at the rejection of the exclusion bill, taken out on the English Catholics.[36]

The fright of the Plot and the pressure from the Council prodded the magistrates of the shires into enforcing the recusancy laws much more vigorously. In Wiltshire there was a sharp, short-lived rise in the number of convictions in 1678–9, but there were fewer convictions than in 1673. In Middlesex the number of convictions reached a peak of 1203 in 1679. In both counties the majority of those convicted were Papists. In Warwickshire the period 1678–81 saw almost the only convictions of the reign, apart from a few in 1673–4. Norfolk again proved the exception. The figures for 1678–9 were low; they included a high proportion of Papists, but by no means all the Papists that there were. The number of convictions began to rise sharply in 1680 and reached a peak in 1684.[37]

A parliamentary investigation of Papists in London late in 1680 led to 327 more convictions in Middlesex. All but nine of those convicted in 1680–1 and all but sixty of those convicted in 1678–9 came from the cities of London and Westminster and the western suburbs. This was the area where there were most Catholics, but also parliament and the Council were more sensitive to the presence of Papists there, close to parliament and the court, than in the outlying parts of the county. Even in this area, however, many Papists escaped conviction. In November 1680 Thomas Beaver, constable of Suffolk Street ward in the parish of St. Martin's in the Fields, made a census of his ward. He found 287 adults and thirteen 'families' of unspecified size. Of these twenty-nine individuals and one family were Papists and

---

[36] *ibid.* pp. 222–5; Clifton, thesis, p. 206; *CJ*, ix, 679.
[37] Williams, *Wilts.*, p. 272; Appendices 1 and 2; *Warwick County Records*, vii, pp. lxix–lxxxii.

eight persons were reputed Papists. Taking them together, eighteen persons and the 'family' (that of lord Dunbarton) were Scots, Irish or aliens and nineteen were English. Only six persons, three of them aliens, had been convicted of recusancy; this is remarkable, considering that the constable who here returned them as Papists was supposed to present them as recusants. It should be noted that this ward had an unusually high concentration of Catholics; a survey of the city of London showed only seventy-seven Papists out of 6,253 inhabitants in twenty wards.[38]

Besides trying to have more Papists convicted of recusancy, the Council struggled to overhaul and activate the machinery for raising money from them. Under an order of 5 March 1680 counties were grouped in 'receipts', each with a receiver-general and subordinate officials, whose function was to inquire into the value of recusants' lands, prior to commissions being issued to the sheriffs to seize the lands. The receiver-general was to manage the evidence for the crown in the inquiries and was to lease out the lands seized on behalf of the king. He could opt to levy the fine of £20 per month if the ownership of land was obscured by trusts and conveyances.[39] This initiative went some way towards reactivating the old machinery. Its effects were not apparent before 1681 and the overhauled machinery was used most in 1681–4, when the recusancy laws were being used as much against Dissenters as against Papists. Before 1681, however, the government was more concerned with Papists than with 'peaceable' Dissenters, and some Dissenters convicted of recusancy managed to have the proceedings against them stopped.[40]

The standard procedure for securing convictions for recusancy was slow and cumbersome, however, and the king and Council had recourse to simpler, quicker procedures. On 17 November 1678 the king issued a proclamation which ordered all constables and churchwardens to draw up lists of Papists and reputed Papists. The names from these lists were to be put into commissions, which were to be sent to J.P.s, to tender the oaths of allegiance and supremacy. Some commissions were issued

---

[38] Middlesex R. O., WR/RR(L)/2; *HMC House of Lords 1678–88*, pp. 169–71.

[39] PC/2/68, pp. 423–4; *CTB*, vi, 529–30, 552.

[40] Morrice MS P, pp. 263, 305; Granville, ii, 52n.; *CTB*, v, 1256–7; Barillon au Roi, 15 July 1680 NS, Baschet 146.

before the end of December; some were found to be defective and many more were issued in 1679 and 1680.[41] On 22 November 1678 the Commons, at the speaker's suggestion, ordered its members to bring in lists of suspected Papists in their counties; these were to be inserted in the bill for the easier conviction of Papists that was drawn up in April 1679. In December 1679 a committee of the Council was set up to consider how the enforcement of the laws against Papists could be improved. It recommended that the lists which had been brought into the Commons should be passed on to the lord chancellor, who was to put the names into new commissions to tender the oaths. In February 1680 the Council ordered that the lists be passed on to the assize judges who were to see that those named in them were presented and convicted as recusants.[42] A proclamation of 20 December 1678 ordered magistrates to disarm actual or reputed Papists and to require them to enter into recognisances for their good behaviour.[43]

The tendering of the oaths and the exaction of recognisances for good behaviour were two of the main weapons used by the Council against the Catholics. In the city of London the exaction of recognisances was almost the only procedure used. To make a Papist appear at each sessions to be bound over, on pain of losing his recognisance, served either as a rough check on his whereabouts or as a crude pecuniary mulct. Another procedure used in London was the prosecution of those who remained in or came into the London area without licence, in defiance of the king's proclamations.[44] In its efforts to have the oaths tendered to Papists and suspected Papists, however, the Council was often hampered by a lack of comprehension or co-operation at the local level. It ordered J.P.s to tender both the oath of allegiance and the oath of supremacy and to 'prosecute to a *praemunire*' those who refused them. It is clear, however, that many J.P.s felt that the penalties

---

[41] *CSPD 1678*, p. 527; Steele, i, no. 3663; Bodl., Rawl. MS A 136, pp. 132, 455, 459; *HMC Kenyon*, pp. 118, 120.

[42] *CJ*, ix, 544; PC/2/68, pp. 327–8, 406; *HMC Ormond*, N.S., iv, 478–479, v, 282–3; *HMC le Fleming*, p. 165.

[43] *CSPD 1678*, pp. 580–1.

[44] H. Bowler (ed.), *London Quarter Sessions Records 1605–1685* (CRS, xxxiv, 1934), passim (seventeen recognisances were forfeited in the city; the total value of the fifteen whose value was given was £2460); PC/2/69, p. 279.

involved in this procedure were too drastic and that its use was of dubious legality. The relevant statute, 3 & 4 Jac. I, cap. 4, imposed the penalties of *praemunire* only for refusal of the oath of allegiance. It did not mention the oath of supremacy, which the law imposed only on office-holders.[45] J.P.s in Monmouthshire and Yorkshire tendered only the oath of allegiance. In Warwickshire a commission to tender the oaths to a number of local Papists does not seem to have been acted upon. In Buckinghamshire, although many persons were presented for recusancy, the oath of allegiance was tendered to only fourteen suspected Papists. Thirteen of them took it; the fourteenth refused both the oaths and was imprisoned for a while. She was later released on bail, pending her appearance before the court of King's Bench.[46] Of 143 Herefordshire Papists named in a commission of 1680, thirty-eight took the oaths, thirty undertook to appear before King's Bench and fifty-three failed to appear. Little action was taken against any of them.[47]

The Council complained particularly of the failure to tender both the oaths in Lancashire. Of 1406 persons indicted as recusants, only 124 were bound to keep the peace; those who refused both the oaths were sent to prison, but those who took the oath of allegiance were bound over, often for several sessions. Those recusants who were bound over did not have their recognisances estreated if they defaulted. Roger Kenyon, the receiver of recusant revenues for the county, thought that this was because so many Protestants had stood as sureties for Catholics. Also the right to collect the money from these estreats had been farmed out to one Heywood; he paid only £25 10s 0d a year for the right, but the sum now due was, on paper, £60,000.[48] In March

---

[45] It is possible that the Council justified the tendering of the oath of supremacy by a rather stretched interpretation of 5 Eliz., cap. 1, which imposed the penalties of *praemunire* for maintaining a foreign jurisdiction; see Steele, i, no. 3705.

[46] PC/2/67, p. 58; Bodl., Rawl. MS A 136, pp. 163–4; *HMC Various Collections*, ii, 164; *Warwick County Records*, vii, p. lxxv; W. le Hardy (ed.), *Buckinghamshire Sessions Records*, i (Aylesbury, 1933), pp. 14, 25, 32 and passim.

[47] O'Keeffe, chap. 5, especially p. 159.

[48] Lancs. R. O., DDKe/7/8 (papers 2 and 3) and DDKe/7/28; *HMC Kenyon*, pp. 118–22; *CSPD 1680–1*, p. 56; *CTB*, vii, 563. 'Estreat' was used both as a verb, meaning to fine or mulct, and as a noun, meaning the paper instrument implementing or recording that fine.

1680 the Council sent a special commission to the Lancashire J.P.s to prosecute certain recusants to a *praemunire* if they refused both the oaths. None of the recusants appeared and nothing was done. At the October quarter sessions J.P.s at Lancaster, Preston and Wigan refused to sign the estreats which the judges had drawn up in July. Daniel Fleming, J.P., wrote that he would tender only the oath of allegiance and would bind over those who appeared and took it from one sessions to another. The J.P.s agreed with the counsel for the recusants that those who did not appear should forfeit their recognisances but that there should be no further proceedings against those who took the oath of allegiance until the king's pleasure was known. The Council answered that they should be prosecuted to a *praemunire*, but it is far from certain that they were.[49]

The Council's huffing and puffing was not wholly ineffectual. A number of Catholics were imprisoned for refusing the oaths and were not released for some years. On the whole, however, it is clear that, despite the fears aroused by the Plot, the laws were not enforced to the full. The Council itself was not always severe. As early as January 1679 it examined with considerable courtesy some Staffordshire gentlemen mentioned by the informer Dugdale as being privy to the Plot. They were released, and at least two were not even asked for bail, although they had all openly admitted that they harboured priests, which by law was a capital offence.[50] Nevertheless the laws were enforced far more rigorously than they had been hitherto, particularly those against the priesthood. No priests had been executed between 1660 and 1678 but eighteen, including an Irish archbishop, were executed between 1678 and 1681, and others died in prison. The mission was considerably disrupted; by 1680 the Catholics of Worcester had not seen a priest for over a year. Its finances were weakened by confiscations of property devoted to 'superstitious uses'. The Catholic laity suffered far less, except for the few accused by Oates and his imitators. Many Catholic peers and gentlemen thought it wise to go abroad for a while and the Plot must have imposed a considerable psychological strain on those who re-

---

[49] *HMC Kenyon*, pp. 120–2; *HMC le Fleming*, pp. 171–2; Lancs. R. O., DDKe/7/5.
[50] Bodl., Rawl. MS A 136, pp. 126–30, 139, 158, 165.

mained.[51] During the Exclusion Crisis Charles allowed the investigation of the Plot and insisted that the penal laws should be enforced to the full in order to remove the stigma of Popery from the court. Out of political necessity, he sacrificed the English Catholics in order to safeguard the succession of his Catholic brother.

THE POLITICAL EXPLOITATION OF THE PLOT

There were two main phases in the political exploitation of the Plot. The first involved the removal of Danby and the army and so of the fears that they aroused; the second involved James's exclusion from the throne. The Whigs' use of anti-Catholicism was brutally simple. They harped on the dangers of Popery and arbitrary government (which became interchangeable terms), uncritically asserted the reality of the Plot, insisted that exclusion was the only practicable solution to the problem of a Popish successor and branded everyone who disagreed with them as a Papist or a favourer of Popery.

If the Whigs' use of anti-Catholicism was unedifying, they relied on it so much because it was the only real weapon they had. Basically their position was not very strong; it was far weaker than that of the opposition leaders in 1640–2. There were now no distractions from Scotland or Ireland; the Scots revolt of 1679 was quickly crushed. Charles II kept control of the city of London and, in particular, of the lieutenancy and the trained bands, the main means of maintaining order in the city.[52] The Whigs controlled the Commons but not the Lords. The peers were always more attentive to the king's wishes than the Commons were, and they showed irritation at the Commons' hysteria and extremism as early as December 1678.[53] The Whigs' efforts were concentrated on parliament but it was the king who decided when it should meet and for how long. The Whigs therefore tried to mobilise support outside parliament in order to put pressure

---

[51] R. Challoner, *Memoirs of Missionary Priests 1577–1684*, ed. J.H. Pollen (London, 1924), pp. 519–82; Zimmerman, p. 333; Kenyon, *Popish Plot*, chap. 7.

[52] Allen, *EHR*, lxxxvii, passim; 'A Seasonable Address to Both Houses', (1681), *Somers Tracts*, viii, 235.

[53] Kenyon, *Popish Plot*, pp. 129, 131.

on the king (and, through him, on the Lords) to a point where he would surrender and accept exclusion. At the heart of the Whigs' strategy was the assumption that Charles would back down if enough pressure were put on him. It was not an unreasonable assumption. Charles had withdrawn his declaration in favour of toleration of 1662 and the Declaration of Indulgence of 1672; he had made peace with the Dutch in 1674 and had declared war on France in 1678. Many of those closest to the king – including that most astute of politicians, the earl of Sunderland – believed that Charles would eventually surrender.[54] But he did not, and the radicalism of the Whigs' tactics drove a substantial, conservative part of the political nation to rally blindly to him. The Whigs' appeal to the people raised a spectre of civil war, but in fact their popular support was mobilised from above and was concentrated on the single issue of exclusion; careful organisation created an exaggerated impression of spontaneous mass pressure. Except for a few tense days in August 1679, when Charles was dangerously ill, the threat of civil war and of social upheaval was far more spectral than real.[55] However, the spectre of 1641 scared the Tories so that they thought that an uncritical acquiescence in the consolidation of royal authority was the lesser of two evils, especially as it gave them the chance to pay off scores accumulated during the Exclusion Crisis. When the king refused to bow to their pressure, civil war was the Whigs' only hope, but they were not prepared to go that far.

The Whigs were in no sense a united party; they were an agglomeration of groups and individuals held shakily together by the single common aim of exclusion.[56] They were deeply divided on questions as basic as that of an alternative successor. Their arguments, too, were often contradictory. Their case against James rested on an appeal to reason, to positive necessity. The unprecedented situation of the heir to a Protestant crown turning Papist required an unprecedented remedy: that followed logically from Protestant assumptions about the probable be-

---

[54] J. R. Jones, *The First Whigs* (Oxford, 1961), pp. 59–60, 130–3; J. P. Kenyon, *Robert Spencer Earl of Sunderland* (London, 1958), pp. 51ff.; Haley, *Shaftesbury*, pp. 599–600; Ailesbury, i, 38; BM Add. MS 25361, fols. 11–12.

[55] Jones, *First Whigs*, pp. 86–7, 115–18, 167–72, 212–15.

[56] *ibid.* chap. 1.

haviour of a Popish king. But parliamentary convention and the Common Law tradition, which the great majority of seventeenth century Englishmen accepted, decreed that the case should be argued in terms of law and precedent. They therefore tried to show that parliament could alter the succession and had often done so in the past, using precedents that were often bogus or irrelevant. At the same time they tried to hammer home the need for exclusion by a mixture of rational argument and crude anti-Catholic scaremongering. The tensions and the contradictions in Whig ideas were, in fact, analogous to those faced by parliamentarians in 1640–2, who had also had to wrestle mentally with an unprecedented situation.[57] Anti-Catholicism and the emotions aroused by the Plot were the only means that the Whigs had of covering up the divisions in their ranks and the contradictions in their ideas. As it became harder to cover them up and the situation reached a crisis, the stridency of the Whigs' anti-Catholicism increased, for it was becoming apparent that it was not going to work. The stridency further deepened the gulf between Whigs and Tories.

When parliament met in October 1678 it began to investigate the Plot, but soon showed concern about Popery at court and in the army. On 12 November Henry Powle urged that the oaths should be tendered to suspected Papists at Whitehall: 'By this means,' he said, 'you will in a great measure take off the aspersion of this being a state plot'.[58] The Commons was horrified to hear of some Popish officers in the army and sent secretary Williamson to the Tower for signing their commissions. One M.P. talked of 'tolerating Popery in an army of 22,000 men'. Another thought that 'It is a Popish army and officers that put the king's life in danger, though the magistrates be Protestants.' A third talked of putting castles in the pope's hands. Lord Cavendish said that the Popish plotters had been encouraged by the existence of a Popish successor and of a standing army.[59] Fears of the Papists, the court and the army were clearly intermingled.

*   *   *

[57] See B. Behrens, 'The Whig Theory of the Constitution in the Reign of Charles II', *Cambridge Historical Journal*, vii (1941), 42–71; J. H. Hexter, *The Reign of King Pym* (Cambridge, Mass., 1941), pp. 175–84.

[58] Grey, vi, 190; Josselin, pp. 175–7.

[59] Grey, vi, 166–9, 174, 216–25, 230–6; *CJ*, ix, 542; Miller, *EHR*, lxxxviii, 44.

When Charles refused to call out the militia, some M.P.s accused those who had advised him to refuse of doing the Jesuits' work for them. William Williams, who was to become speaker in 1680, grumbled ominously that 'This bill was for the safety of the kingdom, and to tell us of prerogative when the kingdom is in danger.' On 16 December a bill to raise money to pay off the army passed the Commons, but it was lost with the prorogation.[60]

In inveighing against the Popish army the Commons implicitly attacked Danby. His position was fairly secure until on 19 December Ralph Montagu, a man devoid of political principle even by normal Restoration standards, produced some letters which he had received while he was ambassador in Paris. He had told Barillon over two months earlier that he might produce them. Montagu's prize exhibit was a letter from Danby which suggested making peace with France in return for a subsidy. The Commons were furious and Danby was impeached. The fact that the letter had been written at the king's command was brushed aside by the solicitor-general, Sir Francis Winnington, with the remark that it could not be so as Charles had, in parliament, declared his intention to be the opposite. (Winnington lost his place in 1679.) Charles's acknowledgment of the letter must have reinforced the suspicions of the king and his brother created by Coleman's correspondence.[61] The crux of the charges against Danby was that he had raised an army, on pretence of making war against France, in order to introduce arbitrary government. He was accused of concealing the Plot and of being 'Popishly affected'. Popery and arbitrary power were now regarded as virtually the same thing. 'Lay Popery flat,' said Sir Henry Capel in April 1679, 'and there's an end of arbitrary government and power; it is a mere chimera or notion without Popery'.[62] Distrust of the court was increased still further by the fact that the army still had not been disbanded by the time a new parliament met in March 1679. M.P.s noted that Coleman's scheme had included the raising of an army with French money; one described the army as a 'limb of Popery, set up by this great

[60] *CJ*, ix, 541, 558; Grey, vi, 303, 306, 307.
[61] Barillon au Roi, 24 Oct. 1678 NS, Baschet 141; Grey, vi, 383; Burnet, ii, 175–6; Reresby, pp. 162–3; Kenyon, *Popish Plot*, p. 87.
[62] Grey, vi, 383–7, vii, 149, viii, 100; *CJ*, ix, 561–2; Browning, *Danby*, ii, 74–5.

minister [Danby] who is not yet quite out of the way'. Another thought that 'if we had had no army, we should have had no Plot'.[63] In fact most of the forces raised in 1678 were disbanded in the summer of 1679, after the dissolution of parliament.

Until the spring of 1679 the Commons' fears were not only of the Papists but also of the court, in particular of Danby and the army. Once both of these were out of the way, the Whigs turned to the future and to exclusion. The court tried hard to keep James's name out of Coleman's trial but two of his letters were published illegally, with a statement that they had been written with James's approval.[64] In the Commons on 4 November 1678 lord Russell suggested that James be removed from the king's counsels; lord Cavendish claimed that his being heir-apparent had encouraged the plotters; William Sacheverell hinted broadly at exclusion. The debate was adjourned without a vote being taken. On 21 November the court just managed to muster a majority in the Commons in favour of a proviso exempting James from the Second Test Act. Sir Thomas Lee's attack on the proviso anticipated later Whig arguments; the danger came, he said, 'not so much from the Papists, as the Protestants that act the part of Popery to do their own work. Those that support the interest of the Papists, however they call themselves Protestants, do more to support Papists than Papists themselves.'[65]

The idea of outward Protestants doing the Papists' work in setting up Popery and arbitrary government was not new. Marvell had used it in *The Growth of Popery*; so had Sacheverell and Sir Thomas Meres, as early as 1 November 1678.[66] For the Whigs to accuse all those who stood in their way of Popery was an obvious and effective tactic; its use was made inevitable by the terms in which the debate was conducted. Almost all M.P.s believed to some extent in the Plot and in the dangers from Popery. Court speakers had to argue that the prosecution of the Plot and the suppression of Popery did not necessarily require that James be excluded from the Lords or from the crown. Such arguments were often unconvincing. The Tories were afraid that

[63] *CSPD 1679–80*, p. 21; *Grey*, vi, 265–6, vii, 5, 8, 64, 68, 159–61.
[64] Kenyon, *Popish Plot*, pp. 118, 123–4.
[65] *Grey*, vi, 133–49, 240–53. (Quotation from p. 250.)
[66] *Grey*, vi, 129.

exclusion involved a major attack on the prerogative, the legitimate succession and the traditional constitutional order. But to urge moderation or compromise left them wide open to charges, direct or indirect, of favouring Popery. Three Tory M.P.s were expelled in 1679–80 for impugning the reality of the Plot; an old Royalist pamphleteer, Sir John Birkenhead, was called a favourer of Popery for daring to mention 'forty-one'. The Whigs reduced the issue to one of Protestantism or Popery; if they did not override all laws now (which they denied they were doing) a future Popish successor would do so: 'The Protestant religion is so intermixed with the civil interests of the nation that it is not possible to preserve them if a Popish successor comes.'[67] The Whigs had a majority in the Commons and the advantage of a debating position that was extreme but, in the terms in which it was argued, logical. Tories said little against them in parliament, therefore, but in their pamphlets and their loyal addresses they raised their cries of rebellion and 'forty-one' and waited for revenge. There was a Cavalier tradition as well as an anti-Catholic one.

On 9 November 1678 Charles made it clear that he would allow no permanent alteration in the succession and no permanent diminution of his prerogative. On the 22nd speaker Seymour proposed certain limitations on a Popish successor and draconian measures against the Papists, but stressed that there could be no alteration in the line of succession. The witnesses soon began to hint and then to assert that James was involved in the Plot. By March 1679 Dugdale and Needham were accusing him openly.[68] On 27 April the Commons resolved that James's being a Papist and the hope of his coming to the throne had given the greatest encouragement to the Papists' designs. The chamberlain of the city of London, Sir Thomas Player, said openly that James had been the main agent in setting up Popery and arbitrary government. Despite Charles's insistence that he would accept limitations but not exclusion, an exclusion bill was read on 15 May, but it was lost with the dissolution.[69]

On 27 May parliament was prorogued and later dissolved.

---

[67] Grey, vi, 309, vii, 55, viii, 272; *CJ*, ix, 642–3.
[68] Grey, vi, 172; *HMC Ormond*, N.S., iv, 478–9; *CSPD 1678*, p. 550; *HMC Fitzherbert*, pp. 137, 145–6.
[69] Grey, vii, 137–51, especially pp. 141–2.

The new one did not meet until October 1680. In the interim both sides gathered their resources for the struggle which was to come. Charles unsettled and frustrated the Whigs by successive prorogations and delays. The Whigs responded with a campaign of petitions that parliament should meet, which were answered by Tory 'abhorrences' that the Whigs should try to dictate to the king on what was a matter of his prerogative. Charles also gave orders so often for the laws against Catholics to be enforced that Barillon, for one, grew cynical: 'c'est une chose ordinaire quand les séances des parlements approchent'.[70] He also began to discriminate against Whigs and Dissenters and to favour Tories in local government and in public offices. In December 1679 he ordered the lord mayor of London to ensure that all common councilmen had qualified under the Corporation Act; similar orders were later sent to other towns.[71] Officers and soldiers of the militia were to be made to take the oaths and sacrament and a few Tories were added to the commissions of the peace. The judges were told to discountenance petitioning and the government tried to regain control of the press, which they had lost with the lapsing of the Licensing Act. Oates and Bedloe had their pensions cut and Henry Care was convicted of publishing a scandalous pamphlet.[72] As 'abhorrers' rallied to the king and the number of Tory pamphlets grew, the Treasury commissioners assured the king that he could survive financially without parliament.[73]

The Whigs, meanwhile, could not do all that much. Those on the Council had little real power, those outside concentrated on electioneering, petitioning and propaganda. They were greatly helped by the clumsy efforts of Elizabeth Cellier, the Popish midwife, and her little Catholic coterie to blame the Plot on to the Presbyterians. The conviction for treason of viscount Stafford also revived the Plot's credit for a while. But on the whole the flood of Whig and anti-Catholic pamphlets and broadsides could

---

[70] Barillon au Roi, 3 Oct. 1680 NS, Baschet 146. See also the same, 28 Dec. 1679, 1 and 4 Jan. 1680 NS, Baschet 143-4; BM Add. MS 25359, fol. 234.

[71] *CSPD 1679–80*, pp. 312–13, 433–4, 438, 467, 479–80, etc.

[72] *ibid.* pp. 393, 437, 536; N. Luttrell, *A Brief Historical Relation of State Affairs 1678–1714* (6 vols., Oxford, 1857), i, 37; BM Add. MS 25359, fol. 343.

[73] Barillon au Roi, 15 April 1680 NS, Baschet 145.

not entirely offset the increasing mediocrity of the new witnesses and a slow waning of the belief that the Papists still constituted an immediate threat to the English Protestant nation. Between the acquittal of Sir George Wakeman in July 1679 and Stafford's trial in December 1680, nobody was convicted in London of complicity in the Plot; although a number of priests were convicted for their priesthood after June 1679, none of them were executed.[74] The dying speeches of those executed in 1678–9, which denied all knowledge of the Plot, must have shaken the belief of many, despite a stream of allegations that Papists could get dispensations from the pope to lie even on the point of death.[75] Some, such as the king, Richard Legh and the marquis of Worcester had doubted the truth of the Plot from the start. Others doubted part of it: Evelyn thought that Godfrey had been murdered by the Papists but did not believe the accusations against the queen and Wakeman. He and Sir John Reresby both had serious doubts by the time of Stafford's trial, although Evelyn was still uncertain.[76] As Burnet remarked, 'there are seasons of believing as well as of disbelieving; and believing was then [late 1678] so much in season that improbabilities or inconsistencies were little considered'. By the end of 1680 more men were beginning to disbelieve.[77]

The aim of Whig propaganda was to keep the Plot in the public eye in order to maintain people's belief in it, to keep up hatred of Popery and Papists and to try to channel and direct the energies thus aroused towards the universal remedy of exclusion. The growth of Tory feeling and Tory political activity in 1680–1 reflected a growing belief, first, that the Plot, while it had existed, was now under control and, secondly, that under cover of the

[74] Kenyon, *Popish Plot*, pp. 167, 195; see also Kenyon, 'The Acquittal of Sir George Wakeman, 18 July 1679', *HJ*, xiv (1971), 693–708.

[75] Burnet, ii, 220; Warner, pp. 270–1; Kenyon, *Popish Plot*, pp. 180–3; BM Add. MS 29910, fol. 114; *State Trials*, vii, 482, 543–70, 580–2, 679; E. Tonge, *The New Design of the Papists Detected* (1679); J. Williams, *An Impartial Consideration of those Speeches* (1679); *The Mistery of Inquiry Unfolded* (1679); *Lying Allowable with Papists* (1680), etc.

[76] Reresby, pp. 153–4, 203, 206–9; Burnet, ii, 168; Newton, *House of Lyme*, p. 289; *HMC Beaufort*, pp. 71–2; Evelyn, 21 Oct., 24 Nov. 1678, 18 July 1679, 6–7 Dec. 1680, *Diary*, iv, 155, 158, 174–5, 230–4.

[77] Burnet, ii, 186; Arundell MSS, 'Letters to and from Sir John Arundell', Sir Thomas Chicheley to Arundell, 5 Jan. 1680 (1?), 2 Jan. 1681 (2?).

Plot the Whigs were mounting an attack on the most basic principles of the monarchy and the ancient constitution which raised uncomfortable echoes of the situation on the eve of the Civil War.

There were some Catholic pamphlets which attacked the details of the informers' evidence and pointed out the general implausibility of the Plot, but these were usually not widely distributed and the fact that they were written by Catholics would make Protestants less receptive to their arguments.[78] By far the most important figure to cast doubt, in print, on the reality of the Plot was the most influential pamphleteer of the period, Roger L'Estrange. In the summer of 1679 he published a factual account of the trials, which gave ample prominence to those inconsistencies in Oates's evidence which the accused had pointed out, but did not comment on them. This led to accusations that he himself was a Papist.[79] He defended himself in a series of pamphlets in 1680, in which he expressed an increasingly ironical deference to the unimpeachable credit of Titus Oates.[80] He seized especially on Oates's reference in his *Narrative* to the fanatics and Dissenters being manipulated by the Papists. If this were true (and Oates said that it was) then surely the fanatics were just as dangerous as the Papists.[81] L'Estrange himself did not think that it was true, however. Whatever Oates and Prynne might have said, the Papists had been loyal in the Civil War and the fanatics had not. Now there was far more to fear from the Presbyterians than from the Papists. He still did not deny that there had been a Popish Plot but he argued that it was now

---

[78] T. A., *Remarks on the Trial of Mr Ireland, Mr Pickering and Mr Grove* (1679, not in Wing); F. P., 'A Letter to Both Houses of Parliament' (1679), *Somers Tracts*, viii, 109–15; 'A New Narrative of the Popish Plot' (1680), *Somers Tracts*, viii, 61–6; J. Corker, 'Roman Catholick Principles' (1680), *Somers Tracts*, ix, 59–63; *The Earl of Castlemaine's Manifesto* (1681). Perhaps the most widely distributed was Castlemaine's *Compendium* (1679).

[79] L'Estrange, *History of the Plot* (1679), esp. pp. 6, 21, 32–40, 54–6, 84–5, 88; H. Care, *History of the Damnable Popish Plot* (2nd edn, 1681), preface, sigs. A3–A4; *Strange's Case Strangely Altered* (1680), etc.

[80] *L'Estrange's Narrative of the Plot* (1680), p. 8; *A Further Discovery of the Plot* (1680) (Wing L 1252), p. 14; *Discovery upon Discovery* (1680), pp. 10–11, 18–19.

[81] *L'Estrange's Narrative*, pp. 4–9, 29–30; *A Further Discovery*, pp. 12–13, 25–32.

under control and distinguished between sworn evidence in a court of law and the rumours, often untrue, which had proliferated and which had been accepted equally readily as true.[82] He complained that the Whigs and fanatics had built upon the original Plot a crazy structure of rumours and inventions, which brought in 'reputed Papists' (or good Churchmen) as well as real Papists. Their aim was to use the fears that these lies and rumours aroused among the 'rabble' in a bid to overthrow the monarchy and the established government:

The Popish Plot has bounds and limits; the king's witnesses tell us what it is and where it lies, and we have had nothing new of that Plot now a good while. But this imaginary plot is a plot upon a perpetual plot and to keep the nation so long in awe of the Popish Plot till the faction may execute another plot of their own.[83]

He claimed that the Whigs were not really concerned about Popery at all:

A legal and effectual provision against the danger of Romish practices and errors will never serve their turn, whose quarrel is barely to the name of Popery without understanding the thing itself. And if there were not a Roman Catholic left in the three kingdoms they would be never the better satisfied, for where they cannot find Popery they will make it, nay, and be troubled too that they could not find it. It is no new thing for a popular outcry in the matter of religion to have a state faction in the belly of it. The first late clamour was against downright Popery and then came on Popishly affected (that sweeps all). The order of bishops and the discipline of the church took their turns next; and the next blow was at the crown itself; when every man was made a Papist that would not play the knave and the fool, for company, with the common people.[84]

Thus L'Estrange moved from insinuations about the inconsistencies of Oates's evidence to the formulation of the cliché that was to become a Tory orthodoxy: that there was now a Presbyterian plot against crown and church, just as there had been in

---

[82] *An Answer to the Appeal from the Country to the City* (1679), pp. 10–11, 14–23; *Discovery upon Discovery*, pp. 9, 23–7; *L'Estrange's Narrative*, pp. 13–15; see also Glanvill, *Zealous and Impartial Protestant*, p. 59.

[83] *L'Estrange's Narrative*, pp. 25–6.

[84] *History of the Plot*, preface; reprinted verbatim in *A Further Discovery*, p. 8.

1641. Unlike L'Estrange, most Tory writers simply regurgitated this cliché; they lacked L'Estrange's courage and did not expose themselves to vilification and possible physical danger by publicly undermining the credit of Oates and his Plot. Besides the common cry that 'forty-one is here again', some Tory writers claimed that the fanatics were doing the Papists' work for them.[85] Others stressed James's personal qualities and the practical difficulties in the way of exclusion: James would still be king of Scotland; he would have the support of all the Catholic Irish and he might well receive help from Catholic princes abroad. Some of the more perceptive stressed that it would be impossible for a Catholic king to introduce Popery, since the Papists were too few to be of any weight; a Catholic king would be able to do nothing without an army and he would not be able to raise one unless a parliament provided the money to pay it. Some writers argued that a king's religion was irrelevant: it was 'now out of fashion for kings to be priests and prophets', wrote one; 'kings are not nowadays priest-ridden', wrote another.[86] All assumed that a Catholic king would be bound by conscience, religion and the law to keep faith with his subjects. The risks involved in a Popish succession – if it ever happened – were far less than those inevitably involved in exclusion.[87] Such arguments appealed to the conservative, the cautious and the old Cavaliers who did remember 1641; they were given extra strength by the fact that Charles made his opposition to exclusion quite clear.

Whig pamphlets tried to show first that parliament had the power to exclude James from the throne,[88] and secondly that it was essential to do so. Like the Tories, the Whigs claimed that the ancient consitution was in danger, but they saw the danger

[85] *Some Observations upon the Tickling Querie* (1681), p. 3; J. Nalson, *A Letter from a Jesuit at Paris* (1679), passim; Nalson, *Foxes and Firebrands* (1680), pp. 25–33.

[86] M. R., *Three Great Questions Concerning the Succession* (1680), p. 16; 'England's Concern in the Case of His R. H.', *Somers Tracts*, viii, 175; see also Glanvill, *Zealous and Impartial Protestant*, pp. 46–50; 'A Seasonable Address to Both Houses', *Somers Tracts*, viii, 233–6.

[87] L'Estrange, *A Reply to the Second Part of the Character of a Popish Successor* (1681), pp. 9, 21, 29; L'Estrange, *Answer to the Appeal*, pp. 24–5.

[88] *A Brief History of the Succession* (1681); J. Phillips, *The Character of a Popish Successor ... Part the Second* (1681), pp. 2–17.

as coming from James and the Popish and despotic court, not from Whig radicalism. The necessity for exclusion was demonstrated by reference to beliefs about Catholicism that were inherent in the anti-Catholic tradition, illustrated by the Plot and by parades of horrors. The basic premise was that Catholics in general, and Catholic princes in particular, were bound to strive to extirpate heresy; a Popish ruler of a Protestant nation would be under constant pressure from his confessor and from the pope to establish Popery; the breaking of oaths and laws would count for nothing in such a meritorious cause. In other words, a Catholic king was a slave to the pope.[89] He would, if he could, overthrow all laws, rule by means of an army and fill all places with Papists or with men of no religion who would turn Papist. Popery was thus inseparable from absolutism. Limitations on a Popish king would last only until he had the power to break through them, which would not be long. Mary's promises at the start of her reign were often cited as evidence of the duplicity of Popish princes.[90]

The Plot was used to show the hopes that the Papists had of James, Coleman's letters were cited to show his complicity. All the unpleasant features of the court's policies in the last decade were blamed on to him. All this was backed up by lurid accounts of the horrors to be expected under a Popish king – arbitrary rule and bloody persecution.[91] Much of the literature wobbled uncertainly between legalism and scaremongering:

'Tis a maxim among lawyers that *Lex facit Regem* and maxims must not be denied; if so, then to speak out after the true intendment of law, he that comes not to the crown *satiatim*, as the laws [sic]

[89] E. Settle, 'The Character of a Popish Successor' (1681), *State Tracts*, i, 149–57; *The Narrative of John Smith* (1681), pp. 1–4; D. Clarkson, 'The Case of Protestants in England under a Popish Prince' (1681), *Somers Tracts*, viii, 158–61; Grey, vii, 404–5, 451, viii, 264, 278–9.

[90] Settle, *State Tracts*, i, 149–57; C. Blount, 'An Appeal from the Country to the City', *State Tracts*, i, 401–2; 'An Account of Queen Mary's Methods' (1681), *Somers Tracts*, vii, 324–7; *Memoirs of Queen Mary's Days* (1679), pp. 1–3.

[91] Settle, *State Tracts*, i, 153; Blount, *State Tracts*, i, 401–2; *Memoirs of Queen Mary's Days*, p. 3; *The Instrument or Writing of Association* (1679), pp. 3, 5–6; D. Y., *A Most Serious Expostulation with Several of My Fellow Citizens* (1680), pp. 2–3; Clarkson, *Somers Tracts*, viii, 151–3; 'A Letter to a Person of Honour', (1680), *Somers Tracts*, viii, 204–7; Grey, vii, 406.

notifies and prescribes, 'tis no lawful succession, but downright usurpation. And without scruple, 'tis the endeavour of every good Christian to withstand an usurper, it being undoubtedly more pleasing to God to put one man by, who thus wilfully disables himself, and withal most shamefully usurps, than expose millions of souls to damnation and the streets to flow with blood by suffering that religion to creep in, whose reformation (at the mildest rate) will certainly prove fire and faggot.[92]

Such arguments were, of course, based on garbled and exaggerated misrepresentations of Catholic beliefs. But they convinced the majority of the Commons and of the electorate of the need for exclusion. They show the strength of the anti-Catholic tradition and the identification of Popery with absolutism. One should remember that the Whigs' fears of what would happen when James became king proved correct, if greatly exaggerated. At a time when it was out of fashion for kings to be priests and prophets, James was determinedly unfashionable. If the Whigs' pictures of Catholicism and the papacy were highly inaccurate, their assessment of James's political and religious proclivities was far more accurate, as many Tories were to realise by 1688. Nevertheless the Tories deserve some credit for their refusal to condemn James untried.

The final meetings of parliament and the propaganda that followed the Lords' rejection of the exclusion bill showed merely an intensification of existing themes. Frustrated of their only aim, Whig M.P.s thundered in near-hysteria at the judges, the Lords and the marquis of Halifax, all of whom were accused of favouring Popery. One M.P. talked of 'Protestant Papists', another said that 'Popery in a great measure is set up for arbitrary power's sake; they are not so forward for religion.' Winnington advocated a Protestant association on the lines of that of 1585. The House voted to impeach a High Tory parson for reflecting on the Plot in a sermon and accused lord chief justice Scroggs of bringing in Popery and arbitrary government.[93] As it was dissolved the Commons passed a resolution that the Papists had fired London in 1666. The pattern was repeated in the Oxford Parliament. After that was dissolved the hysterical extremism of Whig pamphlets increased further, but this reflected

[92] 'Pereat Papa' (1681?), *Somers Tracts*, viii, 165.
[93] Grey, viii, 157–8, 166, 219, 237.

a growing sense of impotence and often verged on the absurd; it was alleged in 1681 that Tories as well as Papists had started the Great Fire.[94] Without parliament there could be no exclusion and no effective Whig party. The Whig pamphlets of 1681–2 were full of sound and fury and signified very little.

POPULAR PRESSURES AND POPE-BURNINGS

One further aspect of the Catholic question in the Exclusion Crisis remains to be discussed: the use of anti-Catholicism to stir up the 'mob' and the influence of the 'mob' on politics. Tories like Roger North stressed its importance and referred to elaborate organisation and to 'mob-masters'. But the Whigs' use of mass pressure and of mass petitions, although it greatly annoyed the Tories, was not the same thing as mob pressure or mob rule, in the sense that they had existed in 1641. On the contrary the pressure was basically peaceful and legal. There were election riots – that was nothing unusual – and bonfires and drinking to celebrate popular political events. But there was little or no violence against Catholics and no mobs attacked Whitehall and Westminster, although neither was strongly defended.[95]

One reason for this must be that in the period of greatest tension in London, between October 1678 and May 1679, king and parliament seemed in harmony, prosecuting the Plot and putting down Popery, despite the tension over the army. The breach over the first exclusion bill came in May. Then members of the Green Ribbon Club drew their swords to prevent the porters of the Temple, who had been sent by the benchers, from putting out a fire that they had lit to celebrate the first reading of the exclusion bill. But no riot ensued. In June papers were scattered in the London streets which urged the apprentices to go to the king, ask him why the Popish lords had not been executed and press him to call a parliament. Again there was no riot. In May 1680, after an alleged assault on John Arnold, Catholics' houses were marked with a cross, as if for a massacre. None occurred.[96] As exclusion replaced the Plot and the fear of

---

[94] Grey, viii, 289–90; *CSPD 1680–1*, p. 435.
[95] North, *Examen*, pp. 570–1; Warner, p. 416.
[96] *HMC Ormond*, N.S., iv, 514; *HMC 7th Report, Appendix*, p. 472; *CSPD 1679–80*, p. 177; Warner, pp. 437–8.

the army at the centre of politics, spontaneous fears and tensions declined; exclusion was simply not such an intense emotional issue.

Most of the emphasis on mob pressure in the Exclusion Crisis has been made by Tory propagandists and historians. Professor Jones has exploded the myth that the Whig Green Ribbon Club was an all-powerful manipulator of mobs and riots; its importance in this field extended only to financing or helping to finance, the two great 17 November pope-burnings in 1679 and 1680, which North regarded as contrived by the club.[97] But pope-burnings were not new in the Exclusion Crisis; those financed by the club were the biggest but not necessarily the only ones there were; and their direct political importance was probably small.

The practice of burning the pope in effigy seems to have revived in 1673. Before that the custom had been merely to light bonfires and fireworks on 5 November.[98] In 1673 the fifth of November fell at a time of great tension over the prorogation of parliament, the duke's marriage and the French alliance. This excitement was manifested in anti-Catholic sermons and great numbers of bonfires and fireworks. Apparently spontaneously children and apprentices made effigies of popes and carried them in procession. A larger pope, still small enough to be carried on a pole, was burned in the Poultry; it was also shot, as was an effigy of a Frenchman. About a thousand people were present; having filled themselves with liquor 'every man and boy went to his own home and so the play ended'.[99]

The last phrase is a telling one. Pope-burnings were not necessarily political demonstrations. They became bigger and better as the Catholic question came to dominate politics and as more money was spent on them. They were a response to anti-Catholic tensions, but they were also reaffirmations and celebrations of the Protestant past and they were fun. 'Persons of quality went to see it as they did my lord mayor's show,' noted one writer in

[97] J. R. Jones, 'The Green Ribbon Club', *Durham University Journal*, xviii (1956), 17–20; North, *Examen*, pp. 571–4.

[98] Pepys, 5 Nov. 1660 and 1661, *Diary*, i, 283, ii, 208; *CSPVen 1666–8*, p. 321.

[99] *Letters to Williamson*, ii, 67, 71; Evelyn, 5 Nov. 1673, *Diary*, iv, 26; *CSPVen 1673–5*, p. 174; BM Add. MS 25122, fol. 165; *The Burning of the Whore of Babylon* (1673); Newton, *House of Lyme*, pp. 259–60.

1679.[100] The crowds which went were quite different from the one which had tried to frighten Charles I into sacrificing Strafford. The cult of queen Elizabeth had probably grown up in her own time partly as a spontaneous compensation for the loss of the old Catholic ceremonies and processions.[101] A more overtly political element was injected into the ceremonies of 1679–81; they were obviously intended to be offensive to James and to pander to, and show the strength of, anti-Catholic feeling. But for all that they remained a national festival, a pageant, a ritual, an entertainment. Ale and wine flowed freely. In 1679 a room at Temple Bar to watch the show cost £10: it was, after all, a remarkable spectacle. And as Southwell noted with surprise and relief, after all the squibs and confusions everybody went home to bed.[102] If the pope-burnings were, in rather a diffuse way, massive expressions of popular feeling, they had little or no coercive influence on a government that was determined to ignore them.

Many popes were burnt in 1673, including one worth £50 at Southwark on 26 November, the day the new duchess of York arrived. (This is a very rare instance of a pope-burning that did not take place on 5 or 17 November.) I have come across no reference to any pope-burnings in 1674–5, but on 17 November 1676 and 1677 a larger pope, with devils whispering in his ear, carried in a chair by several persons, was burned at Temple Bar, now the normal venue. Persons of quality provided drink for the common people. A pope was burnt at the Monument on 5 November 1677. On 5 November 1678 several expensive popes were burned, the best being at Temple Bar. Though there were no references to the Plot on that occasion, in one place Coleman and Langhorne were also burned in effigy.[103]

On 5 November 1679 Exclusionist politics intruded into the ceremony. Sir Robert Peyton, unpopular because of his alleged overtures to James, was burned in effigy along with the pope.

100 Verney, iv, 259–60.
101 Strong, *Journal of the Warburg and Courtauld Institutes*, xxi, 88, 91 and passim.
102 *HMC 7th Report, Appendix*, p. 477; *HMC Ormond*, N.S., iv, 561.
103 *CSPD 1673–5*, pp. 40, 44; *The Pope Burnt to Ashes* (1676), pp. 2–4; *Hatton Correspondence*, i, 157; *CSPD 1677–8*, p. 446; *HMC Ormond* N.S., iv, 472; *The Manner of the Burning the Pope in Effigies* (1678); Wood, ii, 422.

But the 5th was now a much less solemn and important occasion than the 17th, which implied a deep criticism of the court as falling far short of Elizabethan perfection.[104] The pageant of 17 November was the first to be financed in part by the Green Ribbon Club. It was said to have cost £2500; ten members of the club were said to have paid £10 each but others thought that the Templers had paid for it. (The club met at the King's Head tavern, by Temple Bar.) A great statue of Elizabeth was decked out with Magna Carta and the Protestant religion and the pope was made to bow before it. He now had a string of followers – cardinals, friars, Jesuits and so on. Two hundred porters were hired at two shillings a man to carry lights. The Plot was represented by Godfrey and one of his murderers and by Peyton. It was said that there were two hundred thousand people there. Terriesi was shocked and amazed: he had never seen anything like it. Fireworks flew in all directions. After the pope had been burned, Godfrey's effigy was carried to Somerset House, where he was believed to have been murdered.[105] On 5 November 1680 there were many popes burned,[106] but the big occasion was 17 November, which fell only two days after the Lords rejected the exclusion bill. The king sent to the lord mayor to stop the pope-burning; the mayor said he could not stop it but he could guarantee that there would be no disorders. The guard of the trained bands was doubled, from 400 to 800 men. The pageant was again huge; it included Mrs Cellier, Jeffreys (the recorder of London) and various abhorrers and 'Protestants in masquerade'. There was no direct mention of exclusion or of James, and although the queen's Catholic ladies trembled behind the bolted doors of Somerset House in fearful anticipation, there was no violence. The Whigs were not prepared for it.[107]

[104] *Hatton Correspondence*, i, 201; BM Add. MS 25359, fol. 184.
[105] *Hatton Correspondence*, i, 203; Warner, pp. 186–7; *HMC 7th Report, Appendix*, p. 477; BM Add. MS 25359, fols. 193–4; *London's Defiance to Rome* (1679); Verney, iv, 259–60.
[106] BM Add. MS 25361, fol. 46; Newton, *House of Lyme*, p. 296.
[107] Verney, iv, 259–60; BM Add. MS 25361, fol. 81; Barillon au Roi, 28 Nov. and 2 Dec. 1680, Baschet 147; Allen, *EHR*, lxxxvii, 301; Arundell MSS, 'Letters to and from John Arundell', Lady Anne Arundell to Sir John, 18 Nov. (1680) (in blue folder); *The Solemn Mock Procession or the Trial and Execution of the Pope* (1680), pp. 1–4.

There seem to have been few pope-burnings outside London. There was one at St Edmund Hall, Oxford on 5 November 1678. Students in Edinburgh were prevented by troops from completely burning a pope on Christmas Day 1679; they were no more successful a year later, when they felt the heavy hand of James's government. Other popes were burned at Salisbury and Taunton and at Abergavenny, in the heart of Catholic Monmouthsire. This last was a scaled-down version of the London processions and included such delights as a four-foot midget with a blunderbuss as master of ceremonies and 'two lusty sow-gelders with very large and shrill flagellets'. It aimed specifically to point out and intimidate local Catholics, but it was not altogether popular, as it interfered with the fair.[108]

On 5 November 1681 the boys of Westminster school burned an effigy of Jack Presbyter, a sign of changing times. On the 17th there was another large pope-burning, this time at Smithfield. In 1682 bonfires were allowed on 5 November but some rowdiness developed and the pope-burning planned for the 17th was prevented. The trained bands were called out and some half-made 'monsters' were found near Bishopsgate. Bonfires and squibs were banned as well after a riotous assault on the Dutch ambassador on 5 November 1683; an attempt to burn a pope in 1684 was frustrated by the lord mayor.[109] Bonfires were prohibited in 1685, 1686 and 1687, although no objections were raised to Oates's being burned in effigy on the king's birthday. In 1685 shops were shut on 5 November and there were sermons in the churches. There were some bonfires and many fireworks; many people put candles in their windows and displays of candles were arranged on barrels.[110] In 1686 there were more bonfires, including a large one at Southwark; there were also far more candles,

---

[108] Wood, ii, 422; *HMC Dartmouth*, i, 42–3; *The Scots' Demonstration of their Abhorrence of Popery* (1680); Luttrell, i, 61–2; *CSPD 1680–1*, p. 150; S. Williams, 'The Pope-burning Processions of 1679, 1680 and 1681', *Journal of the Warburg and Courtauld Institutes*, xxi (1958), 117; *The Pope's Downfall at Abergavenny* (1679), pp. 3–4.

[109] Luttrell, i, 142, 144, 287; *HMC 10th Report, Appendix 4*, p. 174; *The Procession or the Burning of the Pope in Effigie* (1681); North, *Examen*, pp. 579–81; *CSPD 1682*, p. 545; PC/2/69, p. 566; PC/2/70, p. 60; Morrice MS P, pp. 343–5; BM Add. MS 25369, fol. 91.

[110] BM Add. MS 25371, fol. 78; Luttrell, i, 359, 362; *CSPD 1685*, no. 1860; Morrice MS P, pp. 483, 490, 492, 633.

including a large display on the Monument and on the conduits; there were displays in the shape of a triple crown 'and other reflecting figures'. There were several popes burned in London and elsewhere. The lord mayor and aldermen and the J.P.s of Middlesex and Westminster were severely rebuked for allowing this to happen and the keeper of the Monument was dismissed.[111] In 1687 the authorities took greater precautions and there were only a few fireworks and some displays of candles. The shops were still shut on 5 November, the church bells were rung and there were sermons in the churches. In 1688 popes were burned to celebrate the acquittal of the Seven Bishops.[112]

The great pope-burnings, spectacular as they were, represented only the intensification of a traditional practice; their immediate political impact was small. By definition they took place on only two days a year. Even in 1679–81, though they aroused a general anti-Catholic feeling, they could not be described as instruments of mob pressure. They grew in size because of the increased fear of Popery and, most important, simply because much more money was spent on them. Those who spent it hoped that they might have some political effect. The government feared that such large concourses of people could be dangerous. In fact for their size the pope-burnings were remarkably innocuous, and a small force of the city-trained bands proved quite sufficient to maintain order while they were going on. The real battles were fought elsewhere, in elections, in wars of pamphlets and petitions and above all in parliament. The mob was not very important in the Exclusion Crisis, but this fact has been obscured by the vast crowds at the pope-burnings and by Tory propaganda; the Tories, concerned to draw a parallel with 1641, represented the largely non-violent mobilisation of popular support as mob rule.

The mob's lack of importance can be explained by several factors. Charles II kept a far tighter control of the machinery of government and of law and order than Charles I had done in 1640–2 or James II did in 1688. He was helped by the consistent co-operation of the city of London lieutenancy and trained bands. There was not the same alienation of king and nation in

---

[111] Morrice MSS P, pp. 654–5, 658, Q, p. 33; BM Add. MSS 25373, fols. 46–7, 29561, fol. 546, 29910, fol. 203.
[112] BM Add. MSS 25375, fols. 30–1, 25376, fols. 176–7, 209; Morrice MS Q, pp. 193–4, 205; Luttrell, i, 419; Campana, ii, 235.

1678–81 as there had been in 1640–2 or as there was to be in 1688. Charles kept the support of a substantial section of the political nation and was able to exploit the Tory backlash for all it was worth. The Plot and the eventual confrontation over exclusion, though causally linked, were separated in time; the emotional excitement generated by the first had waned by the time of the second. There were not the recurring crises, the standing armies (after the summer of 1679) or the fears of Irish Papists that there were in 1640–2 and 1688. The threat from Popery and arbitrary government seemed immediate in 1640–2 and 1688; in 1679–81 it was only a possible threat, somewhere in the future. This lower level of intensity and of immediacy made the battles of the Exclusion Crisis more superficial than they might appear at first sight. Both Whigs and Tories, for different reasons, exaggerated the extent of popular involvement in the campaign to exclude James. There was on the Whig side neither the depth of feeling nor the preparedness necessary for civil war.

9

THE TORY REACTION (1681-5)

After the Oxford Parliament the Catholic question gradually dropped out of politics until it re-emerged late in 1684. Whig propaganda concentrated less on anti-Catholicism than on abusing the Tories. There were incidents of violence which were expressions of anger and frustration. In November 1681 the queen's lacemaker lit a small bonfire to celebrate her birthday; a crowd put it out, saying that it was a Popish fire, and smashed his windows. Several violent affrays, mostly against Tories, followed the *ignoramus* verdict in Shaftesbury's case. Huguenots in Norwich were attacked, apparently because they were thought to be Papists.[1] But the government soon got the upper hand, banning pope-burnings and even bonfires in London. Charles at last undertook an Anglican, authoritarian policy of the kind Danby had advocated. He appealed to 'gentlemen who go on the Church of England and the old Cavalier principles, which. . . . are the only principles that are safe for the government and comfortable to the conscience'.[2] This policy was very successful. The Exclusion Crisis had reopened divisions in the political nation similar to those left by the Civil War, which had been slurred over by fears of James and the court and by the Popish Plot. The Tories had rallied to the king; now they were to have their reward, in the form of a monopoly of places and the persecution of Dissenters and Whigs. Meanwhile, to prevent mistrust, no open favour was to be shown to Catholics.

In the spring of 1681 the hesitant Tory measures of early 1680 were renewed with greater vigour. In December 1680 Charles had repeated his order of the previous year than London common councilmen should be qualified under the Corporation Act. In March 1681 a purge of the commissions of the peace began and in November the court was careful to appoint reliable sheriffs.[3] In his declaration of 8 April, after he had dissolved the

---

[1] *CSPD 1680-1*, pp. 571, 583-4, 588-9, *July-Sept. 1683*, p. 363.
[2] *CSPD 1680-1*, p. 376.
[3] *ibid.* pp. 104, 175, 182, 204, 209, etc.; Barillon au Roi, 24 Nov. 1681, NS, Baschet 150.

Oxford Parliament, Charles compared the excesses of that parliament to those which had preceded the Civil War, stressed that monarchy, religion and property would stand or fall together and appealed to his subjects' loyalty. He ordered that the declaration be read in every parish church. By April informers were coming forward to discredit the Whigs; grand juries presented conventiclers and asked that the laws against Papists and Dissenters should be enforced; one described Dissenters as disguised Jesuits.[4] In June the king ordered that conventicles and seditious meetings should be suppressed and the Council decreed that London alehouse-keepers were to lose their licences if they did not take the Anglican sacrament. The Council also tried to ensure that the laws against Catholics were enforced, especially in London.[5] Meanwhile the Treasury Commission brought the royal finances to something approaching solvency by means of economies and more efficient collection.

The last vestiges of the Plot were disposed of. In July 1681 the Council repeated an earlier order that no priest was to be executed except at the king's positive command. This did not save Oliver Plunkett, archbishop of Armagh, who was executed for treason on 1 July, mainly because the government wanted to use his trial to establish the credit of the worthless Irish witnesses whom it planned to use against Shaftesbury and the Whigs. More typical was the case of the seven condemned priests who were transported to the Scilly Isles, despite the opposition of the London sheriffs. The pensions of the Plot witnesses were stopped, Oates's in September 1681, Bolron's and Mowbray's in December 1682 and those of most of the minor informers in March 1683. The only exceptions were the two priests, John Sergeant and David Morris, whose pensions were paid until the end of the reign. The extent to which the times had changed was shown in March 1683, when a man who gave information of a Jesuit plot was whipped and sent to the house of correction, in order to discourage such rogues in the future.[6]

[4] *His Majesty's Declaration to All His Loving Subjects* (1681); *CSPD 1680–1*, pp. 232, 250–1, 301, 360, *1682*, p. 534.

[5] PC/2/69, pp. 279, 294, 365, 386, 395, 408, 425, 497, 563; *CSPD, 1680–1*, pp. 549–50, 630, *1682*, p. 59; Barillon au Roi, 11 Dec. 1681 NS, Baschet 150.

[6] PC/2/69, pp. 319, 415, 446; Jones, *First Whigs*, pp. 187–8; Akerman, pp. 35, 39, 59, 67–9, 98; *CSPD Jan.–June 1683*, pp. 111–13, 116.

In its efforts to enforce the laws against all types of religious nonconformity, the government tried once again to make the recusancy laws work. However, in Yorkshire, Warwickshire and many other counties the number of convictions for recusancy declined rapidly after 1681. In Wiltshire there was a sudden up-surge of convictions in 1683 (150, as against 124 in 1678); the majority of those convicted were Dissenters. In Middlesex there were 191 convictions in 1683. Only six per cent of those convicted can be identified as Papists, as against seventy per cent in 1679 and fifty-eight per cent in 1681. Sixty-six per cent of the convictions now took place outside the cities of London and Westminster and the western suburbs, as against five per cent in 1678–9. It seems clear that the recusancy laws were now being used mainly against Dissenters and the persecution of Dissenters seems to have intensified after the Rye House Plot. There were also many more convictions for attending conventicles; there survive nearly 750 certificates of conviction for 1682–3 and 111 for 1684 from Middlesex alone. Each contains a number of names. The only other convictions in the county in Charles II's reign were forty-eight in 1664–5, after the first Conventicle Act, five in 1670, after the second Conventicle act and ten in 1674–5, during Danby's drive against nonconformity. In Norfolk, too, the recusancy laws were used primarily against Dissenters. The number of convictions rose each year, from 213 in 1680 to 666 in 1684. The proportion of definite Catholics fell from between forty and sixty per cent in 1676–9 to only six and a half per cent in 1684. On the other hand the number of Quakers convicted increased from fifty-nine in 1680 to 166 in 1684. The number of convictions fell off rapidly in 1684–5 in Middlesex and Wiltshire and a year later in Norfolk.[7]

Once the recusants had been convicted, however, there remained the problem of levying the fines prescribed by the law. In July 1682 it was clear that less money from recusancy fines was coming into the Exchequer than the government would have liked. There was a suggestion that it might be more sensible to levy at discretion a sum of less than £20 per month, which would bring in more money and would allow the recusants to be

[7] Aveling, *Northern Catholics*, pp. 332–4; *Warwick County Records*, vii, pp. lxxxiii–cii; Williams, *Wilts.*, p. 272; Appendices 1 and 2; Middlesex R. O., MR/RC/1–6.

mulcted steadily rather than ruined. Although large sums had
been collected, the problem was to ensure that the receivers and
sheriffs paid into the Exchequer the money that they had collected: 'The king has not had a full fifth part of what it has cost
the recusants.'[8] There were many cases of individual hardship.
Sir John Southcote forfeited two-thirds of his lands but the
sheriff also demanded £80 per month in fines, which he was
quite unable to pay. However, he was lucky enough to be able
to state his case to the attorney-general, who wrote him out a
quietus on the spot. Two of the Giffards of Blackladies, in a
similar situation, were less lucky and remained in gaol. Some
needy Cavaliers had their fines remitted in recognition of their
loyalty in the Civil War. In Yorkshire only sixty-one gentlemen
had had any lands seized by 1685 and only one (Sir Philip Constable) had had lands seized which were worth more than
£30 a year (£120 a year in his case). Nevertheless the revenue from recusants had risen steadily, from a total of £668
1s 7½d in the years 1675–8, to £5,089 3s 1d in 1678–81 and
£18,241 11s 7½d in 1681–4. Even in 1684–8 the total raised
was £5, 038 9s 7d.[9]

A rough statistical estimate of the financial burden on recusants
can be made for Lancashire from three documents in the papers
of Roger Kenyon. Two are accounts of sums levied in two of the
four law terms (Easter and Michaelmas) in 1682 and the other
is an estimate of the annual value of recusants' estates in three of
the county's six hundreds and part of a fourth.[10] The annual value
of the estates totalled £18,962 10s 0d. The sums levied in the
two terms totalled £768 0s 2d and £707 11s 2d. From this the
annual value of recusants' estates for the whole county can be
estimated as, very approximately, £30,000. If similar sums were
levied in the other two terms, the total levied in a year would be
approximately £3000, or about ten per cent of the income of the
Lancashire Catholic community. It is very possible, however,

[8] *CTB*, vii, 334, 532, 580.
[9] *CTB*, vii, 752, 989, 1019, 1081; Morris, i, 405–7; *CSPD July–Sept.*
1683, p. 324; Aveling, *Northern Catholics*, pp. 326–7; Chandaman, pp.
704, 706. (Each date refers to Michaelmas of that year.)
[10] Lancs. R. O., DDKe/7/19–21. The three hundreds were West Derby,
Lonsdale and Amounderness, the first two of which had substantial
Catholic populations.

that nothing was levied in the other two terms, in which case the proportion would be only five per cent, which was much less than the two-thirds demanded by the law, but was still a noticeable amount.

The burden fell on rich and poor alike. Of 217 estates whose value is given, sixty-six were worth less than £10 a year (average about £5), 125 were worth between £10 and £99 a year (average £28) and twenty-six were worth £100 a year or more (average £583). Lord Molyneux, with £3500 a year, paid £60 and £100 in the two terms, as did Richard Sherburne (£3000 a year). Sir William Gerard (£1000 a year) paid £20 and £20, Robert Dalton (£600) paid £20 and £30 and Henry Blundell of Ince Blundell (£200) paid nothing and £5. With the exception of Blundell, all these sums represent between four and eight and one-third per cent of the recusant's income; if they made other payments in the other terms the proportion would be higher. Poor Catholics fared similarly. Margery Tickle of Altcar, with an income of £20 a year, paid £3 10s 0d and nothing; John Aynsworth of Little Crosby (£2 10s 0d a year) paid fifteen shillings and nothing; Ellen Worrall and Thomas Rothwell, also of Little Crosby (£2 and £3 a year), each paid ten shillings.[11] These fines must have represented a substantial, even vital, part of the incomes of these poor recusants. Richer Catholics had more to spare and had the money and legal knowledge to make conveyances that would conceal the ownership of their lands. The poorest Catholics probably suffered most.

In the summer of 1684 the government tried once more to reorganise the machinery. Sheriffs were to be allowed one shilling in the pound commission on moneys levied on (significantly) 'Dissenters'. In July the local receivers were abolished and their functions were taken over by one Edward Ange, who became manager of recusant revenues, and who was to try to make the receivers pay to the Exchequer the money they had collected. The persecution of Dissenters by predominantly Tory magistracies continued vigorously. When other procedures failed, conventiclers were accused of rioting. In 1684 dragoons were almost used against Dissenters in Shropshire and elsewhere and many Dissenters were made to give recognisances as Papists

---

[11] All of these were probably Catholics, see above, pp. 13, 62.

had been in 1679. This persecution had not abated by the end of the reign.[12]

In May 1684 came the first signs of changes in government policy. James was restored to the Privy Council and to his old office of lord admiral. He began an action of *scandalum magnatum* against Titus Oates. Several priests were released from prison and in July the duchess of York's mother, the duchess of Modena, hinted to the Brussels internuncio that James thought that conditions were now favourable for the appointment of a vicar apostolic for England. A new oath of allegiance was drawn up and approved by Rome; it was planned to tender it to Catholics when they were released from prison.[13]

In the autumn the first moves were made in a more authoritarian and pro-Catholic policy. James and Sunderland told Barillon that the judges had found many Catholics in prison and that the king wanted to free them, if he could do so without attracting opposition. Jeffreys raised the matter in the cabinet council and stressed the Catholics' loyalty in the Civil War. Lord keeper Guilford replied that many of those in prison were not Catholics but Dissenters, who were enemies of the government. He said that the king could pardon individuals, if he was satisfied of their loyalty, but that he, as lord keeper, could not in all conscience affix the Great Seal to a general pardon, which is apparently what Sunderland had suggested. Guilford's advice was taken; though the king wished to relieve the Catholics, he did not want to seem to act contrary to law.[14] Meanwhile it was planned to recall Ormond from Ireland and to send Rochester (the son of lord chancellor Clarendon) to be the new lord lieutenant. Also the Irish army was to be purged of 'Cromwellians' and filled with loyal officers, some of whom were to be Catholics and all of whom were to be men 'dont sa Majesté Britannique puisse être sûre s'il arrivait quelque mouvement dans

---

[12] *CTB*, vii, 1165, 1228–30; Morrice MS P, pp. 402–3, 409, 415, 453; *CSPD 1684–5*, pp. 238, 252, 302; D. R. Lacey, *Dissent and Parliamentary Politics in England, 1661–89* (New Brunswick, 1969), p. 161; Luttrell, i, 316.

[13] Luttrell, i, 308, 313; *CSPD 1684–5*, pp. 8, 11, 18; Nunz. Div. 228, fol. 46, 232, fols. 164–5, 167–8; BM Add. MS 25369, fols. 35–6.

[14] Barillon au Roi, 5 and 16 Oct. 1684 NS, Baschet 159; North, *Lives of the Norths*, i, 309–11.

aucun des trois royaumes'.[15] James, Sunderland and Jeffreys were the chief advocates of this new forward policy. On 15 January 1685 a pardon was issued to a long list of persons, including many Catholics, for all trespasses, treasons, *praemunires*, pains and penalties. Rumours abounded of a general toleration for Catholics but Guilford would have no part of it. Barillon wrote that James was anxious to overcome the legal obstacles to a toleration of Catholics and that Charles was much more cautious.[16] A few days later Charles was dead, but the pattern for the new reign had already been established.

[15] Barillon au Roi, 13 and 23 Nov. 1684, 8 Jan. 1685 NS, Baschet 159, 160; Kenyon, *Sunderland*, pp. 100–1; Burnet, ii, 447–9; Carte, iv, 668–669, v, 176–7.
[16] Barillon au Roi, 28 Dec. 1684, 8 Jan. and 8 Feb. 1685 NS, Baschet 159, 160; SP/44/335, pp. 329–39 (printed without lists *CSPD 1684–5*, p. 287); Luttrell, i, 326; Macpherson, i, 144.

10

JAMES II AND THE CHURCH
OF ENGLAND MEN (1685–6)

JAMES'S MOTIVES AND PROBLEMS

James II ranks as one of the great villains of Whig historiography, the English equivalent of Louis XIV. According to most of his contemporaries and most subsequent historians, James tried during his reign to destroy English liberties and the Common Law, to establish a military despotism, to impose Catholicism and to subject England to the pope. Even when the naked anti-Catholicism of the seventeenth century became less respectable, the Whig and liberal historians of the nineteenth century still stressed each act of illegality and each violation of the letter of the law as the Whigs understood it; thus Macaulay even quibbled with the strict legality of the brutal sentence imposed on Titus Oates in 1685 for his monstrous perjuries.[1] There has been a tendency to see the establishment of absolutism as James's primary concern and to regard his conversion to Catholicism as something of secondary importance. The implicit anti-Catholicism which has remained a central feature of the Whig interpretation of history has led historians to assume that no rational man could possibly be convinced of the truth of Catholicism, since Catholicism, in their eyes, depended for its survival on ignorance, superstition and the denial of rational inquiry. Considered in this frame of mind, it appeared that James's conversion must have been both superficial and sinister, merely the religious corollary of his alleged desire to establish a political despotism. One finds echoes of this attitude even in the work of perceptive modern historians who have otherwise dealt harshly with the Whig interpretation of this period.[2]

In my opinion the Whig interpretation of the reign of James II has three main flaws. First, whether or not it is dominated by an overt anti-Catholicism it accepts uncritically the main elements

---

[1] Macaulay, i, 487–8.
[2] See for instance J. R. Western, *Monarchy and Revolution: The English State in the Sixteen Eighties* (London, 1972), pp. 187–8.

of the seventeenth century anti-Catholic tradition, particularly its identification of Popery with absolutism and the assumptions which it inculcated about the behaviour of Papists in power. It also accepts, equally uncritically, the contemporary dread of Louis XIV and the assumption that James was both the tool and the imitator of the French king. Professor Jones has now shown that insofar as James had a foreign policy it was not one of subservience to France.[3] Nevertheless, most historians have started with the assumption that James *was* subservient to France and then looked for evidence of this in the dispatches of Barillon which are at best of dubious reliability. Secondly, I am quite convinced that James's Catholicism was sincere and that his primary aim was to improve the position of Catholicism in England by peaceful means. There was not the slightest possibility of imposing Catholicism by force. James's 'arbitrary' and 'illegal' actions were all directed towards the single end of allowing greater liberty and civil rights to the English Catholics and securing that liberty and those rights by means of an act of parliament. Thirdly, Whig historians have looked at James's reign in terms of absolute constitutional propriety, noting carefully each occasion on which he violated the letter of the law. They have not looked at the events of the reign in their historical context and in particular they have failed to take sufficient account of one fact of enormous importance – until the end of 1687 there was no prospect of a Catholic heir. It is wildly implausible that James should have tried to create an absolute monarchy in England for the benefit of his Dutch son-in-law, whom he disliked. On the other hand, it is quite reasonable to assume that he wanted to do all he could to improve the condition of his co-religionists both during his lifetime and after his death.

Since his conversion James's main concern had been to advance his new religion and to protect the English Catholics. From 1669 to 1673 his hopes had centred on the 'grand design' envisaged in the Secret Treaty of Dover. In 1673–4 he had urged Charles

[3] J. R. Jones, *The Revolution of 1688 in England* (London, 1972), pp. 176–187. Professor Jones's book appeared after my typescript was completed. He gives an excellent analysis of the campaign to pack parliament as well as of the European context of the Revolution; his interpretation of James's motives does not differ fundamentally from mine.

to make no concessions that could harm the Catholics. In 1675 he was driven into temporary opposition to the court by Danby's intolerant Anglicanism; he even considered co-operating with the Dissenters, whom he regarded normally as enemies of the monarchy.[4] By 1678 he had resumed his earlier authoritarian position, urging Charles to use his newly raised forces for a military coup; this would have helped to protect the Catholics against an increasingly anti-Catholic parliament. During the Exclusion Crisis he had been in the political wilderness, but his influence revived after his time in Scotland and in the autumn of 1684 he advocated a policy that would strengthen the crown, afford relief to Papists (but not to Dissenters) and open the way for the employment of Catholics in Ireland. As a rule James had urged his brother to stand firm on the authority of the crown, in the interests not only of the monarchy but also of the Catholics, who could expect no relief from parliament. But when Danby tried to strengthen the position of the court while pursuing an anti-Catholic line, James showed that the Catholic interest was his first concern by wobbling towards opposition.

James's natural proclivities were for authority on the part of the crown and for unquestioning obedience on the part of its subjects. In this he had much in common with the Tories who had made effusive professions of the sanctity of non-resistance in the early 1680s when the Whigs had been on the run, the top positions in the church had been filled with James's supporters and James had shown himself a tough defender of the episcopal church in Scotland. It was therefore unfortunate that James was a militant Catholic and that the Tories, his natural supporters, would not stomach Popery. James systematically destroyed the very strong political position bequeathed to him by Charles in a vain attempt to make them do so. He may have realised this but he regarded it as his mission in life to re-establish Catholicism in England. 'Having received the crown from God,' he told d'Adda, the papal nuncio, '. . . he must consider no other measures but those which would serve Him well and take all the steps that would lead to the greater glory of His Divine Majesty. He considered that he had still done little compared with what he knew he was obliged to do.'[5]

[4] Feiling, *Tory Party*, p. 180; above, pp. 107, 130–7.
[5] 'Havendo ricevuta la coróna da Dio . . . non doveva guardare altre

In achieving this he faced enormous problems. To the anti-Catholicism of the great majority of the political nation was added his lack of a Catholic heir. James was fifty-one when he became king. He had been married to Mary Beatrice for over eleven years; none of their children had lived. His heir was his daughter by his first marriage, Mary, married to William of Orange. Both were Protestants and so, despite attempts to convert her, was Mary's sister, Anne. James indignantly rejected suggestions that he should alter the succession.[6] The Protestantism of the heir-apparent to the throne helps to explain the lack of open opposition from Protestants during much of the reign and also the reluctance of many Catholics to co-operate with James's Catholicising measures. Both Protestants and Catholics realised that these measures were likely to be reversed by a Protestant successor, probably with added severity against the Catholics.[7]

This situation, as Terriesi pointed out, made the forcible imposition of Catholicism quite impossible. I have found no evidence that James ever considered following Louis XIV's example and dragooning Protestants into embracing Catholicism. Indeed the situation of the two kings was quite different. Louis used a very large Catholic army to coerce a small localised minority. James's army was quite small – just under 20,000 officers and men – and less than one eighth of its officers were Catholics. It was hardly conceivable that it could have been used to convert a nation of over five million people, the overwhelming majority of whom were at least nominally Protestants. Catholicism could spread in England only by making willing converts and for this some relaxation of the laws affecting Catholics was essential. Only then could all the Protestants' misconceptions about Catholicism be dispelled.[8] James (like Coleman) hoped and believed

misure che quelle di ben servirlo e fare tutti li passi che puotessero condurre alla maggior glòria di Sua Divina Maiestà, ed haverebbe stimato di fare sèmpre pòco a riguardo di quello che si conoscèva in òbbligo di dover fare': BM Add. MS 15395, fol. 390; see also *ibid.* fols. 366–7; Barillon au Roi, 25 March 1686 NS, Baschet 165.

6 Barillon au Roi, 27 June 1686 NS, Baschet 166; BM Add. MSS 15395, fols. 455–6, 34512, fol. 50; Western, pp. 203, 205.

7 BM Add. MS 25369, fol. 265; H. C. Foxcroft (ed.), *Supplement to Burnet's History of My Own Time* (Oxford 1902), pp. 152–4; Bredvold, pp. 160–1.

8 Miller, *EHR*, lxxxviii, 46–7; BM Add. MSS 25369, fol. 268, 25371, fols. 340–2, 25374, fol. 37; Foley, v, 150, 153–4.

that as soon as the artificial restraints on conversion imposed by the penal laws were removed, the essential and (to him) obvious rightness of Catholicism would become apparent to all and converts would come forward in large numbers. Like many Protestants, he had an exaggerated opinion of the ability of the Catholic priesthood to make converts and he believed that there were innumerable secret Papists waiting for the opportunity to declare themselves.[9] He had very little understanding of or respect for the genuineness of Protestants' beliefs, which he tended to regard as self-interest or faction in the guise of religion. Sunderland even told d'Adda that once the penal laws were taken off England would be Catholic within two years.[10]

If conversions were to be made and if the Catholics were to have any security after his death, James had to have the penal laws removed permanently and legally by a parliament. Two possible courses of action were open to him. He could try to secure the repeal either of the laws affecting Catholics only or of the laws affecting both Catholics and Dissenters. Each scheme had its advantages. The former would have to be done by an Anglican parliament, which would be better disposed towards monarchy than one composed of Dissenters, whom James usually regarded, not without reason, as hostile to monarchy and to himself. On the other hand, if all penal laws were taken off the divisive tendencies inherent in Protestantism would come into play as they had done during the Interregnum, and the triumph of Catholicism, as the epitome of unity and authority, would be accelerated. At first James hoped to get an Anglican parliament to take off the laws affecting Catholics, leaving in force those affecting Dissenters. In 1685–6 the government persecuted Dissenters but not Catholics and distinguished between 'loyal' and 'disloyal' religious nonconformity. James abandoned this policy when it became obvious that it was not going to work. Even when the Tories refused to co-operate, he tried fruitlessly for over a year to bully or cajole them into submission, before finally reversing his policy and, taking a stand on a general toleration, trying to create an alternative basis of political support among the Dissenters.

[9] Ranke, iv, 277, 310; Bodl., Tanner MS 28, fols. 54, 175–6.
[10] Barillon au Roi, 22 Nov. 1685 and 4 Feb. 1686 NS, Baschet 162, 163; Bodl., Rawl, MS D 91, p. 28; BM Add. MS 15395, fols. 284–5, 492–493; Burnet, iii, 207.

For James the free exercise of Catholicism was the essential thing which, he believed, would lead inevitably to its re-establishment in England without any need for coercion. He thought that once Englishmen could see how Catholicism had been misrepresented they would willingly turn to the true faith, especially if that had the weight of royal approval behind it. So long as Catholic worship were freely allowed, other details of the toleration were of secondary importance, merely a matter of tactics. Whether James wanted toleration for Dissenters as well as for Catholics varied according to circumstances. He was not a tolerationist in the sense that he believed that honest differences of opinion could be or should be permitted within a state or that no one church had a monopoly of truth: in fact he believed the opposite. His advocacy of toleration was the product of the self-confidence of his bigotry: if Catholicism were tolerated, it would triumph completely and inevitably and then the question of toleration would lose all meaning.

That this view was extremely naive goes without saying. But James never believed that anyone could honestly and sincerely hold opinions different from his own. He explained opposition in terms of personalities, faction, self-interest, misrepresentation or conspiracy but never in terms of principle. He believed that Tory gentlemen opposed him because they feared for their abbey-lands and that Anglican clergymen did so because they feared for their benefices. He did not understand that after a century and a quarter of continuous Protestantism Englishmen could not be (and did not wish to be) disabused of their misconceptions about Catholicism by a missionary effort as puny as the one that he mounted. He failed to appreciate that Protestants could be sincerely attached to their beliefs.

His schemes were doomed to eventual failure because the vast majority of Englishmen would not willingly turn Papist, a fact made even more certain by the apparent inevitability of the Protestant succession. The Anglicans, the natural supporters of monarchy, were solidly against toleration. Some of the Dissenters were more favourable, but James's reluctance to trust them was reinforced by their involvement in Monmouth's rebellion. He failed to secure the wholehearted support of either Anglicans or Dissenters for a legal toleration that included Catholics, so he resorted to prerogative action of dubious legality to secure immediate benefits for the Catholics, to prepare the way for a tractable parliament and to encourage converts to come forward. Throughout he observed the forms of law. As Barillon delicately put it, 'tout ce qui se fait est selon l'ordre des lois établies ou du moins il y a une espèce de formalité gardée qu'on peut soutenir être conforme aux lois'.[11] But the dubious legality hardened the resistance of both Churchmen and Dissenters and James's schemes were on the verge of collapse when William invaded in 1688.

James's Catholicising policy might seem insane; it can be explained only by his naive and grossly inflated expectations of conversions. Fortified by his sense of divine mission, he believed with a conviction born of faith than converts would appear, not because he had any rational grounds for thinking that they would but because he desperately wanted them to. So he pressed blindly on, hoping somehow to repeal the penal laws with some show of legality and to present his successor with the *fait accompli* of a Catholic England. He was eager to accept the assurances of his bigoted and sycophantic courtiers that the obstacles which he met were the product of the intrigues of William's supporters rather than the sullen and disillusioned hostility of the great majority of the political nation. He refused to believe that the Tories whom he turned out of one office after another were sincere in their religion and loyalism and that they would dearly have liked to obey him but that the demands which he made on their consciences were just too great. When he was convinced that the Anglicans would not obey him he turned to the Dissenters. One act of dubious legality followed another, rubberstamped by a carefully selected bench of judges. He blundered on with the blind optimism of a man whose mind was determinedly closed to any thought of failure. Ironically in June 1688 his wife bore him a son and heir, the want of which had led originally to his haste. By then his plans were disintegrating all around him; when William invaded, few were prepared to resist him. In less than four years James had destroyed the strongest political position that any Stuart ever enjoyed. He had turned the Tories from vociferous loyalty to sullen apathy. And he had achieved this by concentrating single-mindedly on the line of action that the Tories could not stomach – the promotion of Popery.

[11] Barillon au Roi, 27 Oct. 1687 NS, Baschet 173.

THE BREAK WITH THE TORIES

When James first came to the throne, some leading Catholics favoured a general liberty of conscience and James's confessor wrote that it was the king's intention to grant one. However, by the end of February James had rejected the idea after opposition from the Council (which consisted mainly of Tories). He decided instead to press parliament to take off the laws against Catholics. Barillon thought that parliament might agree to this and perhaps to the employment of Catholics in household posts.[12] James was still uncertain how parliament would behave and tried to extract money from Louis XIV; he appealed to Louis's prejudices, saying that he needed the money to strengthen his authority and to help the Catholics, but Louis was reluctant to pay up without some assurance of positive benefits for himself. James doubted whether parliament would agree to relax the laws affecting Catholics but he continued to express optimism and praised a paper of Buckingham's which advocated a general toleration. Some Catholic gentlemen told Sir John Reresby in May that the king expected parliament to take off the penal laws against Catholics. When parliament met in May it voted James an ample revenue but showed itself very hostile to Catholicism, so James did not dare to propose any changes in the laws. However, Monmouth's rebellion gave him a chance to enlarge his army and parliament voted him the money to pay it. Louis used this as an excuse to cut off his subsidy. When parliament met again in November it vigorously attacked the keeping up of the army and the king's insistence on retaining some eighty-five Catholic officers whom he had commissioned during the summer. James refused to compromise and so rendered unusable the most compliant parliament of the century, although it was over a year before he finally accepted that it was unusable.[13]

In the first weeks of his reign James took steps to suspend the

---

[12] BM Add. MS 25369, fols. 268, 278, 285; Nunz. Div. 232, fol. 162; C. J. Fox, *A History of the Early Part of the Reign of James II* (London, 1808), Appendix, pp. xxxiii, xlv; Lingard, x, 203; Ranke, iv, 229n.

[13] Fox, Appendix, pp. lxxxiii–lxxxiv, lxxxviii, xcix–c, cii–cxvii; Barillon au Roi, 7 and 28 May 1685 NS, CPA 155; Reresby, pp. 363–4; Miller, *EHR*, lxxxviii, 35, 45–7.

working of the laws affecting Catholics. On 27 February 1685 he ordered that persons in prison for refusing the oaths or for not coming to church should be released if they gave recognisances for their good behaviour and if they produced certificates that they or their nearest relatives had suffered for their loyalty in the civil wars. On 18 April he gave a similar order to those exercising ecclesiastical jurisdiction. Ange, the manager of recusant revenues, was ordered on 19 March and 14 April to delay the execution of writs that had already been sent out. In May there were issued the first of many stays of processes against individual recusants who had produced certificates attesting their loyalty; this continued the policy that had begun with the pardon of 15 January.[14] Having stopped the proceedings against Catholics the king set out to refund the money that they had paid in fines. On 6 June he stated that he wanted such money which had not yet been paid into the Exchequer to be repaid to the recusants. He renewed Ange's patent, which still included the term 'Popish recusants' and ordered that Ange should take charge of the repayment of the moneys to recusants in order to prevent the sheriffs' accounts from becoming too complicated. The first refunds were being made before the end of July, when Ange authorised the repayment to Sir Philip Constable of £60, less various fees which came to £10 19s 6d.[15]

It was made quite clear that the laws were to be enforced against all recusants other than those who produced certificates of loyalty. These certificates were used during 1685 and much of 1686. In one case where proceedings against some recusants had been stopped, they were resumed when it was discovered that the certificate had been obtained 'by surprise'.[16] By the beginning of 1687 the certificates had become a formality: a very long list of Warwickshire recusants was covered by a rather general certificate by Robert Brent and Henry Parker. Many of the warrants to stop the proceedings against recusants bore in the margin the name of Brent, a Catholic lawyer who played an important but shadowy role in James's administration. This implies that many of the recusants involved were Catholics.

[14] *CSPD 1685*, nos. 243–6, 558, 746; *CTB*, viii, 66, 132, 176.
[15] *CTB*, viii, 214–15, 217–18, 255; East Riding R. O., DDEV 68/248/(viii). I am grateful to Mr J. A. Williams for this reference.
[16] *CSPD 1685*, nos. 1750, 1866–7.

In the margin of one warrant which was drawn up after the relaxation of the laws against Quakers in 1686, Brent's name has been erased and William Penn's has been substituted.[17]

For the predominantly Tory magistracy Dissent was closely identified with disloyalty and Catholics were far more likely than Dissenters to be able to prove their loyalty to the crown in the Civil War. In December 1685 Ange was put in charge of the revenues from recusants, conventiclers and excommunicates and it was ordered that all those without loyalty certificates were to be prosecuted. In February 1686 Ange was ordered to use the records of the ecclesiastical courts of the diocese of London to identify excommunicates and those who had been presented for nonconformity and to levy the money due from them. In March the king issued a dispensation to allow a large number of English and Scottish Catholic nobles and gentry to travel freely and to come to court without taking the oaths.[18]

In 1685 and much of 1686 Dissenters were persecuted vigorously, often under the Conventicle Act rather than the recusancy laws. This severity may have dated from the time of Monmouth's rebellion, when the Council took steps to secure Nonconformist ministers and other suspect persons. There survive well over three hundred certificates of conviction for conventicling from Middlesex alone between February and June 1686; many contain twenty names or more. As a meeting of five persons constituted a conventicle under the act of 1670, one may assume that more conventiclers were convicted in Middlesex in six months in 1686 than there were Papists convicted of recusancy in 1679, the worst year of the Plot. The general pardon of 10 March 1686 would not have affected most of these convictions. Meanwhile money from recusancy fines still came into the Exchequer, much of it the backlog from the early 1680s. £3041 1s 7½d was received between Easter 1685 and Easter 1686 and £1214 10s 10½d during the following year.[19]

[17] *CSPD 1686–7*, nos. 488, 490, 717, 1025; BM Add. MS 17018, fol. 194; *CTB*, viii, 1128–9. For Brent, see J. R. Jones, 'James II's Whig Collaborators', *HJ*, iii (1960), 67–8.

[18] *CTB*, viii, 467, 594; *CSPD 1686–7*, no. 268.

[19] *CSPD 1685*, no. 957; BM Add. 41823, fol. 115; Lee (ed.), *Diaries and Letters of Philip Henry*, pp. 325, 340; Parkinson (ed.), *Life of Adam Martindale*, pp. 233–4; Middlesex R. O., MR/RC/9 (315 certificates), plus a few in MR/RC/7–8; Chandaman, p. 706.

Until James had abandoned all hope of getting his way with the Anglicans in parliament he did nothing to propitiate the Dissenters, whose seditious reputation seemed to have been confirmed by the involvement of some of the West Country Dissenters in Monmouth's rebellion. The use of loyalty certificates was a convenient way of distinguishing between Catholics and Dissenters without doing so in overtly denominational terms. One may assume that if James had succeeded in obtaining a parliamentary toleration in 1685 it would have embodied the distinction between loyal and disloyal nonconformists that the government was already making in its enforcement of the laws. When James wanted the Dissenters' political support, this distinction was quietly abandoned and James took his stand on a general toleration which, he claimed, had been his aim all the time.

During and after the November session of parliament divisions appeared among the Catholics. The 'country' Catholics, fearing for their estates, wanted the king to act cautiously; they would be satisfied with the non-execution of the laws or with the repeal of the penal laws only. They feared that any attempt to repeal the Test Acts as well would be bound to provoke a reaction against the Catholics under a Protestant successor. The 'court' Catholics urged James to press ahead. 'Ils voient bien', wrote Barillon, 'que s'il [James] ne prend pendant sa vie de fortes précautions et qu'il n'y ait un changement dans les lois à leur égard, ils se trouveront exposés à une ruine entière dès que M. le prince d'Orange viendra à la couronne'.[20] (It apparently never occurred to them that William could re-enact the laws that they had repealed.) This forward party at court contained few men who possessed talent for any political activity other than court infighting and intrigue. Bonrepos, a special envoy from Louis XIV, had an extremely low opinion of their ability: 'Il [d'Adda] n'est point capable non plus qu'aucun des autres de donner un bon conseil ni de faire prendre une résolution décisive, tellement que toute cette grande affaire si importante pour la religion Catholique est dirigée par milord Sunderland, Protestant.'[21] The forward party had one great strength, however: it told James what he wanted to hear, that he should press on with his Catholicising

[20] Barillon au Roi, 12 Nov. and 13 Dec. 1685 NS, Baschet 162; Fox, Appendix, p. cxxxv.
[21] Bonrepos's report, 11 Feb. 1686 NS, Baschet 164.

mission. For this reason and because its enemies at court were his enemies Sunderland led, followed or used the forward party, but it eventually caused James to dismiss him. He controlled it (as far as control was possible) through a 'Catholic council' established during the first weeks of the reign.[22] The forward party described all who opposed it as friends of the prince of Orange. Like James, it could understand opposition only in terms of personality and conspiracy and had no great awareness of political realities. Sunderland alone probably had such an awareness but he could not afford to tell James unpleasant truths if he wished to keep his job. Even as late as the spring of 1688 Sunderland seems to have convinced himself that James's schemes had some chance of succeeding, but by the summer he was urging the king to make concessions.[23]

After James had prorogued parliament in November 1685 he dismissed from their offices some M.P.s who had voted against the court in order to 'retenir les autres dans leur devoir'. Barillon reported that he intended to purge the army of unreliable officers and to put the army in England and the government of Ireland into the hands of Catholics and other reliable men. But although the employment of Catholics proceeded rapidly in Ireland very few additional Catholic officers were put into the English army.[24] Rumours abounded of a general toleration but Barillon thought that the Dissenters distrusted James and that they feared he would use his army to impose Popery.[25] He also thought that James distrusted the Dissenters. 'Leurs principes sont fort opposés à la royauté et il est difficile d'espérer un bon succès par le moyen de ceux qui ne respirent que l'abaissement de l'autorité royale aussi bien que celle des évêques.' James was therefore in a quandary. 'Il connaît que le parti episcopal sera fort mal aisé à ramener en faveur des Catholiques: il voudra...

---

[22] Fox, Appendix, p. xlviii; Barillon au Roi, 25 March 1686 NS, Baschet 165.

[23] For a first-class account of court politics under James II and particularly of the role of Sunderland, see Kenyon, *Sunderland*, chaps. 4–6.

[24] Barillon au Roi, 24 Dec. 1685 and 7 Feb. 1686 NS, Baschet 162, 164; J. G. Simms, *Jacobite Ireland 1685–91* (London, 1969), pp. 19–29; Miller, *EHR*, lxxxviii, 39, 47.

[25] BM Add. MSS 25371, fol. 223, 34510, fols. 102–3; Luttrell, i, 367; Barillon au Roi, 7 Jan. 1686 NS, Baschet 163.

tenter encore si a fermeté ne surmontera point les accoûtumer à souffrir le religion Catholique plutôt que d'être exposés à voir toutes les sectes différentes s'établir.'[26] This was James's dilemma in 1686: he wanted to secure toleration for Catholics without allowing it to Dissenters, whom he regarded as seditious. He tried to resolve it by trying more and more heavy-handedly to break down the Anglicans' aversion to Popery, but without success. As it became apparent that he was not going to succeed he began, very slowly, to edge his way towards allowing toleration for Dissenters.

James did what he could to encourage converts to come forward. He published two documents found among Charles's papers which purported to give the late king's reasons for his conversion. James left the see of York vacant and planned to use its revenues to make good the losses suffered by converts (which aroused fears that the next archbishop of York would be a Papist) and his priests approached various courtiers, with little success.[27] He also tried to persuade the usually compliant Scots parliament to allow toleration to the Scottish Catholics, and hoped that this might encourage the passing of a similar measure in England. Barillon reported that James 'avait fort envie que les Catholiques eussent seuls la liberté de l'exercice de leur religion', but the king's Scots advisers said that this was impossible. He eventually agreed that the Presbyterians should also be allowed a limited toleration and that it would be too risky to try to repeal the Scottish Test Act. The Scots parliament offered unexpectedly stiff resistance and the project was abandoned. James's courtiers blamed the opposition on to the machinations of cabals in London and of the Dutch.[28]

In the summer of 1686 there was a definite change of policy which was manifested in three ways. First, James began to employ Catholics in civilian posts. Earlier in the year James had allowed Obadiah Walker and others to keep their fellowships at Oxford despite their conversion to Catholicism. Another convert,

---

[26] Barillon au Roi, 7 Feb. 1686 NS, Baschet 164.

[27] 'Copies of Two Papers', *State Tracts*, ii, 273–4; Barillon, 4 Feb. 1686 NS, Baschet 164; BM Add. MSS 15395, fols. 459–60, 15396, fols. 63–4; Comber, i, 21; Ailesbury, i, 154; Burnet, iii, 114–15.

[28] Barillon au Roi, 25 March, 29 April, 27 and 30 May, 3 and 13 June, 22 July 1686 NS, Baschet 165, 166; BM Add. MS 15395, fols. 440–1.

Edward Slater, the parson of Putney, had been allowed to keep his benefice. The creation of a fourth troop of horse guards for lord Dover marked the first employment of a Catholic in a semi-household post.[29] James began to move forward after the verdict in the case of *Godden* v. *Hales* on 21 June. The judges upheld the king's right 'to dispense with the penal laws in particular cases and upon particular necessary reasons' and ruled that the king was the sole judge of the necessity of such reasons.[30] In July a few Papists appeared on grand and petty juries. By the end of the year there were five Catholics (lords Tyrconnel, Dover, Bellasis, Powis and Arundell of Wardour) on the Privy Council. In October James declared his intention to send one or two Catholic J.P.s to each county. A committee of the Council was set up to inspect the commissions of the peace, to see what alterations were needed for the king's service. Most of its information about those who were suitable to be appointed came from Arundell of Wardour, Dover, Powis and Tyrconnel, who relied in turn on the information of Catholics in the localities. Apart from the bishop of Durham, the Protestant councillors took little part in the deliberations. By January 1687 the committee had finished its task and the new commissions were issued in February. Of 455 J.P.s who were put in, just under sixty-four per cent were Catholics.[31]

The second new trend in James's policy was a concerted attempt to gag and humiliate the Church of England. Shortly after his accession James had told archbishop Sancroft of Canterbury and bishop Compton of London to prevent their clergy from preaching against Catholicism and he implied that if they did not do so his promises to protect the Church of England might prove to be conditional. Soon after, when the clergy continued their anti-Catholic sermons, James renewed his order and his warning. In February 1686 he reissued the directives against seditious and controversial preaching first issued by Charles II in 1662. In May 1686 John Sharp, the rector of St

[29] *CSPD 1686–7*, no. 342; *HMC House of Lords 1689–90*, p. 301; Barillon, 14 March 1686 NS, Baschet 165.

[30] W. C. Costin and J. S. Watson, *The Law and Working of the Constitution* (2 vols., London, 1952), i, 256–8.

[31] Morrice MS P, pp. 570–1, 645, 658; BM Add. MSS 15396, fol. 139, 25373, fol. 38; PC/2/71, p. 325; PRO, Index 4215, pp. 167–9; Appendix 3.

Giles in the Fields, preached a sharp sermon against Popery. Compton was ordered to suspend him, but refused and was eventually suspended himself. In July the king set up the Ecclesiastical Commission which was to be used, as Sunderland told d'Adda, 'to regulate the licence of the Protestant ministers and to curb the audacity of the bishops'. It was also to be the king's main weapon in his efforts to force the universities to admit Catholics.[32]

Thirdly, the king's attitude towards the Dissenters slowly relaxed. For much of 1686 Dissenters were still vigorously persecuted, as they had been since 1681. Although some of the initiative for this may have come from the court at first, there is no doubt that it was carried on enthusiastically by Anglican bishops, clergymen and magistrates.[33] The first sign of the court's change of attitude came in March. The king issued a general pardon which seems to have included religious offences in which judgment had not yet been given and a general warrant was issued to discharge all Quakers from imprisonment, to stop collecting fines from them and to suspend all proceedings against them. Significantly this came six days after a similar order in favour of the Penn family. There followed an order to stop the proceedings against a large number of individual Quakers.[34] These orders were not always obeyed, but in June the Dutch ambassador noted that the London trained bands had protected a Catholic chapel, broken up a Nonconformist conventicle and ignored a Quaker meeting. In May the king ordered that the proceedings against a few London Dissenters should be stopped. There were rumours of a general toleration and James is said to have said that he would grant one if his affairs permitted it.[35]

Early in July some Anabaptists from Abingdon petitioned the king for relief from the burdens of the laws, stressing that they were loyal and obedient subjects. James received their petition kindly and gave them a pardon and a patent under the Great Seal which stated that they were not to be prosecuted further in

[32] Lingard, x, 203; Ranke, iv, 218–19, 293–4; T. Sharp, *Life of Archbishop John Sharp* (2 vols., London, 1825), i, 69; Granville, ii, 249–51; BM Add. MS 15396, fols. 26–7.

[33] Morrice MS P, pp. 524–7, 547–8, 569, 574, 581, 602, 616–17, 634.

[34] Steele, i, no. 3828; *CSPD 1686–7*, nos. 248, 274; *CTB*, viii, 629–34.

[35] *CTB*, viii, 1303; Morrice MS P, pp. 532–3, 550, 554, 563; BM Add. MS 34512, fol. 36.

matters of religion. It added that they had produced loyalty certificates, although it was alleged by others that these certificates had been obtained from two J.P.s who did not know them. The pardon and patent covered twenty-five men and their families and cost £25 in fees.[36] Late in August some Anabaptists from Tewkesbury made a similar petition. James again granted it and said that the removal of all the penal laws would have the approval, not only of himself, but also of a parliament, if his friends would concur. He talked often of the harshness of the church's persecution of Dissenters. It was now assumed that any Dissenters could get dispensations from the penal laws if they would petition for them. In September James allowed freedom of worship to the wool manufacturers of Scotland.[37] But although the harassment of conventicles continued, the two largest Dissenting groups, the Presbyterians and the Independents, refused to petition for relief. They feared that the conditions attached to the king's offer of freedom of worship would include liberty for the Papists. The court now put out frequent feelers towards the Dissenters, notably through a Presbyterian called Sir John Baber, who had acted as a contact between the court and the Dissenters in 1668 and 1671. As early as 7 August Roger Morrice, a Presbyterian, believed that James would try to secure the election of a parliament consisting mainly of Dissenters.[38]

By November 1686 many congregations were securing dispensations from the penal laws. Among the agents who were most active in procuring dispensations were the Catholic councillor lord Powis, Robert Brent and Sir Nicholas Butler, a disreputable ex-Baptist who turned Catholic in about July 1686 in order to keep his place in the customs and who became an important political figure thereafter.[39] A licence office was set up where a payment of fifty shillings would secure a dispensation for a whole family against all proceedings for recusancy and nonconformity,

---

[36] Morrice MS P, pp. 563, 568, 572, 576, 584.

[37] *ibid.* pp. 601, 615, 618, 626.

[38] *ibid.* pp. 594, 611, 615–17, 625; see Thomas in Nuttall and Chadwick, pp. 198, 208.

[39] Morrice MSS P, pp. 584, 611, 635, 639, Q, pp. 16, 53; *An Account of the Convincement of Richard Davies*, pp. 147–8. For Butler's conversion, see G. J. W. Agar Ellis (ed.), *Ellis Correspondence* (2 vols., London, 1829), i, 133–4, 138; Morrice MS P, pp. 556, 562, 611.

together with a licence to worship freely in the future. Richard Baxter, who had been in prison since the previous year, was now released.[40] Tory magistrates were clearly taken aback when conventiclers produced these dispensations but most eventually allowed them. Some conventicles were still disturbed and the government still found it difficult to stop the persecution of Quakers.[41] Supersessions of proceedings against Quakers and other recusants now referred, not to loyalty, but to good testimony of peaceable behaviour.[42] The court's change of policy was perhaps impeded by Rochester's continued presence at the Treasury. As late as 2 December he was pressing the Leicestershire J.P.s for the king's share of conventicle fines. However, Rochester's credit was already tottering after a prolonged assault from Sunderland, and at the end of December he was dismissed. In January James continued to stop proceedings against conventicles and began to refund some of their fines. By February many were meeting openly. On 8 March he ordered that all proceedings against Catholics should be stopped, whether they had produced loyalty certificates or not, 'the king being well satisfied in the loyalty of all his Roman Catholic subjects'.[43]

The 'closeting' campaign of early 1687, James's last attempt to win over the Anglican M.P.s elected in 1685, should be seen against this background of the appointment of Catholics to office, the harassment of the Church of England and the gradual suspension of the laws affecting Protestant Dissenters. All these, particularly the dismissals from office, must have embarrassed and irritated the Tory M.P.s. Those who still held offices were now given the choice of complying with the king or losing their places. James purged his household of all who were not unequivocally behind him. Rochester lost the treasurership for refusing to turn Catholic; James told Barillon: 'Il lui avait fait remarquer à lui-même que son attachement à la religion Protestante l'empêchait de lui donner de bons conseils et de juger sainement les

---

[40] Morrice MS Q, pp. 15–16; BM Add. MSS 29910, fol. 203, 34510, fols. 136–7.

[41] Morrice MS Q, pp. 9, 17, 20, 33, 38, 44, 71; *CSPD 1686–7*, nos. 1160, 1215, 1281.

[42] *CTB*, viii, 1005–6; *CSPD 1686–7*, nos. 1146–53, 1179, 1201.

[43] *CTB*, viii, 1040, 1246, 1262; *CSPD 1686–7*, no. 1361; Luttrell, i, 393; Morrice MS Q, pp. 70, 74, 80; Bodl., Ballard MS 12, fol. 21.

affaires.'[44] James tried to extract from M.P.s written, or at least verbal, assurances that they would do as he wished. The king interviewed some in his closet, others were sounded out by the judges and by trusted magnates. James wrote to the duke of Beaufort asking him to speak to M.P.s 'about what I intend to endeavour to have done when they meet next, which is to have the two tests and penal laws repealed that my Catholic subjects may be in the same condition the rest of my subjects are'. He told Beaufort to 'take pains with such as make difficulty to promise to comply with my so reasonable desires'. James hoped to bully, persuade or even bribe M.P.s into submission and expressed confidence of success.[45] But the closetings were the last spasm of a policy which he had virtually decided to abandon. On 12 February 1687 he issued a declaration of indulgence in Scotland. He was about to commit himself completely to an appeal to the Dissenters.

[44] BM Add. MS 15396, fols. 196–8; SS Ing. 12, fols. 2–6; Barillon au Roi, 9 Jan. 1687 NS, Baschet 168.

[45] Barillon au Roi, 16 and 20 Jan., 10 Feb., 10 March 1687 NS, Baschet 168; SS Ing. 12, fols. 11, 21, 30; Sir J. Mackintosh, *History of the Revolution of 1688* (London, 1834), p. 637; Reresby, pp. 447–9; *HMC Beaufort*, pp. 89–90; *HMC le Fleming*, p. 203; Ellis, i, 235–6, 255–6; Ranke, iv, 310n.

11

JAMES II AND THE DISSENTERS
(1687–8)

The failure of the policy of closeting marked the end of James's efforts to persuade the members of his Tory parliament to agree to the removal of the penal laws affecting Catholics. Although both Houses had proved loyal and compliant on most issues, they had made it clear in both sessions that they would not allow the toleration of Papists. After all the Tories' over-effusive protestations of loyalty and obedience during the earlier 1680s, their obstinacy on this point seemed to James like a slap in the face. Much of his later vindictiveness against the church, the universities and the Seven Bishops can be explained by his bitter sense of betrayal. The Declaration of Indulgence was not motivated solely by pique, of course. It had been apparent for some time that if James could not persuade his Anglican parliament to repeal the penal laws, he might try to get a Dissenting parliament that would do so, whatever he had thought of Dissenters in the past. If he wished to maintain the slightest pretence of legality, this parliament could contain no Catholics, as they were excluded by the 1678 Test Act. James considered dispensing with this act but his legal advisers told him firmly that such an action would be indefensible in law.[1]

James had been edging towards an appeal to the Dissenters for some time but he hesitated to commit himself until it was absolutely clear that he had nothing to hope for from his old supporters. At the end of February 1687 Sunderland told Barillon that parliament would not comply with the king, but that James had to find this out for himself, as Sunderland had told him that Rochester was the cause of its resistance. By early March James was convinced that Dissenters and Catholics together formed the majority of the population. By 18 March he had decided to issue a declaration of indulgence in England. He told the Council that it would be an interim measure, pending the granting of liberty of conscience by parliament. James

[1] Barillon au Roi, 16 Oct. 1687 NS, Baschet 173; Mackintosh, p. 645.

claimed that it would make the benefits of liberty of conscience apparent to all, but Barillon thought that

le véritable motif qu'a eu Sa Majesté Britannique a été de jeter de la division entre l'Église Anglicane et les non conformistes et de faire que ces derniers se joignent aux Catholiques en sorte qu'ils puissent ensemble former un parti assez puissant contre le parti episcopal qui a traversé et fait manquer les mesures prises en faveur de la religion Catholique.[2]

James believed that the Dissenters would rejoice at being freed from the Anglican yoke and that many converts to Catholicism would come forward. Nevertheless Barillon thought that James was not entirely happy about the situation: 'Je crois que, dans le fonds, si on ne pouvait laisser que la religion Anglicane et la Catholique établies par les lois, le roi d'Angleterre en serait bien plus content.'[3]

In James's Scottish declaration he had, by virtue of his absolute power, taken off all the disabilities of the Catholics and some of those of the Presbyterians and Quakers.[4] The English Declaration of Indulgence was issued on 4 April. The king stated: 'We cannot but heartily wish ... that all the people of our dominions were members of the Catholic church.' He believed that attempts to coerce conscience usually failed and damaged the economy; he cited as evidence 'the conduct of the four last reigns' (but not that of Mary). He guaranteed to the nation and to the established church the free exercise of religion and the secure enjoyment of property (including abbey-lands). He suspended all penal laws by 'our royal will and pleasure' and dispensed all his subjects from the need to take the oaths and test. After the declaration had been issued, the king ordered that all proceedings for recusancy should be stopped as he had decided that his favour should extend to Dissenters.[5]

There remained certain problems which had arisen from the working of the penal laws during the past decade. In December

---

[2] SS Ing. 12, fol. 81; Barillon au Roi, 10 and 31 March 1687 NS, Baschet 168; Mackintosh, p. 639.

[3] Barillon 10 Feb. and 3 April 1687 NS, Baschet 168; SS Ing. 12, fol. 87; Mackintosh, pp. 639–40; BM Add. MS 34502, fols. 82–3.

[4] G. Burnet, 'Some Reflections on His Majesty's Proclamation' (1687), *State Tracts*, ii, 281–7.

[5] Kenyon, *Stuart Constitution*, pp. 410–13; CTB, viii, 1321, 1393.

1687 commissions were issued to inquire into moneys which had been levied on recusants and Dissenters since 1677 and which had not been accounted for. The commissioners included a few Catholics. New commissions were issued several times in 1688. There are some references to the commissioners meeting with obstruction but those in Devon accumulated a large amount of information between July and September 1688 and seem to have discharged their task with diligence and efficiency. In Essex, according to Sir John Bramston, the commissioners took so much money from constables, churchwardens and parishioners that in some places they collected more than had been levied originally. Then people began to refuse to pay and the commissioners gradually ceased to operate.[6] The Exchequer still tried to extract money from the receivers, whose office had been abolished in 1684. Some, like Edward Clark, seem never to have cleared their accounts. Thomas Lemmon of Middlesex apparently never acted at all and Venables Lynd of Westminster claimed to have spent more than he raised. William Christian showed a deficit of £272 9s od on his final account, although he may have paid money in earlier. The sheriffs had also collected large sums and some recusants had compounded directly with the Exchequer. Although in some cases the Exchequer did try to enforce the repayment of recusancy fines, most of the money levied from recusants was probably never repaid. There was no question of repaying money already accounted for in the Exchequer.[7]

These measures represented the tying up of loose ends. On the political front the Dissenters' reaction to the indulgence was mixed. The more radical sects, like the Quakers and Anabaptists, tended to be well pleased. The more cautious Presbyterians were less enthusiastic. 'To say their general design is to bring in Popery is to say nothing,' wrote Roger Morrice, 'for that is acknowledged; but the question is . . . how giving liberty to the Protestant Dissenters and letting them into the government can answer to this end'. Oliver Heywood, another Presbyterian, was made sus-

---

6 *CTB*, viii, 1695–7, 1803–6, 1933, 1981–2, 2028, 2032–5; Bodl., Rawl. MS D 372 (much of the information was recorded on specially printed forms); lord Braybrooke (ed.), *Autobiography of Sir John Bramston* (Camden Soc., 1845), p. 305.
7 *CTB*, viii, 528, 1191–2, 1242–3, 1572, 1645, 1759; Williams, *Wilts.*, p. 35.

picious by James's sudden change of heart, but decided never-theless to use thankfully the liberty which the king had granted. Elsewhere, although ministers might have reservations, their congregations pressed them to open the meeting-houses and to preach publicly.[8] Only a minority of Dissenters were prepared to make addresses to the king, thanking him for the declaration, but most were willing enough to take advantage of the liberty that it gave them. While a Protestant succession seemed certain, there could not be much danger in doing so.

James, however, hoped that the declaration would enable him to create a new basis of political support made up of Catholics and Dissenters. He was now convinced that the Church of England had survived only because it had possessed the power to coerce others into conformity and he confidently expected that the declaration would lead to many conversions to Catholicism. He claimed that William feared that Catholicism would now develop such deep roots that it would be impossible to prevent its establishment. After sounding the existing M.P.s once more, he dissolved parliament in July. Sunderland was now losing his nerve. He told d'Adda that it would be dangerous to alienate the Anglicans; they were well-affected towards monarchy, but the Dissenters hated both the monarchy and the Catholics. He now doubted the reliability of the army, which he had not done a few months before. He said that the king should be content with moderate gains and that he should not lose all in trying to gain too much. But James had 'decided all other considerations to be far inferior to the principal one of advancing the Catholic religion'. By September Barillon was also becoming pessimistic. James had been impressed by his reception on his progress to the West, but 'les repects extérieurs qui ont été rendus à sa personne ne peuvent être tirés à conséquence quand il sera question de faire les choses qu'on croit pouvoir être avantageuses aux Catholiques'.[9]

After dissolving his first parliament, James set out to obtain another which would repeal the penal laws and Test Acts. He was prepared to use persuasion, fraud and force. A committee,

---

[8] Morrice MS Q, pp. 85, 179; J. Horsfall Turner (ed.), *Autobiographies, Diaries &c of Oliver Heywood* (4 vols., Brighouse, 1882), iv, 124–5; Bodl.. Tanner MS 29, fol. 10.

[9] Barillon au Roi, 5 May, 12 June and 29 Sept. 1687 NS, Baschet 169, 170, 172; Mackintosh, pp. 636, 643–5.

whose members included Sunderland, Jeffreys and Fr Petre, was set up to prepare for the parliamentary elections by remodelling the commissions of the peace and the corporations of the parliamentary boroughs. During the campaign for an amenable parliament many more Catholics were admitted to the commissions of the peace and other offices. Throughout his reign James's appointments to office were influenced by several conflicting considerations. First, he wanted to employ Catholics freely, to show his favour to them and to encourage converts to come forward. These appointments were intended, in Terriesi's words, 'to make these Catholics a little more considerable in the country ... and in time to do the king good service in the election of members of parliament'.[10] Secondly, from the spring of 1687, James's appointments were intended to build up enough support among Dissenters to enable him to secure a Protestant parliament that would repeal the penal laws. Thirdly, while doing this, he wanted to avoid losing the support of Anglican magnates like the dukes of Beaufort, Newcastle and Norfolk or the earls of Bath, Derby and Lindsey. Naturally these contradictions made success even harder to achieve. Neither Anglican magnates nor Dissenters relished the employment of Papists; James's illegal favours to Catholics made the achievement of a legal toleration for Catholics even more difficult.

By early in 1687 some 290 Catholic J.P.s had been appointed. Between April and June 1687 the new commissions were reissued with a clause dispensing all J.P.s from taking the oaths and test, and some new J.P.s were added.[11] In October the second major remodelling of the commissions began. J.P.s were asked, by means of the notorious 'three questions', to commit themselves to support the repeal of the penal laws and Test Acts. Very many who refused to comply were put out and new commissions were issued, mostly between February and April 1688. This time most of those put in were Dissenters. Of 709 new J.P.s only ninety-nine, or fourteen per cent, were Catholics, as opposed to sixty-four per cent in the first remodelling.[12] Most suitable Catholics had been

[10] BM Add. MS 25373, fol. 29. 'Per rendere éssi Cattolici un pòco più stimabili alla campagna ... e con il tèmpo per fare de' buòni ufitii alla Mtà del Re nella eletióne della mèmbri del parlaménto.

[11] *CSPD 1686–7*, no. 1665; PRO, Index 4215, pp. 174ff.

[12] SP/44/56, pp. 389–90; Duckett, passim; PRO, Index 4215, pp. 186–

put in during the first remodelling, the purpose of which had been to show favour to Catholics and to encourage would-be converts, at a time when James had not given up hope of winning over the Anglicans. The aim of the second remodelling was mainly to build up an alternative basis of support to the Tories, which was to be made up of Dissenters and a few compliant Anglicans.

By 1688, of 1714 J.P.s and deputy lieutenants (most deputy lieutenants also serving as J.P.s) in all but five counties of England and Wales, at least 410, or 23.9 per cent, were Catholics. As Catholics comprised little more than one per cent of the population, this would suggest that James pressed most of the available Catholics into service. In the North Riding most of the leading Catholics were appointed. In Buckinghamshire, according to Jeffreys' unreliable figures, ten J.P.s were Catholics in 1688 (in fact there were eight), three of them newly put in. Seven (in fact nine) were Anglicans, none of them new. Twenty-one were Dissenters, all of them new. The only members of prominent Catholic families who were not made J.P.s were Charles Dormer, a minor, and Sir John Fortescue, a lunatic.[13]

With the exception of the army, where Catholic and Protestant officers were employed on roughly equal terms,[14] all available Catholics were given places in most areas of employment simply because they were Catholics. James's claim that he only wanted to place Catholics on an equal footing with Protestants was not borne out by his actions. By 1688 thirteen out of forty-three Privy Councillors were Catholics, including five converts.[15] The first Catholic lord lieutenant, lord Dover, was appointed in November 1686. No more were appointed until August 1687, but by March 1688 there were thirteen. Most had replaced Anglicans who were put out for refusing to co-operate in the tendering of the three questions. Allowing for the converts

191; Appendix 3. The data for the second remodelling are rather less complete than those for the first

[13] Appendix 3; Aveling, *Northern Catholics*, p. 336; Duckett, ii, 148–54, 296–7; CRS, lx, 291, 300–2; T. B. Trappes-Lomax, 'Some Homes of the Dormer Family', *RH*, viii (1966), 183.

[14] Miller, *EHR*, lxxxviii, 48.

[15] Apart from the five appointed in 1686, there were the following: Castlemaine, Fr Petre, Sir T. Strickland and the five converts: Perth; Melfort, Peterborough, Sir N. Butler and Sunderland. PC/2/71, p. v; PC/2/72, p. 707.

Sunderland and Peterborough (the latter holding two lieutenancies) Catholics held sixteen out of forty-three lieutenancies in 1688, one of them jointly. (This does not include London and counts Wales as a single lieutenancy.)[16]

Apart from Herbert Masters, who was sheriff of Herefordshire from 1686 to 1688 and who was converted to Catholicism, the first Catholic sheriffs were appointed in November 1687. Terriesi thought James had appointed no Catholic sheriffs in 1686 for reasons of caution. In 1687 thirteen Catholics were appointed and served, counting one whose place was taken by his son.[17] Three were appointed and failed to serve and two were appointed in April and July 1688 and served.[18] William Gower, apparently a Catholic, was appointed sheriff of Worcestershire in November 1688, but refused to serve. Thus while James was trying to obtain a House of Commons that would repeal the penal laws and Test Acts, fourteen or at most sixteen of the county shrievalties were held by Papists. Sheriffs played a vital part in county elections. That so few Papists were appointed must reflect either awareness that to appoint a Catholic would be politically damaging in many counties or a dearth of Catholics suitable or willing to serve.

In the law, too, the employment of Catholics was hindered by a lack of suitable personnel. Few Catholics managed to practise law. Although some entered an Inn of Court as part of their education, a survey of the Inns in 1679 revealed only

---

16 Duckett, i, 3–18 gives a list taken from the patent rolls, the dates of which are slightly later than those in the secretary's entry book (SP/44/164). The Catholics were Dover, Nov. 1686; Waldegrave, Aug. 1687; Molyneux, Sept. 1687; Aston, Carrington and Fairfax, Nov. 1687; Berwick, Dec. 1687; Teynham, Jan. 1688; Powis, Petre and Montagu, Feb. 1688; Yarmouth (joint with lord Pembroke) and lord T. Howard, March 1688.

17 *Orange Gazette*, no. 3 (3–7 Jan. 1689); BM Add. MS 25373, fol. 38. The Catholic sheriffs were: T. Wollascott (Berks.); Sir E. Longueville (Bucks.); H. Curwen (Cumb.); J. Rowe (Devon); Sir T. Manby (Essex); H. Hall (Glos.); P. Jones (Mon.); G., then F. Willoughby (Notts.); Sir H. Browne (Oxon.); P. Draycott (Staffs.); Sir J. Gage (Sussex); R. Sheldon (Warwks.); Sir W. Blount (Worcs.). From 'A List of Sheriffs for England and Wales', *Public Record Office Lists and Indexes*, vol. ix. Mackintosh, p. 189, gave the number of Catholic sheriffs as thirteen.

18 The three: Sir H. Hunloke (Derbys.); B. Moor (Herts.); M. Wynn (Denb.). The two, J. Digby (Rutland) and R. Vaughan (Radnor).

twenty-three English and Welsh Catholics, most of whom were country gentlemen rather than practising lawyers. Catholics like Richard Langhorne (executed during the Plot) or Brent, who built up substantial practices, were exceptional. Brent even undertook some Treasury business in 1675–8.[19] James appointed three Catholic judges. Sir Christopher Milton, a convert, the brother of John Milton, was appointed in 1686 and discharged as superannuated in 1688. Sir Richard Allibone and Sir Charles Ingleby were appointed in 1687 and 1688. It is possible that another judge, Sir Robert Wright, became a Catholic; there is some evidence that he considered doing so.[20]

Few Catholics attained positions of eminence in the central administration, partly because so few possessed real ability and experience, and partly because Sunderland was determined to stomach no rivals. Arundell of Wardour, an octogenarian, became lord privy seal in 1687. In December 1686 Bellasis, verging on decrepitude, and the swaggering Dover were made Treasury commissioners, along with the experienced Protestant administrators, Godolphin, Ernle and Fox. Melfort, the Scottish secretary, and Sunderland, after his conversion, were the only other Catholics to hold major offices. The Catholics' strength at court lay in their influence on James, not in the offices that they held. Those Catholics who held court posts or who undertook diplomatic missions – Castlemaine, Waldegrave, Albeville, Thomas Howard – were not in themselves men of great political weight or ability.[21]

Catholics were employed at all levels of the administration. Papists ejected from the customs service after the Revolution

[19] House of Lords R. O., Main Papers, no. 114 (3 April 1679); *CTB*, v, 491, 910; PC/2/67, p. 46.
[20] For Milton, Allibone and Ingleby, see *DNB;* Wright was pardoned and dispensed from taking the oaths in 1687, SP/44/337, p. 299. A. F. Havighurst, 'James II and the Twelve Men in Scarlet', *Law Quarterly Review*, lxix (1953), 533 says that Wright may have been converted. G. W. Keeton, *Lord Chancellor Jeffreys and the Stuart Cause* (London, 1965) states that both Wright and Sir William Williams became Catholics, but he adduces no evidence (pp. 342, 357, 367). The latter seems very unlikely in view of his Whig past; he made his peace with William as early as 16 Dec. 1688, see DNB.
[21] PC/2/71, p. 410; *CSPD 1686–7*, no. 1286; *Memoirs of the Life of Sir Stephen Fox* (1717), p. 115; Barillon au Roi, 22 July 1686 NS, Baschet 166.

ranged from the hon. William Molyneux, customer of Chester, to humbled tidewaiters, searchers and boatmen.[22] Catholics were also intruded into municipal corporations. At Gloucester the mayor, John Hill, turned Catholic; the king ordered that he be kept in for another term; Catholic mayors were elected by the king's command at Stafford and at Newcastle-upon-Tyne.[23] The Cambridge corporation successfully resisted an attempt put in a Catholic mayor in 1687, but the next year the mayor was a Catholic. At Worcester the mayor was dismissed for making a bonfire on 5 November 1687; his successor was a Catholic.[24] At Carlisle and no doubt elsewhere Catholics were made aldermen. But in most towns there were few Catholics. If suitable M.P.s were to be elected, the king would need the co-operation of the Dissenters. The more radical sects heeded his advances more than did the moderates; the latter had been so alarmed by events by the beginning of 1688 that they started to listen to the advances of the Church of England. Perhaps more significant than any intrusion of Papists was the dissolution of the Norwich corporation in 1688 for refusing to admit Quakers.[25]

The purges of the commissions of the peace and of the corporations and the employment of Catholics in them were part of a revolutionary attack on the existing political order and on the sensibilities and monopoly of office of the Anglican gentry. James hoped somehow to secure the appearance of the consent of the political nation for the repeal of the penal laws and Test Acts. But if many Protestants did not object too strongly to the Catholics' being allowed to practise their religion, for the great majority of Englishmen it was a basic axiom that Papists should be kept out of political life and out of positions of power. Once there, it was believed, they would press the king to rule in their interest until the Protestants could trust no magistrate. Hoffmann, the Imperial envoy, understood this: 'It is impracticable to allow [Protestants and Catholics] to mix in public office, and to make

[22] *CTB*, viii, 2151, 2153, 2156–8, 2162, 2165, ix, 2, 9, 12–13.
[23] SP/44/337, pp. 300, 361; Luttrell, i, 396, 415; BM Add. MSS 25373, fols. 8–9, 25374, fol. 212; J. Brand, *History and Antiquities of Newcastle upon Tyne* (2 vols., London, 1789), ii, 194–5, 498.
[24] *HMC Downshire*, i, 269; *HMC le Fleming*, p. 216; BM Add. MS 25375, fol. 72.
[25] *HMC le Fleming*, pp. 209–10 (the Catholics were Sir F. Salkeld, H. Curwen and W. Fletcher); BM Add. MS 34487, fols. 19, 25.

them live in harmony, since the two religions are so strongly
opposed and since it is impossible for the king to extirpate the
zeal and the animosity which the two sides hold for each other.'
He argued that it would therefore be a mistake to intrude Catholics into offices: 'It would be unjust for a few to unsettle the
calm of a whole nation.'[26] Few Protestants would have disagreed
with that. Whatever Dissenters thought of the repeal of the penal
laws, they had little interest in the repeal of the Test Acts, which
affected them far less than they affected the Catholics.[27]

It is very difficult to find first-hand evidence of what the
Catholics thought of James's plans. There is little Catholic
family correspondence for this period and I have found virtually
none for 1687–8. General evidence suggests that the Catholics
were unenthusiastic. Terriesi repeatedly stated that the lay
Catholics were reluctant to support James, fearing severe persecution under a Protestant successor. Barillon wrote in November
1685:

Les Catholiques riches et établis craignent l'avenir et appréhendent
un retour qui les ruinerait; ainsi ils voudraient admettre tous les
tempéraments possibles et se contenteraient des plus médiocres avan-
tages qu'on leur voudrait accorder, comme serait la révocation des
lois pénales sans s'attacher à la révocation du test.

The court Catholics wanted to repeal the Test Acts as well.[28]
Protestant observers also noted that the Catholic landowners
were more cautious than the courtiers. They were slow to thank
the king for the Declaration of Indulgence and produced only
one address.[29] There were reports that some wanted the moderate
Powis, rather than Tyrconnel, to be made lord lieutenant of
Ireland, that some asked William's envoy Dijkveld in 1687 to
assure the prince that they would do nothing contrary to his
interests, that the Catholic peers urged James to act with moderation in the case of the Seven Bishops and that lord Bellasis urged
James to negotiate with William at the beginning of December
1688. Some were said to have refused to serve as sheriffs while

---

[26] Campana, ii, 163.

[27] BM Add. MSS 25374, fol. 90, 25376, fol. 201; SS Ing. 12, fol. 267.

[28] BM Add. MSS 25369, fol. 265, 25371, fol. 346, 25374, fols. 64–5, 155,
25375, fol. 41; Barillon au Roi, 12 and 22 Nov. 1685 NS, Baschet 162.

[29] Portland MSS 2104, 2126; *Supplement to Burnet*, p. 210; Halifax,
Works, p. 338; Ailesbury, i, 152, 165; BM Add. MS 25374, fol. 120.

others who agreed to serve allegedly said that they would not make false returns in elections.[30]

Evidence about the attitude of individuals is harder to find. Lord Bellasis told the earl of Ailesbury that he regretted the tone of James's speech to parliament in November 1685; he later told Reresby that he had opposed James's policies but that he had been ignored as one who was old and timorous and feared to lose his estates. He described Tyrconnel as madman enough to ruin three kingdoms.[31] Sir William Goring is said to have reproached Catholics for serving as J.P.s and deputy lieutenants, saying 'you will ruin us all by it'. But if he refused to serve, his name still appeared in the commissions of the peace for Sussex. Sir John Gage, sheriff of Sussex, 'a gentleman of a very plentiful estate and for that reason a moderate man', said in March 1688 that there was no need for the Catholics to make an address to the king as he knew their feelings already.[32] Of eight Catholic J.P.s appointed in Warwickshire only three acted at sessions and only one of the three Catholic peers included in the commission acted. On the other hand, of six Catholic J.P.s appointed in Suffolk early in 1687, at least four appeared at sessions.[33] (It was by no means unusual for Protestant J.P.s to appear very rarely at sessions or not at all.) I have found no definite evidence of Catholics who refused to be made J.P.s, although some who appear in the lists for early 1687 are not in those for 1688. Three Catholics refused to be made sheriffs in 1687, but Protestants were also often reluctant to take on this expensive charge. Charles Trinder apparently refused to be made a judge in July 1688.[34]

It is also clear, however, that many Catholic gentlemen took office willingly and gave active support both to the missionary effort and to the campaign to secure the repeal of the penal laws

---

[30] *Supplement to Burnet*, pp. 210, 255; Comber, ii, 144; Barillon au Roi, 5 May 1687 and 13 Dec. 1688 NS, Baschet 169 and CPA 167; BM Add. MSS 25373, fol. 38, 34510, fol. 123; Macaulay, ii, 335n., 431; Portland MS 2113.

[31] Ailesbury, i, 126; Reresby, p. 561; Portland MS 2100; Dalrymple, i, 98.

[32] Ailesbury, i, 152; Bodl., Ballard MS 11, fol. 183.

[33] *Warwick County Records*, vii, pp. li–lii, lvii; Ipswich and East Suffolk R.O., B. 105/2/11; I am grateful to Marion Clark, the assistant archivist, for supplying me with lists of the J.P.s at each sessions.

[34] BM Add. MS 29563, fol. 215.

and Test Acts. The Lancashire Papists were said to be particularly aggressive, seizing and saying Mass in chapels that belonged to the established church. Elsewhere there were reports of provocative and tactless behaviour by Papists.[35] At least three of the Catholic sheriffs insisted on hearing Catholic sermons in their county towns; another empanelled an almost wholly Catholic jury; other Catholic notables encouraged grand juries to address the king and to thank him for his indulgence. Judge Allibone, the Catholic lords lieutenant and some of the Catholic J.P.s campaigned for the repeal of the penal laws and Test Acts, but their approach was rather too restrained and gentlemanly and in the spring of 1688 James had recourse to more experienced and less scrupulous canvassers, who were mostly Dissenters.[36] In short, most Catholic peers and gentlemen seem to have been willing to accept the local offices from which they had been excluded for so long because of their religion and to support the mission, which could operate at last without restriction. There is less evidence that they wholeheartedly supported James's increasingly ruthless campaign to secure a compliant parliament, in which he came to rely increasingly, not on Catholic officials, but on organisers and electioneers who had learned their skills under Shaftesbury and the Exclusionist Whigs.

If this campaign met with considerable difficulties, the missionary effort was going little better. James assured d'Adda that conversions were being made but Terriesi repeatedly stated that although there were many converts among the lower classes, there were few of wealth or social consequence.[37] The few converts of rank were mostly associated with the court. It seemed, however, that one of the greatest obstacles to conversions, the lack of a Catholic successor, might soon be removed. By

---

[35] SP/44/56, p. 415; Morrice MS P, p. 481; *HMC Kenyon*, p. 203; Bodl., Tanner MS 29, fol. 133; BM Add. MS 29563, fol. 312; *Clarendon Correspondence*, i, 198.

[36] SP/44/56, p. 406; BM Add. MSS 25375, fol. 241, 36707, fol. 38; Bodl., Ballard MSS 11, fol. 183, 12, fols. 38–9, Tanner MSS 28, fol. 138a, 259, fol. 55; P. C. Vellacott, 'The Diary of a Country Gentleman in 1688', *Cambridge Historical Journal*, ii (1926), 51–2; *HMC le Fleming*, p. 209; Jones, *HJ*, iii, 67 and passim.

[37] BM Add. MSS 15396, fols. 390–1, 25373, fol. 242, 25374, fol. 112, 25376, fol. 72.

the beginning of January 1688 the queen was definitely pregnant and James had great hopes of a son.[38] Thus encouraged, he stepped up his campaign for a parliament. As he could conceive of no other means of achieving his ends, he responded to rebuffs and to the absence of results by intensifying his existing policy. His obstinate persistence can best be explained by the fact that his sources of information were, in Professor Kenyon's words, 'polluted by sycophancy, wilful optimism or sheer ignorance' and also by 'the emotion that leads men without hope to cling to their illusions even in the face of self-evident fact'.[39]

As the campaign came to rely increasingly blatantly on force and fraud and as the possibility of a Catholic heir loomed larger, Dissenters and Anglicans moved closer together. The birth of the Prince of Wales and the trial of the Seven Bishops brought matters to a head. The fact that James now had a Catholic heir made an invasion much more likely. After the Bishops' acquittal Sunderland urged James to make concessions but he refused. Then, in the latter part of September, he finally realised that invasion was imminent; he undid all he had done since 1687 and even restored all the charters that had been forfeited since 1679 and reinstated those who had served under them.[40] Catholics were put out of all civilian appointments, but not out of the army, where their reliability made them far too valuable to lose. But these concessions were all too obviously designed to recover support in the face of invasion and did the king little political good.

James now became cautious. He rejected Barillon's advice to bring troops over from Ireland, as he feared that to do so would alienate his subjects. He decided instead to see what the Church of England men would do.[41] As his schemes crumbled he pinned his hopes on divine intervention. D'Adda wrote that he had confidence in his army 'but he trusts more in the assistance of God, who will defend a cause that is His'. Four days later he was less sure of the army and had the Host exposed in his

---

38 Barillon au Roi, 15 Jan. 1688 NS, Baschet 175.
39 Kenyon, *Sunderland*, p. 193; Jones, *HJ*, vol. iii, passim; Lacey, p. 206.
40 Barillon au Roi, 19 July 1688 NS, CPA 166; BM Add. MS 15397, fol. 154; Kenyon, *Sunderland*, pp. 217–19.
41 Barillon au Roi, 18 Sept. 1688 NS, CPA 166; *Clarendon Correspondence*, ii, 190.

chapel to implore divine assistance. He later claimed that this explained the scattering of the Dutch fleet in a storm. On 26 September he was persuaded to summon parliament but then changed his mind. Jeffreys fumed that 'some rogues had changed the king's mind; that he would yield in nothing to the bishops; that the Virgin Mary was to do all'.[42] His self-confidence collapsed with his plans and he took refuge in blind faith. He finally agreed to summon a few regiments from Ireland and assured d'Adda that he had not given up his plans for the advancement of Catholicism in England and that he was trusting in God.[43] Just over a month later he was on his way to France.

Throughout his reign, James's aim was to secure a full, open and legal toleration for Catholics in the fond belief that, once this was achieved, England would revert to Catholicism within a few years. Seventeenth century Protestants failed to understand that Catholics found more in their religion than empty ceremonies and blind obedience to the pope or that Catholicism was more than a crafty imposition by avaricious priests and megalomaniac popes on a populace deliberately maintained in ignorance. Similarly James and his entourage could not believe that Protestants had a genuine spiritual attachment to their mode of belief. They attributed their remaining Protestant either to timidity, in the face of the penal laws, or to self-interest – the clergy wanted to keep their tithes and benefices, the laity feared for their abbey-lands. To James nothing but fears for their property could explain men's attachment to a type of belief that seemed to him so obviously false. He therefore took pains to soothe what he regarded as the most basic Protestant fears and included explicit assurances tbout abbey-lands and benefices in the Declaration of Indulgence.[44] In fact the abbey-land question was a minor feature of the much broader and deeper anti-Catholic tradition. James did not understand this and attributed

---

[42] BM Add. MS 15397, fols. 289–90, 293–8; Dalrymple, i, 157; *Clarendon Correspondence*, ii, 190–1.

[43] Barillon au Roi, 14 and 18 Oct. 1688 NS, CPA 166; BM Add. MS 15397, fol. 406.

[44] BM Add. MS 15395, fols. 301, 367–8; Akerman, p. 179; Barillon au Roi, 8 Nov. 1685 NS, Baschet 162; Weldon, pp. 229–30; Kenyon, *Stuart Constitution*, pp. 411, 413.

all opposition to self-interest, factiousness or sedition. He was not a genuine believer in toleration. His concessions to Dissent were dictated by expediency. He had no respect for the beliefs of others, however sincerely held. He later explained his expulsion in 1688 in terms of rebellion and conspiracy. He could not or would not understand that his blind zeal for Catholicism and the actions that it had led him to undertake had alienated his subjects to a point where even d'Adda noted that they were 'indifferent to say the least' in the face of William's invasion.[45] He had failed totally to appreciate the strength and depth of the English anti-Catholic tradition.

[45] BM Add. MS 15397, fols. 447–8.

12

JAMES II AND ROME

Before he came to the throne, James II's relations with the Holy
See had not been entirely happy. For a long time the curia had
resented his marrying Mary Beatrice without its approval. When
he became king James did little to endear himself to the pope by
either the matter or the manner of his dealings with him. James
concentrated on the personal gratification of himself and his
queen rather than on the needs of the English mission. In particular he tried for over three years to bully the pope into making
Edward Petre SJ either a bishop or a cardinal. He ignored
Innocent XI's arguments and obstinately refused to take 'no'
for an answer.

James's high-handedness in his dealings with Rome seemed a
conscious imitation of that of Louis XIV, who had carried on a
long series of disputes with successive popes. Louis combined his
plundering and oppression of the French church with claims of its
virtual independence of Rome. His ambassador to the Holy See
claimed an excessive degree of diplomatic immunity. To these
long-standing sources of friction was added the dispute over the
election to the archbishopric of Cologne in 1688. It was not
surprising, therefore, that the dominant feature of Innocent XI's
diplomacy was antipathy to France. It was thus singularly unfortunate that James should choose to imitate the French king's
manner and that a close political connection should be believed
to exist between them. Although James's ambassador did not
claim the wide immunities claimed by his French counterpart, he
renounced them with such excessive self-congratulation on
his own moderation that he must have dissipated any good
impression that the renunciation might have created. Moreover,
the pope, advised by cardinal Philip Howard (also known as
cardinal Norfolk), had grave doubts about the wisdom of James's
religious policy. He continually urged that James and the English
Catholics should be content with moderate gains and that they
should not ruin all by trying to gain too much.[1] So when James

---

[1] Cibo MS 88, pp. 20–1; B. Neveu, 'Jacques II Médiateur entre Louis

demanded in a clumsy and high-handed manner favours of which the pope disapproved and which had nothing to do with the needs of the English mission, he was unlikely to meet with a favourable response.

James's reign started smoothly enough. There had been some preliminary moves about the appointment of a vicar apostolic in 1684. Howard told the Chapter that Rome regarded its present constitution as illegal and that it would never appoint an ordinary for England. The Brussels internuncio remarked that he knew little of the situation in England, which he thought was Howard's concern.[2] When Charles died, the Chapter petitioned James not to admit a vicar apostolic but on 3 April the king asked Rome to appoint one, and suggested that John Leyburn (Howard's secretary) was a suitable candidate. In August a congregation at the Quirinale appointed Leyburn vicar apostolic, with the title of bishop of Adrumetum *in partibus infidelium* and with the faculties granted to Bishop in 1623 and to Howard in 1672.[3]

Having provided a head for the mission James concentrated on gratifying the queen and himself. In May he asked the pope to make Rinaldo d'Este, the queen's uncle, a cardinal. In October he asked that Petre, the dean of the chapel royal, should be made a bishop, announced that he would send an ambassador to Rome and asked the pope to send a nuncio to England. A papal agent Ferdinando d'Adda, arrived in November, but not until May 1687 was he raised to the dignity of nuncio and consecrated a bishop *in partibus* in a public ceremony. The pope was more fearful of the reaction of English Protestants than was the king; he delayed as long as possible conferring on d'Adda the title of nuncio and giving an audience to James's ambassador.[4]

Innocent XI did not want to promote Rinaldo for several reasons. His uncle, also called Rinaldo, had been a cardinal and a

XIV et Innocent XI', *Mélanges d'Archéologie et d'Histoire*, lxxix (1967), 714, 716–18, 723, 755–6 (especially p. 756 n. 3); Ranke, iv, 373; Burnet, iii, 78–9; CUL Add. MS 4879, fol. 71.

[2] Nunz, Fian. 75, fol. 8; Nunz. Div. 228, fols. 49–50, 232, fols. 159–60; AAW A34, pp. 920–1.

[3] AAW A34, p. 931; James II to the pope, 3 April 1685, Rom. Tr. 100A, fol. 331; Nunz. Fian. 75, fols. 371–2; Nunz. Div. 232, fol. 168; Prop. Ang., fols. 782–91.

[4] Ailesbury, i, 152–3, 165.

bull of Sixtus V forbade that the cardinalates should become hereditary. Besides the last cardinal d'Este had been an active partisan of France and the pope feared that his nephew would be the same. James claimed that Rinaldo would depend on nobody but the pope. He had never heard of the bull of Sixtus V. In September 1686 the pope gave in and raised Rinaldo to the purple.[5] The pope was even less willing to agree to the promotion of Petre. Innocent XI was generally regarded as being hostile to the Society of Jesus, although his hostility was tempered by his even greater antipathy to France and by the election of an anti-French general of the Society in 1687.[6] He did not want to appoint a Jesuit to either a bishopric or a cardinalate, especially at the request of a prince. To do so would establish a precedent at a time when the king of Spain was pressing for a similar favour and when many other princes had Jesuit confessors. When popes had promoted Jesuits in the past it had been for their own exceptional merits and the initiative had come from the pope and not from a prince. The pope resented what he regarded as improper and unpleasant signs of ambition on the part of a member of the Society. He stressed that he would willingly consider promoting members of any other order, provided that they were personally suitable.[7]

In November 1685 the pope politely refused to make Petre a bishop on the grounds that he was a Jesuit and asked James to recommend another candidate.[8] In February the earl of Castlemaine, the complaisant husband of one of Charles II's mistresses and an active Catholic pamphleteer, left to become James's ambassador at Rome; he had been instructed to press for the promotion of both Rinaldo and Petre. At Rome he established himself in sumptuous magnificence. His palace bore the arms of the king and the pope, with various devices showing true religion crushing heresy. (In the official English account of his

[5] BM Add. MSS 15395, fols. 503–4, 518, 15396, fols. 98–9, 131–2, 25372, fol. 230; Burnet, iii, 156n.

[6] E. Michaud, *Louis XIV et Innocent XI* (4 vols., Paris, 1882–3), i, 267–268, 289–93, 299–301; Neveu, pp. 715–16; BM Add. MS 25373, fol. 48; Clarke, ii, 78; Ranke, iv, 378; Burnet, iii, 159.

[7] BM Add. MSS 15396, fols. 142–3, 335–8, 25375, fols. 135–6; SS Ing. 12, fols. 276–7.

[8] BM Add. MS 15395, fols. 294–5.

embassy 'rebellion' was substituted for 'heresy'.)[9] His carriage towards the pope was no more tactful. When the pope postponed his audience several times on the pretext that he was ill, Castlemaine grew impatient. Late in August, acting on James's orders, he threatened to go home unless d'Este was promoted. The pope was highly offended, but James had become increasingly impatient at the pope's resistance to a request so 'reasonable' as that for d'Este's promotion, and meant what he said.[10] When Innocent gave in to this bullying, James was encouraged to try it again in the case of Petre.

Petre had been gaining an increasing ascendancy over James for some time; a contemporary Jesuit account suggested that James's influence had saved Petre from coming to trial during the Plot. By the end of 1686 he had eclipsed all his rivals.[11] James pressed with increasing impatience for his promotion. Barillon thought that as a bishop Petre would be able to perform his functions in the king's chapel with greater dignity. James claimed that he had few subjects worthy of promotion, that Petre was a man of great merits who had suffered during the Plot and who was not pressing for his own advancement and that his promotion would greatly help the Catholic religion in England. (He did not explain how.) Sunderland told d'Adda that the king wanted Petre to have a more conspicuous character so that he could introduce him into the management of affairs.[12] D'Adda had a hard task when he tried to explain to James the reasons for the pope's refusal. In June 1686 James interrupted him several times, complained that Jesuits had been promoted in the past and threatened to recall Castlemaine. In February 1687, when James said that Castlemaine had led him to expect the promotion, even the urbane d'Adda was nettled. He replied that he did not know how Castlemaine could have got that impression and started wearily to go over the pope's reasons for refusal for

---

9 BM Add. MS 10118, fol. 143; Luttrell, i, 393; J. M. Wright, *An Account of His Excellence Roger Earl of Castlemaine's Embassy* (1688), pp. 27–9, 65, 78 and the various illustrations.

10 BM Add. MSS 25372, fols. 137, 230, 28226, fol. 19.

11 Foley, v, 148; Ellis, i, 20–1, 47, 68, 155, 196, 224; BM Add. MS 25373, fol. 88.

12 Barillon au Roi, 27 June 1686 NS, Baschet 166; BM Add. MSS 15395, fols. 527–8, 15396, fols. 181–5; SS Ing. 12, fols. 40–2; Cibo MS 88, pp. 19, 22–4.

the umpteenth time. He even read to James the decree of the
Council of Trent against the promotion of Jesuits, but to no
avail. James ignored all d'Adda's arguments and endlessly repeated his own.[13]

Obstinacy on both sides was bound to lead to a clash. The
instructions of Sir John Litcot, who was to succeed Castlemaine
as James's agent in Rome in the spring of 1687, show clearly the
high-handed attitude of the English court. James insisted that
no one whom he had not recommended should be promoted to a
bishopric. He claimed that, during the long hiatus of Catholic
church government in England, the crown might have acquired
new rights or just claims to peculiar methods. 'We directed him
[Castlemaine] not [to] be diverted by precedents and practices of
other kingdoms from prosecuting such means, though unusual,
as we should think fit to preserve or suggest towards the attaining
of our ends.'[14] James was as impatient of Rome's concern for
legal niceties as he was with the technicalities of the Common
Law when they stood in his way.

The clash came in April 1687. Castlemaine demanded that the
pope should promote Petre and threatened that, if he did not, the
king would recall Castlemaine and expel d'Adda from London.
He added that the pope's refusal was an affront to the king's
honour and belittled him in the eyes of other princes and in those
of his subjects. The pope was bitterly angry at such treatment
and this time he was not going to give in to it. He said that he
presumed that Castlemaine was not expressing the king's opinion.
In June James wrote asking pardon for Castlemaine's behaviour
and requested that Petre should be made a cardinal instead.
The pope refused.[15] James and his queen continued to proceed
with a fine disregard of the wishes of everyone but themselves. In
August 1686 James had said that he wished to make d'Este
cardinal protector of England when he was raised to the purple.
D'Adda reported that d'Este wanted the office, not knowing that
it was held by Howard, who had been protector since 1680. In
October 1687 the queen suggested that d'Este be made the

---

[13] BM Add. MSS 15395, fols. 516–22, 15397, fols. 281–2 (the latter dispatch is misdated in the transcripts; it should be 3 Oct. 1687 NS, not
1688); Cibo MS 88, pp. 25–6; SS Ing. 12, fols. 40–1.

[14] BM Lansdowne MS 1152 B. fols. 260–1.

[15] Cibo MS 88, pp. 1–5, 22, 29; BM Add. MSS 9341, fols. 3–5, 15396,
fols. 294–5, 25374, fol. 106.

English ambassador to Rome, to show that he was independent of France. When the pope pointed out that cardinals were not allowed to hold such posts, James declared that he would give d'Este the protectorship, at a salary of £5000 a year, which would help to ensure a 'perfect correspondence' between king and pope. James wrote to Howard, urging him not to take the change in bad part, and made him his lord almoner, at a salary of £2000 a year; Leyburn was to act as his deputy. James told Howard that he was in no way dissatisfied with his behaviour, but that 'I think it will be best for my service to employ in that station the cardinal d'Este who is so nearly related to the queen my wife and therefore I am fully persuaded that you will readily acquiesce therein.'[16]

It is possible that d'Este's 'appointment' was a by-product of the Petre campaign. The French ambassador in Rome reported that Howard was turning the pope against Petre. D'Adda reported that James believed that Howard had given the pope the impression that Petre was anxious for promotion and that he had pressed the king to make representations on his behalf. James assured the pope that Petre was in no way ambitious. D'Adda tried unsuccessfully to convince Sunderland that the pope's refusal expressed his own wishes and was not just the product of Howard's influence. Howard certainly had grave reservations about James's forward policy and probably had little time for Petre. But Terriesi and an anonymous writer of November 1687 both thought that Howard was not hostile to Petre's promotion; according to Terriesi, it was not on Howard that the Jesuits blamed the pope's refusal. I think it probable that the king and queen simply regarded the queen's uncle as a more suitable protector of England than an English cardinal; they may also have thought that d'Este would press more energetically than Howard would for Petre's promotion. Whatever they thought, it made no difference. The protectorship was a papal appointment and Howard remained protector until his death.[17]

16 BM Add. MSS 10118, fol. 161, 15396, fols. 131–2, 25372, fols. 230, 294, 25375, fols. 13, 38; BM Lansdowne MS 1152B, fol. 13; SS Ing. 12, fols. 242–4; AAW A35, p. 443; Akerman, p. 191.
17 Michaud, ii, 113, 118; BM Add. MSS 15396, fols. 382–3, 25374 ,fol. 264; Burnet, iii, 78–9; unsigned letter of 20 Oct. 1687, Rom. Tr. 100B, fol. 180; Anstruther, pp. 359–60.

In late 1687 and early 1688 James mounted a sustained diplomatic campaign for Petre's promotion and also made it clear that it had nothing to do with the organisational needs of the English mission by asking for and getting three more vicars apostolic; he had mentioned the need for these over a year earlier.[18] The Spanish ambassador at Rome and the grand duke of Tuscany made representations to the pope on Petre's behalf. James made Petre a privy councillor as a determined if irrelevant demonstration of his favour to him. As Terriesi explained, if the pope would not promote Petre in the ecclesiastical sphere, the king would promote him in the temporal. It made no difference to Petre's influence, which was essentially of a private and unofficial kind.[19]

As usual, when James's plans failed to work, he and his entourage did not consider whether they had been attempting the impossible but explained their difficulties in personal terms. The Jesuits were now a dominant element in the 'forward party' at court. James had always shown a fondness for the order but after the Plot he had been forced to take a non-Jesuit as his confessor, a Lorrainer called Mansuet who took no part in politics. In February 1687 James was persuaded to dismiss him and to take as his confessor John Warner SJ, on the flimsy pretext that a certain woman was often at Mansuet's lodgings and that there was a fear of scandals. As d'Adda sarcastically pointed out, Mansuet was seventy.[20] The influence of Petre and Warner was essentially secret and so is hard to evaluate. It was almost certainly greatly exaggerated by contemporaries who, fearful at the prospect of members of the dreaded Society close to the centre of power, ascribed every unpopular feature of James's policies to their malign machinations. I think it probable that Petre was more concerned with court and ecclesiastical in-fighting than with national politics and this impression is supported by two men who knew far more of what went on at James II's court than either bishop Burnet or lord Macaulay. The earl of Ailesbury thought Petre 'a hot-headed ignorant churchman' who 'had

---

[18] BM Add. MSS 9341, fols. 20, 22, 15396, fols. 87–8.
[19] CUL Add. MS 4879, fol. 120; BM Add. MS 25375, fols. 11, 25–6, 111–12.
[20] SS Ing. 12, fols. 55–8; ASJ, Foley MS i, 183; Morrice MSS P, pp. 532, 628, Q, p. 210; Ellis, i, 47, 68, 155.

nothing in view but a cardinal's hat'. Terriesi thought that the Jesuits' influence was usually exaggerated: 'in fact all essential matters spring from the king with the advice of the lord chancellor [Jeffreys] or of lord Sunderland'. Some saw Petre as no more than the tool of Sunderland.[21] The Jesuits were only one among several Catholic influences at court; it is clear that Sunderland and later Melfort, and also perhaps the queen and Barillon, were the most powerful influences on James and that many of the king's policies originated in his own mind. The strength of the Jesuits, of Sunderland and of the forward party generally lay in the fact that they all told James what he wanted to hear.

The Jesuits both in the English court and at Rome had a great interest in the elevation of Petre to the purple; Litcot kept Petre informed of how 'the affair' was going. The Jesuits came increasingly to ascribe the pope's refusals to d'Adda's misinforming the pope. They urged James to recall Litcot and to expel d'Adda, and to tell the pope that James could be a good Catholic while doing without the court of Rome; in other words they urged James to adopt Louis XIV's approach. Petre himself blamed d'Adda for the pope's refusal; he had never liked the nuncio and there was even a story that Petre had told the king that d'Adda was a Whig.[22] In a conversation with Terriesi in January 1688, Petre railed incoherently against the nuncio and even against the pope. He praised James's patience and moderation in tolerating their behaviour. 'He then burst out in threats of royal resentment; he foretold very considerable changes and promised severe revenge against the pope and his supporters; he exaggerated this and a thousand other ambiguities so confusedly that I could make no sense of it.' Petre added that he was sure that the pope had not been informed of the harm his refusal was bringing on the Catholic religion.[23] Soon afterwards

[21] Ailesbury, i, 152; BM Add. MS 25374, fol. 219: 'Le còse essenziali scaturiscano tutte in effètto da S. Mtà col consìglio del Gran Cancellière o di Milord Sunderland'; Clarke, ii, 76–7.

[22] ASJ, Anglia Epist. Gen. 1642–98, fol. 472; PRO, SP/85/12, fol. 238; BM Add. MSS 25374, fols. 320–1, 25375, fols, 10–12, 108, 34510, fol. 61; Morrice MS P, pp. 628, 650.

[23] BM Add. MS 25375, fols. 110–11. 'Prorompeva pòi in minàcce de' Reali risentiménti; prediceva novità rilevantissime et annunciava vendétte severissime cóntro del Papa e de' sua fautóri, facendo di

James and the Spanish ambassador reproved the unfortunate nuncio. (The Spanish ambassador worked closely with the king and the Jesuits on this matter, perhaps hoping that if the pope granted James's request, he would have to grant the similar request of the king of Spain.)[24] The pope took refuge in dignified silence, and ordered the general of the Jesuits to write to Petre and tell him to desist from putting any pressure on the king to seek his promotion. The general was upset by this and wrote instead to John Keynes, the English provincial, asking him to intimate to Petre that the pope would like him to desist. After making inquiries among Petre's friends, the general was convinced that the allegations of ambition were unfounded.[25] In February 1688 the Jesuits at court began to claim that d'Adda was under the influence of Sunderland (who was now drifting away from Petre) and of Barillon. In July, after the acquittal of the Seven Bishops, some of those close to the king ascribed their difficulties in large part to the pope's refusal to promote Petre.[26] With advisers like this it is not surprising that James's policies often had only a tenuous connection with reality.

In October 1687 James began to consider asking Louis to moderate the claims of his ambassador in Rome; he hoped thus to induce the pope to promote Petre. In January he offered to mediate between the pope and the French king. In June he sent lord Thomas Howard, the cardinal's nephew, to Rome as an ambassador extraordinary. He was to suggest negotiations in London through Barillon and d'Adda and was to ask once more for Petre to be promoted. James no doubt hoped that the pope might agree to this if the mediation succeeded. Both sides were now looking for a way to back down without losing face and there were signs in October that the pope might be ready to compromise, but the mediation was brought to an abrupt halt by the Revolution.[27]

At least as late as September 1688 James still hoped for Petre's

tutto ciò e di mille altre ambiguità che esagereva una catàstrofe tale che mai potetti ritrarne sènso di sòrte veruna.'

[24] BM Add. 25375, fols. 12, 38, 121–2.
[25] ASJ, Anglia Epist. Gen. 1642–98, fols. 478, 480–1.
[26] BM Add. MSS 25375, fols. 189, 212, 25376, fols. 44–5, 172, 34512, fols. 75–6; Portland MSS 2129, 2149.
[27] BM Add. MS 25374, fol. 313; BM Lansdowne MS 1152B, fols. 137–8; Michaud, ii, 124; Neveu, pp. 723–33.

promotion, almost three years after the pope's first refusal.[28] James's behaviour in his dealings with Rome was typical of him. He pursued his objectives with blinkered obstinacy, ascribing difficulties and failures to misinformation or intrigue. He assumed that, as he had become a Catholic and hoped to make England Catholic, he could dictate to the pope, who would do as he asked.[29] He failed to appreciate that at Rome there were forms and conventions which had to be respected and which could not be boorishly overridden. He also failed to understand that Innocent XI was also an obstinate man who hated France and did not like Jesuits. As so often, James could not conceive how anybody could in all sincerity hold an opinion that differed from his own. The pope did all that he could to please James. He appointed four vicars apostolic and eventually agreed to make d'Adda a nuncio and d'Este a cardinal. But he would not make any Jesuit a bishop or a cardinal at the instance of a prince, especially a prince who was suspected of having a close political connection with Louis XIV and who seemed determined to ape the manner of the French king in his dealings with Rome.

[28] BM Add. MS 15397, fols. 243–4.
[29] SS Ing. 12, fol. 276; Cibo MS 88, pp. 19–24, 27–8.

13

THE MISSIONARY EFFORT UNDER
JAMES II

James II's efforts to convert England to Catholicism were doomed to failure. He did not have the resources to convert a Protestant kingdom and anyway, quite apart from the anticipation of a Protestant successor, it became clear that after over a century of Protestantism Englishmen simply did not *want* to turn Catholic and James had no means of coercing them. As Halifax pointed out, the whole scheme was impossible:

The great design cannot be carried on without numbers; numbers cannot be had without converts, the old stock not being sufficient; converts will not venture till they have such a law to secure them as hath no exception to it; so that an irregularity, or any degree of violence to the law, would so entirely take away the effect of it that men would as little run the hazard of changing their religion after the making it as before.[1]

Terriesi reported on several occasions that although many converts were being made among the lower classes, there were very few among the nobility and gentry, except for courtiers anxious to curry favour with the king.[2] The Franciscans' figures for reconciliations to Catholicism in Worcestershire and at Birmingham do not suggest that the number of conversions was very large even among the poor, although it was higher than it had been during the last two decades of uncertainty and intermittent persecution. In Worcestershire there were twelve reconciliations in 1685, eleven in 1686, four in 1687 and two in 1688, a total of twenty-nine in four years. There had been thirty in the four years 1660–3 and there were forty-six in 1693–6. In Birmingham the picture was similar: forty-five reconciliations in 1685, forty-one in 1686, forty-one in 1687 and twenty in 1688. There had been forty-one in 1660, thirty-five in 1661 and forty-five in 1662. These figures suggest that in the west Midlands at least there were

[1] Halifax, *Works*, p. 335.
[2] BM Add. MSS 25371, fol. 33, 25373, fols. 39–40, 242, 25374, fol. 112, 25376, fol. 72.

more converts under James II than there had been since the years immediately after the Restoration but there are no signs of a mass movement towards Catholicism.[3]

There were few converts among persons of quality. Some who became Catholics in the hope of places or of quick promotion hastily reverted to Protestantism after the Revolution. These included Sunderland, the earl of Yarmouth, Sir Thomas Stradling (a lieutenant-colonel in the army and a J.P. for Glamorgan), Herbert Masters (sheriff and J.P. for Herefordshire), Sir Nicholas Butler (almost certainly) and even a humble waggoner.[4] Others however remained firm to the faith. The earls of Perth and Melfort and Sir Edward Hales went into exile with James. The earls of Salisbury and Peterborough both suffered imprisonment and they, John Dryden and Sir John Curson of Oxfordshire all remained Catholics until they died. However, neither Salisbury nor Peterborough left a Catholic heir and it is unlikely that conversions among the peers and gentry under James II compensated for apostasies at the time of the Plot.[5] There were some converts among the Anglican clergy: Terriesi reported in 1687 that thirty had been converted in the last two years. I have found records of ten who were converted, two of whom (Edward Slater and Mr Gibbs of Gissing, Suffolk) recanted in 1689. At least eight fellows of Oxford colleges became Catholics and Joshua Basset, another convert, became master of Sidney Sussex College, Cambridge. Most seem to have remained Catholics after the Revolution.[6]

[3] J. D. McEvilly, 'Worcestershire Entries in Franciscan Registers 1657–1824', *Worcestershire Recusant*, xiv (1969), 34–7; 'The Franciscan Register of St Peter's Birmingham', *Warwickshire Parish Registers*, iii, ed. W. P. W. Phillimore, J. L. Whitfield and J. H. Bloom (London, 1906), 1–17. (I am grateful to Fr Howard Docherty OFM for the latter reference.) Those reconciled at Birmingham included people from various parts of Worcestershire, Warwickshire and Staffordshire. For a Protestant comment on the small number of converts in Worcestershire, see Bodl., Ballard MS 12, fol. 21.

[4] J. P. Kenyon, *The Nobility in the Revolution of 1688* (Hull, 1963), p. 14; *HMC le Fleming*, p. 224; *POAS*, iv, 153–8; *Orange Gazette*, no. 3 (3–7 Jan. 1689); Luttrell, iii, 43; *CSPD 1689–90*, p. 73.

[5] *DNB*, under James Cecil, 4th earl of Salisbury and Henry Mordaunt, 2nd earl of Peterborough; Ailesbury, i, 153; *VCH Oxon*, v, 308.

[6] BM Add. MSS 25374, fol. 67, 36707, fol. 20, 40160, fols. 45, 49–52, 72–3; *HMC Downshire*, i, 175, 286; Macaulay, ii, 86; Wood, iii, 214;

James's missionary effort was hampered by the size and nature of the resources at his command. The few hundred priests in England were quite adequate for the needs of the small English Catholic community but hardly enough for a programme of nationwide evangelism. The seminaries abroad set over all the priests that they could, but the numbers could not be increased overnight. The Franciscans brought over ten Belgian friars and gave two friars priest's orders when they were still a year below the canonical age.[7] The usefulness of the available priests varied considerably. Many were not temperamentally or technically equipped for evangelism; their prime concern had been to hold the Catholic community firm in the faith rather than to win new converts. Many were unused to preaching and some had been abroad so long that their English was poor.[8] Many of the foreign priests were undisciplined and disorderly; some of the English ones dragged their feet, fearing reprisals under a Protestant successor. On the other hand, a minority of zealous priests at court urged the king on to further works of evangelism.[9]

The English mission had few funds of its own after the depredations of the years following the Popish Plot, so it had to depend on the zeal and generosity of the Catholic laity and above all of the king. 'As for the interests of religion,' wrote Terriesi, 'the king alone is zealous to struggle to advance it, against the friars, against the priests, against the Catholic laymen and against all the Protestants'.[10] There is no doubt that James's example and enthusiasm dominated the missionary effort. On 1 January 1686 he met Leyburn and the superiors of the regular orders and

DNB, under Joshua Basset, John Massey, Robert Charnock and Obadiah Walker.

[7] BM Add. MS 25373, fol. 78; Foley, v, 148; Thaddeus, pp. 103–4; AOFM, Acta Capitularum 1625–1746, pp. 208–9.

[8] Morrice MS Q, pp. 88, 91; *A Pastoral Letter from the Four Catholic Bishops* (1688), p. 2; Blundell, *Cavalier*, p. 185; Beales, pp. 232–3; Burnet, iii, 79; Macaulay, ii, 111n.

[9] BM Add. MSS 15395, fols. 401–5, 15396, fols. 177–9, 25371, fols. 342–3, 346, 25372, fols. 82, 217–18, 25373, fol. 39, 25374, fols. 64–6.

[10] BM Add. MS 25371, fol. 346. 'Nel propòsito della religióne, sia ùnico e sólo il zelo della Mtà Sua a pugnare per avanzarla, cóntro li frati, cóntro li prèti, cóntro li Cattolici secolari e cóntro li Protestanti tutti.'

exhorted them to love and unity in the common cause. He said that 'for his part he would endeavour as much as lay in him and as he could do by law [to] propagate the Catholic faith and that he would be a most obedient child to Mother Church and desired their advice and counsel from time to time'. He did what he could to prevent disputes between the secular clergy and the various orders, but there were some disputes about the possession of chapels in which James was accused (probably rightly) of favouring the Jesuits.[11] He opened his own chapels to the public and provided sermons in English. His financial support for the mission was very generous. He gave £1250 to the two Jesuit schools in London, £600 to the Scots mission and £100 each to four Scots foundations abroad. He paid Leyburn and the other vicars apostolic £1000 a year each and paid the Catholic chaplains in several garrisons. He spent over £10,000 from the secret service money alone on the chapels at Whitehall, Windsor, St James's and Southwark.[12]

However Terriesi's allegations that James alone bore the burden of the missionary effort and that the Catholic laity was apathetic or hostile are not fully borne out by the facts. Some wealthy individuals financed chapels or schools. The earl of Salisbury opened chapels at London and Hatfield; the Eyre family opened a chapel near Hathersage; lord Powis supported a school and a chapel at Welshpool; the Eystons opened a public chapel at East Hendred (Berkshire).[13] Where there was no one individual or family who could afford to build and equip a chapel the missions depended on the support of the laity, rich and poor alike. Mr Hesketh gave £200 to support the Franciscan mission to the poor Catholics of Goosnargh, Lancashire. The Franciscan residence at Abergavenny was financed by local Catholics, notably a Mrs Gunter. A Mrs Walmesley probably provided a house for the Franciscans at York. Local Catholics contributed £225 7s 2½d towards a chapel at Fernyhalgh,

---

[11] Weldon, p. 228; E. L. Taunton, *History of the Jesuits in England* (London, 1901), p. 446; Foley, v, 943–5; Kirk, pp. 98–9; SS Ing. 20, fols. 196–7.

[12] Foley, v, 266–8; *CSPD 1689–90*, p. 383; Akerman, pp. 184, 190–1, 194, 196–7, 208–9 and passim.

[13] BM Add. MS 25375, fol. 127; Luttrell, i, 433; Foley, v, 488, 943; Thaddeus, pp. 149–51.

Lancashire.[14] A total of £1334 8s 11d was contributed towards the building of St Peter's, Birmingham. Of this goods or money to the value of £180 came from the king, £190 from Sir John Gage and £250 from a Mrs Gregg. The priest, Leo Randolph OFM, contributed £60 and £40 more came from Franciscan funds. Twelve other gifts of between £10 and £40 brought in £200 15s 0d. There were also 177 gifts of between £1 and £7 4s 0d (total £369 8s 0d) and 148 gifts of less than £1, some of as little as threepence (total £44 5s 11d). Money and goods to the value of £27 were marked as coming from Protestants. Among those who contributed were Catholic gentlemen, not only from the west Midlands, but from all parts of the country. They included Sir William Goring of Sussex, lord Arundell of Wardour, Charles Trinder of Gloucestershire, Sir Robert Throckmorton of Warwickshire, Sir Edward Golding of Nottinghamshire, Mr Walmesley of Lancashire and Sir John Webb of Hampshire. Most of these gave between five and ten pounds – not a great deal, perhaps, but something; most kept priests themselves and doubtless had other calls on their pockets. The contributors also included twelve priests.[15]

Occasionally, as with the Jesuits at Bury St Edmund's, an order was able to buy a house for a chapel out of its own funds. Elsewhere the houses that were used for chapels were only rented, so money was needed only to equip them. Often an existing public building was taken over, like the sessions house at Holywell (Flintshire) or the Manor at York. One or two disused Anglican chapels were converted for Catholic use.[16] On special occasions, such as the assizes, Mass might be said in a school-house or even in a town hall. Three chapels were opened in Oxford colleges by newly converted fellows and the mayor of Gloucester, also a convert, opened one there. In garrison towns, such as Chester, Plymouth and Bristol, the king simply sent a priest to minister

---

[14] AOFM, 'An Inventory of the Writings &c Belonging to the Province (1704)', p. 22; Thaddeus, p. 135; Aveling, *City of York*, p. 104; Blundell, *Old Catholic Lancs.*, i, 169–70.

[15] Phillimore, Whitfield and P. E. Williams (eds.), *Warwickshire Parish Registers*, ii (London, 1904), 6–14.

[16] Taunton, *History of the Jesuits*, p. 446; Foley, v, 538, 943–5; AAW A34, pp. 1063–4; Reresby, p. 457; SP/44/56, p. 415; BM Add. MS 29562, fols. 111, 151, 184.

to the garrison and ordered that he be given somewhere to say Mass. There were, therefore, Mass-places or chapels in most provincial towns of any size by 1688.[17]

Thus the mission received considerable support from Catholic laymen and women, rich and poor, who added their gifts and goodwill to the meagre resources of the clergy. Despite this wide involvement, however, one is constantly struck by the dominant role of the king. His financial contribution was very large. He laid great stress on the value of his personal example and practised his religion with an openness that verged on the provocative. Most important of all, he used the full weight of his authority to secure facilities and protection for missioners all over the country. He alone could protect chapels from hostile crowds and discourage Protestant preachers from attacking Catholicism.

Behind the missionary effort lay the belief that converts would flock to the church once they could see Catholicism as it really was and not as its enemies said it was. Works were published (many of them by Henry Hills, the official printer) which set out the principles of Catholicism clearly and simply. Important among these were translations of Bossuet, Charles II's reasons for his conversion and a number of works by John Gother. This literature aimed to show, in the title of one of Gother's works, *A Papist Misrepresented and Represented*. A separate stream of pamphlets of 1687–8 defended the Declaration of Indulgence, mostly in terms of the natural equity of liberty of conscience and the indefensibility of persecution. The authors were mostly Protestants of very varying viewpoints, including Samuel Parker, bishop of Oxford, Sir Roger L'Estrange, John Northleigh, an Anglican physician, Henry Care, one-time author of the violently anti-Catholic *Weekly Pacquet of Advice from Rome*, and William Penn, the Quaker, also living down his Whig past.

In August 1685 John Leyburn was made vicar apostolic with strict orders not to recognise the Chapter. The Holy Office ordered that the regulars should be subject to him in the matter

17 Blundell, *Old Catholic Lancs.*, iii, 6; Bodl., Ballard MS 12, fols. 38–9; Wood, iii, 194, 244; Luttrell, i, 436; BM Add. MS 15396, fols. 155, 213; J. Hunter (ed.), *The Diary of Dr Thomas Cartwright* (Camden Soc., 1843), pp. 75–6; *CSPD 1686–7*, nos. 1486–7.

of the granting of missionary faculties.[18] The Chapter implored
the king not to admit a vicar apostolic but to no avail. With
Leyburn's appointment the Chapter lost all effective power and
became primarily an honorary and philanthropic body.[19] The
Jesuits submitted to Leyburn's authority. The Benedictines refused
at first but then, at the king's request, submitted with reservations.[20] Leyburn modified the existing organisation of the secular
mission, dividing the country into four districts with rural
deans to assist the vicars-general. One of his first concerns was to
administer the sacrament of confirmation, of which English
Catholics had been deprived for over fifty years. In 1687 he confirmed over 20,000 people in the North and Midlands. He exhorted the clergy to preach zealously and urged the laity to give
generously to spread the faith, so that the Catholics would not
lag behind the Dissenters.[21] In January 1688 three more vicars
apostolic were appointed so that now there was one for each of
the four districts. The new organisation had barely got under
way before the Revolution.

The missionary effort was most obviously effective in London
where there were at least eighteen chapels by the autumn of 1688.
These included three royal chapels (the old ones at Somerset
House and St James's and a new one which opened at Whitehall
at Christmas 1686), the five existing chapels of the French,
Spanish, Portuguese, Venetian and Florentine representatives and
ten new chapels.[22] Most of the old chapels provided English
sermons by the beginning of 1686. There were also two Jesuit
colleges and the Benedictines and Franciscans each had two
communities and the Carmelites had one. Hoffmann reported

[18] Prop. Ang., fol. 782; AAW A34, pp. 957–8, 961, 964–5.
[19] AAW A34, pp. 931, 941–3, 977–86, 995–7, 1003–4, 1055–6; Hemphill,
pp. 10–11; Williams, *Wilts.*, pp. 111–12.
[20] ASJ, Anglia Epist. Gen. 1642–98, fols. 459, 461; BM Add. MSS 10118,
fols. 128–9, 422–3, 25375, fols. 46, 103, 194.
[21] AAW A34, pp. 1027–8, 1046–7, 1057, 1059; Hemphill, pp. 11–14.
[22] The new chapels were, in order of opening: (1) Stanford's, Lime Street,
April 1686; (2) d'Adda's, St James's park, May 1686; (3) Imperial
envoy's, 1686(?); (4) Jesuits', the Savoy, May 1687; (5) Carmelites',
July 1687; (6) Southwark chapel, 1687(?); (7) Dominicans', Lincoln's
Inn Fields, Jan. 1688; (8) Franciscans', Lincoln's Inn Fields, Feb. 1688;
(9) The Tower, May 1688; (10) Elector of Cologne's representative
(Benedictines'), St John's Clerkenwell, June 1688. The Dominicans'
chapel was endowed by the earl of Salisbury.

that these establishments all depended on the generosity of the laity and in particular on that of the king.[23]

The first and the most contentious of the new chapels was that opened by Stanford, the representative of the Elector Palatine, at Lime Street. As Stanford had no money of his own, the money to equip it came partly from the king, partly from Catholic merchants in the city of London and partly from the funds of the secular clergy. James told Stanford in February 1686 that he wanted to open a chapel in the city and that the only way that he could do so was through a foreign representative. In that case it could be represented as an ambassadorial chapel and the king could protect it on the pretext that he was preserving Stanford's diplomatic immunity. The city authorities complained that it was unprecedented both for an ambassador to have his chapel in the city itself and for that ambassador to be an Englishman. (The other chapels were in the western suburbs and Westminster, the area around the court.) The lord mayor shut the chapel up and ordered that the work on it should cease but the king told him to reopen the chapel and to ask pardon.[24] The first two Sundays on which the chapel was open there were major riots which were suppressed only with difficulty. The elector, who had not been informed of the opening of what was nominally his chapel, now dissociated himself from it. He said that as the Catholic ruler of a predominantly Protestant state he had no wish to interfere in the internal religious affairs of another country. James dismissed with contempt the elector's pleas that the chapel should be moved to somewhere less controversial. The chapel remained open and by June it was largely left alone.[25]

Its later history was not entirely happy. Terriesi reported in May 1686 that many friars were attracted to the chapel by the money that was collected there and that it was proving difficult to keep them in order. The first chaplains were secular priests, but they were soon replaced by Jesuits. According to the

[23] BM Add. MSS 15395, fols. 367, 379–80, 25371, fol. 46; Campana, ii, 185.
[24] G. Macdonald, 'The Lime Street Chapel (Part I)', *Dublin Review*, clxxx (1927), 263–4; Ranke, iv, 295; BM Add. MSS 15395, fols. 385–6, 421–5, 34508, fols. 110–11.
[25] Macdonald, *Dublin Review*, clxxx, 264 and (Part II), *ibid.* clxxxi (1927), 2–6; Barillon au Roi, 6 June 1686 NS, Baschet 166; see also Miller, *HJ*, vol. xvi (1973).

Jesuits, the king removed the seculars after they had quarrelled with Stanford. The seculars claimed that the Jesuits turned the king against them by means of accusations that they were Blackloists and Jansenists. Stanford's reports to the elector tend to support the seculars' claim. Early in 1688 the chapel was taken away from Stanford, who was heavily in debt, and the king helped the Jesuits to buy neighbouring houses and gardens so that they could open a school.[26] After the furore over Stanford's chapel, there was little open opposition to the opening of new chapels, either because better security precautions were taken or because they were in less provocative situations.[27] The chapels enabled the Catholics of London to worship much more freely than before and this no doubt encouraged conversions. There are many reports of chapels being crowded in 1688 when new ones had been opened and some old ones had been enlarged.

Outside London chapels were opened in most provincial towns of any size. The Franciscans, who had far fewer missioners than the seculars, the Jesuits or the Benedictines, opened new residences and chapels at Abergavenny, Birmingham, Hexham, Holywell, Leominster, Monmouth, Warwick, Whitehill (near Goosnargh, Lancashire) and York. They already had residences at Osmotherley and Hereford and others were planned at Canterbury and St Michael's Mount.[28] Catholic evangelism under James II, like Puritan evangelism fifty or a hundred years earlier, concentrated mainly on the towns. Although urban Catholicism was weak, a market town acted as a focus for the social and economic life of the surrounding countryside. If large numbers of converts were to be made in a short time, this could be done only in the centres of population. The clergy's hopes of making converts in the towns led to the maintenance of ecclesiastical establishments far larger than would have been necessary if only the needs of the existing Catholic population had been considered. Thus at York up to six chapels, including two domestic chapels, catered for a native Catholic population of about sixty, to which should be added a few Catholic soldiers

---

[26] Macdonald, *Dublin Review*, clxxx, 257–9, 265, clxxxi, 9–13; Kirk, pp. 98–9; SS Ing. 20, fol. 196; BM Add. MSS 25372, fol. 82, 25375, fols. 220, 241–2, 25376, fol. 9.

[27] SS Ing. 12, fols. 185–6; BM Add. MS 25372, fol. 69.

[28] AOFM, Acta Capitularum 1625–1746, p. 200; Thaddeus, passim.

in the garrison and the households of Catholic gentry who visited the city. At Lincoln, where the Catholic population was very small, there was a chapel served by three priests.[29]

These provincial chapels, like those in London, often depended on the protection of troops; when James told his Benedictine chaplains to wear their habits in public he provided an armed guard to escort them through St James's Park.[30] Almost all the chapels were destroyed in the Revolution. Of the Franciscan residences which existed under James II six were still functioning in 1704 – Osmotherley, Abergavenny, Birmingham, Hexham, Monmouth and Whitehill. The rest (Hereford, Holywell, Leominster, Warwick and York) no longer existed and the large Franciscan chapel in Lincoln's Inn Fields had been totally destroyed in 1688.[31] The secular clergy had a number of town missions in 1700 (Durham, Edgbaston, Newcastle-upon-Tyne, Tamworth, Wolverhampton and York) most of which probably dated back no further than James II's reign.[32] Under James it seems that the mission did at least gain a foothold in a number of towns which it was to use to good effect in the second half of the eighteenth century but which, at the time, did not produce any spectacular results in terms of conversions.

A handful of schools were also set up. The Jesuits opened twelve and others were opened by Anglican clergymen who had been converted to Catholicism or by individual schoolmasters.[33] The main Jesuit school in London, which was in the Savoy, was a considerable success. It was explicitly non-denominational and taught nothing controversial, although it had a Catholic chapel attached. Within months of opening it had attracted over four hundred pupils, most of them Protestants.[34] A similar girls' school was opened in St Martin's Lane and the Jesuits planned to open another school in Lime Street. The success of these schools stimulated the opening of rival Protestant schools; the

---

[29] Aveling, *City of York*, pp. 103–5; Hill, *Tudor and Stuart Lincoln*, p. 190; Foley, v, 621.

[30] BM Add. MS 34510, fol. 55; Morrice MS Q, p. 200.

[31] AOFM, 'An Inventory of the Writings &c', pp. 22–9.

[32] AAW A38, no. 2. The Tamworth mission dated back thirty years.

[33] Beales, pp. 248–55; BM Add. MS 40160, fols. 72–3; J. Gutch (ed.), *Collectanea Curiosa* (2 vols., London, 1781), i, 290–3.

[34] Beales, pp. 236–7, 255; Barillon au Roi, 5 June 1687 NS, Baschet 170; BM Add. MSS 25374, fols. 110, 297, 25375, fol. 241.

endowment of one of these was diverted after the Revolution to the maintenance of poor vicars.[35]

The missionary effort was not very successful but it had no real chance under the circumstances. It only really got under way late in 1686, so it had barely two years to prove itself. It was hampered by a dearth of suitable priests, by the lethargy of some Catholics and by the hostility of most Protestants. It was carried on under the shadow of an apparently inevitable Protestant succession. Above all its hopes of success rested on a serious misconception, the belief that the tiny Catholic minority could convert the enormous Protestant majority. Over a century of Protestant hostility to Catholicism could not be dissipated overnight simply by giving the Catholics freedom to state their case. If some Protestant antipathy to Catholicism was based on misapprehensions, much rested on reasons which seemed adequate to those who held them; there were genuine differences of opinion. Most Protestants did not believe that their religion was a mass of inaccuracies and misrepresentations imposed on them by a self-interested clergy any more than Catholics believed it of theirs. This James II could not or would not understand and his failure to understand cost him his throne.

[35] *HMC Downshire*, i, 282; BM Add. MSS 15397, fols. 51–2, 25375, fols. 106, 241–2, 25376, fols. 9, 21, 53, 72; *Autobiography of Symon Patrick*, pp. 127–8.

14

THE OPPOSITION TO JAMES II

Much of the opposition to James II that existed in 1688 had not existed in 1685, but had been created by his actions. By the late summer of 1688 Sunderland at least had come to realise the extent of the alienation of the political nation and to understand that James, however he tried, could not obtain a parliament that would repeal the penal laws and Test Acts. The threat of William's invasion accelerated James's decision to reverse his Catholicising policy but he would have had to abandon it anyway as it simply was not going to work. If William had not invaded and if James had reverted to a policy more acceptable to the Tories, he would probably have survived. Until William's invasion or a parliament provided it with a focus, the opposition was not strong enough to bring down James's regime. He had an army of nearly twenty thousand men and his financial position was strong after the generous parliamentary grants of 1685. He had no serious financial problems until late in 1688 when William's invasion started a slump in trade and a financial panic.[1]

The Williamite conspirators were too few to bring down the regime on their own. The rest of the opposition consisted mainly of, first, refusals to co-operate with the agents and policies of the king; secondly, a pamphlet literature that gradually increased in volume and in effectiveness and, thirdly, spontaneous but unco-ordinated popular violence against manifestations of Catholicism.

After parliament had refused to acquiesce in his employment of Catholic army officers in 1685, James began to dismiss from office those who would not comply with his wishes. Used sparingly this strategy might have worked. Used, as it was, on a large scale it was self-defeating. It progressively alienated the political nation and encouraged men to lie in order to keep their places. It was impossible to obtain a parliament that would repeal the penal laws with even the most specious appearance of consent when the overwhelming majority of the political nation was clearly opposed to doing so. But opposition of this type was

[1] *HMC le Fleming*, p. 213; BM Add. MS 25377, fols. 16–17, 59–60.

mostly negative and passive. Anglican clergymen refused to read the second Declaration of Indulgence in their churches or to report those who had refused to read it. Disgruntled Tory squires sulked on their estates and often refused to co-operate with the new Catholic or Nonconformist magistrates. Some like Halifax and colonel Titus saw no need for drastic action as the whole design was bound to collapse anyway. The Anglican earl of Nottingham thought in September 1687 that the Anglicans would carry most of the elections, and this opinion was shared by the Presbyterian Morrice and by an anonymous Jesuit. Only the timid bishop of Norwich thought that James might have a chance of success.[2]

By the summer of 1688, though the court might be elated at the birth of the Prince of Wales, there were signs that its control of the localities was weakening. The Catholic lords lieutenant and J.P.s were finding it difficult to get their Protestant neighbours and underlings to obey them. The first challenges to their authority came late in 1687 and early in 1688. The J.P.s of Somerset told their new Catholic lord lieutenant, lord Waldegrave, that they could not obey him unless he took the oaths. In Lancashire lord Molyneux, another Catholic lord lieutenant, found the old J.P.s still in the commission of the peace while the new ones had not yet been put in. Lord Lovelace told constables that they need not obey Catholic J.P.s as they were not qualified according to law.[3] After the acquittal of the Seven Bishops the situation grew worse. Magistrates found it difficult to prevent popular rejoicings or to punish those who took part and grand juries refused to present them.[4] There were more refusals to obey the king's *mandamuses* and to recognise the validity of his dispensations. Grand juries at Winchester, Shrewsbury and elsewhere presented Catholics for holding office contrary to law. The judges on their circuits were met by few who were not Catholics and their advocacy of the repeal of the penal laws and Test Acts

---

[2] Dalrymple, ii, Appendix, Part I, pp. 204–6; Portland MS 2135; Morrice MS Q, p. 291; ASJ, Foley MS i, 291; Bodl., Tanner MS 28, fol. 183.

[3] BM Add. MSS 25375, fol. 29, 34487, fol. 9, 36707, fol. 16; SP/31/4, fol. 18; Luttrell, i, 432.

[4] BM Add. MSS 25376, fols. 188–9, 226, 34487, fol. 15, 34510, fol. 137, 36707, fol. 38; Morrice MS Q, p. 283; *HMC le Fleming*, p. 212.

aroused little response.[5] According to a newsletter 'there is now but one [*sc.* legally qualified?] justice of peace in all Shropshire and he is carried to gaol for debt; where to people are forced to go to him for their freedom and the poor devil cannot have it himself'. When William invaded, the newly reinstated Protestant lords lieutenant and deputy lieutenants showed great reluctance to act energetically or to mobilise the militia against him and a sizeable minority defected to the invaders.[6]

It eventually became apparent that an amenable parliament was not to be had. Even in December 1685 the court candidate had been heavily defeated in a violent by-election at Bristol, of which Southwell wrote ominously: 'The worst is that there has been nothing of Whig and Tory in this matter but an undervaluing the recommendation given [by the court] . . . as if it were high time for Protestants of all sorts to be friends.'[7] James would have had a far rougher passage if he had tried to hold a general election in 1688.

There were two main types of 'opposition' literature under James II. The first consisted of straightforward controversial works which attacked various aspects of Catholic doctrine and practice. The great majority were by Anglicans. A catalogue of 1689 listed 228 pamphlets against Popery which had been published by Anglicans in 1685–8 as against two by Dissenters and one by Henry Care, who seemed to fall outside normal categories. Some Dissenters claimed that they would have published more if the bishops had not refused to license their books.[8] The second type of pamphlet began to appear in ever-increasing numbers from 1687. Pamphlets of this type were overtly political and were unlicensed. They were printed secretly in England or were imported from Holland. Their main purpose was to persuade the Dissenters not to fall in with James's design of repealing the penal laws and Test Acts. They did not usually attack the principle of toleration, at least for Dissenters, but alleged that James's

---

[5] BM Add. MSS 25376, fols. 235–7, 245, 280–1, 36707, fol. 20; Ellis, ii, 100–2, 108–9; Clarke, ii, 168.

[6] BM Add. MS 34487, fol. 19; Miller, *HJ* (1973).

[7] *HMC Ormond*, N.S., vii, 404–5; see also *HMC Egmont*, ii, 168.

[8] *A Catalogue of all the Discourses Printed Against Popery* (1689); Burnet, iii, 98–101; Morrice MS Q, p. 140.

offers of toleration were insincere and were part of a design to impose Popery. They relied for their arguments firstly on James's record and secondly on the assumptions about the behaviour of Papists in power which were a central part of the anti-Catholic tradition. They stressed that James and the Papists had 'made their first courtship to the Church of England and when they were rejected there, they made their application to you [the Dissenters] in the second place'. James could not be trusted 'after what we know of his Majesty's natural genius and religious bigotry and after what we have seen and experienced in the whole course of his government'.[9] As for the principles of Popery, Halifax wrote in his highly influential *Letter to a Dissenter*: 'This alliance between Liberty and Infallibility is bringing together the two most contrary things that are in the world. The church of Rome doth not only dislike the allowing liberty, but by its principles it cannot do it.'[10]

Perhaps the most important pamphlet to be published in these years was *A Letter Written by Mijn Heer Fagel . . . to Mr James Stewart*, which appeared in January 1688. It stated that it was William's opinion that all the penal laws should be repealed but not the Test Acts. This made it clear that Dissenters and even Catholics could expect a legal toleration under James's presumptive successor, without those conditions (notably the admission of Catholics to public office) which James demanded.[11] The Dissenters had not previously looked forward to William's succession to the throne with unreserved enthusiasm. In September 1686, when James began to relax the enforcement of the laws against Dissenters, Morrice feared that William would maintain the existing laws against Dissenters and that he would throw in his lot with the Anglicans, as those most wedded to strong monarchy. In May 1687 William's special envoy Dijkveld had contacted a number of leading Dissenters. Some got the impression from him that William would put them on equal terms with the

---

[9] Halifax, *Works*, p. 106; 'Some Reflexions on a Discourse', *State Tracts*, ii, 368. See also R. Ferguson, 'A Representation of the Threatening Dangers' (1687), *State Tracts*, ii, 395–6; *A Letter to a Dissenter from his Friend at the Hague* (1688), p. 3.

[10] Halifax, *Works*, p. 106; see also Burnet, 'A Letter containing some Reflexions' (1687), *State Tracts*, ii, 292.

[11] *State Tracts*, ii, 334–7; Burnet, iii, 202–5.

Anglicans but others still thought that William would fall in with the Tories.[12] Thus *Fagel's Letter* reassured the Dissenters of William's goodwill towards them just as they were beginning to be seriously alarmed by the extremism of James's campaign for a parliament and by the possibility, distant as yet, of a Catholic successor. Their alarm grew with the further intensification of the campaign and with the birth of the Prince of Wales and it was reinforced by increasing numbers of pamphlets. Despite the rather feeble efforts of the court to cast doubt on the authenticity of *Fagel's Letter*, it soon became apparent that it was quite genuine.[13]

Large numbers of opposition pamphlets were printed in 1688 and many were distributed free of charge. Many asserted that the queen's pregnancy was not genuine.[14] Bogus letters from Jesuits purported to set out James's designs for England.[15] Astrological works predicted the downfall of James's regime.[16] Among the numerous other works produced were a number by Gilbert Burnet, who spent the reign in exile at William's court. The dissemination of these pamphlets showed considerable organisation. *A Letter to a Dissenter* had been distributed simultaneously in towns all over the country (a technique used by Catholic propagandists under Elizabeth). James Johnstone, an agent of William's confidential aide, Hans Willem Bentinck, urged that the same should be done with *Fagel's Letter*, but in fact only about half of the ten thousand copies originally printed were distributed in the country. Later another thirty thousand were printed but by now the government was looking out for them and it was more difficult to distribute them. Nevertheless, the demand for copies was

---

[12] Morrice MSS P, p. 628, Q, pp. 124–5, 132, 140.

[13] BM Add. MS 25375, fols. 143, 205; Portland MS 2126; *State Tracts*, ii, 338–62.

[14] Wood, iii, 254–5; BM Add MS 25375, fol. 168; Burnet, iii, 236; *Revolution Politicks* (1733), part iv, 43–4, 47–8, 66–9; *Idem Iterum or the History of Queen Mary's Big Belly* (1688).

[15] 'Father La Chaise's Project for the Extirpation of Heretics' (1688) *Somers Tracts*, ix, 86–8; 'A Letter from a Jesuit of Liège' (1687) and 'A Letter from the Reverend Father Petre ... to the Reverend Father La Chaise' (1688), both in *A Third Collection of Papers* (1688). See also Burnet, iii, 169–70; Morrice MS Q, pp. 239–43; Portland MS 2100.

[16] *Revolution Politicks*, part vi, 60–2, part vii, 62–3; Rutt (ed.), *Life of Edmund Calamy*, i, 180.

very great and the pamphlet made a great impact.[17] Other pamphlets were also distributed all over the country. In August 1687 a bookseller in York received a number of copies of three 'seditious' pamphlets, which he took to a J.P. Early in 1688 many copies of *Reflexions on Monsieur Fagel's Letter* were distributed free of charge; Johnstone and Halifax each found that two dozen copies had been left at his lodgings. In May 1688, while the clergy of York were debating whether they should obey the king's order to read the Declaration of Indulgence in their churches, a special messenger arrived from London with five hundred copies of a paper which argued against reading the Declaration. They resolved not to read it and distributed the papers instead. The Seven Bishops' petition to the king was also quickly printed and widely dispersed.[18]

The court encouraged refutations of these pamphlets and, where it could, suppressed them and punished their authors and printers. Under pressure from France, James tried to suppress accounts of the persecution of the Huguenots which followed the revocation of the Edict of Nantes.[19] Nevertheless, accounts of the Huguenots' sufferings soon reached England, together with news of a speech by the bishop of Valence in which he urged Louis to join with James in extirpating heresy in England.[20] The news of what was happening in France caused great anxiety among English Protestants. Roger Morrice looked for parallels between James's actions and those of Louis XIV and at times expected a *dragonnade*, although in his calmer moments he realised that James would not be able to use his army to impose Popery.[21]

[17] Portland MSS 2124, 2126, 2126(2), 2141, 2145; Rostenberg, p. 37.
[18] BM Add. MS 41804, fols. 311–15; Portland MSS 2141, 2159; Comber, i, 20, ii, 157–8; R. Thomas, 'The Seven Bishops and their Petition, 18 May 1688', *JEH*, xii (1961), 66–7; see also Wood, iii, 182, 187; BM Add. MS 41804, fols. 129, 142, 151; Ellis, i, 159, ii, 139; Luttrell, i, 434.
[19] Barillon au Roi, 19 Nov. 1685, 7 Jan. and 13 May 1686 NS, Baschet 162, 163, 166; BM Add. MS 15395, fol. 275.
[20] Evelyn, *Diary*, iv, 484–7; Morrice MS P, pp. 480, 484, 488, 498, etc.; BM Add. MS 29561, fol. 538; J. Claude, *An Account of the Persecutions and Oppressions* (1686); for the bishop of Valence's speech, see Barillon au Roi, 8 Nov. 1685 NS, Baschet 162; Morrice MS P, p. 490; Granville, i, 215.
[21] *Supplement to Burnet*, p. 207; 'Some Reflexions on a Discourse', *State Tracts*, ii, 363, 368; Morrice MSS P, pp. 595, 628, Q, pp. 89, 179.

Early in 1686 the government managed to seize many copies of the rev. Samuel Johnson's *Humble and Hearty Address to All the English Protestants in this Present Army*; Johnson was degraded from holy orders, pilloried and whipped. Apparently no separate copies of the broadside survive but it was distributed widely at the time. Some five hundred copies were found in Hugh Speke's cell in King's Bench prison, a figure which Speke later enlarged to twenty thousand.[22] The government tried hard to stop unlicensed printing and to seize unlicensed works, but inevitably many got through. It also tried to restrict the sending of newsletters and produced its own weekly news-sheet, *Publick Occurrences*, written by Henry Care.[23]

In January 1686 Henry Hills was appointed king's printer. He had just turned Papist after having £4000 damages awarded against him on an action of *scandalum magnatum* brought by the earl of Peterborough. Obadiah Walker was allowed to set up a press at Oxford.[24] These presses concentrated at first on producing Catholic books, but their distribution met with some obstruction. In February 1686 the Stationers' Company seized some Catholic devotional works. They were told to return them to the printer but nine months later Sunderland was still trying to get them back from the archbishop of Canterbury, to whom the stationers had delivered them. In 1687 advertisements for Catholic books began to appear in the *Gazette* but James would not allow anti-Catholic works to appear in the term catalogues.[25] In 1688 the government responded to the distribution of opposition pamphlets by distributing its own. In May Johnstone reported that twenty thousand copies of John Northleigh's *Parliamentum Pacificum* and of something which he called *A Letter to one at*

---

22 *State Tracts*, ii, 429; Macaulay, ii, 104–7; BM Add. MS 34508, fol. 120; Wood, iii, 178; H. Speke, *Some Memoirs of the Late Happy Revolution* (Dublin, 1709), pp. 73–4 and *The Secret History of the Happy Revolution* (1715), p. 15.
23 *HMC le Fleming*, p. 204; Evelyn, 18 April 1686, *Diary*, iv, 507–8; Portland MSS 2141, 2143, 2159; BM Add. MSS 25375, fols. 149, 194, 241, 34487, fol. 17, 34510, fol. 76; Wood, iii, 180; Ellis, ii, 243.
24 Evelyn, 12 March 1686, *Diary*, iv, 503–4; Morrice MS P, pp. 520–1; Wood, iii, 198.
25 *CSPD 1686–7*, nos. 149, 1161; Bodl., Tanner MS 30, fols. 100, 102; Bramston, p. 301; N. Sykes, *William Wake* (2 vols., Cambridge, 1957), i, 42.

Amsterdam had been distributed free, at the king's expense, making a total of a hundred thousand papers in one month. James's electoral agents were ordered to distribute government propaganda and to report on that of the opposition.[26] However hard the government might try to suppress its enemies' propaganda and to gain acceptance for its own, it was fighting a losing battle. The police resources of a seventeenth century government were insufficient to eradicate unlicensed literature, especially when so much was smuggled in from abroad. The opposition's literature found much greater acceptance than the government's. However inaccurate and alarmist much of it might be, it interpreted events in a way which Protestants were prepared to understand. One reason why William's invasion met with so little opposition was because opposition propaganda had carefully fed the doubts and fears created in English minds by the simple fact of having a Popish king, who now had a Popish heir, and by the actions which that king had undertaken, which seemed to threaten to overthrow all laws and parliaments. This propaganda was supplemented by the many wild rumours which flew round England in November and December 1688, particularly the rumours that James had made a secret alliance with the French king and that a French or Irish army had come over to England. The propaganda and rumours alone cannot explain James's defeat, but they did reinforce his subjects' existing reluctance to resist William's army.[27]

The opening of chapels often provoked riots and violence, but such opposition was essentially spontaneous and sporadic and was easily put down by troops. Sometimes priests or Catholic officers gave the crowds considerable provocation. In February 1687 Richard Trappes, a Franciscan, was sent by the king to say Mass at Guernsey. He demanded that he should be given the use of a disused chapel in the churchyard. The local magistrates refused to clear it of lumber and complained to the king. Trappes said Mass in the castle at first, for about twenty people, but he was forced to move out by the debauched behaviour of the deputy governor, Maccarty, an Irish Catholic. (The governor, lord

---

[26] Portland MS 2161; Morrice MS Q, p. 294.
[27] Morrice MS Q, pp. 288, 290–1, 293, 308, 324; *A Diary of Several Reports* (1704), pp. 6, 9–15, 28; Miller, *HJ* (1973).

Hatton, was away in England.) On 3 March Trappes was abused by some women and children with 'some songs and scurrilous words in derision of priests and the Mass'. Maccarty, nursing a heavy hangover, called out his troops, stones were thrown, and only pacifying action by the women prevented bloodshed.[28] Soon after, an order came from the king that Trappes was not to insist on having the chapel in the churchyard and that the magistrates were to find him somewhere else. Trappes however greatly exaggerated his sufferings, saying 'how he is sent there like an apostle and how he has suffered like an apostle'; he disliked the alternative Mass-places and insisted on having the chapel in the churchyard. Maccarty duly got workmen in and the chapel was soon opened, apparently without any further disturbance.[29]

Where Catholic chapels were opened it seems to have been a common practice to crowd them out, so that Catholics could not get in or worship in peace. In some cases there was more violence. At Bristol a priest was beaten up and imprisoned, apparently after he had behaved provocatively, and a crowd held a pageant mocking the Virgin Mary and the Host. It was dispersed by troops.[30] At Stanford's chapel in London there were riots on successive Sundays, despite the lord mayor's efforts to prevent disorders. Henry Savile said that people were frightened to attend the chapels because of the crowds,[31] but other reports suggest that they were usually crowded.

The extent to which James had alienated his subjects was shown by the petition and trial of the Seven Bishops. The foremost advocates of non-resistance dared to criticise the king, albeit in the most respectful terms, and, somewhat to their surprise, they found that they were popular heroes. It was typical of James's mentality that he regarded the petition as expressing sedition verging on treason and that he later saw it as part of a design to force him to imprison the bishops so that archbishop Sancroft would be unable to attest to the imminent birth of the Prince of

[28] BM Add. MS 29562, fols. 9, 65, 68, 70.
[29] *CSPD 1686–7*, no. 1535; BM Add. MS 29562, fols. 92, 111, 151, 184.
[30] Wood, iii, 213, 254, 264; BM Add. MS 25372, fol. 46; *HMC Portland*, iii, 396; *HMC Ormond*, ii, 304; Macaulay, ii, 100–1; Barillon au Roi, 30 May 1686 NS, Baschet 166.
[31] W. D. Cooper (ed.), *Savile Correspondence* (Camden Soc., 1858), p.290.

Wales.[32] The rejoicing at the bishops' acquittal strained the government's ability to maintain order. In London the pope was burned in effigy in front of Whitehall palace and various Catholics' houses were attacked. In Somerset the Prince of Wales was burned in effigy as well as the pope and at Exeter magistrates who tried to put out the bonfires were in danger of being burned themselves.[33]

William's invasion and the breakdown of law and order which had started a little before led to sporadic violence against Catholics throughout the nation, particularly in the towns. For several years Protestants had watched helplessly as Catholic officials were imposed on them, as priests paraded and said Mass openly and as the presence of Catholic soldiers in garrisons had increased the usual friction between soldiers and civilians. Now the Protestants had their revenge. In Newcastle a new equestrian statue of the king was toppled into the Tyne. At Cambridge a priest's robes were burned and a Papist was made to dance naked in a ditch until he agreed to change his religion. In London there were a number of riots at Catholic chapels which led to one chapel being destroyed and most of the rest being closed. A precarious order was maintained with increasing difficulty until after James's flight in the early hours of 11 December. Then other chapels were attacked and destroyed and the situation was out of control for a while, but order was soon restored.[34]

In the second week of December James's army broke up and the Irish contingents headed for home as best they could. The fact that Irish troops were wandering round the country started a nationwide panic reminiscent of that of 1678. At Dover there were rumours of a French invasion and of the approach of Irish troops as early as 9 December.[35] On the night of 12–13 December the fear reached London. Seven thousand Irish were rumoured to be advancing on the city, killing all whom they met. 'The watch called all up that the Irish were near and at Knightsbridge had killed man, woman and child and were resolved for to fire and massacre.' The rumour seems to have started after a

[32] Clarke, ii, 159.
[33] BM Add. MS 25376, fols. 172, 176–7, 188–9, 209.
[34] *HMC le Fleming*, pp. 218, 226; Reresby, pp. 487–90; Brand, *History and Antiquities of Newcastle*, ii, 499; Miller, *HJ* (1973).
[35] *HMC 7th Report, Appendix*, p. 421.

scuffle when some Irish soldiers from the garrison at Tilbury had tried to commandeer a boat to take them home. In fact there were only 'six hundred poor disbanded unarmed fellows, who had scarce a knife to cut their victuals and were begging their way into their own country'. The citizens of London were extremely alarmed, however. They rushed to arms, kept their lights burning and beat drums and fired off muskets all night; the women banged their pots and pans. Not until four in the morning did people begin to go to bed, leaving one person on guard in each house.[36]

The rumours spread North and West. At Ampthill the inhabitants blocked the gates, hearing that Bedford and other towns were on fire. At Wendover many of the inhabitants fled when they heard that the Irish were coming; in fact some Irish soldiers who had been refused quarters nearby had killed two or three people and had plundered their homes. There were rumours of Papists in arms around Northampton and of Irish troops landing in Lincolnshire. The Irish were also rumoured to have fired Birmingham; the people of Lichfield and Burton prepared to defend themselves. On 15 December the mayor of Wigan heard that over eight thousand Irish and Scots had committed a massacre at Birmingham and had fired Stafford and were now heading North. A guard was set on Warrington bridge; on a general summons to arms, 4600 men appeared.[37] The main current of fear was felt in the days immediately after James's first flight. It followed the route, from London towards Chester, which the Irish would have followed on their way home. However, ripples of the Irish panic spread further afield and lasted considerably longer. There were panics as far east as Norfolk, as far west as Cornwall and Pembrokeshire and as far north as Berwick. Even in Yorkshire fears of the Irish persisted as late as 28 December, but over most of the country calm had been restored well before the end of the month.[38]

[36] *Hatton Correspondence*, ii, 125; *HMC Portland*, iii, 420–1; Luttrell, i, 487; BM Add. MS 25377, fols. 216–17; Ellis, ii, 356–7; *A Diary of Several Reports*, p. 40; *London Courant*, no. 2 (12–15 Dec. 1688); Verney, iv, 447.

[37] Ailesbury, i, 200; *Universal Intelligence*, nos. 3 and 5 (15–18 and 22–26 Dec.); *HMC 5th Report, Appendix*, p. 399; *HMC Portland*, iii, 420–1; *HMC Hastings*, ii, 211; *HMC le Fleming*, p. 229.

[38] B. Cozens-Hardy (ed.), *Norfolk Lieutenancy Journal 1676–1701* (Nor-

These panics and the general reaction against James's regime gave rise to considerable violence against the persons and property of Catholics.[39] This was something which had not occurred after the Great Fire or during the Exclusion Crisis. People had gone home to bed after the great London pope-burnings, but no one slept on 'Irish night'. In the second and third weeks of December 1688 the violent outburst of resentment at James's regime and policies was made more intense by the panic fear aroused by the disbanded Irish troops and by the temporary disorganisation of the machinery of law and order after James's flight. Hugh Speke later claimed to have initiated 'Irish night' by means of the spurious *Third Declaration of the Prince of Orange*, but in fact the *Declaration* had been distributed on about 7 December and had merely added to the fears and rumours that were everywhere. The fears of the Irish were too widespread and corresponded too closely to earlier patterns to have been produced merely by one man's machinations.[40]

With the Revolution of 1688 there came to an end what had been neither a ruthless campaign to impose Popery and absolutism nor a sincere attempt at a general religious toleration that was centuries ahead of its time. In fact James's Catholicising policy had been the expression of the faith and fantasies of one man, a man who was far more a fool than a villain. He had made totally unrealistic assumptions about the possibility of making converts to Catholicism; he had gone ahead despite the fact that he had no Catholic heir; he had destroyed the strongest political position that any Stuart had ever enjoyed by deliberately and persistently flouting an unchallenged and unchallengeable axiom of seventeenth century Englishmen, that Papists should be kept out of politics and out of positions of power. In the words of Professor Kenyon: 'It is a tragedy that James, whose character

folk Record Soc., 1961), p. 97; *English Currant*, no. 5 (21–26 Dec.); *Universal Intelligence*, nos. 6 and 10 (26–29 Dec. and 5–8 Jan. 1689); *London Mercury*, no. 8 (3–7 Jan.).

[39] *HMC le Fleming*, p. 228; *VCH Staffs.*, viii, 272; Reresby, pp. 531, 542–3. See also the rather sketchy accounts by M. Beloff, *Public Order and Popular Disturbances in England 1660–1714* (Oxford, 1938), pp. 40–3 and W. L. Sachse, 'The Mob in the Revolution of 1688', *Journal of British Studies*, iv (1964), 23–40.

[40] See my forthcoming article in *HJ* (1973).

fitted him so admirably for the leadership of a powerful conservative faction, should have been united by religious whim to a persecuted sect whose fortunes could be advanced only by the exercise of subtlety and cunning.'⁴¹ Charles II had had his share of
subtlety and cunning. He had done as much as he could to help
the Catholics but he had known when to retreat, as he had had
to do, when James's conversion altered the political situation.
James, unfortunately, had none.

In the short run James's policies exposed the Catholics to
violence and looting. It made apparent what many Catholics
already realised, that the best they could hope for was for the
laws to be in force but not enforced. This was what had happened
in the 1660s, but then the laws had been enforced more and more
after James's conversion had become known. In the long run
the reign perhaps did the Catholics some good. It added yet
another episode to the anti-Catholic tradition but it killed, at last,
the myth that there were innumerable secret Papists waiting to
declare themselves. The Catholics had emerged to be counted and
had been seen to be few. Their association with Jacobitism made
them seem dangerous for some time more, but gradually the active
animus against them died away. The eighteenth century
approached religious issues less enthusiastically than the seventeenth had done. English Protestants would not allow Catholics
to bear office or to worship openly for some time. But they were
to be relatively free from persecution in the eighteenth century.

Although overt anti-Catholicism gradually became unfashionable, an implicit anti-Catholicism has remained an integral
feature of Protestant historiography and Protestant thinking. It
is still widely assumed that Catholicism is inimical to free intellectual and theological inquiry, that it is irrational and feeds on
ignorance and that Protestantism is not. It is also an essential
assumption of Whig historiography that Catholicism is identified
as closely with tyranny and absolutism as Protestantism is identified with liberty and with representative institutions. That there
is much truth in these commonplaces cannot be denied. But as
the Catholic church makes slow and hesitant moves towards
greater democratisation and lay participation, and as more and
more Catholic priests all over the world advocate radical or revo-

⁴¹ Kenyon, *Sunderland*, p. 112.

lutionary political action, it is perhaps time to take a new, more critical look at these commonplaces and stereotypes. In particular, it is time to reconsider the image of the Catholics and of Catholicism in England which has been handed down to us by generation after generation of Protestant historians.

Year	City RC	City Other	Westminster and western suburbs RC	Westminster and western suburbs Other	County and eastern suburbs RC	County and eastern suburbs Other	Totals RC	Totals Other	Totals Total
1661–2									
1663		2	8	13		4	8	19	27
1664–5									
1666				1		2		3	3
1667					1	8	1	8	9
1668						6		6	6
1669						15		15	15
1670						2		2	2
1671–3									
1674	38	133	301	196	31	40	370	369	739
1675			2			7	2	7	9
1676–7									
1678			4		8	1	12	1	13
1679	8	16	809	319	24	27	841	362	1203
1680			43*	38	5	2	48	40	88
1681	7	22	132	76	1	1	140	99	239
1682						2		2	2
1683	2		10	52		127	12	179	191
1684			2	3		12	2	15	17
1685				1		2		3	3
	55	173	1311	699	70	258	1436	1130	2566

* This does not include 141 Catholic peers and gentlemen who were convicted late in 1680 'in order to keep them from coming to London, or the liberties thereof, or within ten miles of the same city': PDB, c3.

SOURCES

BM Add. MS 20739, printed in CRS, vi, 286–8 (list of recusants convicted 1660–71).

PRO, E/377/65–81 (recusant rolls) except for E/377/69, which was too damaged to be used. The rolls are dated according to the king's regnal year, which for Charles II began on 30 January. I have followed this practice, for when someone was convicted in January, the proceedings against him must have started in the previous year. Often the roll for a given year also contains convictions from other years; I have used the date of conviction in all cases. When someone was convicted more than once in one year I have counted it as one conviction. The first one or two sheets of the 1678 roll for Middlesex are missing, so the figures for late 1678 and early 1679 will be too low; this is confirmed by the extracts from the quarter sessions records printed (neither in full nor very accurately) in J. R. Jeaffreson (ed.), *Middlesex County Records* (4 vols., London, 1886–92), vol. iv.

IDENTIFICATION

As there were so many Dissenters in Middlesex, I have concentrated on identifying Papists, using the following:

House of Lords R.O., Main Papers, nos. 22 (18 Nov. 1678), 40 (3 Dec. 1678) and 321 (PDB, c2 and c4).

G.L.C. (Middlesex) R.O., Dartmouth Street, MR/RR/1–4; WC/R/1, pp. 33–55; WR/RR(L)/2.

Corporation of London R.O., MSS 7/14–16, 63/14–15, 112/15, Sessions Papers 1678.

A Catalogue of Such Persons as are, or are reputed to be of the Romish Religion . . . within the County of Middlesex, Cities of London and Westminster &c (1680?).

Guildhall Library, MSS 9537/19, 9800A.

Jeaffreson, *Middlesex County Records*, iv, 92, 96–7, 100–19, 122, 123, 126–31, 134–5, 142, 150, 154.

H. Bowler (ed.), *London Quarter Sessions Records 1605–1685* (CRS, vol. xxxiv, 1934).

I have assumed, where a husband and wife were both recusants, that if one was a Catholic the other one must have been a Catholic as well; I have done the same where children appear as recusants after their parents, but I have not tried to link people where they do not appear together on the recusant rolls. I have followed the same practice for Norfolk. It should be stressed that the figures given represent only identifiable Catholics and that many of those appearing as 'others' must also have been Papists.

APPENDIX 2 : RECUSANCY CONVICTIONS IN NORFOLK

Year	P	Q	N	?	Total	%P	%Q	%N+?
1661–3								
1664	38	42		108	188	20	22	57
1665	33	13		82	128	26	10	64
1666–8								
1669	12	21		54	87	14	26	62
1670–3								
1674	18	10		34	62	29	16	55
1675	27	17		33	77	35	22	43
1676	23	8	3	13	47	49	16	33
1677	33	11		10	54	61	20	18
1678	33	18	2	25	78	42	23	35
1679	36	16	3	29	84	43	19	38
1680	43	59	6	105	213	20	28	52
1681	70	106	21	220	417	17	25	58
1682	53	129	25	226	433	12	30	58
1683	51	138	25	262	476	11	29	60
1684	44	166	48	408	666	6½	25	68
1685	2	22	3	91	118	2	19	80
	516	776	136	1700	3128	16½	25	58½

192	369	75	1113	1749	–	Number of persons identified in each category.
2.69	2.10	1.81	1.53	1.80	–	Average number of convictions per person.

(P stands for Papists, Q for Quakers, N for Nonconformists and ? for those whose religion cannot be identified. The figures in the last three columns are percentages.)

SOURCES

CRS, vi, 289–96 (checked against the original) and the recusant rolls. The latter have some peculiar features as far as Norfolk is concerned. The first to contain any conviction for the county is that for 1679 (E/377/74), which contains convictions going back to 1674. As no other roll does this, it is possible that these convictions represent the entire total. After 1679 there are many records of conviction on each roll.

Appendix 2

IDENTIFICATION

Norfolk and Norwick R.O., VIS/7, Case 34 Shelf D, QS Box 46.
Friends' House Library, London, Abstracts of the records of
monthly meetings for births, marriages and burials, Norfolk.
Dr Williams's Library, Harmer MSS 2 and 6.
House of Lords R.O., PDB, c54.
G. Lyon Turner, *Original Records of Early Nonconformity* (3 vols.,
London, 1911–14), vol. iii.
Bate, Appendix vii.
J. Besse, *A Collection of the Sufferings of the People called Quakers* (2
vols., London, 1753), vol. i.
E. E. Estcourt and J. O. Payne (eds.), *English Catholic Non-Jurors
of 1715* (London, 1886).
The Quakers' Challenge to the Norfolk Clergy (1699).
The Suffering Case of the People Commonly Called Quakers (1701).
N. Penney (ed.), 'Extracts from State Papers relating to Friends,
1654–72', *Friends Historical Journal*, Supplements 8–11 (1913).

Using these sourses, my identifications of the religious allegiance of
recusants will be most accurate for Quakers and least accurate for
other Nonconformists. I have usually treated an identification as
positive only when the recusant's parish was given, although some
recusants were presented in two or three contiguous parishes.
Whatever their limitations, the figures show how the recusancy
laws were used more and more against the Dissenters and Quakers
in the 1680s and they also show that Papists were, on average, convicted more times than other recusants.

APPENDIX 3 : THE COMMISSIONS OF THE PEACE UNDER JAMES II

In the following tables, the arrangement of columns is as follows. The first shows the number of J.P.s put into commission by the committee of the Council that was set up in October 1686 and the second shows the number of these who were Catholics. The third shows the number of Catholic J.P.s who were not put in by the committee but who were in commission when the 'three questions' were tendered at the end of 1687 or during 1688, and so must have been put in later in 1687 or early in 1688. In some cases it is not clear whether they were put in before or after the tendering of the three questions. These are marked with an asterisk. The fourth and fifth columns show the number of J.P.s put in in the second remodelling, after the three questions, and the number of them who were Catholics. The sixth shows the number of Catholic J.P.s put in during 1687 or 1688 who for some reason do not appear in the final lists for 1688. The seventh and eighth columns give the total numbers of deputy lieutenants and J.P.s in the final lists and the ninth and tenth show the number of each who were Catholics. The last column shows the percentage of Catholics in the final lists of deputy lieutenants and J.P.s for each county.

For some counties the figures are incomplete. For Cheshire and the Isle of Ely, marked (a), the lists are of J.P.s only, although some of them were probably deputy lieutenants as well. For Huntingdonshire, marked (b), there is only a list of new J.P.s. For the West Riding, marked (c), there was probably no remodelling in 1688, as the answers to the three questions date mostly from August of that year.[1] For Rutland there is only a short list of deputy lieutenants from 1688. As for the last four English counties, I have found no lists at all for Suffolk and Westmorland. For Middlesex there is only a list of deputy lieutenants for 1688, but the nearest I have found to a list of J.P.s is one for Westminster, dated 4 February 1688.[2] The Westminster commission of the peace was not identical with that of Middlesex (the property qualification for J.P.s was lower, for one thing), but there was considerable overlapping of personnel. Thirty-one of the thirty-four J.P.s put into the Middlesex commission in 1687 were on the Westminster commission in 1688, as were nineteen of the twenty-five men who became deputy lieutenants for Middlesex in 1688. There were 111 J.P.s in the Westminster commission; fifteen were Catholics, including fourteen put into the Middlesex commission in

---

[1] Duckett, i, 87–90.   [2] Middlesex R. O., WJP/CP/2.

1687. In Warwickshire there seems to have been no commission issued after that of 12 July 1687.[3] Sunderland, the lord lieutenant, does not seem to have tendered the three questions in the county.[4] The proportion of Catholics (eight out of forty, or twenty per cent) is close to the national average.

SOURCES

PC/2/71, pp. 363–79 (list of changes in 1686–7).
SP/44/165, pp. 3–65, 128 (new deputy lieutenants, 1688).
Duckett, checked against the originals: Bodl., Rawl. MS A 139, fols. 111–15 and MS Arch. f. c. 6 (formerly Rawl. MS A 139B), fols. 199–274 (details of the responses to the three questions and the changes that followed).

IDENTIFICATION

For the identification of individual Catholic J.P.s see my Ph.D. thesis, 'The Catholic Factor in English Politics, 1660–1688' (Cambridge, 1971), pp. 365–79. I have included only men for whom reasonably reliable evidence of Catholicism can be adduced. The main means of identification used are Duckett, PDB and Estcourt and Payne, *English Catholic Non-Jurors of 1715*. One Catholic J.P. whom I have identified since completing the thesis is H. Metcalfe (North Riding), for whom see Aveling, *City of York*, p. 258.

County	In 1686–7 All	In 1686–7 RC	In 87–8 RC	Out 1688 All	Out 1688 RC	87–8 RC	Total 1688 DLts	Total 1688 JPs	RCs 1688 DLts	RCs 1688 JPs	1688 %RCs
ENGLAND											
Beds.	8	1		19	1		13	15		2	7
Berks.	10	7	1	15	7	2	7	20	4	9	48
Bucks.	5	4	3	24	3	2	17	21	6	2	21
Cambs.	4	2		10		1	5	21		1	4
Ches.	7	3					(a)	32	(a)	3	9
Corn.	6	1		28	1		10	27	1	1	5
Cumb.	7	7		3		1	4	13	2	4	35
Derbys.	5	4	1	14	1	1	7	16	3	2	22
Devon	15	5	1	8			14	40	3	3	11
Dorset	5	4		37			17	32	4		9

[3] Warwickshire R. O., QS/1/1/14; PRO, Index 4215, p. 176.
[4] Macaulay, ii, 331; there is no mention in Kenyon, *Sunderland*, or in Duckett that he ever tendered the three questions.

Appendix 3

County	In 1686–7 All	In 1686–7 RC	In 87–8 RC	Out 1688 All	Out 87–8 RC	Out 87–8 RC	Total 1688 DLts	Total 1688 JPs	RCs 1688 DLts	RCs 1688 JPs	1688 %RCs
Durham	15	13	5*			4	16	27	6	8	33
Essex	8	8	1	32	2	2	14	41	4	5	16
Glos.	12	8	2	14	1	1	9	29	3	7	26
Hants.	21	9		11	3		8	36	4	8	27
Herefs.	15	14	2	2			11	21	4	12	50
Herts.	5	1	1*			1	10	25	1		3
Hunts.	7			11			8	(b) 7			
I. Ely	1	1		4			(a)	21	(a)	1	5
Kent	13	13	4	32	2		28	83	6	13	17
Lancs.	12	10	15*				15	29	9	16	57
Leics.	4	3		15	6	1	7	17	2	6	33
Lincs.	9	9	3	17	1	2	15	26	8	3	27
Mon.	7	5		16	11		8	17	4	12	64
Norfk.	5	4	1	37	6		10	39	5	6	22
Northants.	5	3	1	14	1		9	21	1	4	16
Northumb.	12	11	9*			2	12	29	9	9	44
Notts.	1	1	1	18	2		10	12	4		18
Oxon.	10	10	4	24	7	5	10	30	3	13	40
Rutland	1	1	2*				5	?	3		
Salop.	9	9	1	28	1	1	13	28	8	2	24
Som.	3	3	2	41	2	3	12	36		4	8
Staffs.	21	11	1	17	5	1	10	27	4	12	44
Surrey	13	2	1*				8	44	1	2	6
Sussex	24	9	4*			1	20	33	9	3	23
Wilts.	9	4	1	24	7	1	15	26	5	6	27
Worcs.	8	8	3	16	2		13	22	5	8	37
Yks. E.	9	8		28	6		12	25	8	6	38
Yks. N.	10	10		19	5		10	24	4	11	44
Yks. W.	9	9	4*	(c)			20	54	10	3	18
	350	235	74	578	83	32	432	1066	153	207	
Middx.	34	14					25		4		
Suffk.	6	6									
Warwks.	6	6	2								
Westmor.	5	5									
	401	266	76	578	83	32	457	1066	157	207	

(N.B. Of the fifteen Papists in the third column for Lancashire, ten were certainly put in before the three questions and the other five were probably put in after they had been tendered.)

WALES County	In 1686–7 All	RC	In 87–8 RC	In 1688 All	RC	Out 87–8 RC	Total 1688 DLts	JPs	RCs 1688 DLts	JPs	1688 %RCs
Anglesey	1	1		5	1		5	4	1	1	22
Brecon	4	2	2	13	3		7	16	3	4	30
Cards.	2		2	11		2	5	7			
Carms.	1			9			4	7			
Carns.	7	3	1	9	2		4	10	2	4	43
Denb.	6	3		13	3		5	14		6	32
Flint	7	6	1	8	2		6	12	2	7	50
Glam.	6	3	2	15			7	17	2	3	21
Merion.	10	2		13			3	13	1	1	13
Montg.	4	1	2	12	2	2	6	10		3	17
Pemb.	2	1		9			4	8	1		8
Radnor	4	2		14	3		4	13	3	2	29
	54	24	10	131	16	4	60	131	15	31	24

(The earl of Castlemaine and viscount Montgomery appear as deputy lieutenants for every county: if they were included, the figures would be 39 Catholic deputies out of 84, and the percentage of Catholics would be thirty-three.)

TOTALS, ENGLAND AND WALES

Early 1687: 455 J.P.s put in, including 290 Catholics (63.75%).
Later in 1687 or early in 1688: 55 Catholics put in.
Before or after the tendering of the three questions: 31 Catholics put in.
After the three questions: 709 J.P.s put in, including 99 Catholics (14%).

TOTALS IN 1688

Deputy lieutenants: 517, including 172 Catholics (33.3%).
Justices of the peace: 1197, including 238 Catholics (19.9%).
Overall total: 1714, including 410 Catholics (23.92%).

SELECT BIBLIOGRAPHY

(Further bibliographical information about the period can be found in W. L. Sachse, *Restoration England 1660–1689*, Cambridge, 1971.)

Abernathy, G. R., jnr, 'Clarendon and the Declaration of Indulgence', *JEH*, vol. xi, 1960.

Ailesbury, T. Bruce, earl of, *Memoirs*, ed. W. E. Buckley, 2 vols., Cambridge, 1890.

Akerman, J. Y., *Moneys Received and Paid for Secret Services of Charles II and James II 1678–88*, Camden Soc., 1851.

Albion, G., *Charles I and the Court of Rome*, London, 1935.

Anstruther, G., 'Cardinal Howard and the English Court', *Archivum Fratrum Praedicatorum*, vol. xxviii, 1958.

Aveling, H., *Catholic Recusancy in the City of York 1558–1791*, CRS monograph no. 2, 1970.

The Catholic Recusants of the West Riding of Yorkshire 1558–1790, Proceedings of the Leeds Philosophical and Literary Society, vol. x, 1963.

Northern Catholics: The Catholic Recusants of the North Riding of Yorkshire 1558–1790, London, 1966.

Post-Reformation Catholicism in East Yorkshire, 1558–1790, E. Yorkshire Local History Soc., 1960.

'Some Aspects of Yorkshire Catholic Recusant History', in G. J. Cuming (ed.), *Studies in Church History*, vol. iv, Leiden, 1967.

Bate, F., *The Declaration of Indulgence 1672*, London, 1908.

Baxter, R., *Reliquiae Baxterianae*, ed. M. Sylvester, London, 1696.

Beales, A. C. F., *Education under Penalty*, London, 1963.

Birrell, T. A., 'English Catholics without a Bishop, 1655–72', *RH*, vol. iv, 1958.

Blundell, F. O., *Old Catholic Lancashire*, 3 vols., London, 1925–41.

Blundell, M., *Cavalier: Letters of William Blundell of Crosby to his Friends*, London, 1933.

Bosher, R. S., *The Making of the Restoration Settlement: The Influence of the Laudians 1649–62*, London, 1951.

Bossy, J., 'The Character of Elizabethan Catholicism', in T. Aston (ed.), *Crisis in Europe 1560–1660*, London, 1965.

Brady, W. M., *The Episcopal Succession*, 3 vols., Rome, 1877.

Bramston, Sir J., *Autobiography of Sir John Bramston*, ed. lord Braybrooke, Camden Soc., 1845.

Bredvold, L. I., *The Intellectual Milieu of John Dryden*, Ann Arbor, 1956.

Brown, T., *Miscellanea Aulica*, 1702.

Browning, A. (ed.), *English Historical Documents 1660–1714*, London, 1953.

Thomas Earl of Danby, 3 vols., Glasgow, 1951.

Burnet, G., *History of My Own Time*, 6 vols., Oxford, 1823.

A Supplement to Burnet's History of My Own Time, ed. H. C. Foxcroft, Oxford, 1902.

Campana di Cavelli, E., *Les Derniers Stuarts à Saint-Germain-en-Laye*, 2 vols., London, 1871.

Caraman, P., *The Years of Siege: Catholic Life from James I to Cromwell*, London, 1966.

Care, H., *The Weekly Pacquet of Advice from Rome, or the History of Popery*, 4 vols., 1679–82.

Carte, T., *An History of the Life of James, Duke of Ormond*, 6 vols., Oxford, 1851.

Castlemaine, Roger Palmer, earl of, *The Catholique Apology, with a Reply to the Answer*, 3rd edn., 1674.

Chandaman, C. D., 'The English Public Revenue, 1660–1688', unpublished Ph.D. thesis, London, 1954.

Clarendon, E. Hyde, earl of, *The Life of*, 3 vols., Oxford, 1827.

Clarendon Correspondence, ed. S. W. Singer, 2 vols., London, 1828.

Clark, R., *Strangers and Sojourners at Port Royal*, Cambridge, 1932.

Clarke, J. S., *Life of James II*, 2 vols., London, 1816.

Clifton, R., 'The Fear of Catholics in England, 1637 to 1645', unpublished D.Phil. thesis, Oxford, 1967.

'The Popular Fear of Catholics during the English Revolution', *P & P*, no. 52, 1971.

Comber, T., *Autobiographies and Letters*, ed. C. E. Whiting, 2 vols., Surtees Soc., 1946–7.

Corker, J., *Stafford's Memoires*, 1681.

Dalrymple, Sir J., *Memoirs of Great Britain and Ireland*, 2 vols., London, 1771–3.

Dockery, J. B., *Christopher Davenport, Friar and Diplomat*, London, 1960.

Dodd, C. (*vere* H. Tootell), *Church History of England*, 3 vols., 'Brussels', 1742.

Duckett, Sir G. F., *Penal Laws and Test Act 1687–8*, 2 vols., London, 1882–3.

Select Bibliography

Ellis Correspondence, ed. G. J. W. Agar Ellis, 2 vols., London, 1829.

Essex Papers: vol. i ed. O. Airy, vol. ii ed. C. E. Pike; 2 vols., Camden Soc., 1890, 1913.

Evelyn, J., *Diary*, ed. E. S. de Beer, 6 vols., Oxford, 1955.

Feiling, Sir K. G., *British Foreign Policy 1660–72*, London, 1930.

History of the Tory Party 1640–1714, Oxford, 1924.

Foley, H., *Records of the English Province of the Society of Jesus*, 7 vols. in 8, London, 1877–83.

Fox, C. J., *A History of the Early Part of the Reign of James II*, London, 1808.

Foxe, J., *Acts and Monuments*, ed. S. R. Cattley, 8 vols., London, 1841.

Granville, D., *The Remains of Denis Granville*, ed. G. Ornsby, 2 vols., Surtees Soc., 1861, 1867.

Grey, A., *Debates in the House of Commons 1667–94*, 10 vols., London, 1763.

Guilday, P., *The English Catholic Refugees on the Continent 1558–1795*, London, 1914.

Haley, K. H. D., *Charles II*, Historical Association, 1966.

The First Earl of Shaftesbury, Oxford, 1968.

William of Orange and the English Opposition 1672–4, Oxford, 1953.

Halifax, G. Savile, marquis of, *Complete Works*, ed. J. P. Kenyon, Harmondsworth, 1969.

Haller, W., *Foxe's Book of Martyrs and the Elect Nation*, London, 1963.

Hartmann, C. H., *Clifford of the Cabal*, London, 1937

The King my Brother, London, 1954.

Hatton Correspondence, ed. E. Maunde Thompson, 2 vols., Camden Soc., 1878.

Havran, M. J., *The Catholics in Caroline England*, Oxford, 1962.

Hay, M. V., *The Jesuits and the Popish Plot*, London, 1934.

Hemphill, B. (*vere* Whelan), *The Early Vicars Apostolic of England*, London, 1954.

Hughes, P., *Rome and the Counter-Reformation in Enlgand*, London, 1942.

Jones, J. R., *The First Whigs*, Oxford, 1961.

'James II's Whig Collaborators', *HJ*, vol. iii, 1960.

Josselin, R., *The Diary of the Rev. Ralph Josselin*, ed. E. Hockliffe, Camden Soc., 1908.

Kenyon, J. P., *The Nobility in the Revolution of 1688*, Hull, 1963.

The Popish Plot, London, 1972.

Select Bibliography

Robert Spencer Earl of Sunderland, London, 1958.

The Stuart Constitution, Cambridge, 1966.

Kirk, J., *Biographies of English Catholics in the Eighteenth Century*, ed. J. H. Pollen and E. Burton, London, 1909.

Lacey, D. R., *Dissent and Parliamentary Politics in England, 1661– 89*, New Brunswick, 1969.

Lamont, W. M., *Marginal Prynne*, London, 1963.

Lee, M. D., *The Cabal*, Urbana, 1965.

Lindley, K. J., 'The Part Played by Catholics in the English Civil War', unpublished Ph.D. thesis, Manchester, 1968.

Lingard, J., *History of England*, 6th edn, 10 vols., London, 1855.

Lister, T. H., *Life of Clarendon*, 3 vols., London, 1838.

Luttrell, N., *A Brief Historical Relation of State Affairs 1678–1714*, 6 vols., Oxford, 1857.

Macaulay, T. B., lord, *History of England*, 2nd edn, 5 vols., London, 1849–61.

MacGrath, P., *Papists and Puritans under Elizabeth I*, London, 1967.

Mackintosh, Sir J., *History of the Revolution of 1688*, London, 1834.

Macpherson, J., *Original Papers containing the Secret History of Great Britain*, 2 vols., London, 1775.

Marvell, A., *An Account of the Growth of Popery and Arbitrary Government*, 1677.

Poems and Letters, ed. H. Margoliouth, rev. by P. Legouis and E. E. Duncan Jones, 3rd edn, 2 vols., Oxford, 1971.

Michaud, E., *Louis XIV et Innocent XI*, 4 vols., Paris, 1882–3.

Mignet, F. A. M., *Négociations Rélatives à la Succession d'Espagne*, 4 vols., Paris, 1835–42.

Miller, J., 'Catholic Officers in the Later Stuart Army', *EHR*, vol. lxxxviii, 1973.

'The Militia and the Army in the Reign of James II', *HJ*, vol. xvi, 1973.

Morris, J., *The Troubles of our Catholic Forefathers*, 3 vols., London, 1872–7.

Neveu, B., 'Jacques II Médiateur entre Louis XIV et Innocent XI', *Mélanges d'Archéologie et d'Histoire*, vol. lxxix, 1967.

Newton, lady, *The House of Lyme*, London, 1917.

Lyme Letters 1660–1760, London, 1925.

North, R., *Examen*, London, 1740.

Lives of the Norths, ed. A. Jessopp, 3 vols., London, 1890.

Ogg, D., *England in the Reign of Charles II*, 2nd edn, 2 vols., Oxford, 1956.

Select bibliography

O'Keeffe, M. M. C., 'The Popish Plot in South Wales and the Marches of Hereford and Gloucester', unpublished M.A. thesis, University College, Galway, 1969.

Pepys, S., *Diary*, ed. R. C. Latham and W. Matthews, 11 vols., London 1970–4. (Vols. i–v have appeared at the time of writing.)

Poems on Affairs of State 1660–1688, 4 vols., New Haven, 1963–8: ed. (i) G. de F. Lord, (ii) L. F. Mengel, jnr, (iii) H. H. Schless, (iv) C. M. Crump.

Ranke, L. von, *A History of England, Principally in the Seventeenth Century*, 6 vols., Oxford, 1875.

Reresby, Sir J., *Memoirs*, ed. A. Browning, Glasgow, 1936.

Rostenberg, L., *The Minority Press and the English Crown 1558–1625*, Nieuwkoop, 1971.

Sergeant, J., *An Account of the Chapter erected by William, Titular Bishop of Chalcedon*, ed. W. Turnbull, London, 1853.

Simms, J. G., *Jacobite Ireland 1685–91*, London, 1969.

Somers Tracts, ed. Sir W. Scott, 13 vols., London, 1809–15.

State Tracts, 2 vols., 1689–92.

State Trials, ed. W. Cobbett and T. B. Howell, 33 vols., London, 1809–26.

Steele, R., *Tudor and Stuart Proclamations*, 2 vols., Bibliotheca Lindesiana, Oxford, 1910.

Strong, R. C., 'The Accession Day of Queen Elizabeth I', *Journal of the Warburg and Courtauld Institutes*, vol. xxi, 1958.

Thaddeus, Fr, *The Franciscans in England*, London, 1898.

Thomas, R., 'Comprehension and Indulgence', in G. F. Nuttall and O. Chadwick (eds.), *From Uniformity to Unity 1662–1962*, London, 1962.

Treby, G., *A Collection of Letters and Other Writings* and *The Second Part of the Collection*, 2 vols., London, 1681.

Turner, F. C., *James II*, London, 1948.

Verney, M. M., *Memoirs of the Verney Family*, 4 vols., London, 1892–9.

Warner, J., *The History of the English Persecution of Catholics and the Presbyterian Plot*, ed. T. A. Birrell, 2 vols. (CRS, xlvii–xlviii, 1953–5.

Warwick County Records, vols. vii and viii, ed. S. C. Ratcliff and H. C. Johnson, Warwick, 1946 and 1953.

Weldon, B., *Chronological Notes . . . of the English Congregation of the Order of St Benedict*, London, 1881.

Western, J. R., *Monarchy and Revolution: The English State in the Sixteen Eighties*, London, 1972.

Select bibliography

Whiteman, A., 'The Restoration of the Church of England', in G. F. Nuttall and O. Chadwick (eds.), *From Uniformity to Unity 1662–1962*, London, 1962.

Wiener, C. Z., 'The Beleaguered Isle: A Study of Elizabethan and Early Jacobean Anti-Catholicism', *P & P*, no. 51, 1971.

Williams, J. A., *Catholic Recusancy in Wiltshire, 1660–1791*, CRS monograph no. 1, 1968.

Williamson, Sir J., *Letters Addressed from London to Sir Joseph Williamson 1673–4*, ed. W. D. Christie, 2 vols., Camden Soc., 1874.

Witcombe, D. T., *Charles II and the Cavalier House of Commons 1663–74*, Manchester, 1966.

Wood, A. à, *Life and Times*, ed. A. Clark, 5 vols., Oxford Historical Soc., 1891–1900.

Wormald, B. H. G., *Clarendon: Politics, Historiography and Religion 1640–60*, Cambridge, 1951.

Zimmerman, B., *Carmel in England*, London, 1899.

INDEX

(RC indicates Roman Catholic)

Index

Index

Index

Index

Index

Index

Worcester House declaration (1660), 97

Worrall, Ellen, RC, 193

Wright, Sir Robert, 221

Yarmouth, earl of, *see* Paston, William

York, duchess of, *see* (i) Hyde, Anne, (ii) Mary Beatrice

York, duke of, *see* James II

Yorkshire
Catholicism in, 7, 10, 11, 15n, 16, 20–1, 35
enforcement of penal laws in, 60, 62, 132–3, 142, 167, 191, 192